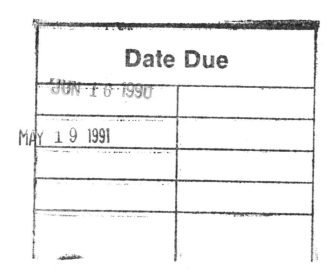

Date Due

JUN 16 1990	
MAY 19 1991	

Building Europe

Building Europe:
Britain's Partners in the EEC

Edited by
Carol and Kenneth J. Twitchett

London
Europa Publications Limited
1981

Europa Publications Limited
18 Bedford Square, London WC1B 3JN

HC
241.2
B 757

British Library Cataloguing in Publication Data
Building Europe.
  1. European Economic Community countries –
Economic integration
  2. European Economic Community countries –
Political integration
  I. Twitchett, Carol   II. Twitchett, Kenneth J.
  338.91'4   HC241

ISBN 0 905118 61 8

Printed in Great Britain by
Unwin Brothers Limited
The Gresham Press
Old Woking, Surrey

To our parents

Contents

Abbreviations*

AAMS	Associated African and Malagasy States
ACP	African, Caribbean and Pacific
ASEAN	Association of South East Asian Nations
BEB	Directoraat-Generaal voor Buitenlandse Economische Betrekking
BLEU	Belgo-Luxembourg Economic Union
CAP	Common Agricultural Policy (of the EEC)
CCEIA	Coordinatie Commissie voor Europese Integratie en Associatie Problemen
CET	Common External Tariff (of the EEC)
CFP	Common Fisheries Policy (of the EEC)
CGIL	Communist-allied trade union federation (of Italy)
CIPE	Inter-Ministerial Committee for Economic Programming (of Italy)
CMSG	Common Market Study Group
COMECON	Council for Mutual Economic Assistance (also referred to as CMEA)
COREPER	Committee of Permanent Representatives
COREU	European Community Telegram Network
CTP	Common Transport Policy (of the EEC)
DC	Christian Democratic Party (of Italy)
DGES	Directoraat-General voor Europese Samenwerking
EAGGF	European Agricultural Guidance and Guarantee Fund (see also FEOGA)
EC	European Community
ECSC	European Coal and Steel Community

---

* Separate acronym tables for Dutch and Belgian political parties are contained in appendices at the end of Chapters V and VI.

EDC	European Defence Community
EDF	European Development Fund
EEC	European Economic Community
EFTA	European Free Trade Association
EIB	European Investment Bank
EMS	European Monetary System
EMU	European Monetary Union
EPC	European Political Community
ERDF	European Regional Development Fund
ESF	European Social Fund
EUA	European Unit of Account
Euratom	European Atomic Energy Community
FDP	Free Democratic Party (of West Germany)
FEOGA	French version of EAGGF
FRG	Federal Republic of Germany
GATT	General Agreement on Tariffs and Trade
GDP	Gross Domestic Product
GDR	German Democratic Republic
GNP	Gross National Product
GSP	Generalized System of Preferences
ICEM	Irish Council of the European Movement
ILO	International Labour Organisation
IRA	Irish Republican Army
ISM	Irish Sovereignty Movement
KKE	Greek Communist Party
LDC	Less Developed Country
LO	Danish Trades Union Congress
MCA	Monetary Compensation Amount
MEP	Member of the European Parliament
MP	Member of Parliament
MRC	Market Relations Committee (of the Danish Folketing)
NATO	North Atlantic Treaty Organization
NECC	Nordic Economic Co-operation Committee
Nordek	Nordic Economic Union
OECD	Organisation for Economic Co-operation and Development
OEEC	Organisation for European Economic Co-operation
PASOK	Greek Socialist Party
PCE	Spanish Communist Party
PCF	French Communist Party
PCI	Italian Communist Party
PEP	Political and Economic Planning
PSI	Italian Socialist Party
PSOE	Spanish Socialist Party
REZ	Raad voor Europese Zaken

ROW	Rest of the World
RPR	Rassemblement Populaire Républicain
SACEUR	Supreme Allied Commander Europe (NATO)
SHAPE	Supreme Headquarters Allied Powers in Europe
SPD	Social Democratic Party (of West Germany)
TUC	Trades Union Congress
UACES	University Association for Contemporary European Studies
UDF	Union pour la Démocratie Française
UKREP	United Kingdom Permanent Representative
UN	United Nations
UNCTAD	United Nations Conference on Trade and Development
UNIDO	United Nations Industrial Development Organization
USSR	Union of Soviet Socialist Republics
VAT	Value Added Tax
WEU	Western European Union
WHO	World Health Organization

Preface

During fifteen years or so of research and teaching on Western European integration, we have regretted the absence of a textbook encapsulating in one volume the aims and aspirations of each of the member states as they relate to the European Community. There are some excellent studies dating from the middle 1960s on the roles of France and Germany in creating the 'new Europe', and many more on the origins and evolution of the EEC. The extensive bibliography at the end of this book itself demonstrates the wealth of literature dating from the 1970s on European co-operation in general and the EEC in particular. It lists the very large number of books currently available on the United Kingdom and the European Community, written from a wide variety of perspectives. But to our knowledge no single symposium in English has attempted to embrace the ambitions of all the Ten and, indeed, the prospective Community members.

When approaching the contributors we asked them to focus on a series of specific points. We knew that each of them would look at the issues from their idiosyncratic perspectives as they were all experienced commentators on the European Community with individual interests and styles of analysis. We requested each of them to consider a particular EEC member state (except for Adrian Poole who tackled both Belgium and Luxembourg, and Geoffrey Edwards who valiantly took on the task of assessing the motives of the then three candidate members – Greece, Portugal, and Spain), and to examine the following questions: first, why did that particular state opt for EEC membership; second, the predominant attitudes evidenced by successive governments towards various aspects of EEC endeavour, notably common policy formation; third, the extent to which the EEC is perceived to further specific national interests; and fourth, the differences of opinion within each of the states under consideration regarding Community membership and the desired direction of future EEC development.

We believe that the excellent responses of all the contributors to these

requests collectively provide a unique guide to the part played by each of
the United Kingdom's partners in building Community Europe. We have
attempted in Chapter I to place the other contributions within the broader
context of the contemporary problems confronting the countries of Western
Europe and to probe the EEC's role as a diplomatic framework for the
external relations of its member states. We also comment briefly on the
United Kingdom's involvement in Community affairs, particularly the
factors underlying the unfavourable British response to EEC membership.

Annette Morgan surveys French policies towards 'building Europe' in
Chapter II. She notes the pioneering role of such great French patriots as
Jean Monnet and Robert Schuman, and assesses President de Gaulle's
impact on French attitudes towards European integration. She provides a
guide to contemporary French policies and interests *vis à vis* the Community
and its future development. Similarly, in Chapter III, Roger Morgan
analyses the West German motives underpinning the Federal Republic's
participation in the Community and evaluates German interests in an EEC
context. He highlights the differing attitudes evident in the major political
parties regarding the Community's future, especially its role in the world.
In Chapter IV Geoffrey Pridham explores the origins, motivation, and
party-political bias of Italian policies towards European integration. He
emphasizes that Italy regards her Roman heritage as an integral, living
part of her history, and that this assists in promoting a broad-based sense
of identity with European-wide institutional endeavour, especially the EEC.

In Chapters V and VI, Richard Griffiths and Adrian Poole respectively
investigate the overwhelmingly pro-European policies of the Netherlands
and Belgium-Luxembourg. Professor Griffiths assesses the Dutch contribution towards promoting greater Western European integration and surveys the interests of the Netherlands in various aspects of EEC endeavour.
Adrian Poole examines Belgian attitudes to the EEC and analyses the
notable impact which the Community has had on Belgium itself. He also
looks at the Luxembourg experience and briefly comments on Benelux as
an example of European co-operation.

Clive Archer analyses the origins of Danish accession to the EEC in
Chapter VII. He examines the pursuit of Denmark's interests in the
Community and the divisions in her domestic opinion regarding continued
membership. He ably demonstrates that Denmark shares with the United
Kingdom the perhaps dubious distinction of being one of the two EEC
member states with the most vociferous body of anti-Market opinion. In
marked contrast, the other newcomer to the Community, Ireland, is an
enthusiastic participant in EEC affairs. Her involvement in the Community
is commented on by Trevor Salmon in Chapter VIII. He traces the evolution
of Irish attitudes towards the EEC since the 1960s and assesses the various
ways whereby Ireland furthers its national interests through Community
membership.

In the final chapter Geoffrey Edwards probes the challenge presented to the Nine by the admission of Greece to EEC membership in 1981 and the potential adhesion of Portugal and Spain. He underlines the significance of the fact that Greece, Portugal, and Spain are among the very few examples of countries which have recently exchanged dictatorial for democratic regimes and the importance which EEC membership has for their new freely-elected governments. Their return to democracy was followed almost immediately by applications for EEC membership.

François Mitterrand's victory over Valéry Giscard d'Estaing in the French presidential election of May 1981 occurred when this book was at the proof stage. Annette Morgan, therefore, has added a brief postscript on the possible implications to her chapter on France and the European Community. President Mitterrand's socialist government is likely to be just as tenacious as its more conservative predecessors in defence of France's national interests within the Community context. One immediate consequence was that Claude Cheysson, the EEC Commissioner for Development Policy, became French Foreign Minister. His appointment itself indicates that at the highest political level the new French administration like previous ones will have an intimate knowledge and understanding of the European Community. The close relationship which France and Germany had under President Giscard d'Estaing and Chancellor Schmidt (their lingua franca being English!) is also likely to be perpetuated; both Helmut Schmidt and François Mitterrand are socialists and the new French President has close ties with Willi Brandt, the actual leader of Chancellor Schmidt's German Social Democratic Party. Insofar as differences occur, they could well be over such matters as reform of the common agricultural policy and the financing of the EEC generally. Indeed, Germany was moving closer to the United Kingdom on these issues even before Valéry Giscard d'Estaing's departure from the French Presidency. The Paris–Bonn axis, however, will probably remain the dominant feature of politics at the Community level for the foreseeable future.

In some chapters a problem arises regarding the use of the term *community*. The term itself is frequently employed to denote an especially close relationship between a group of states, but *the Community* is also often used to refer to the EC or to all three European Communities – EEC, ECSC, and Euratom. Indeed, the term European Community or the acronym EEC are used by most of the contributors to this symposium as shorthand terms for all three Communities; a practice followed by many other commentators on European affairs. Usually in this book the context clarifies the meaning in which the terms *community* etc. are used, though there might be a few instances where readers themselves need to decide whether reference is to a particular form of co-operative endeavour, to all three Communities, or simply to the EEC.

We deeply regret that William Pickles died while writing his contribution on the United Kingdom and the EEC to this book. We would like to pay tribute to his role in stimulating research in British universities on Western

European integration. Although one of the most critical observers of Community Europe, he encouraged several of the present contributors to pursue their studies on the EEC. His chapter is sadly missed and we would like to thank his widow, Professor Dorothy Pickles, for her kind consideration. She herself, of course, is a very distinguished commentator on European affairs. As editors, we would also like to express our thanks to all the contributors for their willing co-operation and to the editorial staff of Europa Publications for their courtesy and generous assistance. Finally, we are very grateful to Lyn Rycroft for her invaluable secretarial services in preparing this manuscript.

August 1980   Carol and Kenneth J. Twitchett

I

The EEC as a Framework for Diplomacy

Carol and Kenneth J. Twitchett

The European Community is an established feature of the international diplomatic scene. Externally, it is accepted as a significant international actor in its own right. On the global stage its member states collectively are frequently seen as in fact possessing a greater sense of purpose and cohesion than may well be justified when viewed from within the EEC itself. To most developing countries of the Third World, for example, the Community is the most important trading bloc and their principal source of concessional finance. They tend to overlook the deep divisions which in practice have prevented the formation of a dynamic EEC development policy. So far as the two superpowers are concerned, the United States looks to the Community for coherent responses within the context of a vaguely-defined Atlantic partnership, and the Soviet Union remains deeply suspicious of the form of political unity emerging from Western European economic integration. The Community has long been regarded as an important participant in international economic relations. The 1979–80 Afghanistan and Iranian crises did prompt a greater general recognition of its political legitimacy as an international actor, but in actual practice Community responses to both crises have been somewhat muted and inadequate.

Internally, the EEC's member states appreciate the value of the Community as a basis for diplomatic actions and initiatives. Their individual and collective commitment to common EEC policies in general, however, often contrasts sharply with the divergence of views between them regarding specific issue areas. Each member state conceives individual common policy endeavours as essentially reflecting its own national priorities. They seek to use the Community as a vehicle for the projection and achievement of particular national goals. The EEC constitutes a successful framework for diplomacy only to the extent that the predominant national policies of the member states coalesce in a mutually compatible linkage of interests. Where there is no recognized compatibility of interests, the prospects for common

1

policy endeavours are minimal. Yet the EEC can and does function as a framework for diplomacy as long as no single member state asserts national views dramatically opposed to those of its partners.

The other contributors to this book examine the national goals and specific allegiances of Britain's partners in the EEC. This chapter itself primarily seeks to provide an overall perspective by assessing the extent to which the member states have actually succeeded in providing a diplomatic framework for 'building Europe', especially one which can respond to the demands made on the EEC by non-member states. That endeavour is undertaken in the first three sections of this chapter. The first section traces the evolution of the basic ideas associated with building the European Community and then proceeds to outline some of the current problems affecting its ability to project a coherent external image. The second section is concerned with the nature of the EEC's external relations and is divided into two parts: the first one looks at the Community's role in the world and other international organizations, while the second examines the operational base and subsequent policy initiatives which underpin the Community as a framework for diplomacy and the pursuit of external relations. The third section investigates the record of political co-operation between the Nine, particularly in the late 1970s, and the tentative moves towards what might, albeit rather optimistically, be termed a common foreign policy. It also briefly surveys the ways in which individual member states have used the EEC as a framework for diplomacy.

The extent to which any member state can and does utilize the EEC as an instrument for achieving its diplomatic and other national goals is a function both of the problems relating to its Community membership and the perception of them within its own domestic society. As the other chapters in this book demonstrate, the internal debate within the United Kingdom on the benefits or otherwise of EEC membership, have their counterparts among Britain's partners. To help place those other debates within a sharper perspective, the fourth section of this chapter briefly looks at the problems relating to British membership of the EEC. In the modern world, the framework for diplomacy is often shaped almost as much by national as international considerations.

1. The EEC in the 1980s

The European Community on the threshold of the 1980s is confronted by a bewildering range of complex problems. Within the EEC itself, some of the most urgent include the need to streamline the policy-making process, the pending prospect of bankruptcy of Community institutions unless their budgetary and financing mechanisms are drastically revised, the reform of the common agricultural policy (CAP) currently absorbing nearly three-quarters of the Community budget, and the integration of Greece and probably Portugal and Spain within the EEC framework. If the EEC is to withstand these and other challenges, the member states will need to demonstrate strong and coherent commitment to common action.

The national governments themselves, however, are confronted with the chilling legacy of the 1970s, especially as manifested by inflation and mass unemployment. These and other seemingly intractable problems confront all the member states to a greater or lesser degree. If they act on the assumption that the problems are more likely to be susceptible to Community-level palliatives, then the EEC will continue to be seen as a framework for tackling these difficulties. At the present time, most if not all the ruling élites in the member states appear to accept this view. But, as is evident from the other chapters in this book, the extent of each member state's commitment is difficult to gauge as the priority accorded to EEC goals varies depending on a wide range of predominantly domestic factors.

The original architects of the EEC themselves had a remarkably clear conception of the Community's ultimate goal and the means whereby it should be achieved.[1] A quarter of a century later the goal of West European unity still appears to be a long way off, and the path mapped out by the 1957 Treaty of Rome seems to have meandered into a bleak and rocky wilderness. For Jean Monnet and the other founding fathers, the new Europe had to be organized on a federal basis. This goal was to be achieved through the artful interplay of economics and political institutions. From inception it was recognized as a highly political process which would have to dislodge what Monnet denoted as 'the accumulated obstacles' of the past.[2] An early draft of the revolutionary Schuman Declaration which eventually led to the creation of the European Coal and Steel Community (ECSC), emphasized that the plan for pooling French and German coal and steel resources had 'an essential political objective: to make a breach in the ramparts of national sovereignty which will be narrow enough to secure consent, but deep enough to open the way towards the unity that is essential to peace'.[3]

The ECSC was itself an experiment in sectoral integration. The 1951 Paris Treaty clearly defined the scope and institutions of the ECSC, with the High Authority having an explicitly supranational character.[4] A supranational organization is defined as one 'whose member states have given its central institutions the right and the ability to exercise functions and to take decisions independently of and even in spite of the member states in fields traditionally within their preserve'.[5] In marked contrast, the 1957 Rome Treaties establishing the EEC and Euratom were much less specific and

---

[1] See, for example, Jean Monnet, *Memoirs* (Collins, 1978), p. 295.
[2] *Ibid.*
[3] *Ibid.*, p. 296.
[4] Article 9 of the Treaty setting up the ECSC specifically refers to the 'supranational character' of the High Authority.
[5] See K. J. Twitchett, *The Evolving United Nations* (Europa, 1971), pp. 6–7.

3

more open-ended in their commitment to integration. But, as Jean Monnet perceived it, integration still remained as the key to European unity. It would shift from sectoral or vertical integration to more general or horizontal integration, leading eventually to full economic union.[6]

The EEC Treaty set in motion among the member states the creation of a common market resting on a customs union. Within the customs union all barriers to the free movement of goods, peoples, services, and capital were to be removed. The emergence of an industrial common market was to be accompanied by an agricultural common market, which itself would require special collective measures to take account of governmental intervention in the agricultural sector. The logic of integration, as seen in the 1950s would lead to wide-ranging harmonization of policy, both internally and externally, and gradually (yet inexorably) embrace all aspects of economic and social intercourse between the member states.

The Rome Treaty's drafters set no specific timetable for this process, beyond the initial removal of customs duties between the member states – which was in fact achieved between the original Six ahead of schedule in 1968. Rather, it was assumed that the integration process itself would propel the member states forward as anomalies became evident; logic would dictate that these could only be resolved by further steps down the road to economic union.[7] Moreover, the Community's institutional framework was devised as a positive means of encouraging the integration process. The member states were represented as a collective identity in the Council of Ministers, while the Commission was conceived as the independent motor-mechanism, exclusively responsible for proposing measures in the *Community* interest, not just an amalgam of the *national* interests of the member states.[8]

Buoyant economic conditions throughout the 1960s helped to encourage the original Six to implement the EEC Treaty and formulate the CAP. The success of the Community experiment was endorsed by the membership of Denmark, Ireland, and the United Kingdom in 1973. By then, however, the Commission was already experiencing great difficulty in prodding the member states further down the road of economic integration. The removal of barriers between the Six and the Nine, especially if, like customs duties, they can be unambiguously identified, proved a great deal easier to accomplish than creating political initiatives in areas where the Rome Treaty provided no specific requirements. Negative integration could proceed without the active political commitment of all the participants, but positive integration, especially beyond the specific letter of the three founding

[6] Monnet, *Memoirs*, op. cit., p. 401.
[7] For an examination of this theory of economic integration, see Leon Lindberg, *The Political Dynamics of European Economic Integration* (Oxford University Press, 1963).
[8] For a discussion of the nature of the EEC and a brief survey of its operations, see Carol Cosgrove Twitchett, 'The EEC and European Co-operation', in K. J. Twitchett (ed.), *European Co-operation Today* (Europa, 1980), Chapter III.

treaties, has proved an elusive goal. And the difficulties in building sufficient consensus to achieve positive integration were complicated in many ways by first expanding the EEC from six to nine, and then to ten.

An example of the pitfalls met by the Community internally may be found in the fields of economic and monetary policy. The so-called logic of integration embodied in the EEC Treaty was clear: the creation of the common market and the CAP would require harmonized fiscal and monetary systems and exchange rate co-ordination. The concept of Economic and Monetary Union (EMU) as understood in the 1960s implied fixed exchange rates and the progressive convergence of national economic and monetary policies. Given the imbalance between richer and poorer Community states, an integral part of EMU was the establishment of a regional development fund – the ERDF – to offset the problems of adjustment in the weaker member states. In the 1970s the actual growing divergence rather than convergence in economic performance among the Nine gravely compromised the implementation of Community goals relating to EMU. Italy, Ireland and the United Kingdom found their economies to be too weak to sustain the impact of the international monetary and economic upheavals of the early 1970s without essentially *national* controls. France, too, later left the joint float (the so-called snake in the tunnel) of EEC currencies as her economy seemed to be under threat from outside forces. Thus the continued fluctuation of currency parities within the EEC caused enormous complications for its budget and the CAP, the latter resting on common prices denominated in common units of account.

To some extent the European Monetary System (EMS) of the later 1970s ameliorated these difficulties, although to date without the participation of the United Kingdom. The EMS, however, is not the product of EEC policy-making.[9] It is the result of essentially national deliberations between national decision-makers taken within the broad political context of the Community. The integration process envisaged by the EEC Treaty in fact has become bogged down in this field. While the end result is as difficult and anomalous as the treaty drafters foresaw, the member states apparently lack the collective political will to overcome the obstacles in the way of further progress.

This kind of impasse is evident in nearly all areas of Community endeavour. The Rome Treaty itself offers relatively limited means for common action to redress the evils of galloping inflation and unemployment. Its *laisser faire* principles are a far cry from the essentially national, interventionist policies advocated by the leaders of the Nine at the Venice summit meeting in June 1980. Chancellor Helmut Schmidt and Prime Minister Margaret Thatcher both called for national policies based on strict financial and monetary controls and industrial discipline, with only a

---

[9] For a discussion of this point, see Geoffrey Dennis, 'European Monetary Co-operation', in K. J. Twitchett (ed.), *European Co-operation Today, ibid.*, Chapter VIII.

passing reference to the EMS.[10] Similarly, energy supplies, a crucial determinant of Western Europe's prosperity, continue to remain outside the Community package. Little now survives of the European Commission's plans for a common energy policy spanning the ECSC, Euratom and EEC Treaties. The Venice summit showed that France, Germany and the United Kingdom do not intend to allow their energy policies to be controlled at the EEC level, involving the Commission's allegedly 'explosive ideas of harmonizing prices and taxes and laying hands on the huge funds needed for energy investment'.[11]

The Venice summit itself provided a pointer towards the possible evolution of the European Community in the 1980s. It confirmed that the member states were almost totally absorbed in their own problems and unwilling to risk collective ventures if national ones appeared to present viable alternatives. The summit took place at a time of considerable international tension and uncertainty, against the background of the Soviet invasion of Afghanistan and the divergent responses of the NATO allies to the plight of the American hostages in Iran. It assured the maintenance of the so-called EEC initiative on the Middle East (albeit a rather circumspect move in itself), and made bland statements about measures to assist the poorer states of the Third World. Although not breaking any new ground, the Venice meeting at least confirmed the EEC's role, even if only half-heartedly, as a framework for diplomacy at the same time as it cast doubt on the prospects for the Community's internal political development.

Indeed, it is perhaps somewhat surprising that despite the similar nature of the adverse domestic pressures prevailing throughout the member states, especially regarding unemployment, the pressures are eliciting national rather than Community responses. EEC institutions as such seem likely in the foreseeable future to play only a residual background role. In terms of policy initiative, the Commission's role has visibly diminished in recent years. Admittedly, its Treaty role remains and in principle the monopoly right of initiative is retained. Yet this right is only effective within the confines of the EEC Treaty itself.[12] In the late 1970s it became increasingly apparent that the member states were moving away from the strict letter of the Community treaties as bases for their common endeavour. Common policies in such EEC-defined sectors as transport, regional aids, and social policy effectively have been blocked by intransigence on the part of some member states. Although usually in dispute between themselves, general intransigence towards the EEC is a shared characteristic of France and the United Kingdom, with smaller Community members like the Netherlands demonstrating this characteristic on particular issues such as transport. At the same time, the member states have established a broad consensus on the desirability of common action if not yet the precise details, beyond the treaty

[10] *The Sunday Times*, 15 June 1980.
[11] *Ibid.*
[12] Michael Shanks elaborates on this point in *The Times*, 8 Aug. 1980.

framework in other areas such as education and counter-terrorist measures. Initiatives in these areas stem from outside the Commission and formal treaty orbit.

It is likely that in the 1980s the Commission, initially under the Presidency of the very experienced Luxembourg politician, Gaston Thorn, will be confronted with a series of unpleasant choices. It could continue to insist on its right of initiative – and hence find itself increasingly bypassed by the foreign office network of intra-EEC contacts (the Political Co-operation Machinery) and by the Committee of Permanent Representatives (CORE-PER). Or it could tacitly accept that the locus of initiative-taking has shifted to COREPER and allied bodies under essentially national control, and so run the risk of prejudicing its treaty status. It could concentrate on its role as independent guardian and implementor of EEC legislation. Yet that could result in it becoming increasingly regarded as a technical body, admittedly fulfilling a vital regulatory role but hardly constituting a decisive political influence. The experience of administering the EEC's harmonization process has surely underlined that it is all too easy for the Commission to become bogged down in technical desiderata of a relatively trivial and often unpopular nature, such as the installation of tachographs in heavy goods vehicles, thereby compromising its credibility on major issues like the actual provision of Community finance for a common transport policy.[13]

Gaston Thorn and his colleagues have yet to face the perhaps perverse logic of these choices. It is not without significance, however, that M. Thorn himself has been a key participant in the European Council and its subsidiary political co-operation machinery. Indeed, in the latter half of 1980, Luxembourg was the EEC Presidency state and as its Foreign Minister, Gaston Thorn represented the Community on the world stage. It may be that Thorn, given his unique experience in EEC policy-making, will be well-placed to forge new links between the Commission and the European Council: links which might redress the centrifugal tendencies currently so evident in the Community today. The task will be difficult and the chances of success limited to say the least.

2. The Community's External Relations

The EEC in the World – From its inception, the European Community has been involved in diplomatic relations with non-member countries. The ECSC found itself concerned with diplomacy from its very establishment in 1952. Only days after the High Authority started work, diplomatic missions were accredited to the ECSC, initially by the United Kingdom and then by the United States; other West European countries following suit very speedily. In 1957, even before the Treaties of Rome were ratified,

[13] For an elaboration of this point and the general problems relating to policy harmonization in the European Communities, see Carol Cosgrove Twitchett (ed.), *Harmonisation in the EEC* (Macmillan, 1981).

the six member states of the new EEC had perforce to consider the diplomatic relations of the new Community with a wide range of other countries and international organizations. Since then, the EEC has been the recipient of a multiplicity of demands from non-member states.

In considering the EEC's role in the world, it is necessary to make a general distinction between those areas of external relations where the member states are required by the basic treaties to act through Community institutions, and those where the member states have chosen to use the EEC even though not specifically required to do so. The latter area of foreign policy activity relates directly to what has come to be called *political co-operation* among the member states, and is considered in the third section of this chapter. In this section, the analysis focuses on those areas where the founding treaties require the EEC to act on behalf of the member states.

In the realm of external relations, European Community institutions have tended to act as a central clearing house rather than a repository of principles and a major source of innovation. This suggests that there are differences of emphasis in the role of Community institutions in external policy formation compared with such intra-Community ones as the formation of the CAP. It could also be maintained that within the domestic framework of EEC endeavour, the Commission's role during the 1970s came much more to resemble its traditional role in external relations than its initial seminal role in formulating the CAP. The Community's farm policy may well in hindsight prove to be the one single area of EEC policy endeavour where Community institutions have made a really dramatic and fundamentally decisive contribution to policy formation among the member states; an achievement which in British eyes at least is hardly likely to evoke enthusiasm for further endeavours.

To some extent the Commission's role in external relations means that the outcome of EEC initiatives will of necessity represent a diplomatic compromise between the competing interests of the member states. As with all diplomatic compromises, they may well be founded on the lowest common denominator of agreement. This creates a basic structural problem for the EEC in international negotiations. In effect, any Community policy proposal made to a third country or in the context of wider multilateral diplomatic activities, will itself represent the outcome of already hard-fought compromises. As a result, the EEC position is hardly likely to be susceptible to further compromise in wider diplomatic frameworks. As a consequence the EEC tends to engage in international diplomacy from a position of inflexibility. Recent examples of the problems resulting from this lack of flexibility in the EEC negotiating position are to be found in the diplomatic bargaining which took place prior to the conclusion of the second Lomé Convention of 1979, and the GATT negotiations for the Tokyo Round. In both instances, the EEC as a unit was severely constrained in reacting to the initiatives of its negotiating partners. In the case of the negotiations for Lomé II, the African, Caribbean and Pacific (ACP) states found it extremely frustrating to obtain positive responses from the European Community as the mandate given to the EEC negotiators was itself the result of long and bitter bargaining among the Nine themselves. This led to a generally negative impression being gained by the ACP states regarding EEC willingness to take account of their problems. Similarly, but in a very different context, the other developed industrialized countries in the GATT found it a frustrating exercise to attempt to obtain concessions from the EEC during the Tokyo Round negotiations of 1978-79, especially regarding temperate agricultural products subject to the CAP – the latter itself being a major issue of contention between the Nine themselves.

The nature of the European Community as an international actor has been examined extensively elsewhere.[14] In the present context it is sufficient to assert that the preservation of the European Community has acquired a very high priority in the foreign policy formation of all the member states, and the EEC is regarded as an important international actor in its own right by most third countries. In 1980, some 109 countries had diplomatic missions accredited to the European Community in Brussels. The only significant group of countries not to have accredited missions to the Community are those under direct Soviet influence, although it is worth noting that Romania and Vietnam both maintain missions to the EEC in Brussels. The European Community itself maintains delegations throughout the world. In particular, it has delegations to other international organizations in Paris, Geneva, and New York, together with delegations accredited to the United States in Washington, to Canada in Ottawa, and to Japan in Tokyo. The European Commission also maintains a delegation in Caracas, Venezuela, accredited to the Latin American countries and regional organizations there. In the context of the EEC-ACP partnership, the Community maintains some 43 missions in the various ACP states; in some cases the EEC delegation is accredited to more than one state in the region.

Other international organizations in fact have played a very significant role in establishing the EEC as an important diplomatic framework. The EEC Treaty itself requires the Commission to negotiate on behalf of the European Community in international economic organizations of direct relevance to the founding treaties. In practice the EEC has gone far beyond the minimal treaty requirements in establishing itself as an international actor in other international organizations. The EEC has long had observer status in the United Nations General Assembly and various other United Nations institutions.[15] In addition, the Community has been an active participant in the GATT, and is a party to a wide range of international commodity agreements including the GATT multifibre arrangement, the International Tin Agreement, and the International Cocoa Agreement.

[14] For example, see Carol Cosgrove and Ken Twitchett, *The New International Actors: The UN and the EEC* (Macmillan, 1970).
[15] For an elaboration of this point, see K. J. Twitchett, *Europe and the World* (Europa, 1976), pp. 29-33.

During the so-called 'North–South dialogue' at the 1976–77 Conference on International Economic Co-operation in Paris, there was one single delegation only for the European Community and its member states to deal with the multitude of points arising from a very wide and complex agenda. At the international level, non-member countries increasingly assume that the Community member states will 'speak with one voice' even on aspects of international relations not directly within the competence of the founding treaties. In actual fact, the European Commission has become the acknowledged negotiator for the EEC in most international economic organizations, and it is generally accepted that the EEC Presidency state will speak on behalf of the Community as a whole at the United Nations General Assembly and other international diplomatic gatherings. The Nine member states themselves maintained a high degree of voting consistency in the United Nations General Assembly debates during the 1970s, differing only on about ten per cent of the issues under discussion. Ireland tended to be a 'rogue state' out of voting alignment with its Community partners. She, of course, has never been a member of NATO and has long been established within the United Nations system as a leading member of the non-aligned countries. Ireland obtains a range of diplomatic benefits from her reputation as one of the few white, western neutral countries acceptable throughout the Third World as a political mediator. As is shown by Trevor Salmon in Chapter VIII, the Irish in practice tend not to place much emphasis on the differences between Dublin's perception of international affairs and the view from the other capitals of their Community partners. Overall, the Nine generally have been able to act together within the United Nations context with a high degree of homogeneity.

In international economic organizations generally the EEC Commission has established a very high reputation for its technical competence and diplomatic agility. Even before the Rome Treaties were ratified in 1957, the EEC became the focus of diplomatic negotiations within the GATT as the Six were required to comply with the GATT provisions regarding the creation of their new customs union. This was only the beginning of an intense relationship between the EEC and the GATT which can be traced through the Kennedy Round of the 1960s to the Tokyo Round of the 1970s. In addition, the EEC has established itself as a major actor in UNCTAD, and in other United Nations forums such as UNIDO and the United Nations Conference on Science and Technology for Development. The role of the EEC in international organizations has a particular significance in that during the 1970s such forums have become the primary diplomatic instrument for many states. The richer OECD countries can still maintain a network of embassies throughout the world and they use the facilities possessed by international organizations only as secondary instruments. In contrast, the bulk of the new states acting on the contemporary world stage rely to a very considerable extent on international organizations as the principal focus of their diplomacy. Most Third World countries send their ablest diplomatic personnel to the organizations based in such cities as Geneva, Paris, Brussels and New York; using them to negotiate with the other diplomats based there. As a result, the European Community finds itself increasingly involved in international diplomacy deriving from its role in international organizations generally. As the European Commission rather than the member states tends to represent the EEC on a day-to-day basis in these organizations, this itself tends to enhance the Commission's own diplomatic status.

The operational base for external relations – None of the founding treaties establishing the three European Communities contain specific commitments obliging the member states to collaborate in creating common foreign policy initiatives. When establishing the three Communities, the founding members were primarily concerned to 'further trade and co-operation among themselves and to promote their own prosperity. Although it would be wrong to describe them as simply selfish and inward looking, the processes they set in motion of necessity involved their own economies first and foremost. These processes, however, have since proved to have very important external consequences both for the Six themselves and now for the Nine, and for third countries outside the Community framework.'[16]

The EEC's involvement in external trade relations stems directly from the Common External Tariff (CET) and the CAP. As already mentioned, the basis of the EEC is the customs union to which all the member states are committed. Article 111 of the EEC Treaty gave the Community the express task of negotiating with third countries on the basis of the CET from the very beginning of the Community's existence. Thus from its very emergence the EEC was rightly viewed as an international negotiating body in its own right, replacing the member states in international trade talks and becoming the bargaining partner confronting other countries in their search for trade concessions from the Six.

Three broad phases can be identified when looking at the EEC's operational bases for external relations since the mid 1950s. The first, dating from the founding of the EEC until the early 1960s relates to the need for the Community to make special arrangements with traditional trading partners; substituting the EEC as the partner in place of the Six individually in special trading relationships. During the second phase, spanning the remainder of the 1960s until the early 1970s, the EEC found itself subject to increasing international pressures from particular groups of countries. While the EEC's external posture was essentially responsive to external initiatives, the nature of its responses became increasingly more haphazard, leading to what can be described as an entangling web of external commitments. The third phase, broadly spanning the years since 1972, has been one in which the EEC's external relations have been dominated by essentially

---

[16] *Ibid.*, p. 15.

responsive characteristics, but where the beginnings of a framework for positive external policy initiatives can also be identified. The emergence of these Community-level external policy initiatives was based on the member states' recognition of the EEC's collective economic and political strength, especially in the aftermath of Community enlargement from six to nine.

During the first phase of external relations, the member states were confronted with the need to amend, adapt, and substitute new collective arrangements consistent with their obligations under the EEC treaty for pre-existing commitments. The first of these, as already mentioned, was the need for the member states to represent themselves collectively via EEC institutions in the GATT. In addition, and in many ways more dramatically, there was the obligation imposed by the Rome Treaty itself (Part IV, articles 131 to 136) to create multilateral trading links between the new Community and those colonies and dependencies of the member states in Africa, the Caribbean and other parts of the world who previously had special economic relations with one or more of the Six. Clearly, the most far-reaching obligations in this respect arose from the French empire in Africa, and the association links subsequently created by Part IV of the Rome Treaty have survived the upheavals of the last twenty-five years or so. Part IV Association itself evolved in the early 1960s into the Yaoundé Association regime providing the Associated African and Malagasy States (AAMS) with privileged trade and aid relations with the EEC.[17] In addition, article 238 of the Rome Treaty provided the basis for the EEC to negotiate association arrangements with other third countries. Many Mediterranean countries who were anxious to maintain trade access to the EEC market in the face of the CET and the CAP sought arrangements under its auspices.

Article 113 of the EEC Treaty provided the basis for the Common Commercial Policy, 'based on uniformly established principles, particularly in regard to tariff amendments, to the conclusion of tariff and trade agreements, to the establishing of uniform practice as regards methods of liberalization, to export policy, and to commercial protective measures including measures to be taken in cases of dumping or subsidies'. Within the general framework of its move towards a common commercial policy, the EEC in the early 1960s negotiated non-preferential trade agreements with several countries, providing concessions under the CET and the CAP for a range of products. In particular, dating from this period, were the trade agreements with the Lebanon, Iran and Israel; in each case the arrangements related to fairly specific lists of products for which the countries concerned were the main EEC suppliers. It was not until the third phase of external relations that the EEC considered establishing positive preferential trade agreements with third countries.

Throughout this early period of the EEC's existence, however, its external

---

[17] This aspect of the EEC's association regime is dealt with in Carol Cosgrove Twitchett, *Europe and Africa: from association to partnership* (Teakfield, 1978).

relations were dominated by the need to find accommodations with the other Western European countries who had declined to participate in the integration process, but nevertheless desired relationships with the EEC. The United Kingdom and the Scandinavian countries took the lead in proposing a wider free trade area within the framework of the OEEC in 1958–59, which would encompass the newly established EEC. In the aftermath of these ill-fated negotiations, the so-called 'seven outside' created the European Free Trade Association (EFTA) amongst themselves, but within a very short time the United Kingdom, Norway, Denmark and Ireland then applied for membership of the EEC itself. The energy demanded by these negotiations doubtless placed a very great strain on the internal mechanisms of the EEC. Simultaneously, the United States proposed what later became known as the 'Kennedy Round' of trade negotiations which led to across-the-board reductions in international tariffs of an unprecedented nature; these involved the Community in additional extensive readjustments of its CET and common commercial policy framework.

The second stage of the Community's external relations broadly spans the years from the aftermath of the abortive first British entry negotiations which ended in 1963, to the October 1972 summit presaging the enlargement of the Community to Nine. These years were a period of dramatic internal change amongst the Six, with President de Gaulle and France for the most part being in the ascendancy. During these years the EEC came to terms with the increasing range of demands made upon it in the aftermath of decolonization by developing countries throughout the world. In the early 1960s the EEC responded positively to the need to re-vamp its association arrangements and, as already mentioned, created the Yaoundé association links with the AAMS. That Convention lasted from 1964 to 1969 and was replaced by Yaoundé II, which broadly represented an evolution of the association relationship. Under the aegis of Yaoundé Association, the AAMS were afforded a range of reciprocal tariff preferences with the Community and had access to the European Development Fund (EDF) and various other special arrangements. A rather more limited association was concluded with the three East African States of Kenya, Tanzania and Uganda by the Convention of Arusha in 1969, and in 1971 Mauritius became the first Commonwealth country actually to join the Yaoundé association system.

At a broader international level, UNCTAD called for and obtained a positive Community response to its demands for special arrangements in respect of manufactured and semi-finished products from developing countries entering the EEC market. As a result of direct negotiations between the EEC and UNCTAD which continued throughout the later 1960s, the European Community pioneered the establishment of the Generalized System of Preferences (GSP), introducing its own GSP scheme in July 1971. At the same time, increasing pressure from Mediterranean countries who were worried about the restrictive impact of the CAP on their hitherto preferential trade with EEC member states led to the negotiation of a range of special agreements. Morocco and Tunisia, for example, concluded five-year arrangements with the EEC in 1969, while Malta did so in 1970, followed by Cyprus in 1972. Taken together with the pre-existing association agreements with Greece and Turkey and the various trade agreements with Mediterranean countries, these were a somewhat haphazard *montage* of external relationships, some of which were undoubtedly mutually contradictory. At the same time, the EEC found itself under increasing pressure from Latin American countries to enter negotiations regarding the impact of the CAP on their exports to Western Europe, and pressure from Asian countries to negotiate regarding the impact of CAP surplus production and the whole question of what came later in the 1960s and 1970s to be called food aid.

During the third phase of the EEC's external relations, a more structured pattern has begun to emerge in terms of Community responses to international pressures. In the 1970s the Nine increasingly appeared to take to heart Edward Heath's message during the British entry negotiations that collectively the Nine could exert preponderant influence in international relations. Since 1973 a distinct set of Community external relations has emerged based on geographical rather than sectoral divisions. At one level, the member states have been called upon to make collective, coherent responses to the other industrialized countries outside the EEC. In Western Europe, the aftermath of British, Danish and Irish membership in 1973, required negotiating coherent arrangements with the EFTA rump which led to a Western Europe-wide Industrial Free Trade Association. Similarly, relations with the United States, Japan, Canada and the other OECD countries have been dominated by the need for the Nine to come to terms with the economic power they wield. The 'Tokyo Round' of GATT tariff negotiations was successfully concluded in the late 1970s, and it is within that context that the Community has emerged as a meaningful diplomatic framework for its member states in international economic negotiations.

The 1970s were also a period during which the common commercial policy was imposed on EEC dealings with Eastern Europe. The last ten years or so effectively have witnessed the end of bilateral trade relations between Community member states and the socialist countries of Eastern Europe, and the emergence of an uneasy but none the less real trading relationship between the two European economic blocs. The Soviet Union has continued to refuse to accord *de jure* recognition to the EEC as an international actor, but in practice the logic of the CET, the CAP, and the emerging Common Fisheries Policy has forced Soviet negotiators to enter into direct talks with the European Community. The other socialist states of Eastern Europe have had fewer ideological difficulties to overcome in establishing direct contacts with the Community; contacts which have broadly worked to their advantage.

In many ways the 1970s proved to be the most dynamic era for relations between the EEC and the Third World. The Yaoundé Association regime was superseded by the Lomé links, the associated states being expanded to the ACP group of states; first in the Lomé Convention of 1975, and then in the second Convention of Lomé signed in 1979.[18] The Lomé link itself epitomized the all-encompassing nature of Community external policy towards developing countries. It created a contractual partnership between the ACP states on the one side and the EEC on the other, based on special non-reciprocal trade arrangements, the provision of aid by the EDF, the stabilization of ACP export earnings, and a range of other details. Outside the ACP group, however, the Community has proved itself less willing to enter into quite such far reaching arrangements with other developing countries. Nevertheless, the last ten years or so have witnessed the development of what have come to be called Commercial Co-operation Agreements with such countries as India, Bangladesh, Pakistan, Sri Lanka, Mexico and Brazil, and the beginnings of links with regional organizations throughout the Third World. In particular, in 1980 the EEC negotiated a special arrangement with ASEAN[19] and began negotiations with the ANDEAN group[20] in mid-1980.

At the global level the Community has tended to move towards a more positive development policy in response to demands by developing countries for a new international economic order based on a more dynamic North-South dialogue. The problems which have emerged from EEC relations with the Third World in many ways epitomize the limits of the Community as a diplomatic framework for its member states, particularly when that framework rests only on the Paris and Rome Treaty provisions. As is evident from the next section, it has only been with the evolution of political co-operation between the member states that a more coherent European Community development policy has begun to emerge; one embracing those areas of EEC competence and those policy areas within the jurisdiction of the national governments. For example, in the late 1970s the EEC has initiated a modest financial aid programme beyond the framework of the Lomé Convention. The member states also maintain independent aid programmes, both bilateral and via a range of multilateral links, which have yet to be subjected to far-reaching co-ordination at the Community level.

3. Towards a Common Foreign Policy

Political co-operation in the EEC: Any consideration of the EEC as a diplomatic framework must focus on the machinery for political co-operation

[18] For an examination of the Lomé regime, see Carol Cosgrove Twitchett, *A Framework for Development: the EEC and the ACP* (Allen and Unwin, 1981).
[19] See *Europe Forum*, 28 Mar. 1980, p. 10. The ASEAN states are Indonesia, Malaysia, the Philippines, Singapore, and Thailand.
[20] See 'The Community and the Andean Group', *The Courier*, no. 52, July-Aug. 1980, p. 86. The ANDEAN states are Bolivia, Colombia, Ecuador, Peru, and Venezuela.

among the member states. It was clear that from the Community's very inception the member states accepted that there would be a wide range of situations calling for a common external response. The previous section identified three broad phases of EEC external relations, and pinpointed some of the problems created by limitations in the basic Community treaties. In the 1970s the contradictions between Community competence and national jurisdiction became increasingly sharp, yet at the same time progressively less relevant as the member states found it more and more convenient to work together in terms of what has been called 'political co-operation', and which in many ways can be denoted as the beginning of a common foreign policy.

It should be stressed at the outset, however, that the question of a common foreign policy as opposed to simply continuing the conduct of external relations, presupposes concern with the security of the member states. Clearly, the Community founding treaties have no competence whatsoever in the field of military security. The Community has not and has no immediate prospect of having a defined military security role. But this does not mean that security policy as such is necessarily and wholly excluded from its purview. The EEC is a civilian power: 'an international polity as yet possessing no military dimension, but able to exercise influence on states, global and regional organizations, international corporations and other transnational bodies through diplomatic, economic and legal factors'.[21] As already mentioned, Ireland is outside the NATO alliance and France, although a signatory of NATO, since the 1960s has maintained its forces outside the framework of SACEUR. Similarly, Greek membership of the EEC in 1981 has meant another Community state which had withdrawn its forces from the common planning framework of NATO; Greece, of course, like France itself remains a member of the Western Alliance. Nevertheless, despite the lack of a defined common defence policy role, the EEC is indisputably influential in international security issues. It may have no legitimate role in defence questions, but few in the 1980s would dispute the enormous overlap between international economic relations and political security! The lessons of the 1970s, and particularly the international economic consequences for the whole world of the Arab-Israeli war of 1973, have underlined the intense and continuing interaction between military conflict and economic diplomacy.

In its widest sense, political co-operation is the essential basis for the continuing existence of the European Community. Without political co-operation, its member states could not sustain their common endeavours. During the 1970s, however, the phrase *political co-operation* acquired a distinct, somewhat artificial meaning, signifying a departure from the original Community method. It has come to imply the continuing attempt by the member states to co-ordinate their external policies and responses

---

[21] Ken Twitchett, *Europe and the World*, op. cit., p. xv.

in matters beyond the competence of the Community treaties. As such, it is a voluntary commitment to work together, and can only proceed at the pace dictated by the least enthusiastic member state. Operationally, the cumulative effect of the political co-operation process has been to promote what could be termed a broad co-ordination reflex among the foreign affairs ministries of the EEC member states. It is alleged that they now accept consultation on a Community-wide basis as an essential and indeed natural part of their policy-making processes. An important basis for political co-operation is the telex network code-named COREU, introduced in 1970, and which by 1979 was in intensive daily use between the member states. In fact, in 1979 some 4,327 messages were passed through the COREU network in all the various EEC languages, and there were more than twenty meetings at the political director level of the member states' foreign ministries. All the Nine acquiesced in the development of the political co-operation process, and appear to regard it as a useful means of overcoming the dilemmas posed by the limitations of the basic Community treaties.

The question of political co-operation was first aired at the summit meeting of the six heads of government in 1961, but not until the 1970s did *political co-operation* acquire a certain degree of institutionalization. In 1969 at The Hague, the then six member states put in motion the sequence of events which led to the Davignon Report of 1970, setting out the principal two objectives of political co-operation: first, the furtherance of improved understanding among the member states through the regular exchange of information between their foreign ministries; and second, the need to strengthen the member states' solidarity through harmonization and where possible the co-ordination of external policy initiatives. This was followed in 1973 by a second report on *European Political Cooperation and Foreign Policy* which broadly defined political co-operation as dealing with the problems of international politics at the intergovernmental level, distinct from and in addition to the external relations activities of the EEC.[22] From the beginning, there was clearly an overlap between political co-operation and EEC external relations. In the early 1970s several member states, in particular France, endeavoured to keep the two sets of activities apart. But as the decade drew to a close less stress began to be placed on the need for a clear distinction between the two. Annette Morgan has ably traced the coalescence of EEC external relations and political co-operation, suggesting that in 1976 the political co-operation machinery no longer rivalled EEC institutions, but rather acted as a buttress reinforcing the Community edifice.[23]

The actual machinery of political co-operation between the member states is fairly simple and uncomplicated. The *European Council* is the principal body, meeting some three times a year and bringing together the executive

[22] For further details, see *European Community*, July 1980, pp. 7–8.
[23] See Annette Morgan, *From Summit to Council* (Chatham House – Political and Economic Planning, 1976).

heads of governments of the member states. Underpinning the European Council are the meetings of the member states' foreign ministers, occurring approximately four times a year, but more often if the international situation so demands. Underpinning these pre-eminently 'political' meetings are those which bring together the political directors of the foreign ministries. They now meet at least once a month (in fact, twenty-one times in 1979) with the intention of keeping a finger on the pulse of international affairs as they affect the EEC member states both individually and collectively.

There is no continuing institutional apparatus to support these political co-operation meetings. However, a number of working groups have been established within the framework of the political co-operation machinery which bring together senior officials from the various ministries of the member states to discuss major issues. At the beginning of 1980 there were some fifteen working groups in existence, each operating with its own clearly defined brief, focusing on either a specific region of the world or a specific issue. There is a working group for each region of the world; for example, there are groups for Africa, Latin America and South East Asia. With regard to 'issue areas', there are working groups on anti-terrorist co-operation, cultural co-operation, and questions relating to the continuing 'European Security Conference'. Each working group has spawned sub-groups bringing together officials of the Nine on a regular basis to consider collective action on more specific issues. Alongside these working groups, the ambassadors of the member states resident in foreign capitals meet regularly and submit joint reports to the political directors. For example, all the EEC ambassadors in Vienna meet regularly to consider collective responses in relation both to Austria specifically and to the various international organizations situated in that city.

There is no established secretariat attached to the political co-operation machinery. The resulting lack of continuity initially gave rise to a whole range of problems in the early 1970s, but these have since become less important. Secretariat functions are performed by the Presidency state; each member state takes responsibility for servicing the political co-operation machinery during its six months' term as President of Community institutions. The practice has developed since 1977 of increasingly close liaison between the existing Presidency state and its designated successor; to ease the eventual change-over, senior officials are seconded from one foreign office to the other. The Presidency places a significant extra burden on the foreign ministry concerned. In particular, the Presidency Secretariat is responsible for drafting the agenda for all the various political co-operation meetings, administering the procedural rules, and providing chairmen for all the various meetings which take place within the political co-operation framework. It also has the task of organizing collective statements by the member states in the wide range of international forums where the Presidency state has been given responsibility for speaking on behalf of the Community as a whole. The lack of continuity resulting from the absence of a permanent secretariat might be offset at least partially by creating a 'flying secretariat'. This could be composed of a core of officials from all the member states who would move with the Presidency; in effect, move from capital to capital to work with the national Presidency team.

The British Presidency of the EEC Council in 1977 proved an onerous experience for the Foreign Office. Matters were aggravated by the death of the Foreign Secretary, Anthony Crosland, during the British Presidency term. To some extent, however, good relations with the Commission were facilitated by the links between its President, Roy Jenkins, and James Callaghan's Labour Government: Roy Jenkins had been a very senior member of the Labour Government and the new Foreign Secretary, David Owen, was a committed European. Some officials from the British Foreign Office have suggested with hindsight that the burdens of servicing the political co-operation machinery proved more onerous than those associated with representing the EEC in the presidency role. The British were able to take some advantage of the sensible suggestions in the Tindemans Report on European Union for reducing the barriers between the political co-operation machinery and European Community institutions. The Commission could attend political co-operation meetings as a 'guest' only, although its staff are frequently invited to participate in working party discussions: Commission views can be made known, but it is not a party to decisions. While these limitations remain, the Foreign Office did promote a forceful pragmatic approach and there were many day-to-day overlaps between European Community business and political co-operation. Overall, as the Presidency state, the United Kingdom sought to involve the Commission more directly in the political co-operation machinery than had previously been attempted. For example, the British generally encouraged the Commission to second officials to United Kingdom missions in third countries (Bangladesh, for instance); an innovation not subsequently emulated by all the other member states, notably France.

The absence of an institutionalized role for the European Commission in the political co-operation machinery inevitably results in greater emphasis being placed on the role of COREPER. Throughout the 1970s the latter played a key liaison role between Community institutions as such and the political co-operation machinery. The Correspondent level is the crucial one for COREPER liaison with the member states' foreign ministries. The Correspondents are themselves senior foreign service officials, responsible directly to the political directors. They keep the political machinery working at the day-to-day level, and it is among them that the COREU direct telex link is operated. The Correspondents generally preside over the routine procedural rules of political co-operation and provide the key continuity element for each Presidency. In the British case, for example, UKREP in Brussels liaises on a day-to-day basis with the other states' equivalent representatives both directly through the Head of the British Mission in Brussels and indirectly via links between the Foreign Office Correspondents.

Originally links between the political co-operation machinery and the European Parliament were extremely weak. During the 1970s, however, direct regular contacts emerged between the Presidency state and the Parliament's Political Affairs Committee. Four annual meetings were arranged between the Foreign Ministers and the Political Affairs Committee under the old unelected parliamentary regime. Since the 1979 direct parliamentary elections there has been increasing pressure from the Parliament to expand the range of contacts with the political co-operation machinery, both officially and less formally. The Presidency state's representative, normally the foreign minister, now meets with the Political Affairs Committee immediately after each political co-operation session; frequently this is followed by a full debate in the Parliament. The member states have also agreed to answer questions from MEPs regarding the processes and content of political co-operation. The Presidency state, or its representative, is now prepared to answer written or oral questions from MEPs on all aspects of political co-operation, thereby taking the parliamentary discourse well beyond the confines of the Community treaties.

The end products of political co-operation are extremely difficult to evaluate. The precise instruments of this process are three: first, joint declarations by the member states, second, joint resolutions, and third, joint diplomatic *démarches*. For example, in 1978, piracy in the port of Lagos in Nigeria had reached such a level that the Nine agreed on a joint diplomatic *démarche* to the Nigerian Government protesting at this infamous activity. Earlier in 1977, the Nine agreed a joint resolution regarding the infringement of human rights in Latin America, particularly with reference to Chile and Uruguay. In 1977–78, the United Nations General Assembly debate on Southern Africa led to intense co-operation between the delegates of the Nine at the United Nations. The latters' African specialists met every day, sometimes twice a day during the Assembly meeting, and the eventual General Assembly Resolution on Southern Africa to a very great extent derived from the collective activity of the EEC member states.

The European Security Conference was a watershed in the progress of political co-operation among the Nine. At the Helsinki and Geneva meetings in 1974–75, the EEC proved that it could function coherently in the security field through the Presidency state at conference meetings in the fields of economics, trade and the environment. At Belgrade in 1977, the Community context proved to be the catalyst for the Nine regarding further extensions of European security issues, especially concerning economic relations between Eastern and Western Europe. In the later 1970s the Nine adopted common positions on independence for Zimbabwe and Namibia, and called on South Africa to abandon its apartheid policies. Through the political co-operation machinery the Nine established a 'code of conduct on employment in Southern Africa', an important collective achievement in its own right, and one all OECD countries are now urged to adopt. In the Middle East, the Nine have spoken collectively in support of a comprehensive and lasting settlement of the Arab-Israeli conflict. In June 1979 they expressed their opposition to settlements by Israeli nationals on the West Bank. Throughout the 1970s, in fact, the EEC states were engaged in what is termed the 'Euro-Arab dialogue', aimed at strengthening ties between them and the Arab world. In 1980, the EEC was at the forefront of diplomatic initiatives to promote the easing of tension between Israel and her Arab neighbours, and to obtain greater momentum towards the peace settlement promised by the Camp David talks between Israel and Egypt under American auspices. While the European Community states have fallen short of calling for direct participation by the Palestine Liberation Organization in talks with Israel, they have succeeded in presenting a relatively united front, more or less independent from the United States, to the Arab world. These attempts to foster a coherent and uniquely *European* view of the continuing Arab–Israeli tension occurred at a time when the United States under President Carter was increasingly preoccupied with its own domestic political crisis.

In the world at large the Nine used the political co-operation machinery throughout the 1970s to seek to alleviate the plight of refugees, especially in Indochina in the aftermath of the wars in Vietnam and Cambodia. The machinery has also been used in the context of direct diplomatic links with the member states of ASEAN, overlaying the EEC–ASEAN accord of 1980. In addition the Nine agreed to implement the European Convention on the suppression of terrorism and, at the end of 1979, they agreed to establish a *European judicial zone* in response to the challenge of international terrorism.

The efficacy of the political co-operation machinery was severely tested by the differing reactions of the Nine to the Soviet invasion of Afghanistan in December 1979. The initial public responses of France and the United Kingdom, for example, were widely divergent. The British Conservative Government, led by Margaret Thatcher, strongly supported the United States' apparently tough line calling for immediate sanctions against the Soviet Union; in contrast France argued that events in Afghanistan should be seen as a 'local episode rather than as evidence of a new era of Soviet expansionism, and that the EEC's response should be tailored accordingly'.[24] At the time of the Soviet invasion, no political co-operation machinery meeting was planned for at least two weeks, and when the Foreign Ministers did get around to discussing the question, some member states had already made known their own independent reactions.

Discussion of any subject under the political co-operation heading depends on agreement by all the member states. France, especially, was reluctant to discuss Afghanistan, and so there was no question of an emergency meeting of EEC Foreign Ministers or Heads of Government in response to the Soviet invasion. Lord Carrington, the British Foreign Secretary, and Mr Francesco Cossiga, the then Italian Prime Minister and President of

[24] *The Times*, 19 Feb. 1980.

the European Council, did attempt to undertake initiatives to improve the procedures. Lord Carrington, in fact, suggested that any future crisis 'should trigger automatic EEC consultations among political directors and Foreign Ministers'.[25] But no firm public agreements have yet been reached on such a formal revision to the hitherto established political co-operation procedures. The conspicuous disunity displayed by the Nine regarding the Afghanistan crisis and the ensuing attempted sanctions against the Soviet Union (such as boycotting the Olympic Games), emphasized the inadequacies of political co-operation. However, as Arrigo Levi proclaimed:

> when the Nine are really inspired to play together each national foreign policy being called into action at the right time like a instrument in a chamber orchestra, the results can be impressive. But, of course, there is no director, no score to follow. Rather than an orchestra, the Nine are a jazzband, improvising in a jam session. Results can also be painfully ear shattering.[26]

The essential problem is to reconcile unity with diversity. The political co-operation machinery is 'a strange animal having one body and nine heads',[27] and rests fundamentally on consensus and voluntary action; unanimous support by the member governments is absolutely essential at all times. Common policies can only evolve from political co-operation if the information fed to the national foreign ministries through the COREU network strikes responsive common chords. Each member state possesses veto power as long as consensus remains the key; a qualification applying as much to the calling of emergency meetings as to the more regular items on the agenda. Lord Carrington's proposals for an automatic mechanism to promote a meeting of the member states in a crisis situation would necessitate something less than unanimous consent to override objections from individual member countries. Perhaps not surprisingly, France, with its Gaullist heritage and long traditions of independence in an EEC context, has proved the least responsive of the member states to the British proposals.

The discordant Community response to the United States' call for economic sanctions against Iran because of the continued imprisonment of American hostages, further emphasized the weakness of the political co-operation machinery in the absence of the active, unanimous consent of all the member states. West Germany, with British and Italian support, took the lead in April 1980 in advocating a tough European Community line in response to President Carter's call for trade sanctions against Iran. On the other hand, France was markedly unenthusiastic in her response; French reluctance to some extent was understandable given the refuge in Paris granted to Ayatollah Khomeini during his exile under the Shah. However, the lukewarm sanctions against Iran agreed by the Nine in April 1980

[25] *The Economist*, 8 Feb. 1980.
[26] *The Times*, 28 Feb. 1980.
[27] *Ibid.*

were immediately undermined in May by the British Conservative Government's decision not to implement them on the agreed timetable. This immediately was seen as a major weakness on the part of the United Kingdom, especially as the Thatcher Government had ceaselessly trumpeted the need for EEC solidarity with the United States on Iran and other international issues. Perhaps, unavoidably, British credibility in the context of political co-operation in particular, and within the European Community in general, took a severe blow.

The diplomatic interests of the member states – Nevertheless, from the perspective of the early 1980s, all the member states seem to desire more far-reaching external Community policies, and are prepared to work with the existing political co-operation machinery to achieve that goal. To date it appears that the Community offers all of them advantages as a diplomatic framework. For the smaller member states, the European Community (whether in the context of the Community institutions as such or within the framework of political co-operation) is a vehicle for increased influence in world affairs. For example, Gaston Thorn, now President of the European Commission, was President of the United Nations General Assembly in 1976 – a post which he as the then Luxembourg Premier could not really have hoped to obtain if he had not been the combined EEC candidate. In 1977, Belgium played a decisive role in the GATT multifibre negotiations, and by virtue of her EEC Presidency exerted a major influence on textile trading policies between industrialized and developing countries. Ireland, for its part, has become involved to a much greater extent than hitherto in the Arab world and in relations with developing countries generally as a direct result of participation in the European Community. Similarly, the Netherlands and Denmark have also found many advantages in participating in international affairs via the EEC.

The advantages of the EEC as a diplomatic framework are no less for the larger Community countries. For Italy, the Community has proved a major platform for Italian diplomacy in Western Europe, in East-West relations, and within the Atlantic Alliance. For West Germany, the Community has offered a convenient vehicle for her emerging global foreign policy and a framework for her *ost politik*. For France, the Community has acquired legitimacy as a basis for French actions in the world at large, and on the whole there has been a happy coincidence between French and Community interests in the propagation of external policy – a fortuitous state of affairs ardently fostered by Paris initiatives.

For the United Kingdom, the 1970s have proved to be a difficult time diplomatically. Successive British Governments were glad to act within the more cosy Community context in response to the continuing crises which have occurred in the Middle East and South East Asia. Both Conservative and Labour Party leaders have seen the Community as a base to support global British initiatives. The British Conservative Party recognized very early in the 1970s that the United Kingdom has a much greater chance of exercising meaningful influence at a global level acting in concert with its European partners than acting alone; and this lesson seems to have been learned at least by some among the Labour Party's higher echelons. As was shown during her 1977 Presidency, the United Kingdom did not readily accept an absolute distinction between Community external relations and political co-operation processes, and the British Foreign Office has worked consistently to promote the involvement of the Community institutions in all aspects of its external policy initiatives. Like the other member states, the United Kingdom has been intent on shaping Community foreign policy initiatives to reflect British interests and priorities. This is hardly surprising given that all the member states try consistently to further so-called 'national interests'!

Since the first British Presidency of January–June 1977, Community relations with developing countries have often been in the forefront of EEC involvement in the world at large. An EEC development policy as such still eludes a successful definition, but there is a wide range of Community policies towards developing countries which have been fostered and encouraged by each member state as they in turn have taken over the Presidency of Community institutions and chaired the political co-operation meetings. For example, when the United Kingdom handed the Presidency over to Belgium in July 1977, the two countries worked together to support France's chairmanship of the so-called 'North–South dialogue', the Conference on International Economic Co-operation then proceeding in Paris. Belgium in turn passed the Presidency on to Denmark in January 1978, and during the first six months of 1978, the Danes attempted to create a more coherent EEC-based framework for financial and technical assistance policies by the Nine to developing countries generally, and especially to those outside the framework of the Lomé Convention. When West Germany took over the Presidency in July 1978, it was immediately confronted with the need to cope with the early negotiations to revise EEC–ACP links; negotiations which led eventually to the second Lomé Convention of 1979. West Germany placed an indelible influence on the Lomé II negotiations, especially through its espousal of the export earnings guarantee scheme to be applied to mineral exports of the ACP countries and extending the so-called STABEX system.

France took over responsibility for negotiating with the ACP countries during the first six months of 1979. The French Foreign Minister, M. François Poncet, went so far as to make the successful conclusion of negotiations with the ACP countries a major priority, indeed the foremost priority, of the French Presidency. In actual fact, the negotiations were not successfully concluded under the French Presidency, but continued in a desultory and divided fashion under the following Irish Presidency until Lomé II was signed in October 1979. Italy presided over the Community during the first six months of 1980, steering the EEC's collective response to the Brandt Commission Report on relations between the industrialized and the developing countries, and attempting to encourage a broadening of Community policies beyond the Lomé Convention itself. Similarly, Luxembourg took over the Presidency for the last six months of 1980 and made an improvement of EEC relations with developing countries one of the principal planks of its presidential diplomacy. M. Thorn spoke on behalf of the Nine at the United Nations Special Session which commenced in August 1980 to review the lack of progress toward a new international economic order. For the first six months of 1981 it was the Netherlands' responsibility to coax the other member states into making a concerted, coherent, and positive response to the demands of the Third World as exemplified in the United Nations debate on international economic relations scheduled to last throughout 1981. Indeed, the second British Presidency, commencing in July 1981, may well be judged in hindsight by its ability to use the European Community as a dynamic diplomatic framework for promoting a consistent and coherent Community image in response to Third World demands. Regretfully, at the present time, there is little evidence that such a dynamic approach will be forthcoming.

4. Britain and Community Europe

In general British responses to attempts to build a new Europe since the end of the Second World War have been characterized by insular suspicion. The Schuman Plan of May 1950 for a European coal and steel community was greeted with grave doubts by both the Conservative and Labour parties. The then Labour Government of Clement Attlee was intensely suspicious of any apparent attempt by Western European countries to embroil war-battered Britain in their problems. Perhaps a greater source of disappointment to Western Europe, however, was the similar response by the Conservative Party when it was returned to office in 1951. Winston Churchill, the Conservative Prime Minister, had won a widespread reputation as the 'Father of Europe' in the late 1940s; in particular, for his Zurich speech of September 1946 calling for the establishment of a 'United States of Europe'. However, his party and he himself when returned to political power, tended to favour closer co-operation in post-war Europe only so long as this did not infringe the United Kingdom's freedom of action and presented no threat to British interests. When the ECSC was set up by the Treaty of Paris of April 1951, full participation by the United Kingdom was ruled out because it was feared that membership would encroach on British sovereignty and undermine Commonwealth ties. These attitudes were echoed in British responses to the proposals for European defence and political communities in 1952-53; the United Kingdom's refusal to participate being a decisive factor in the demise of the EDC project in 1954. Indeed, although prepared to sign a limited association agreement with the ECSC in 1954, the United Kingdom continued to stand aloof from the mainstream of Western European integration throughout the 1950s.

Following the failure of the EDC, the Six, meeting at Messina in June 1955, declared their intention to continue to strive for a more united Europe. They set up an intergovernmental committee under Paul-Henri Spaak to report on prospects for general economic union and union in the nuclear energy field. The Six approved the Spaak Report in May 1956, and invited other European countries to take part in the negotiations for the new communities. The British Conservative Government of Anthony Eden decided not to participate and in October 1956 declared its preference for a wider European free trade area. The British proposals for the free trade area were interpreted by the Six as evidence of a desire to sabotage the embryonic common market venture; the United Kingdom's subsequent negotiations with them under the auspices of the OEEC were inconclusive. The United Kingdom did not adhere to the two Rome Treaties signed by the Six in March 1957 establishing the EEC and Euratom. The two new communities came into operation on 1 January 1958, and the then British Conservative Government of Harold Macmillan was instrumental in the formation of the rival European Free Trade Association in May 1960. Miriam Camps, a veteran commentator on British relations with Europe, maintained that 'there has never been much real understanding in the United Kingdom of the depth of the drive towards real unity, as distinct from intergovernmental co-operation, on the continent'.[28]

The Macmillan Government, however, soon changed its mind, and the United Kingdom submitted an application for membership of the European Communities in May 1961. But it was evident that the United Kingdom still gravely underestimated the overall determination of the Six to achieve a high degree of meaningful European integration. Harold Macmillan declared to the House of Commons in July 1961 that 'no British Government could join the EEC without prior negotiations with a view to meeting the needs of Commonwealth countries, of our EFTA partners, and of British agriculture consistent with the broad principles and purposes which have inspired the concept of European unity and which are embodied in the Rome Treaty'.[29] The Labour Party under the leadership of Hugh Gaitskell opposed the application for Community membership. The negotiations themselves focused on these issues together with the question of British sovereignty and the supremacy of parliament. They were brought to a decisive end by President de Gaulle's veto of January 1963; a veto which came as a considerable shock to France's EEC partners as well as to the United Kingdom.

The Labour Government of Harold Wilson decided to re-apply for Community membership in May 1967. President de Gaulle was still reluctant to accept British accession, and for some three years all that

---

[28] See Miriam Camps, *Britain and the European Community, 1955–63* (Oxford University Press, 1964), p. 339.

[29] Harold Macmillan to the House of Commons, 31 July 1961, *H.C. Debates*, vol. 645, col. 929.

France's EEC partners could do was to leave the British and allied applications on the Community agenda; the British application had been followed by ones from Denmark, Ireland, and Norway. French intransigence was eased with the accession of Georges Pompidou to the French Presidency, and new membership negotiations began at the end of June 1970. They were successfully completed by the end of 1971, and the British Treaty of Accession was signed on 22 January 1972. The United Kingdom along with Denmark and Ireland became full members of the European Community on 1 January 1973 – although Norway had also signed an accession treaty, it had been rejected in the subsequent Norwegian referendum (by 53 per cent to 47 per cent). Although the successful British negotiations commenced under Harold Wilson's Labour Government, they were concluded by a Conservative one headed by Edward Heath. The United Kingdom thus entered Community Europe under Conservative not Labour auspices. In fact, the change of government from Labour to Conservative in part explains the Labour Party's continuing ambivalence to British membership of the EEC. The membership issue became entwined with general domestic hostility to the Heath administration, especially its record in the field of industrial relations. However, the 'Tory terms' negotiated by Geoffrey Rippon were probably not much different to those which George Thomson would have obtained for the Wilson administration.[30]

The successful 1970–71 negotiations focused on a number of crucial issues. These included the future shape of Community political institutions and their impact on parliamentary sovereignty, the implications of EEC membership for ties with the Commonwealth and the United States, the future of EFTA, British adaptation to the CAP, and the balance of payments effect of membership (together with the future role of sterling). Other more minor issues were such interrelated areas as fiscal, regional, and social policies, including the introduction of a value-added tax system. Perhaps the most positive governmental contribution to the domestic debate on British membership was the publication of a White Paper entitled, *Britain and the European Communities: an economic assessment.*[31] This document contained what in hindsight were remarkably accurate predictions of the impact of EEC membership on the United Kingdom in terms of increases in the cost of living index, the balance of payments contribution, and the general equation between what at the time were called the *impact effects* and the *dynamic effects* of entry. The White Paper stated that 'it is clear that any assessment of the economic effects of membership of an enlarged Community must include substantial and continuing balance of payments cost, notably that arising from the Common Agricultural Policy and its financing, which must be set against the substantial economic benefits

[30] For an elaboration of this point, see Uwe Kitzinger, *Diplomacy and Persuasion* (Thames and Hudson, 1973), p. 308.
[31] Cmnd. 4289 (London, HMSO, 1970).

expected from the dynamic effects of membership as well as the expected increase in invisible earnings'.[32]

Unfortunately, the *dynamic effects* of membership have not proved so beneficial as originally envisaged for a variety of reasons, including the United Kingdom's own poor industrial performance. Moreover, since the United Kingdom joined the EEC in January 1973, the prevailing international economic climate has been increasingly disadvantageous. It is therefore extremely difficult to extrapolate the direct impact of membership on the British economy compared with that of the continuing world recession on a country as dependent on international trade and finance as the United Kingdom. Whatever the economic *pros* and *cons*, however, there is considerable evidence to suggest that despite seven years or so of membership, the vast majority of Britons do not accept the logic of Community membership. In fact, public opinion polls and other tests of opinion suggest that there is little identification with Community Europe; most Britons are apathetic if not actually hostile to the EEC. The direct elections to the European Parliament of June 1979 attracted a very low turn-out, and in many British Euro-constituencies under 30 per cent of the electorate bothered to vote. Current interest in the EEC is confined almost totally to the costs of membership – estimated at more than 1,000 million pounds sterling per annum. This British preoccupation with the 'Euro-cash equation' has had adverse effects on the attitudes of the United Kingdom's partners to British interests. At least four main interrelated factors help to explain why many British people still consider the United Kingdom as *in* but not *with* Community Europe: first, historical and geographical legacies; second, continuing political divisions within the two major political parties; third, the very nature of the problems confronting the member states at the present time; and fourth, a general failure on the part of EEC institutions themselves to communicate adequately with ordinary people.

Perhaps the most important single factor, certainly the most basic one, is the historical legacy of British geographical separation from continental Europe. Until comparatively recently the United Kingdom deliberately isolated itself from its European neighbours and concentrated on forging links with other parts of the world. For many Britons today, the peoples of continental Europe are essentially 'foreigners' of a wholly different order to the 'kith and kin' of the old white Commonwealth countries of Australia, Canada and New Zealand, and even the United States. In addition to these somewhat emotional inheritances, differences of tradition between the United Kingdom and her continental partners have been accentuated by the harmonization process which has taken place under EEC auspices since the early 1970s. Not all the Community's harmonization measures have struck an unsympathetic chord in the United Kingdom, but some have undoubtedly aroused the hostility of powerful British interest groups. One particularly

---

[32] *Ibid.*, para. 102.

vexed issue in the harmonization sphere derives from attempts to create a common transport policy. At present there are different weight limits for heavy goods vehicles throughout the Community. The limit is 32 tons in the United Kingdom, but higher in many other EEC countries; the European Commission currently is proposing a harmonized weight limit of 44 metric tons. The geological and geographical factors which have shaped the United Kingdom's road and bridge systems are such that it would be very difficult for rural areas especially to accommodate the resulting heavier lorries – an aspect underlined by the increasingly powerful British environmentalist lobby. Another facet of the common transport policy which has triggered the ire of powerful British interest groups is the attempt to introduce tachographs into all commercial vehicles – the infamous 'spy in the cab' so disliked by the influential Transport and General Workers' Union.

An essential ingredient of the problem is that most British groups and organizations are not European-oriented in their attitudes and outlooks. A good example is provided by the Post Office's reaction to the European Commission's suggestion that national postal rates should not discriminate between different parts of the Community; in other words, letters sent from London to Copenhagen should incur the same postal charge as those going from London to Aberdeen, Birmingham or Coventry. One reason the Post Office offered for rejecting the suggestion was that most Britons correspond far more with countries outside Europe (especially Australia and Canada) than with the EEC's continental member states. The Post Office disputed the rationale of any symbolic need for uniform domestic and Community-wide postal tariffs. Indeed, the United Kingdom's anti-European heritage is such that the EEC is blamed for matters outside its control. A good example is the domestic British debate on replacing *imperial* weights and measures by the continental *metric system*. Many United Kingdom citizens believe that metrication, and the entire decimalization process, has been dictated by Community membership, whereas the British Government had committed itself to these innovations prior to the commencement of the successful British entry negotiations of 1970–71. Needless to say, the decimalization principle is unpopular in the United Kingdom, especially among those who left school prior to the 1970s.

There are very deep political divisions within the United Kingdom on the EEC membership issue. Between 1974 and 1979, the split inside the governing Labour Party between the *pro* and *anti* Marketeers coloured all attempts to assess the results of Community membership. Inside the Labour Party itself there is a long tradition of standing aloof from continental entanglements, which stretches back far beyond the Attlee Government's rejection of the ECSC proposal in 1950. When the Party was returned to power in 1974, it began negotiations for an adjustment in the terms governing British membership. The first national referendum in British political history was held on the renegotiated terms in June 1975. In hindsight the referendum did little to settle the membership question. The fact that in some bewilderment the British people voted to remain in the EEC by a massive two-to-one majority did not represent a lasting victory for the pro-Marketeers nor did it foster a greater sense of identity with Britain's partners in the European Community. The membership debate within the Labour Party itself was equally unfinished. This debate, of course, was not simply a debate about EEC membership, but was also about the balance of power within the Labour Party; indeed, about the very nature of the Party itself. Throughout the 1960s and early 1970s there had been tensions within the Labour Party between, in Uwe Kitzinger's words, the 'well-educated middle-class donnish element in the party' and those from trade union and working class backgrounds. While educational background as such was not a decisive guide to attitudes, one could appreciate the gulf between the predominantly blue-collar rank and file Labour supporters and the views allegedly expressed by a middle-class pro-Marketeer Labour MP during the 1975 Referendum campaign:

'For those of us who love the poetry of Victor Hugo, the music of Beethoven, or the sculptures of Michelangelo, who share the ethics of Aristotle and the Judaic-Christian ideals which are all part of Europe's heritage, today's artificial divisions seem about as sensible as customs posts on the Pennines to keep out Yorkshire wool'.
One could forgive them if they drew the conclusion that for those who did not love Victor Hugo's poetry – might in fact not be quite sure that he had written any – the Channel did not seem all that artificial a division.[33]

The referendum itself took place on the basis of the renegotiated membership terms obtained by Harold Wilson and James Callaghan; therefore logically it was perhaps no longer appropriate for the Labour Party to decry the infamous 'Tory terms'. Unfortunately, however, logic has never been a comfortable bed-fellow beside the emotional appeal of *gut-feelings* among the supporters of all political parties. Within the Labour Party the spectrum of opinion stretches from those who favour EEC membership like Roy Hattersley, to those such as Tony Benn who advocate withdrawal from the Community. In fact, grave disquiet at growing anti-EEC sentiment in the Labour Party was one reason why the Gang of Four (Roy Jenkins, David Owen, William Rodgers and Shirley Williams) and their supporters founded the Social Democratic Party. Gaining growing support is the view that the EEC should become a wider but much looser grouping of states, somewhat reminiscent of EFTA; a grouping where each participating state would remain responsible for its own domestic economic and social policies – the sovereignty of national political institutions being maintained. But the predominant attitude within the Labour Party to the EEC remains one of hostility. Indeed, on 1 October 1980, the annual conference meeting at Blackpool voted by 5,042,000 to 2,097,000 to make the United Kingdom's

---

[33] Kitzinger, op. cit., pp. 324–5.

withdrawal from the Community a priority in the next Labour Party general election manifesto.

Continuing tensions within the Conservative Party have also played a part in frustrating attempts to create a closer feeling of identity between the British people and their fellow Community citizens. There are those such as Edward Heath who favour a strengthened EEC, but a significant minority agree with Teddy Taylor that the United Kingdom's future lies outside the Community. Margaret Thatcher herself is far from being an uncritical admirer of Community Europe. In 1977, for example, she publicly advocated continued British membership, but also proposed a general down-grading of Community institutions including only a very modest role for a directly elected European Parliament.[34] A 1980 Conservative Party report noted a general feeling of disenchantment with the EEC concept among rank and file members. Apparently they are increasingly concerned with the Community's lack of achievement in contributing to the solution of the major problems confronting the United Kingdom and its partners in the world today; the report denoted particular criticism of the member states' failure to present a common front in response to the Afghanistan and Iranian crises and the Moscow Olympic boycott.[35] Indeed, Conservative ministers such as Neil Marten and former Tory Enoch Powell have similar attitudes to Labour critics of the common market idea like Michael Foot and Peter Shore in their suspicion of supranational organizations and the importance they attach to British political institutions, especially parlia-mentary sovereignty. In fact, the response of the House of Commons as a whole to Community membership has been a somewhat 'negative and introspective' concern with 'the effect on its own formal powers and traditional procedures than about the real needs of the interests directly affected and of the general public'.[36] Overall, of all the major British political parties, only the Liberals have remained steadfast in their support of Community Europe.

The third factor underlying the lack of British commitment to the EEC stems from the very nature of the difficult domestic and international scenarios confronting the countries of the Western world during the 1970s. During the last decade or so the United Kingdom and its EEC partners have been beset by a range of complex problems which seem likely to persist well into the 1980s. The international economic crisis which derived originally from the collapse of the dollar in 1971 and grew more acute with the global rise in oil prices following the 1973 Arab–Israeli War, created an international environment hostile to British interests. For their part the

---

[34] Mrs Thatcher's remarks were made in the foreword to John Biffen, *Political Office or Political Power* (Centre for Policy Studies, 1977).

[35] *The Times*, 30 Aug. 1980.

[36] See David Coombes and others, *The British People: Their Voice in Europe* (Saxon House for the Hansard Society, 1977), pp. 50 and 148.

British people appear to assume implicitly that many of the economic difficulties facing them somehow are due to Community membership. There seems to be a general reluctance to accept responsibility for domestic economic problems; problems which in large measure arise from long-term low productivity in manufacturing industry and disruptive industrial relations.[37] While international economic problems may well have complicated the process of mutual adjustment between the United Kingdom and the EEC, a major reason for the failure to make the most of the opportunities provided by Community membership is simply that the British people as a whole have not tried hard enough. The harsh degree of truth in this view must be balanced against the fact that British interests are not necessarily all well served by current Community policies. The contemporary EEC has evolved from negotiations and commitments undertaken by its six original member states; the policies which dominated the Community in the 1970s represented at least a rough balance of interest between the Six from which they could all expect to benefit – many of these benefits, however, have distinct structural disadvantages for the United Kingdom. It was inevitable, moreover, that vexed problems would arise because of attempts to integrate the United Kingdom with its distinctive position 'as a highly urbanised society with a small but efficient agricultural sector whose production is supplemented by substantial imports'. British ministers and officials found 'after entry that their partners were far less willing to change established policies or to entertain requests for different priorities than they had hoped'.[38] Whereas the United Kingdom was a founder member of such international organizations as the League of Nations, the United Nations, and NATO, and played a large role in setting their objectives and priorities, she was a late entrant into the EEC who had to accept a number of policies unpalatable to her as the price of membership.

The CAP has been the most unpalatable of all these policies. Its impact and the resultant excessive budgetary payments by the United Kingdom into the EEC coffers have been major focuses of public hostility to the EEC. During the 1979–80 British campaign to obtain a solution to the budgetary problem, Mrs Thatcher and her colleagues successfully encouraged domestic opinion to dwell on the iniquities of the Community budgetary system and the CAP, alleging that it worked to Britain's bitter disadvantage; the United Kingdom paying 20 per cent of the CAP's cost and receiving only 5 per cent of its benefits. Mrs Thatcher gained a package of concessions to cover the period 1979–82 at the Brussels summit meeting of May 1980. The reform of the CAP in the longer term has also been agreed in principle, and all the member states now recognize that the entire financial system should be

---

[37] For a discussion of these problems, see Carol Cosgrove Twitchett, 'The EEC and European Co-operation', in K. J. Twitchett (ed.), *European Co-operation Today*, op. cit.

[38] See William Wallace (ed.), *Britain in Europe* (Joint Studies in Public Policy, Heinemann, 1980), pp. 1–2.

recast by the end of 1982 as the EEC budget is then almost certain to go beyond the 1 per cent ceiling of VAT contributions. A British refund amounting to some £1,500 million for the years 1979–82 was agreed, but the deal is by no means complete. To some extent it is conditional on the establishment of a Common Fisheries Policy – an issue likely to cause major dissension between Denmark, France, and the United Kingdom; and the CAP, in 'Euro-speak', still has to be 're-structured'. Indeed, as the Labour Party's foreign affairs spokesman, Peter Shore, told the House of Commons, despite the Thatcher deal, the United Kingdom will still end up paying some £1,500 million over a three year period to countries richer than herself simply to increase already unmanageable food surpluses![39] Perhaps the hardest task still confronting the British Government is to ameliorate the domestic anti-Common Market sentiment in part engendered by its own efforts to secure a fair deal over the budgetary question.

Finally, British disenchantment with the EEC has also been aggravated by the increasing 'and often apparently mindless bureaucracy of the European Commission'.[40] The Commission has been accused of ill-conceived, almost silly policy proposals and ineptitude in its public relations. From the British perspective perhaps the most glaring examples have been the sale of subsidized butter to the Soviet Union while British consumers face ever-rising butter prices, and the threat to traditional British foodstuffs posed by various suggested Community harmonization measures – one of the most spectacular being the threat to the Bramley cooking apple due to the proposed EEC rules on the shape and size of apples. Such essentially trivial matters attract wide, unfavourable publicity, counteracting the favourable image which should accrue to the Commission for its useful work in such fields as regional aids and social policy. There is little effort, moreover, to relate the EEC to the lives of ordinary people – itself probably a major reason for the high abstention rate in the United Kingdom in the first direct elections to the European Parliament of June 1979. In fact, in many respects 'the EEC has failed like many an urban district council, to get its usefulness across to all ordinary folk. That is a lesson for the much-reviled Brussels bureaucracy, which though small as it is, nevertheless behaves far too big and bureaucratically far too often.' The fault also lies with 'the national governmental mammoths who, because they in fact dominate Brussels from afar, prevent it from doing many sensible things that ordinary people might understand'.[41] Indeed, as a group the Brussels bureaucrats are humane, well-meaning officials, dedicated to building a peaceful, more prosperous Europe; their essential failure is one of public relations.

Those clumsy edicts and policy endeavours which emanate from Brussels are publicized by the media in the United Kingdom, and the British public

[39] As reported in *Now*, 6 June 1980, p. 8.
[40] *The Times*, 30 Aug. 1980.
[41] *The Economist*, 16 June 1979, p. 13.

often lacks the necessary background perspective for evaluating them. Even when the press, radio, and television do provide adequate background coverage of EEC affairs, the resulting articles and programmes are often boring and dull; or, alternatively, the issues are over-trivialized in an attempt to give them maximum popular appeal. The quality and quantity of the literature and other information issued by the London offices of both the European Commission and the European Parliament is of a high standard, but unfortunately it reaches only a very limited audience – the converted or the informed, not the uninitiated with only a modicum of knowledge regarding British affairs let alone European ones. While there is also a very large body of literature available on Community Europe, much of it is too specialist and often too dull to appeal to the general public. The popular press and the media in general, have a massive task before them if they wish to persuade the bulk of ordinary Britons that the United Kingdom's future does lie irrevocably with Community Europe. Perhaps this task is not properly theirs; the emphasis could well lie more with efforts to inform those of school age about European affairs in general and the EEC in particular. The overall objective should be not so much to instil a sense of Community patriotism, still less a sense of European nationalism, but rather to inculcate a passive acceptance of the EEC similar to that with which people regard district councils and other domestic political institutions. In fact, patriotism in the passive sense and Europeanism in many respects reinforce rather than undermine each other.

Taken together, the aforementioned factors help explain the British people's lack of identification with Community Europe. The original six member states, moreover, had at least two advantages in acclimatizing to the EEC. First, they joined together at a time of economic advancement and prosperity, whereas, as has already been emphasized, the United Kingdom joined in the collective endeavour during a period of international economic recession. There was no time for the British people to become accustomed to EEC membership within the context of overall increases in their prosperity and well-being. Second, and perhaps more importantly, 'the Europeans were used to some extent to co-operating with each other due to their geographical proximity. The degradation which they all experienced during the Second World War helped them to accept that if they did not hang together, they could well hang separately. France with her legacy of empire was perhaps the last to learn this lesson. The United Kingdom, on the other hand, never suffered wartime humiliation in quite the same immediate way as the continental European states, and her pretensions to an imperial role have been much more long-lasting. Indeed, it has been much more difficult for the British people to consider themselves 'European'. 'Fog in the English Channel, continent cut off', perhaps all too aptly still symbolizes the British attitude to European affairs!'[42] A real and permanent British adjustment to

[42] See Ken Twitchett, 'Britain and Community Europe, *International Relations*, Nov. 1979, pp. 713–14.

Community membership, in effect, is more a matter of ambience and nuance than of resolving such technical issues as budgetary contributions and butter prices.

5. Summary and Conclusions

It is clear that the United Kingdom and its fellow EEC member states will speak with one voice in international relations and use the Community as a convenient diplomatic framework if there is no clear and unavoidable clash between defined Community positions and the major interests of individual member states. Increasingly, they are adopting common stands on such issues as trade negotiations with Japan, the international implications of South African apartheid, the search for peace in the Middle East, negotiations with developing countries over textile imports, and debates in the United Nations General Assembly. It is apparent that the world at large expects the Community to speak with one voice, and frequently looks for much greater solidarity on the part of the member states than can reasonably be expected in view of their internal dissensions. The European Court of Justice confirmed in 1977 that the Community treaties themselves provide sound operational bases for EEC activity in the realm of international economic negotiations:

> whenever Community law has created for the institutions of the Community powers within its internal system for the purpose of attaining a specific objective, the Community has authority to enter into the international commitments necessary for the attainment of that objective even in the absence of an express provision in that connection.[43]

The Court thus affirmed that the Community's external powers are parallel with its internal prerogatives despite silence in the founding treaties. The process of political co-operation, moreover, has taken collective member state action in the world at large far beyond the limitations set by the confines of the founding Community documents. The EEC member states themselves have created the machinery through which they could present the Community to the world as a more united, coherent entity. The United Kingdom has participated fully in this process. Unfortunately, however, as is demonstrated by the various contributions to this symposium, in almost all the member states there are powerful interest groups who doubt the efficacy of Community membership. In none of them are the doubts so strongly expressed and the general lack of identification with Community Europe so apparent as in the United Kingdom. A survey of opinion in the nine member states carried out by the European Commission in the summer of 1980 found that only 23 per cent of Britons believed that the European

[43] See The European Communities, *Commission Background Report*, ISEC/B/38/78, 19 May 1978.

Community 'was a good thing compared with 49 per cent who had the opposite view. In all other Member States there [was] a majority which feels the Community is a good thing. The Community average is 55 per cent for and 15 per cent against.'[44]

It should be emphasized that neither this chapter nor the other contributions to this symposium advocate that the Community rather than the countries of their birth should be the ultimate focus of loyalty for the peoples of the EEC. This point causes frequent misunderstanding, especially in the United Kingdom. Patriotism and Europeanism are not mutually exclusive, rather the reverse. Nevertheless, perhaps the 'most difficult point to get across to British public opinion about the European Community is that to be a good European one must first be a good patriot'.[45] Even if a reorientation of loyalty from the national to the European level was desirable, it is certainly unrealistic to anticipate such a change in the foreseeable future. In the words of Christopher Tugendhat, the British EEC Commissioner for the budget, 'A European loyalty should not be expected to take the place of national loyalties that have grown up over the centuries. At this stage only the nation state is able to command loyalty and obedience'. Building 'the European Community is an inspiring task', but for the present it 'can and must co-exist with national loyalties':

> I see the European Community as providing the framework within which the governments and peoples of the member states, helped by the Community institutions, will create something entirely new that is greater than the sum of its parts. I see it as an estuary into which great rivers flow. Each maintaining its own individuality and character, while combining to form something which is simultaneously distinct yet could not exist without them.[46]

Overall the advantages of Community membership seem reasonably clear at least to the governments of the member states. In future great benefits could accrue to all of them if the EEC fulfils its potential as a dynamic diplomatic framework. Will the advantages previously perceived by the member states remain so throughout the 1980s? Will the new Community of Ten, and eventually of Twelve or more, still provide a meaningful diplomatic framework for the new Europe? The British heritage has been difficult enough to digest, and the Greek and Iberian ones may well prove to be no more compatible with those of the original member states. Yet at the very minimum those states have committed themselves along with Denmark, Ireland, and the United Kingdom to joining the Six in their European adventure.

[44] *Euroforum*, 12 Sept. 1980, 13/80, p. 15.
[45] See Christopher Tugendhat, 'How to be a good European', *The Times*, 15 Sept. 1980.
[46] *Ibid.*

II

France

Annette Morgan

1. French Motives for Joining the Community

The Treaty of Rome creating the European Economic Community was negotiated and signed on behalf of the French Government by the Radical-Socialist Secretary of State for Foreign Affairs, Maurice Faure, and ratified on 10 July 1957 by 342 votes against 239 in the National Assembly. It was undoubtedly the most positive achievement of the Government of the Socialist Guy Mollet (which had lasted from January 1956 to June 1957), a man who had had to renege on his liberal electoral platform on Algeria, had suffered the humiliation of the Suez débâcle, and had endured a further deterioration of France's finances which made her dependent on the problematic largesse of the International Monetary Fund and the European Payments Union. The very skilful negotiation by Maurice Faure from Messina to Rome was carried out with the strong support of a Government and a parliamentary majority committed to European unification, but the signature and the ratification of the treaty aroused little passion in public opinion. This relative indifference was due not so much to the technical nature of the treaty as to its timing, coming as it did after the protracted and nerve-racking nationwide debate on the European Defence Community (EDC), and at the beginning of an even more exhausting exercise in soul-searching on the political and ethical implications of the Algerian war and the plummeting international status of France. It was not so much a new departure in French foreign policy as the reaffirmation of the European vocation of the Fourth Republic, which fulfilled one of the most generous and optimistic ambitions of Resistance leaders and writers during and immediately after the end of the Second World War.

In practice, the dynamics of European unification in post-war France originated in a profoundly felt and personally experienced need to lay new foundations for the development of French society which, in the field of foreign policy, found its expression in two antagonistic and irreconcilable orientations: this was the 'great schism' analysed by Raymond Aron in the book of 1948 bearing that very title. After the referendum of 21 October 1945 had given a 96 per cent majority in favour of setting up a new regime rather than returning to the old Third Republican ways, this superficial quasi-unanimity of the French electorate was soon shattered by the debate on the new Constitution. A second and a third referendum on the Constitution revealed profound differences within the electorate, roughly one-third of whom wished or were prepared to accept a radical change of regime advocated by the French Communist Party, another third totally opposed to this change, and the remaining third showing their uneasiness and misgivings through their abstention. This was clear evidence that the French Communist Party, thanks to its crucial and well-publicized role in the Resistance, thanks to the acknowledged heroic part taken by the Red Army in the final victory, and thanks to its very genuine concern for the welfare of French workers and for social equality, had acquired unprecedented status in French politics.

The French Communist Party offered a coherent ideology, the friendship of a formidable and prestigious ally in the Soviet Union, and the guarantee of the forsaking of the selfish bourgeois mentality which had precipitated the collapse of France in 1940. Conversely, to at least two-thirds of the electorate, and probably more, the Communist Party was a dangerous political force striving for power by hook or by crook, servilely pursuing Soviet rather than French interests, and aiming to destroy the very foundations of French political democracy. The heroic behaviour of the Communist *résistants* had not erased the memories of the Russo-German Pact of 1939 for which the bewildered French Communists were made to carry immediate blame, and for which their party was outlawed.

Translated in terms of foreign policy, this polarization of French public opinion gradually clarified a number of issues and contributed massively towards the crystallization of ideological aspirations and the formation of political strategies for European unification. Predictably enough, the overriding preoccupation of the immediate post-war government élites as well as of the citizens struggling with unending shortages, wary of countrywide extensive destruction and appalled by the sight of emaciated deportees, was to prevent the feasibility of a revival of German might. That is why, up to the ill-fated Moscow Conference of Foreign Ministers of the spring of 1947 (at the very moment when the presence of Communists in the French Cabinet proved irretrievably unmanageable), the non-Communist French Foreign Minister tended to side with the Soviet Union's retaliatory behaviour towards Germany and to block Anglo-American attempts to proceed with the orderly reconstruction of the German economy. Increasingly between 1945 and 1948, particularly in 1947–48, the French perceived the contradiction between, on the one hand, their negative policy in relation with France's Western Allies and, on the other, their developing fear of an internal Communist take-over and of the relentless expansion of Eastern European communism westward. The main immediate threat was no longer perceived as German, but as Russian. Spelt out in practical terms, that meant a radical reorientation of French policy towards Germany. If it was no longer possible or even desirable to dismember Germany into smaller state units or to ensure international tutelage of her economy, then it became imperative to secure a normalization of relations with Germany at the same time as channelling her daunting potential towards peaceful and co-operative enterprises.

At the same time, the idealistic aspirations of the Resistance leaders towards a reconciliation with Germany in the framework of a European political entity dedicated to democracy and social justice were beginning to sound like clear-sighted realism. Almost all continental countries involved in the War had suffered political collapse and untold economic and human damage as a result of the monstrous overdevelopment of the nation state in the form of Hitler's Germany, and their leaders were resolved to prevent the recurrence of such a catastrophe. Since those countries had also experienced a further decline of status and influence relative to the political and economic might of the United States and the military and ideological prestige of the Soviet Union, the path to salvation bore the clear signpost 'Europe'. Hence the momentous Congress of The Hague in 1948 which gathered together some 800 statesmen from Western Europe, including Great Britain, who decided there and then to take the first positive steps towards the creation of a Council of Europe.

1948 had already witnessed some important steps towards the consolidation of European solidarity, in military terms through the signing of the Brussels Treaty in March (creating a defensive alliance between Great Britain, France and the Benelux countries), and the founding of the Organisation of European Economic Co-operation in April to co-ordinate the administration of Marshall Aid at the European level, but these were fundamentally intergovernmental organizations, and the French Government as well as non-Communist public opinion was anxious to secure a European commitment that would involve a real transfer of sovereignty from the national to the European level. When governmental delegates expressed their views on the shape of the new Council of Europe, there was profound disagreement between, on the one hand, the French and the Belgians who wanted an Assembly with legislative powers, and, on the other hand, the British and Scandinavians who were irredeemably opposed to the introduction of any supranational element. The Council of Europe was born totally deprived of any political power, and its constitutional impotence signalled the definitive abandonment of any federalist pattern for Europe.

After this considerable setback from the French point of view, the impulsion towards a different form of European unification was given by a handful of experts and politicians under the informal but tenacious guidance of Jean Monnet. Jean Monnet's Europeanism stemmed not from an abstract or emotional form of European patriotism, but from his realization through personal and professional experience of the necessity for European nations to regroup themselves if they were to survive and recover their influence. If constitutional means of uniting Europe proved unacceptable, then other means must be devised, and partly thanks to the relative success of international agencies such as ILO, WHO and other United Nations agencies, partly because of the contingencies of European politics at the time, Monnet opted for a *sui generis* form of functionalism. The genius of Monnet was to convert handicaps and difficulties into assets. In other words, he seized upon the deadlock over international control of the Ruhr, French misgivings about the renascent German economy, and the necessity for the newly established West German State to anchor its barely autonomous foreign policy into firm foundations, to propose a plan by which interested European states would pool together their coal and steel resources. Not only would this make war between the contracting parties virtually impossible, thus reassuring France, but it would also tie Germany securely to Western Europe, and above all it would force the European partners to co-operate on a day-to-day basis and to take together decisions that would be binding on the various governments involved. The method may well have been that of economic integration, but the aims were openly, even provocatively, political. The French Foreign Minister, Schuman, who adopted and launched the plan to a startled press public on 9 May 1950, stated unequivocally: 'This Community of Coal and Steel that we have proposed is only the beginning. It must and will be extended to other areas of public affairs until some day a United States of Europe will emerge.'

While Monnet and Schuman were able to persuade five West European governments and the majority of their public opinion to bring the Schuman Plan to fruition, Monnet subsequently becoming the first President of the High Authority of the Coal and Steel Community. The EDC, another Monnet brainchild, suffered the stresses of a gruesomely protracted gestation abruptly terminated by a negative vote in the French National Assembly on 30 August 1954. The years 1950 to 1954 were not very propitious for the Fourth Republic. Politics at the domestic level were poisoned by the realization of the inadequacies of the new constitution, and the complexities of parliamentary arithmetic due to the presence of blocks of almost total opposition at either end of the parliamentary spectrum which forced governments to adopt politics likely to arouse the least controversy in the centre, thus either shirking controversial issues or devising patchy and ineffectual compromises. At the level of colonial, defence and foreign policy, domestic problems were compounded. France was weakened by a costly and interminable war in Indochina in which she gradually took up the international stance of defending the values of the 'Free World' against communist imperialism, a stance that found few supporters in the world.

Conversely, the war that erupted in Korea in June 1950 highlighted the vulnerability of Europe to Communist aggression and prompted the American Administration to put considerable pressure on its European partners to agree to some form of German rearmament to reinforce Western defences. A mere five years after the end of the Second World War, this prospect was likely to, and did, arouse the worst fears of German militarism in Western Europe and above all in France. That is why Monnet artfully transposed his integrationist model to fit the requirements of a European Defence Community for which a treaty was duly signed in May 1952. But the prospect of a European Army which would bring French and German soldiers side-by-side, unleashed a host of objections and questions which had a profoundly divisive effect on French public opinion and eventually contributed significantly to the demise of European unification as an attainable goal.

The hardline opponents of the very idea of a European Defence Community rallied either round the Communists for whom any form of German rearmament was merely an American-inspired imperialist plot designed both to endanger French security and to prepare aggression against the Soviet Union and her allies, or round the Gaullists for whom any form of supranational control of the French defence system was a dangerous and irresponsible interference with national integrity. In between these ideological adversaries of the plan, there was a whole range of pragmatist doubters who were either worried by the British refusal to commit Britain to the defence of Europe and the safeguard of democratic values against the vagaries of an untried West German state, or unhappy about the very vague provisions of the treaty on the mechanisms of decision-making in a hypersensitive domain like that of defence.

During the long period when the debate gripped French public opinion to such an extent that no government until Pierre Mendès-France became Prime Minister in June 1954 dared call for a ratification vote by the French Assembly, the death of Stalin, the Korean Armistice and the resumption of communications at Foreign Minister level between East and West removed the element of urgency of the plan. Concurrently the failure to capture British interest in European unification and a somewhat dimmed perception of the immediacy and intensity of the Communist threat considerably weakened the position of French Europeans, and no political party except the gradually less numerous Christian Democrats (of the Mouvement Républicain Populaire) remained unconditionally committed to the building of Europe.

The initiative therefore passed from French to Benelux statesmen and the Messina Conference of June 1955, officially convened to choose a successor to Jean Monnet as head of the High Authority, signalled in reality a new determination to extend the successful principles of the Coal and Steel Community to other economic areas. The new French Foreign Minister, Antoine Pinay, was no Robert Schuman, and his manner was prudent rather than imaginative. Nevertheless the French Government endorsed the two proposals to create a European Atomic Community and a European Economic Community.

On 2 January 1956 the French elected a National Assembly with a significant socialist/radical-socialist majority who approved the relaunching of Europe (public support for Europe was in fact broader than the parliamentary base of the socialist government). The draft treaty was scrutinized, on the whole dispassionately, but also meticulously, by the National Assembly in July 1956 and January 1957. The French negotiator, Maurice Faure, handled the negotiations very skilfully, bargaining hard on three chapters:

  (i) the explicit commitment to extend economic integration to agriculture, partly for reasons of coherence, but above all to safeguard French economic interests;
 (ii) the inclusion of the African and Malagasy territories of the French Union in a system of preferential access for trade on a reciprocal basis;
(iii) the drafting of escape clauses which would slow down the dismantling of the French protectionist arsenal in case of severe financial and economic constraints.

Even though the constitutional provisions of the Treaty of Rome markedly toned down the supranational element which had characterized the ECSC model, thus assuaging fears of a further assault on the nation-state, the acceptance of the liberal economic philosophy which underpinned the whole EEC edifice represented a radical, almost revolutionary departure from the French tradition of economic management. The accent was very much on freedom: free movement of goods, capital and people, and on the removal of barriers. It was not at all on economic engineering, which the French had so successfully promoted since the war with the creation of the Planning Commission (not to mention variously successful government agencies created at the time of the Popular Front). Even more strikingly, it called for the dismantling of quotas and tariffs which had been the hallmark of French economic and trade policy for some six decades. French businessmen were therefore particularly apprehensive, and joined their objections to those of politicians like Mendès-France or various Gaullists.

Some objections were of a political character. For instance, the territorial basis of the three Communities was deemed too narrow and not truly representative of Europe. Germany was judged a dangerous partner who might drag Europe into Eastern adventures, or who might desist from Europe altogether if the prospects for reunification should dramatically improve. On the other hand, the negotiators were accused of having too light-heartedly given Britain up as a lost cause, and failed to provide for a satisfactory procedure to ease the membership of potential candidates. Naturally, the relative loss of sovereignty through the power or initiative of the Commission, the weighted majority vote of the Council of Ministers and the supreme jurisdiction of the Court of Justice went neither unnoticed, nor uncriticized. From a strictly economic point of view, French industrialists doubted their resilience when faced with the German challenge, and argued that their heavy social costs created a built-in French inferiority. They appeared convinced that competing and opposed French and German interests would not be sufficiently helped by the size of the European market to guarantee prosperity, and they predicted that the influx of unemployed foreigners would threaten the stability of the manpower market. Finally, although the creation of a European Atomic Community to promote and regulate the peaceful use of nuclear energy was felt to be exciting and imaginative, it also raised the ghost of abuse and danger to national security.

All these fears and criticisms notwithstanding, the French on the whole supported the revitalization of European unification and confirmed their determination, in the words of Maurice Faure, to turn their backs to 'a certain past of war, of ruins and of blood'. The main motivation behind the approval of economic integration remained the pursuit of peace, and the re-emergence of Europe as a distinctive polity.

2. De Gaulle's Impact on France's European Policy

The year 1958 brought about the first serious anxieties over the future of the nascent European Economic Community. While the newly-appointed personnel of the new Community settled down to the job of preparing the first draft proposals to harmonize the intra-Community tariffs, the French Government dramatically lost what grip it had had on the police, the army and the settlers in Algeria, and the 13 May coup in Algiers opened the way for de Gaulle once again to assume responsibility for the destiny of France and correlatively of Europe. This provoked fear in the ranks of European integrationists in the six member states of the Community, perhaps too easily relieved when it was realized that de Gaulle did not intend to denounce France's obligations under the terms of the Treaty of Rome. Indeed one of the very first acts of his foreign policy was to thwart Britain's efforts to push forward the Maudling Plan for a free trade area and that was hailed in France as a successful chasing away of the cuckoo before it had had a chance to lay its egg in the EEC nest. What was perhaps not immediately realized was that de Gaulle merely substituted his own egg, which was meant to hatch a European bird with a strong tricolour plumage, and very different in anatomy from that envisaged by the drafters of the Treaty.

De Gaulle had come to power to find an international system dominated by what he chose to call the 'two hegemonies', one to the East and one to the West, which by their direct territorial confrontation cut Europe into two, a geographical barbarism in his view. His policy would therefore be to correct this barbarism in three basic stages of increasing complexity: he would first restore France's power through a policy of independence and rank (by ending the Algerian war and building up France's nuclear force already begun under the Fourth Republic), because France was the natural European leader; he would then call on France's West European partners to form a political union which would at the same time be strong enough to loosen its strategic and economic dependency on Washington and to resist any imperialist threat coming from Moscow (this would be conditional on a total reconciliation with a Germany whose irritating slavishness to Washington would have to be converted into a loyalty to a 'European Europe'); in a third, much remoter stage, the unnatural Soviet Bloc would disintegrate (ideologies pass, but nations remain) and the East European nations including Russia West of the Urals would recover their independence and freely return to their true European vocation. This romantic long-term vision of Europe rested on a set of clearly conceived and meticulously planned conditions. This explains why the French Government approved the realization of economic integration, which was perceived as benefiting the French economy and therefore strengthening France's political assets. Hence de Gaulle's reassuring acceptance of the constraints implied by the customs union and his uncompromising insistence on the setting-up of a common agricultural policy.

At the same time, de Gaulle was determined not to surrender to forces likely to undermine the development of his own European construction, and that determination is the key to the two major crises which shook the foundations of the EEC and permanently altered the political and constitutional fabric of Europe. The first crisis was brought about by de Gaulle's veto on British membership in January 1963, which was unquestionably motivated by de Gaulle's absolute conviction (merely reinforced by the Kennedy–Macmillan agreement in Nassau) of Britain's inherent incapacity to comprehend and therefore to accept that membership of the European Community automatically precluded any special relationship with the United States.[1] This unilateral and authoritarian gesture symbolized de Gaulle's crucial role but also revealed his isolation in European politics.

The second crisis was the culmination of skirmishes between the Community partners as a result of the irreconcilable contradiction between de Gaulle's Europe and that of the Treaty of Rome. If one of the major obstacles to the development of de Gaulle's Europe was its domination by the United States, the other one was the surrender of national sovereignty to the principle of supranationalism. De Gaulle had therefore proposed an alternative model in which a European union would co-operate in 'political, economic, cultural domains and in that of defence', operating mainly through a council of ministers of heads of state or government and foreign ministers whose decisions would be binding only on those governments which gave their specific approval. That was the ill-fated Fouchet Plan, whose rejection

---

[1] De Gaulle was about to sign a friendship treaty with Germany intended to seal her commitment to the Gaullist concept of Europe; one which signally failed to do so.

in April 1962 shattered de Gaulle's hopes of an early realization of *his*
Europe. After that débâcle, all he could do was to resist vigorously all
potential encroachments by the Community institutions, and that is why in
June 1965 he ordered the French delegation to walk out of the Council of
Ministers rather than discuss any further a Commission package proposal
which linked the financing of the common agricultural policy (beneficial to
France) with an increase of autonomous revenues for the Community and
an extension of the budgetary powers of the European Parliament (thus
displacing financial powers and control from national governments to the
Community institutions). The French boycott was terminated in January
1966 by the Luxembourg compromise, sometimes nicknamed a 'gentleman's
disagreement', which not only shelved the constitutional rule of voting by
weighted majority in the Council of Ministers, but signified that from then
on the Commission's power of initiative would be emptied of any political
substance. Thus had the limits of de Gaulle's formal adhesion to the
European Economic Community been clarified, and the political integrationist impetus of the Community stopped.

De Gaulle's successors, Presidents Pompidou and Giscard d'Estaing,
naturally paid lip-service to his form of Europeanism which was ritualisti-
cally integrated into their rhetoric, but this 'Europeanism' received hetero-
dox application as Pompidou quickly relented on the Gaullist vetoes[2] on
British membership, and Giscard d'Estaing gave his approval to the Treaty
provision that members of the European Parliament should be elected by
universal direct suffrage. Successive French governments have naturally
attempted to orientate Community policies towards French interests but
they have never overtly doubted the wisdom of following the path towards
European union.

3. France's General Attitude to Integration

Whatever may be the reasons for an evolution which constitutes a distortion
of the intentions underpinning the Treaty of Rome,[3] practitioners and
students of the EEC are agreed that policy-making within the Community
is increasingly subjected to the rules of an intergovernmental framework,
to the detriment of the neo-functionalist model which had dominated

[2] The veto of 1963 was followed by a secondary veto in November 1967 when de Gaulle
stated that the British economy would be an intolerable burden on the Six, while the
constraints of the common agricultural policy would be, for structural reasons, a crushing
burden on Britain.
[3] It should be noted that whereas de Gaulle made the most explicit and best publicized
gestures to ensure the containment of supranational propensities within the EEC, France
was by no means the odd man out in the drama which was being played on a backcloth
of evermore sharply outlined nation-states. The vigorous reassertion of the nation-state
principle is convincingly demonstrated in Stanley Hoffmann's classic analysis, 'Obstinate
or Obsolete: the fate of the nation state and the case of Western Europe', *Daedalus*,
Summer 1966.

integration analysis in the 1960s.[4] This does not necessarily mean that the Community is less or more 'European' than it originally was, but that it is recognized that the 'Community interests' are not perceived as automatically identical with 'national interests' and that governments quite naturally give precedence to 'national interests' in the negotiations they undertake at Community level. Member states are well aware of their obligations under the terms of the Treaty of Rome, but the terms are sufficiently vague and the methods of the Community institutions sufficiently flexible to permit very broad interpretations and individualistic behaviour by governments. In October 1972, immediately prior to the first Community enlargement, the nine Heads of state and government met in order to add decorum to the occasion, and set the Community an ambitious programme of policies designed to order its priorities and to update the Treaty of Rome. These provide a useful guide to Community objectives, albeit at a time when no Western recession had yet affected optimistic projections resulting from the economic expansion of the preceding decade.

The two most detailed sections of the Summit Communiqué of 20 October 1972 are devoted to economic and monetary union, intended to be accomplished by the end of 1980, and external relations, in which European responsibilities toward the developing countries and commitments towards the liberalization of international trade were emphasized. Between these two sections were inserted five others dealing with regional policy, social policy, the development of a common policy for industry, science and technology, environmental policy and energy policy; the last two items in vague and brief terms. Finally the Heads of state and government recognized the need to reinforce the institutions of the Community to transform, 'before the end of the present decade and with the fullest respect for the Treaties already signed, the whole complex of the relations of Member States into a European Union'.

The emphasis of the Paris Communiqué was very much on policies rather than on procedures, which was in line with President Pompidou's well-publicized pragmatism and impatience with 'theological disputations'. Economic and monetary union was at the top of the French agenda for European unification, as it would at the same time permit the completion of financial arrangements for the common agricultural policy, stabilize the Common Market threatened by divergent unilateral monetary policies by members of the EEC and by the United States since 1968, and lay the conditions for a truly European posture within the international monetary system. It was indeed no accident that the first Commission memorandum on economic and monetary union, in February 1969, was the brainchild of the French Commissioner, Raymond Barre. Since then the French Government has never ceased to support in principle the programme of economic

---

[4] See Carole Webb's illuminating introductory chapter in H. Wallace, W. Wallace and C. Webb (eds.), *Policy-Making in the European Communities* (John Wiley, 1977).

and monetary union, but it is significant that it was instrumental by circumstances rather than by design in the eventual failure of EMU to take off, while it played a crucial role in the creation of the European Monetary System (EMS) which was officially launched, through no coincidence, during the French Presidency of the Community in March 1979. EMU failed principally because of certain major destabilizing effects: first, of Germany's lack of monetary discipline in May 1971; second, of Nixon's decision to suspend the convertibility of the dollar in 1971; and third, and above all, of the oil crisis of 1973–74. All these factors exaggerated the pre-existing divergences between the various European currencies, eventually forcing the weakened franc to leave the 'Snake' because of its inability to sustain the limits on fluctuation agreed to as a first stage of EMU. But EMU also failed because of a fundamental disagreement between France and Germany on the priority to be accorded to economic or to monetary union. Economic policy co-ordination which would have required a great deal of budgetary discipline and mutual solidarity from European governments was not given serious consideration by the French Government, which was anxious to avoid undue burdens for a fast expanding but very vulnerable French economy. Conversely, the German Government feared that distortions in European economies would render efforts towards monetary union fruitless if not dangerous. EMU languished and was put in limbo in the mid-1970s, but the difficulties which had made it desirable in the late 1960s, far from disappearing, had been further aggravated by the lingering recession. That is why President Giscard d'Estaing welcomed Chancellor Schmidt's initiative to resuscitate the corpse of EMU in the spring of 1978, an initiative itself prompted by soundings of the President of the Commission, Roy Jenkins, in the 1977–78 winter.

The present French Government has demonstrated its commitment to the EMS by giving wholehearted support to the Schmidt initiative, in particular in taking measures to strengthen the Franc in order to prevent damaging stresses within the system.[5] Even though it is too early to judge the effectiveness of EMS, it fits in well within the overall French policy of contributing to the organization of Europe not just for the sake of intra-Community coherence, but also and perhaps primarily to make Europe into a distinctive partner in international financial negotiations.

One of the permanent concerns of successive French governments ever since the original negotiations for the EEC has been the relationship of the Community with developing countries, particularly with the former French territories.[6] It was France that insisted on the inclusion of provisions for an

[5] French support nevertheless became conditional to the acceptance by Germany of the phasing out of compensatory monetary amounts which would have become illogical in a system of stabilized parities and which also gave an unfair advantage to German agricultural exports in relation to French agricultural exports.

[6] For a full treatment of this question, see Carol Cosgrove Twitchett, *Europe and Africa: from association to partnership* (Saxon House, 1978).

47

association between the EEC and most extra-Commonwealth African countries plus some territories in the West Atlantic and South Pacific areas. It was France again who provided the momentum and the necessary Community policy coherence in the negotiations leading to the Yaoundé Convention of 1963 and its amended version of Yaoundé II which was due to lapse at the end of 1974. The enlargement of the Community to include Great Britain provided the occasion for a radical reappraisal of EEC–LDC relationships, as the Community could neither include the whole of the Commonwealth into an association whose resources were finite, nor ignore it.

The developing world played a major part in de Gaulle's foreign policy. First of all, he considered it 'an ardent obligation' for the prosperous industrial Western world to provide financial aid and technical assistance to newly independent but economically disadvantaged countries of the Third World. De Gaulle established a policy of devoting around 1 per cent of the French GNP to this aid, which was relatively more than any other developed country and which was roughly maintained until 1977 when it dropped to 0.6 per cent. Secondly, the building up of a framework of political and economic co-operation between France and newly independent nations would greatly contribute to enhancing the status of France as a major partner in world politics, and would, moreover, weaken the relative position of the superpowers if the bipolar system either disintegrated or shrank. For these various reasons France played the part of advocate of overseas interests in the European Community, meeting less and less resistance from her partners, particularly as she found an ally first in the Commission and, from 1972, in Britain. This policy, moreover, paid handsome economic returns to France by providing secure outlets for French products and investment.

It therefore comes as no surprise that the 1972 Paris Communiqué stressed the 'essential importance (of) the policy of association' and spelt out its components, and that Georges Pompidou and Valéry Giscard d'Estaing endorsed and continued the Gaullist commitment. In a speech to the United Nations General Assembly on 26 September 1972, the then French Foreign Minister, Maurice Schumann, stated that 'the French Government thinks it particularly indispensable that, with regard to the developing countries and in the first place the Common Market's former associates, the enlarged Community should define a policy no less generous than that practised by the Six, a policy worthy of being called European'.

A French Commissioner, Claude Cheysson, played a critical part in the conversion of Yaoundé into the much more comprehensive and generous Lomé Convention signed in February 1975, even though its implementation may have fallen short of the expectations it had aroused. The bulk of negotiations leading to the signature of the Second Lomé Convention were completed during the most recent French Presidency of the Community, in 1979, and the French Foreign Minister, Jean François-Poncet, had indeed announced to the European Parliament on 17 January 1979 that this sector must be given 'high political priority'. He added: 'This point of application of the Community's policy in external relations is important not only for historical reasons and because close co-operation is in the common interest of Europe and those areas, but also because of its exemplary nature in the context of North–South relations.' The official policy of the French Government is therefore close to that of the EEC, though a note of caution must be sounded on the gap between proclaimed principles and implementation: both in terms of aid and opening its markets to manufactured goods from LDCs, the French record has become unimpressive.

The goal-setting ambitions of the 1972 Communiqué could not all realistically be fulfilled with equal determination and vigour, nor were their chances helped by the severe crisis of 1973, during which strained American-European relations, the quadrupling of the price of oil, and the Yom Kippur War, sorely tried the solidarity of the Nine and accelerated reverse of EEC economic performance from one of expansion to one of barely maintained consolidation and retrenchment.

In terms of regional policy France, who had little either to gain or to lose, maintained in 1974 a neutral posture between the protagonists of a Regional Fund (Britain, Ireland and Italy) and the opponent, Germany. In any case, France jealously maintains national control over regional policy affecting French territory. The French Government, which has considerable expertise in the field, co-operates with the Commission in the procedural aspects of regional policy in as much as the Commission does not attempt to develop direct connections with the French regions or to pre-empt financial or policy prerogatives likely to reduce French autonomy in the matter. Likewise, for energy policy, which the French Government considers should remain firmly under national control though in pursuit of commonly agreed, general Community objectives; i.e. the reduction of European dependency on extra-European sources of energy.

President Giscard d'Estaing declared in February 1979: 'Instead of seeking to superimpose a Community policy onto national policies, which has after all failed, we must ensure the convergence of our national policies within the Community so that we can aim for the same results'.[7] The problems of growing unemployment associated with the decline of textile industries and shipbuilding facing competition from the developing world and Japan, and of the steel industry facing contracting demand, have on the whole been resistant to overall Community solutions, because each member state (including West Germany with her historical dread of inflation) has felt its own interests threatened at least in the short term by the kind of discipline that would have been required by the setting up of a coherent industrial policy at the Community level. For instance, the French Government, which faced massive unemployment in Lorraine, in 1980 devised

[7] Press Conference on 15 Feb. 1979.

its radical set of measures for the compensation of redundant workers and reconversion of industry rather than implementing the tentative Davignon Plan for the rationalization of steel production at the European level.

Whereas President Pompidou was above all concerned to focus Community tasks and interests on specific policies, Giscard d'Estaing from the very first months of his Presidency (which almost coincided with France's Presidency of the Community from July to December 1974) evolved a particular interest in the institutional aspect of the Community.[8] This took two forms: the reinforcement of the Community institutions, and the development of political co-operation. Both signalled the end of a state of tension between France and her European partners originating in the Pompidou/Jobert doctrine by which the various organs of the EEC were constitutionally disqualified to deal with matters other than those of economic interest, thus creating a totally artificial demarcation zone, considering the inevitable interpenetration of political and economic domains in any modern international decision-making process. The seminal phase for the reinforcement of Community institutions was the preparation of the summit meeting held at Paris on 9–10 December 1974. This produced a whole battery of proposals ranging from better co-ordination between the existing Community institutions, to the institutionalization of Summit meetings to form a European Council (the Paris one was considered to be the first meeting), to the relaxing of the unanimity rule rigorously enforced since 1966, to the programming of elections to the European Parliament by direct universal suffrage, to take place in or after 1978. This was clearly designed to strengthen the political muscle of the Community which did not appear to have been particularly invigorated by the admission of the three new member states.

In practice, this politicization of the Community structure in the direction of more immediate governmental involvement was received with some degree of trepidation by the 'integrationist' organs of the EEC, the Commission and the European Parliament, but they merely confirmed the orientation of the EEC towards an intergovernmental model. This initiative of President Giscard d'Estaing also heralded a new attitude of France towards the Community, an attitude based on co-operation rather than confrontation. And this attitude of co-operation received its confirmation in the French acquiescence in the evolution of the machinery and activities of political co-operation.

Initiated at the Hague Summit Conference of 1969, the development of political co-operation working through the member states' embassies and foreign offices has been marked since 1974 by the willingness of French foreign ministers and political directors to maintain close working relationships with their Community counterparts, making the preparatory work of

---

[8] See Annette Morgan, *From Summit to Council: Evolution in the EEC* (PEP/Chatham House, 1976).

such meetings as those of the 'Euro-Arab Dialogue', for instance, much easier to co-ordinate. If the progress of that particular set of discussions appears imperceptible to the eye of the observer, it is not due to French restiveness, but to the lack of real communication between European partners anxious above all to secure reasonable terms for access to Arab oil, and Arab partners primarily concerned with European recognition of the right of the Palestinians to an independent state. And the pronouncements of Giscard d'Estaing during his tour of Arab Emirates in 1979 may indicate that he impatiently wishes the Community to act more decisively to bridge the gap. But for the foreseeable future, it will take as many governments to assent to foreign policy co-ordination as there are member states in the Community, and the first three Presidents of the Fifth Republic were all party to this fundamental limitation to political integration.

4. French Interests and the Community

Some form of political union, if not political integration, has been the constant theme underlying French politics, whether it be the open, Atlantic-orientated Europe of Jean Monnet, the 'European Europe' of de Gaulle, the 'European identity' painstakingly outlined in the Copenhagen Declaration of December 1973, or the 'Confederation' advocated by Giscard d'Estaing. France occupies a geographically and historically central position in Western Europe, and therefore has been able to exercise a special influence over the shaping of Europe. Both in drafting the Treaty of Rome and in the subsequent setting up of rules governing the internal organization of Community institutions, notably the Commission and the Court of Justice, France's legal and administrative traditions have made an impact such that French politicians and civil servants alike enjoy a sense of familiarity when operating within the Community framework – contrary, for instance, to their British counterparts who had to accept structures totally alien to British tradition when they took up their posts in 1973. This has enabled French points of view and methods to fit easily into policy-making procedures within the Community, and greatly facilitates coordination between the French and the Community administrative structures. The European Community has also provided a justifiably exploited chance for France to gain ground in its struggle to maintain *francophonie*. From the very beginning of the Community, French has been the main working language, and even the accession of English-speaking countries in 1973 to date has not considerably weakened the position of French.

De Gaulle used a geographical concept of Europe as the starting-point of his European foreign policy, and found plenty of resonance in this in French public opinion which knew at once what he meant. The French have always felt their true vocation to be European (Napoleon sold the Louisiana territories to the United States for a ridiculous price, and Jules Ferry fell because his policy in Tonkin was judged too adventurous and eccentric by the Chamber of Deputies). Moreover, a Community of the Six, of the Nine, and even eventually of the Twelve conveniently ensures that France, whose territory is the largest in the Community and is contiguous with four and soon five member states, continues to be the member state whose physical presence is indispensable to the cohesion of the Community – a state of affairs which de Gaulle exploited fully. In practice, this means that France's foreign policy can easily reconcile French and European interests. Britain may have entertained doubts as to whether her true orbit is European, Atlantic or planetary. Not so France. And above all the European framework provided France with an elegant and immensely fruitful solution to her century-old dilemma: how to contain Germany without having to depend on a fragile system of alliances. The stroke of genius of the Schuman Plan was that it made war between France and Germany virtually impossible, and promoted European unification at the same time. Of all aspects of de Gaulle's European policy, the most durable one is after all the total reconciliation between France and Germany. Into the 1980s the Franco-German partnership remains the most dynamic element of Community policies, as exemplified by the setting up of the EMS, and which the institutionalized diplomatic links between Paris and Bonn make sure will survive beyond the personal friendship of Giscard d'Estaing and Helmut Schmidt. This Franco-German partnership might be clouded by the potential unbalance which could arise if Germany became the leading political as well as the leading economic partner, an evolution of which there were definite signs in 1980. That would be totally unacceptable to France in the narrow context of a strictly bilateral relationship, but it is less likely to become obvious, permanent and unmitigated in the broader context of the European Community. And in the domain of international relations, Germany's recent policy evolution has been rallying towards the arch-Gaullist view that European interests are distinct from American interests, that United States economic, financial and military policies do not necessarily operate in favour of Europe – nor do European trade policies, reciprocally, work to the advantage of American exporters: the Paris–Bonn axis is gaining strength to the detriment of the Washington-Bonn axis.[9]

The Franco-German tandem acquired from the very inception of the EEC, a particular significance in economic terms. One of France's strongest held views at the time of the Val-Duchesse negotiations was that the customs union, which would give Germany a very favourable position for the export of her industrial goods, must be matched by a corresponding EEC-wide market for the expansion of French agriculture. The inclusion of a common

[9] The Washington–Bonn axis remains very strong because of the specifically European conundrum: that the European partners are major world trade partners and are beginning to develop a foreign policy identity, but in terms of European defence they have made no progress at all and must rely for the foreseeable future on the American nuclear shield, French and British *forces de frappe* notwithstanding.

agricultural policy – the terms of which would be hammered out in the early 1960s – was essential to France on three counts. It completed the EEC's ideological cohesion because integration of a major economic sector, agriculture, balanced the integration of the industrial sector. It redressed the perceived disadvantage to the French economy of the customs union boosting a very dynamic German industry. It gave a chance to France's modernizing agriculture to develop its potential as a major exporter. When the principles of the CAP were finally agreed to in 1962 and the first test prices fixed, France's agricultural prices were the lowest in the EEC.[10] Moreover, France had just undergone a radical restructuring of her agriculture, illustrated and reinforced by her agricultural legislation of 1960 and 1962, and was ready to turn her agricultural territory, representing almost 50 per cent of the European total at the time, into the granary and larder of Europe.

For economic and political reasons, France insisted and her partners agreed that liberal market laws were inapplicable to agriculture, and that a European agricultural policy should be based on two principles: the setting up of stable price systems, and the establishment of a Community preference trade policy. Those principles were designed to guarantee a stable minimum income and a stable market to farmers. They also ensured the permanence of the French protectionist tradition in agriculture. In financial terms, the price support system which since its early implementation has absorbed some 90 per cent of the EEC agricultural budget, has undeniably contributed to swell French farmers' coffers. In strict financial terms, France has done well out of the Community. Yet the French response is rather complex. The French Government has a somewhat different perspective from that of French farmers. French farmers, who incidentally do not form a homogeneous economic or social category, have tended to be disillusioned by the results of the CAP and suspicious of French government policies. The CAP may have guaranteed stability to all, but certainly not prosperity. The postwar era has witnessed profound changes in French agriculture which, in the wake of modernization and increased productivity, have halved the agricultural population and created enormous stresses, particularly to the marginal and most threatened farmers. The almost contemporary EEC-Mansholt Plan and French-Vedel Plan designed to ease in the rationalization of agriculture, were received with the greatest suspicion by farmers' unions, and for lack of financial means and political support have only been partially implemented. Whereas the better-off farmers do extremely well out of the price support system, the others derive only marginal benefits from it, and the financial help they may receive to increase and modernize their holdings is perceived as insultingly low and ineffective. As farming incomes, controlled

[10] See Jacques Bourrinet, 'Les incidences de la politique agricole commune sur l'agriculture française', in Joël Rideau et al, La France et les Communautés Européennes (Librairie Générale de Droit et de Jurisprudence, 1975).

by the price system, tend to rise more slowly than farming costs, the majority of French farmers remain sceptical about the benefits brought about by the CAP.

Conversely, successive French governments have been the staunchest upholders of CAP orthodoxy. First of all, it does guarantee French positions on the export market, and France, for instance, is the only net exporter of cereals in the Community. Secondly, it transfers most of the financial burden of agriculture from the national to the Community budget, a not inconsiderable saving. Thirdly, it is a very visible policy which provides the Government with a ready-made forum for publicizing its concern for agriculture. And fourthly, it has enabled France to win laurels in the integration realm, as the agricultural sector is the most integrated in the Community, and even at moments of greatest discord between France and the rest of the Community, the French Government and the Commission have found themselves closely allied in working out Community solutions for agriculture. The present Government recognizes that there are serious problems of CAP malfunctioning, especially the building up of surpluses, but it is not prepared to alter radically the basic principles which have served French interests well.

The governments of the Fifth Republic have all passed a favourable judgement on economic integration, which has helped them to promote the industrialization of France and in reaching the rank of fourth world exporter in 1975, below only the United States, West Germany, and Japan. The recent but lasting recession is affecting France like the rest of the Western world, but the worrying growth of inflation and unemployment is not linked up with membership of the EEC, even though it may be deplored that the EEC policy-makers are unable to devise, let alone agree upon, appropriate solutions. The French are well aware of their vulnerability, and even though national independence is a popular slogan, there are few illusions about its Utopian quality.

5. French Views on the Community's Future Development

One of the most persistent and enthusiastic advocates of Europe is President Giscard d'Estaing himself. The theme of Europe is one of his favourites, and one not just invented in time for the electoral campaign for the European Parliament,[11] though, of course, this enabled him to proclaim his faith even more forcefully than usual:

[11] In an election campaign which was not even ambiguous, since each main political party used it not so much to publicize its views on Europe as to flex its muscles against the other parties, the President of the Republic was supposed to remain neutral. Like other political figures, though keeping closer to relevant European topics, Giscard d'Estaing used the occasion to give a boost to the UDF list headed by one of his ministers, Madame Simone Veil.

Is it necessary, yes or no, to organize Europe? The question will be answered by our children and grandchildren, and I wonder how they will judge in the year 2030 those who, in 1980, would say: 'One must not organize Europe', when we see what is happening all over the world nowadays.[12]

And, to avoid any misunderstanding, the President specified that he meant the 'Europe of the Rome Treaty'. Nevertheless, far from discarding the de Gaulle legacy, Giscard d'Estaing has made clear his rejection of a supranational form of European organization, in favour of a confederation:

What does 'confederal' mean? It means a Europe, as I have already indicated, in which no-one imposes his will on anyone. So it is an organization designed to bring policies closer to each other, to determine guidelines for joint action, but without the possibility of coercing any particular State of Europe that might not agree to a guideline.
Why a confederal structure? In my view, for three reasons: firstly, a political reason which is that today, if there were a federal-type Europe, it would be under the influence of the United States of America. . . The second reason is that today none of the countries of Europe, whatever they may say, would accept decisions contrary to their national interest, imposed by majority decision in a federal structure. . . Lastly, the deepest reason is this: we have to look at Europe as it is. . . Europe is unlike anything that has existed elsewhere. . . So it is normal that Europe's future should reflect this situation and therefore be of a confederal type.[13]

The UDF (Union pour la Démocratie Française), itself a curious confederation of parties which support the President, includes Jean Lecanuet's Centre Démocrate, loyal to its Christian Democratic lineage and therefore even more integrationist than the President. But the other component of the official government majority, the RPR (Rassemblement pour la République) or Gaullist Party, are very critical of Giscard d'Estaing's views. It is a heterogeneous party whose cement is basic allegiance to the Gaullist doctrine, but opinions on Europe range widely from Olivier Guichard, who supports the idea of a European confederation as the only means of safeguarding freedom in society, to Chirac, who from his bed in the Cochin Hospital, launched in December 1978 his 'Appel de Cochin', presumably echoing 'L'Appel du 18 Juin 1940' and calling on the French to resist the new German threat, and Debré who proclaimed his anguish, faced with Anglo-Saxon and German policies with directly opposite orientations to French policies on most matters. The 1979 RPR campaign became notorious for its strident xenophobia, but obviously found relatively little sympathy in the French electorate, since the RPR performed notably less well in the European Parliament election than in the general election of 1978.

[12] Televised broadcast, 18 Apr. 1979.
[13] Press conference, 21 Nov. 1978.

At the other end of the political spectrum, the French Communist Party, a traditional critic of the EEC, emphasized the monopolistic propensities of the Common Market and the restrictions brought about by the EEC on French independence rather than condemning it *in toto*, and became far more intransigent during the direct elections campaign. The Communists see little scope for the working class to influence the Community institutions, whose powers the party tends to exaggerate. They also consider the Community a sphere of influence for the arch-capitalist regimes of West Germany and the United States, and feel that France could develop her own resources and capabilities to a much greater extent if she were freed from Community obligations.

As for the Socialist Party, traditionally a strong supporter of European integration, it applauded the further democratization of Europe as a result of direct elections. The Socialists remain critical of what they perceive to be negative Gaullist policies towards Europe, but at the same time their programme states that 'the quest for independence for France implies that of Europe'. The Socialists have a fairly elaborate programme for Europe, including a thorough reform of the CAP, and approval of Community enlargement.

The French Government is basically favourable to Community enlargement which it considers fundamentally a political issue without underestimating its economic and social implications. The problem for the French Government is that it has met vociferous opposition on the matter from the Communists who see enlargement as a device to reduce further the livelihood of the small farmers, from the Gaullists for whom enlargement spells out 'the ruin of entire French regions', and from the Southern producers of wine and Mediterranean foodstuffs. Even the Employers' Federation is worried about the cost to French industry of the operation, although it approves enlargement in principle. That is why the French President, who nevertheless cordially welcomed the prospective membership of 'ancient Greece and the Greece of today', has to apply to this particular issue his notorious caution, *oui, mais*.

It is now just over fifty years since Aristide Briand on the podium of the League of Nations in September 1929 called for a European confederation. Ever since, with varying degrees of success, France has always been passionately involved in European matters and concerned about the form of European construction. After the voluntarist phase of European unification in the 1940s and 1950s, and the Gaullist bid in the early 1960s for French leadership of a Europe resistant to the lure of supranationalism, France and Europe have settled down to a *realistic Europe*, respectful of national entities and national interests, developing in conformity with the provisions of the Rome Treaty (except for majority voting), pursuing economic integration and prepared to take risks such as setting up the EMS at a time of a great economic uncertainty and relative financial instability, and beginning to make inroads in the domain of foreign policy co-ordination.

No wonder the French President gives himself and Europe a certificate of good conduct. But this picture of virtue and happiness is subjected to serious distortions. French citizens are well aware that neither Brussels nor the European capitals have yet produced convincing blueprints for solving the serious economic recession which threatens the standard of living of all, but more cruelly those of the weak. France's partners are frequently impatient of her tough negotiating methods which all too often masquerade real egoism under the cloak of European orthodoxy, as in the case of the CAP. Even the ACP partners in the Lomé Convention feel that the Europeans have not opened up their markets as much as they could have done, and the French are particular culprits. In spite of these blemishes, however, the performance of France in the EEC is positive, because Europe has solved France's perennial problem of border security, provided the momentum for France to complete her industrial and commercial revolution, and contributed to restoring her international status. For all these reasons, the French Government is committed to continue to play an active part in the maintenance and gradual development of the EEC.

Postscript

This chapter was written before François Mitterrand's victory in the May 1981 French presidential elections and the absolute majority achieved by the Socialist Party in the June elections to the National Assembly. Although reaffirming the need for French independence, the new President is unlikely to depart from the French Socialist tradition of sustained overall support for European integration and European institutions. François Mitterrand is a close friend of the confirmed European, Willy Brandt. He reiterated his support for the European Community of Ten before the first ballot of the presidential campaign, and regretted that present-day Europe 'lacks soul, ideals and conviction.' In the television debate of 5 May with Valéry Giscard d'Estaing, he emphasized his support for Spanish and Portuguese entry into the European Community, provided that economic and regional policy issues could be settled. He chided President Giscard d'Estaing for not having been firm enough with regard to differences with the United Kingdom. On a previous occasion (31 July 1980), however, he publicly noted that if the French Government had not in the past treated the United Kingdom in such an offhand manner, there might have been more understanding now on the part of the British Government.

The appointment of the EEC Commissioner, M. Claude Cheysson, as the new Minister for External Relations confirms the French Government's interest in maintaining an active concern and encouraging positive behaviour in the European Community, and probably in using the EEC to play an increasing role in the North–South dialogue. M. Edgard Pisani, a former prefect and Gaullist minister, who in the early 1960s oversaw the most radical reform of French agricultural structures in the twentieth century, has succeeded M. Cheysson at the European Commission. In 1979 he outlined in some detail proposals for a radical reform of the CAP, and in assuming M. Cheysson's former EEC Development portfolio, will find outlets for his imaginative schemes and proven administrative skills. While the early visit of Chancellor Schmidt to President Mitterrand on 23–24 May confirmed that the Franco-German relationship remains a major dimension in French European politics, it may no longer have the preponderance that it exercised under Giscard d'Estaing. It may not be without significance that Messrs Felipe González (Spain), Andreas Papandreou (Greece) and Mario Soares (Portugal) as well as Willy Brandt, were official guests at François Mitterrand's installation as President of the Republic.

President Mitterrand is unlikely to present a very ambitious programme either on European institutions or on European defence, and he will be careful at sessions of the European Council not to appear to put France in a position of weakness. On the other hand, he will certainly recognize that the European Parliament has a valuable contribution to make to European co-operation (he was after all elected to it on 10 June 1979, though resigned shortly afterwards), and he will continue Claude Cheysson's policies of developing durable trade links with the less developed countries in order to help build their economies and ability to function as important and reliable commercial partners of the EEC. On European, as on other matters, President Mitterrand is likely to be governed by pragmatism rather than ideology, and in negotiations to be a tenacious but not inflexible partner. He will certainly want to reduce the gap now perceived between 'national' and 'European' interests inasmuch as economic and financial constraints permit it, but European integration to him will be a means to further the interests of France. In this aspect, at least, François Miterrand's new Socialist administration will retain continuity with the policies of previous administrations under the Fifth Republic.

FURTHER READING

Erling Bjøl, *La France devant l'Europe* (Munksgaard, Copenhagen, 1966).

John C. Cairns, 'France, Europe, and "the design of the world", 1974–77', *International Journal*, Spring 1977, pp. 253–71.

Sue E. M. Charlton, 'European unity and the politics of the French Left', *Orbis*, Winter 1976, pp. 1448–70.

J. R. Frears, 'The French Parliament and the European Community', *Journal of Common Market Studies*, Dec. 1975, pp. 140–56.

James O. Goldsborough, 'France, the European Crisis and the Alliance', *Foreign Affairs*, April 1974, pp. 538–55.

Michael Harrison, *The Reluctant Ally: France and Atlantic Security* (Johns Hopkins University Press, 1981).

Stanley Hoffmann, 'Obstinate or Obsolete? France, European Integration, and the fate of the Nation-State', in *Decline or Renewal? France since the 1930s* (Viking Press, New York, 1974).

Julian Crandall Hollick, 'Direct Elections to the European Parliament: the French Debate', *The World Today*, Dec. 1977, pp. 472–80.

Pierre Kende, 'La France et l'Intégration Européenne', *Commentaire*, Summer 1979, pp. 181–8.

Michael Leigh, 'Linkage Politics: the French Referendum and the Paris Summit of 1972', *Journal of Common Market Studies*, Dec. 1975, pp. 157–70.

Michael Leigh, 'Giscard and the European Community', *The World Today*, Feb. 1977, pp. 73–80.

Francis O'Neill, *The French Radical Party and European Integration* (Gower, Farnborough, 1981).

Lois Pattison de Ménil, *Who Speaks for Europe? The Vision of Charles de Gaulle* (Weidenfeld and Nicolson, London, 1977).

Joël Rideau *et al*, *La France et les Communautés Européennes* (Librairie Générale, Paris, 1975).

Simon Serfaty, *France, de Gaulle, and Europe* (Johns Hopkins Press, Baltimore, 1968).

Jonathan Story, 'The Franco-German Alliance within the Community', *The World Today*, June 1980, pp. 209–17.

F. Roy Willis, *France, Germany, and the New Europe* (Stanford University Press, 2nd edn., 1968).

III

The Federal Republic of Germany

Roger Morgan*

1. German Motives for Joining the Community

Among the member states of the Community, the Federal Republic has been one of the strongest supporters of integration, both economic and political, ever since Chancellor Konrad Adenauer warmly welcomed the Schuman Plan in 1950.[1] This support, as we shall see, has taken different forms in the course of the thirty-year history of the Community, and it has of course been subject to some reservations reflecting German national interests and perspectives. Broadly speaking, however, support for the aim of European integration has been strong and widespread in all sections of the West German population, and it has also been shared on the whole by all the major political parties. It is true that in the 1950s, when European integration was being promoted by the Christian Democratic Government led by Adenauer (Chancellor from 1949 to 1963), many spokesmen of the Social Democratic opposition party expressed strong reservations about a policy which, by merging the Federal Republic into a West European union, appeared to be blocking any possibility of Germany's reunification. However, as any hope of such reunification faded in the 1960s (Germany's division was dramatically symbolized by the building of the Berlin Wall in 1961) and as the Social Democrats took a share of governmental power from 1966 onwards, these reservations were muted. The first Social Democratic head of a West German government, Willy Brandt (1969 to 1974), committed himself enthusiastically to the goal of 'a European government'; and his successor Helmut Schmidt, after an initial period of strong and

* This chapter draws on research financed by a grant from the Ford Foundation, which the author gratefully acknowledges
[1] The historical background analysed in the first section of the chapter is described more fully in the author's study *West European Politics since 1945* (Butterworth, London, 2nd edn. forthcoming).

obvious distaste for the Brussels bureaucracy and its works, has co-operated actively with the President of France in developing the European Community (including the European Monetary System from 1979 onwards) as an instrument with an important role to play in managing the economic and political problems of the 1970s. Like the two major parties, Germany's third party, the Free Democrats or Liberals, has adopted a generally positive attitude towards the Community: as the SPD's coalition partner since 1969, the FDP has provided influential members for the European Commission, including Ralf Dahrendorf (1970 to 1974) and his successor Guido Brunner, and the FDP's former general secretary, Martin Bangemann, was chosen as leader of the Liberal Group in the directly-elected European Parliament in 1979.

General support for German participation in the Community, and in its future development and strengthening, is thus a matter of common ground among all the major parties in the Federal Republic (as indeed for the trade unions, employers' associations and other interest groups). The precise nature of this support, however, and the reservations to which it is subject, must be explored in some detail. This is best done after a survey of the specific motives which led the Germans to support the concept of European unity in the first place. These motives can be summarized by saying that to participate in 'making Europe' from 1950 onwards offered the Germans advantages of five distinct kinds:

  (i) the prospect of economic recovery and prosperity;
 (ii) the chance of Germany's political and moral rehabilitation;
(iii) support for the strengthening of the Federal Republic's political and social institutions;
 (iv) an enhancement of Germany's external security in Europe;
  (v) a potential basis for the revival of Germany's standing and influence in the world.

These five sets of considerations, of course, were and still are closely interconnected, but they can be disentangled to a considerable extent, and it is important to examine the nature of each of them in turn.

As far as the first issue is concerned – that of Germany's economic problems – it is well known that the country was in a devastated condition after 1945, but it is less widely appreciated how far Germany's pre-war prosperity, and her prospects of recovery, depended on economic relations with foreign countries. As one of the major industrial powers of Europe, Germany had depended since the late nineteenth century on international trade and investment for her growth. The conditions of the Second World War, followed by Germany's division between East and West, the partial dismantling of her industry, and the restrictions imposed by the occupying powers thus deprived her of significant sources of her wealth. After two exceptionally grim post-war years (even worse in Germany than in other parts of Western Europe), the Marshall Plan of 1947, leading to the

European Recovery Programme and the establishment of the Organisation for European Economic Co-operation, offered a chance of Germany's partial reintegration into the international economy: this was of course promoted by the United States for political as well as economic reasons. When the Federal Republic was formed from the three Western Zones of Occupation in 1949, it was still subject, despite Marshall Aid, to considerable economic handicaps: the Eastern part of Germany, primarily agricultural, had been severed from the West, so that the balance of the old German economy was distorted, and West Germany needed to import food to support her large population (including millions of refugees from the East), and hence to pay for these imports through exports of her own; the coalfields of the Ruhr were cut off from their natural complement, the iron-ore desposits of Lorraine and the Saarland, both of which had reverted to French control at the defeat of the Third Reich; and the levels of German industrial production, especially in heavy industry, were strictly controlled by the occupying powers. Even though the last of these restrictions was greatly tempered by the end of 1949, when the new Federal Republic was also allowed to progress towards membership of the OEEC, the Council of Europe, the World Bank and the International Monetary Fund, some limits on Germany's freedom to decide her industrial production levels still remained.

Against this background, it can be seen that the French proposal for a Coal and Steel Community, with German heavy industry subject only to the same controls as that of France, offered very considerable advantages, notably the removal of limits on industrial production and of barriers to the bringing-together of German coal with French iron-ore to make steel which Germany could export to a large tariff-free European market. The plans for a European Economic Community and for an Atomic Energy Community, coming a few years after the Schuman Plan, offered the German economy the further advantages of a large market for all manufactured goods and a possible answer to her shortage of energy: even the Common Agricultural Policy, which the German negotiators of the Treaty of Rome accepted reluctantly, as the price demanded by France for the common market in industrial goods, proved to be advantageous to Germany too.

Germany's second main motive for espousing the cause of European unity was that it contributed powerfully to the political and moral rehabilitation of the German people in the eyes of their neighbours. It was natural, after the horrors inflicted by the Third Reich on Nazi-occupied Europe, that the Germans in 1945 should be regarded politically as suspect and morally as outcasts. The early rules of the Allied occupation regime, which strictly forbade any 'fraternization' with the German people, were an expression of this attitude. The spectacle of a French government proposing in 1950, a mere five years after the war, that the coal and steel industries of France and of Germany should be placed under the same European High Authority, therefore marked a highly symbolic step upwards in Germany's status, and the further French proposal for a European Army in which Germany would have equal status (even though the plan proved abortive) was another step in the same direction. The process of European integration, once it had been started by the Schuman Plan, provided a forum in which German representatives negotiated as equals with their French, Belgian and other interlocutors, and the significance of this, as of the appointment of a German, Walter Hallstein, as the EEC Commission's first President, should, not be underestimated. The Federal Republic's achievement of international respectability was also, of course, helped by her partnership with the United States and her acceptance into NATO, but the reconciliation with France, and other EEC partners which had suffered terribly at the hands of the Third Reich, had a particular emotional meaning for the Germans in the 1950s and 1960s.

West Germany's international rehabilitation through her involvement in European integration was linked with her third reason for pursuing this course, namely its contribution to the consolidation of the Federal Republic's internal institutions. It should not be forgotten that Germany's second attempt to establish a democratic political regime, in the late 1940s, was accompanied by serious doubts about its ultimate success. The politicians who drew up the Basic Law of the Federal Republic, in 1948–49, were acutely conscious of the failure of their predecessors who had designed Germany's first republic in Weimar thirty years earlier, and many provisions of the 1949 constitution were specifically intended to prevent a repetition of the Weimar Republic's decline into dictatorship by 1933. Adenauer and his colleagues in the first years of the Federal Republic were influenced by the further idea that the democratic institutions they had established could draw support from the Republic's incorporation in a West European Community with a political as well as an economic dimension: the more transnational solidarity developed between the political system of European countries – including links between democratic parliamentarians in the directly-elected European Parliament for which the Treaty of Rome provided – the less risk there was of anti-democratic forces undermining the fragile new institutions of German democracy.

It is true that this concept of bringing a European dimension into the new German polity included specific elements of party-political calculation: Adenauer and other Christian Democratic leaders of the 1950s saw 'Europe' partly as a means of securing the basically anti-socialist values for which they stood, including the defence of private property (just as their French and Italian counterparts saw 'Europe' in part as a defence against strong indigenous Communist parties). This helped to make the European cause more suspicious in the eyes of the Social Democratic opposition party in Bonn, but as the 1950s went by the SPD modified its opposition – partly thanks to the pro-European attitude of the trade union movement and of the powerful SPD mayors of Hamburg, Berlin, and other large cities – and the value of a European framework for the Federal Republic's own institutions ceased to be a party issue.

The fourth major motive impelling the Germans to support European unification was that of the Federal Republic's external security. As the Cold War developed, and particularly after the Berlin blockade of 1948-49, Germany's exposed position made her seek the maximum support from partners in Western Europe, as well as the United States. Even before a specifically military element in European integration was suggested – with the French proposal of October 1950 for a European Defence Community which would incorporate German forces in a European Army – and even after this proposal was finally rejected in August 1954, the closer unification of West European countries was clearly motivated in part by their fear of Soviet pressure. The Hungarian crisis of 1956 (coinciding as it did with the revelation of British and French weakness in the Suez crisis) played a part in impelling the Adenauer Government to sign the Treaty of Rome in 1957 (to a lesser extent, the Czech crisis of 1968 contributed to Brandt's wish to enlarge the Community), and the security motivation was underlined by the extremely strong pressure for European integration which was exerted by Germany's main military ally, the United States.

As the open Cold War of the 1950s and 1960s gave way to more complex pressures from the international system – the uncertainties of American policy from Vietnam to Afghanistan, the ongoing energy crisis after the 1973 Middle East war, the continued risk of escalating Middle East conflicts and world economic recession – the Federal Republic has continued to see the European Community as a framework which can help to protect German interests against external dangers. In Chancellor Schmidt's eyes, the Community institutions as such are probably less relevant than the top-level meetings of the European Council, or his close bilateral consultations with the President of France, or even the diplomatic exchanges between Community capitals in the system of European Political Co-operation (which Bonn has worked hard to develop); but all of these channels depend ultimately on the fact that the governments involved are members of the Community. There is thus a direct link between Adenauer's view that European integration could make Germany safer in the early 1950s and Schmidt's view that the Community can contribute to German security in the vastly more complex world of the 1980s.

Germany's fifth main motive for supporting 'Europe', the fact that it offered a vehicle for the recovery of Germany's own standing and influence in the world – economically, culturally, and politically – is the other side of the coin marked 'protection of Germany's security'. The concern with security was dominant in the Federal Republic's early years, and has continued to the present in various forms, as we have seen, but it has been accompanied by the wish to restore Germany's position in international life to the level at which it stood before Hitler. In economic terms, the Second World War meant the temporary loss to Germany of many foreign markets, both in areas politically dominated by the Third Reich (notably Eastern and Western Europe) and further afield, from Latin America to China and Japan. Germany's recovery of her economic position in these areas, in some cases as early as the 1950s, was of course due in part to the intrinsic dynamism of her economy and the enterprise of her salesmen in conquering markets. Her position as a member of the European Community helped considerably, however, both by providing her manufacturers with a guaranteed 'home' market of 200 million people, and also by allowing Germans to appear in many parts of the world as 'Europeans' rather than simply as 'Germans'. In countries with negative memories of the Third Reich this was important. Quite concretely, the Community's relationship with Africa through the Yaoundé and Lomé Conventions, and Germany's participation in economic aid programmes under these Conventions, opened up markets for German exports in new parts of Africa, in addition to those like Namibia (German South West Africa before 1918), where links with Germany were already strong.

The cultural and political benefits to Germany's international standing, from her membership of the Community, are less tangible but no less real. Since the early 1970s the European Political Co-operation framework has made it easier for the Federal Republic to play a discreet role, growing in proportion to its rising economic weight, in the affairs of several parts of the world. In East–West relations, for instance, the Federal Republic's *rapprochement* with its Eastern neighbours through Brandt's *Ostpolitik* has been made more acceptable, both in the East and in the West, by the fact that it is seen to be embedded in the collective *Ostpolitik* of the Nine. In the Arab–Israeli conflict, again, the EPC framework made it easier for Germany to protect her interests by shifting towards the Arab position from 1973 onwards, without a total disruption of her understandably sensitive relationship with Israel; this was facilitated by the argument that a shift in the Federal Republic's position was necessary to keep her in line with the collective view of the Nine.

For the last thirty years, then, the mix of these five main considerations – economic prosperity, moral rehabilitation, internal stabilization, external security, and international influence – has kept the Germans constantly aware of the advantages offered to them by the European Community. Their respective influence has of course varied over time – the importance of the first three is naturally less than it was – but all have been important.

It should be added that, in addition to the considerations which have been presented here as calculations of national *interest* on the part of Germans, there has also been present a profound sense of shock and guilt at the destructive extremes to which the nation state in Germany was led in the Third Reich. A genuine conviction that the nation-state system in Western Europe should be replaced by something better, while it is naturally much weaker in the world of the 1980s than in that of the 1940s, remains a substantial element in German thinking about the Community (it is much stronger than in Britain, France, or even Italy), and neither German politicians nor their European partners can ignore it.

2. Germany's General Attitude to Integration

Against this background, the attitude of successive German governments towards the development of the Community can be summarized in two concepts: firstly, general support for the strengthening of the Community's institutions, in so far as this did not conflict seriously with the views of other Community members or expose German interests to serious risk; and secondly, general support for the development of common policies by the Community, provided that these did not conflict with Germany's existing views on the substance of public policy, or impose undue financial burdens on her.

The institutional aspect of this approach, which should be considered first, reflected the general spirit in which the political institutions of the Federal Republic were conceived. After 1945 the anti-centralist trend in German constitutional thought, which had predominated until the mid-nineteenth century, clearly won the upper hand over the centralizing tendencies which had been dominant in Bismarck's Reich and totally victorious in Hitler's. The very name 'Federal Republic' was chosen in order to emphasize that the German constitution-makers, responding to American examples and French interests as well as to their own particularist tradition, wished to provide for a clear distribution of governmental power between the federal and the regional levels. This principle, in addition to the other factors listed above, explains why Germans were on the whole more ready than citizens of the centralized states of France or Britain to accept the idea of a European Community organized on a federal basis: if power could be shared between Hamburg and Bonn, why not with Brussels as well? The practical effect of this idea on German policy should not be exaggerated, but it did have considerable influence, particularly in the early years of the Community.

It meant, for instance, that German representatives on the High Authority of the ECSC and on the EEC Commission were usually of very high quality. These institutions were also served by German officials of a high calibre in the subordinate ranks of the Luxembourg and Brussels machinery, and the influence of the Bonn Government was usually exerted quite strongly in the interest of strengthening the Community's authorities against the power of its member states. This occurred, for instance, when Adenauer offered resistance to de Gaulle's plans for an intergovernmental structure in the early 1960s (the so-called 'Fouchet Plan'), and when the Erhard Government backed Hallstein and the Commission in the more serious conflict with Paris in 1965–66.

The Community only resolved this conflict at the price of significant concessions by the partisans of supranationalism to those of intergovernmentalism: these concessions included not only the Luxembourg 'agreement' of January 1966, which buried the principle of majority voting, but also the non-renewal of Hallstein's appointment as President of the Commission the following year. By the start of the 1970s, the Brandt administration, although like its predecessors in Bonn it was more outspoken in support of supranationalism than the governments of many other Community members, was declaring its pro-European beliefs in a greatly changed world. Brandt was a spokesman for British entry to the Community in 1969, and for the EPC system after the Davignon Report in 1970; he argued strongly for 'European Union by the 1980s' at the time of the Paris summit conference of October 1972; and he made an impassioned plea for 'a rationally organized European government' in a speech to the European Parliament in November 1973, at the height of Europe's first major energy crisis. However, the Gaullist legacy of the 1960s, and the fact that French doubts about supranationalism were now reinforced by the attitudes of Britain and Denmark, meant that Germany's continuing commitment to the Community's institutional advance was less likely to be put to the test: Bonn remained the most 'pro-European' capital in the Community, but the attitude of her partners made this a progressively less demanding role to sustain.

When Helmut Schmidt replaced Brandt as Chancellor in May 1974, there were strong indications that Bonn's commitment to the Community institutions was itself being down-graded. The new Chancellor publicly criticized the Commission as a 'swollen-up bureaucratic apparatus', and made it clear that he wanted the ultimate political power to remain with the intergovernmental Council of Ministers. At the same time his Finance Minister, Hans Apel, began to make repeated attacks on the Community's accountancy procedures, and indicated that the Federal Republic was not prepared to go on indefinitely functioning as 'the paymaster of Europe'. Chancellor Schmidt also showed his low regard for the Commission when Roy Jenkins replaced François-Xavier Ortoli as its President in 1976–77, by insisting on maintaining the two German' Commissioners, Wilhelm Haferkampf and Guido Brunner, in their posts in Brussels even though there had been widespread criticism of both of them, particularly the former. Again, when the question arose of the European Community being represented at the summit meeting of the leading industrial powers, held in London in May 1977, Schmidt made little or no effort to support the Commission's case against the sceptical or hostile attitude of other national governments.[2]

These indications of declining German support for the Community's institutions can be explained partly by the new Chancellor's relative lack of experience in European affairs: in the SPD's years in opposition, before 1966, he had taken little interest in the Community, and as Defence Minister in the first stage of the Brandt administration, he had not been

[2] See Roger Morgan, *West Germany's Foreign Policy Agenda* (Sage, London, 1978), pp. 45–48.

directly concerned with the Hague summit of 1969 and its sequel in the enlargement of the Community. Even though Schmidt, as indicated above, came after a few years in office to regard the Community as a useful part of the external framework of German political and economic life, his commitment to its institutions has always remained less strong than that of earlier German Chancellors from Adenauer to Brandt. The German Government publicly welcomed the Tindemans Report of 1975, which pressed for faster progress towards the goal of European Union, with much warmer approval than anything expressed in Paris or London, but in the prevailing state of the Community's affairs this resembled a pious statement of good intentions rather than a hard political commitment. The move towards direct elections to the European Parliament, again, was taken much more seriously (and non-controversially) in Germany than in Britain or France, but the postponement of the event from 1978 to 1979 brought no strong protests or statements of regret from Bonn, and in the new Parliament's first trial of strength, its conflict with the Council of Ministers in 1979–80, the German Government took essentially the same position as that of the other major members of the Council of Ministers.

On the institutional aspects of the Community, the attitude of the Schmidt administration has been highly pragmatic. The supranational institutions, the Commission and the Parliament, have not benefited from any particular German support in their struggle to establish their influence against the resistance of other national governments, and there have even been some signs of German reluctance to accept the authority of the Community's Court of Justice, albeit on fairly minor issues; on the other hand, the more intergovernmental elements in the Community mechanism, and other procedures related to it, have been embraced and furthered by German policy. The European Council, for instance, once President Giscard d'Estaing took the initiative in developing the occasional summit meetings of heads of government into this more institutional form, was welcomed by Schmidt as a useful device for managing the affairs of an essentially intergovernmental Community: in July 1978 Schmidt was clearly glad to be able to speak on the basis of a Community position, recently agreed at the Bremen European Council meeting under Germany's Presidency, when the Western economic summit meeting was held in Bonn. The more continuous procedures of European Political Co-operation, again, were actively fostered by the German Foreign Ministry from the time of the Davignon Report of 1970 onwards: it was under Germany's Presidency in 1974 that several improvements in these procedures occurred, including the so-called 'Gymnich Formula' (named after the Federal Government's conference centre near Bonn) for systematic consultations between the Nine and the United States, and the EPC formula has on many occasions proved useful to German interests. It is also interesting to note that in the early months of 1980 the German Minister for European Affairs, Klaus von Dohnanyi, actively pressed on his Community partners a significant new German proposal for an upgrading of the status of the Council of Ministers' Secretary-General: this suggestion embodied the German view that, in a Community increasingly dominated by intergovernmental bargaining both inside and outside the Council of Ministers, the Secretary-General of this body should be given the enhanced status of a German Secretary of State (or Permanent Secretary), to allow him to exercise a mediating role hitherto associated with the Commission.

This pattern of current German attitudes – relative lack of enthusiasm for the Commission, the Parliament and the Court of Justice, and a strong commitment to the European Council, EPC and the Council of Ministers – indicates a prevailing German view that the institutional future of the Community is essentially an intergovernmental one, at least for some time to come.

This institutional perspective, in its budgetary aspects, is closely linked with the Federal Republic's general view of the substance of Community policies: that these are welcome in so far as they, firstly, promote German economic interests, secondly, correspond to Germany's own approach to the principles of public policy, and thirdly, do not entail an excessive German financial contribution.

German economic interests, in the formative years of the European Community, were defined by the post-war handicaps outlined earlier: the severance of industrial West Germany from its Eastern hinterland, the barriers between the Ruhr on the one hand and Lorraine and the Saar on the other, and the general conditions of wartime destruction of economic resources. The answers to all these problems lay, at least in part, in opening up new markets in the West for the exports of a revived German economy. In this process the creation of a tariff-free Common Market played a fundamental part, as did the establishment of free trade in coal and steel in the specific area covered by the Schuman Plan. Germany's main concern in the negotiation of the Rome Treaty was thus to ensure that barriers to free trade were removed (now that German industry had been put in a strong competitive position by the currency reform of 1948), and to apply this principle to trade not only within the Community but externally as well: for German industry the European Community was to form an extensive 'home' market of more than 200 million inhabitants, and its external trade policy should be one which would allow Germany's strong exporting industries the maximum prospects of selling to a world-wide 'foreign' market as well. This of course meant that the Community's posture on world trade issues should be one of free trade rather than protectionism, at least for goods which the German economy was strong in producing: world free trade in industrial goods was the primary objective, and to obtain it the German negotiators (both in 1955–57 and in the later operation of the Community) were ready to accede to France's wish for a rigidly managed CAP which combined price intervention internally with a highly protectionist attitude towards external producers.

With this exception of agricultural policy, Germany's efforts thus went towards the maintenance of an open market, not only through the removal of trade barriers but also through the promotion of an active Community policy on competition: this aspect of the creation of an unregulated market was of great importance to Germany, and was administered in the 1960s by a very active German member of the European Commission, Hans von der Groeben.

The view that the Community's policies should as far as possible reflect and extend those adopted within the Federal Republic – a view which was of course similar to the preference of other member states for European policies to reflect their own domestic ones – was promoted with greater emphasis as Germany emerged as the dominant economy of the Community in the 1970s. In October 1975 Chancellor Schmidt sent personal letters to his fellow heads of government, indicating that increased German financial support for Community policies would only be made available if the other member states adopted economic policies more attuned to Germany's own approach and if the Community's financial procedures were improved. In Europe's long debates about EMU, which will be analysed below, one of the central themes was the unwillingness of the Federal Republic to submit its currency to close links with those of other member states until the latter adopted economic policies more like those of Germany: only when Raymond Barre, French prime minister from 1976 onwards, reversed the previous course of French economic policy and brought it much more closely in line with that of Germany, did the German Government agree to a modified form of monetary union, the European Monetary System, in 1978.

The propensity of German policy-makers to wish to see their own principles of policy adopted by other Community governments applies to external economic relations as well as developments within the narrow Community framework itself: when the French Minister of Foreign Trade, in 1977, spoke of the need for world trade to be better 'organized', the German Economics Minister, Herr Friderichs, addressed to the French Government an open letter inveighing against the dangers of 'any attempt to organize any further the international exchange of goods', which he denounced as 'the first stage towards the abandonment of the rules now operating, the rules of commercial freedom in the world, which in the past has contributed so much to the well-being of our peoples'.[3]

This underlying German attitude towards the Community's economic policies has always been closely linked with a further concern, that these policies should not cost Germany too much money. From the German point of view, policies of 'negative integration' have usually been welcome, because they opened up, at little or no cost, new markets for German exports. Policies of 'positive integration' on the other hand – such policies as the development of an extensive Community regional policy or an interventionist

---

[3] Further details and sources, *ibid.*, p. 72.

policy for industry – have usually met with resistance from the Federal Republic on the grounds that Germany, already a major contributor to the CAP, should not be expected to subsidize other expensive policies as well. This attitude, as will be seen, affects German views not only on Community regional and industrial policy but also on the enlargement of the Community to include Greece, Spain and Portugal, and possible expenditure on raw material stocks and overseas development in general.

The Federal Republic, at the start of the 1980s, still remains in many ways more 'pro-European' than many of its partners. This general attitude, however, is applied only with considerable reservations in certain specific policy areas.

3. German Interests and Specific Community Policies

On the individual policy areas which have become part of the Community's agenda – some to stay as adopted policies, others to languish or fade away – German attitudes have reflected the general guidelines indicated in the previous section.

On *Economic and Monetary Union*, and all the related issues of the joint management of economic affairs, the Federal Republic's policy has been of the kind to be expected from a growing industrial power with a general belief in free market forces, a commitment to world-wide free trade and a historically-conditioned preoccupation with the risks and dangers of inflation. All of these concerns came out very clearly in the position taken by Germany at the time of the Community's great debate on EMU, both before and after the publication of the Werner Report on this subject in October 1970.

On the central issue, of whether integration should be promoted through the monetarist approach of linking national currencies in some form of 'snake', or whether priority should be given to economic measures designed to bring the national economies more closely into alignment, the German approach has been firmly on the 'economist' side of the argument. In contrast to the French preference for the 'monetarist' technique of forcing economic convergence on the states involved through the enforcement of collective monetary discipline, German representatives have strongly argued that such an approach, given the prevailing disparities between national rates of inflation and general economic performance, would be a recipe for disaster. The original Werner Plan foundered on the conflict between these points of view, and the compromise form of EMU actually attempted by the Community failed to survive the upheavals in the international monetary system during the 1970s, especially the floating of the DM in May 1971. The so-called 'mini-snake' or 'DM-snake' which survived the dropping-out of Britain and France from the original EMU in the mid-70s corresponded to the Federal Republic's view of the relationship between economic and monetary integration: only countries with a national economic performance as healthy as that of Germany, and a correspondingly low rate of inflation, were able to keep their currencies linked to the DM. The fact that these countries, as well as including the major EEC members Britain, France and Italy, included the non-Community countries Austria and Switzerland, suggested that German policy was striking a balance between the Community's own development and the intrinsic demands of monetary policy: this situation also lent a degree of unreality to the suggestion unofficially floated by ex-Chancellor Brandt in 1975 that the Community itself should be divided into a closely integrated 'first tier' and a less integrated 'second tier', one of the distinguishing features being their membership of the mónetary snake.

It could be said that the idea of a 'two-tier Community' was implemented, in a sense, when the European Monetary System was introduced at the end of the 1970s: this embraced almost all of the member states, leaving only Britain, and potentially the three new Mediterranean member states, as members of the 'second tier'. Looking back on the experience of EMU, the long-serving head of the European affairs department in the Federal Ministry of Economics has recently remarked, in words which reflect the prevailing German view:

> ... a bold attempt was made to achieve a common policy via Economic and Monetary Union. It was bound to fail: the political and social forces in the Member States cannot be overlaid or neutralized by the automatism of a monetary regulatory mechanism. The Community will continue to depend on the painstaking coordination of national policies. Even the European Monetary System, established at the beginning of 1979, which still allows exchange rate corrections does not alter this situation; on the contrary its success is conditional on how well coordination of economic policy works.[4]

As far as the *Common Agricultural Policy* is concerned, the attitude of the Federal Republic has been marked by a number of contradictions. This is hardly surprising in view of the central role played by the CAP in the Community's development ever since the 1950s, the great importance attached to it by Germany's main partner France, and the fact that successive German administrations have had to reconcile the claims of farmers on the one hand and consumers (and also some EEC partners) on the other in a particularly delicate balance.

At the time when the Rome Treaty was signed, the German Government regarded the CAP, with its distinctly *dirigiste* management of agricultural production, as on the whole an unwelcome accompaniment to the achievement of a free market for industrial goods, but an accompaniment which Gemany had to accept to accommodate the wishes of France. As late as the Hague summit meeting of the Six in December 1969, when Chancellor

---

[4] Ulrich Everling, 'Possibilities and limits of European integration', *Journal of Common Market Studies*, Mar. 1980, p. 218.

Brandt wished to get President Pompidou's agreement to the reopening of entry negotiations with Britain, he saw himself as meeting French wishes rather than German interests when he agreed to the finalization of the financial regulations for the CAP.

During the 1970s, as the anomalies of the CAP became apparent, successive German Chancellors, first Brandt and then Schmidt, have declared themselves in favour of its reform. However, it has at the same time become apparent that the CAP produces substantial benefits for Germany's own expanding and efficient agricultural sector, so that its radical reform would encounter strong resistance here as well as in France. The farm lobby in Germany expresses its interests particularly through the Free Democratic Party, whose precarious position in the Bundestag depends on its retaining the support of agricultural voters in a few critical regions of the country. As the FDP has been part of the governing coalition since 1969, and as one of its leaders, Josef Ertl, has held the post of Minister of Agriculture ever since that date, Chancellor Schmidt has been obliged to temporize in his consideration of any fundamental reform of the CAP. It is likely that some reform will occur in the early 1980s, after the further enlargement of the Community and after the critical German election of October 1980, but Germany is not likely to support any reform which seriously limits the considerable benefits which German farmers have derived from the CAP in its existing form.[5]

The value of the Community's *industrial and competition* policies to Germany is perceived essentially in terms of the way they open up an extensive market to German industry. As indicated above, the promotion of an effective competition policy has been a major concern of the German Government since the earliest days of the Community, and this is still the case.

Germany's relative lack of interest in promoting an interventionist Community policy for industrial development derives partly from the strongly entrenched *laissez-faire* philosophy which has accompanied Germany's own post-war 'economic miracle'; partly from a well-founded belief that Germany's own interests would benefit most from a policy limited essentially to the removal of obstacles to intra-Community trade and investment; and partly from a fear that the cost of a more interventionist policy would be borne in large part by Germany as the most prosperous member of the Community. There have recently been signs of a convergence between West Germany, France and Britain in their approach to this issue, but this has largely taken the form of an evolution of French and British thinking, welcomed by Germany, towards the prevailing German point of view.[6]

[5] See Yao-Su Hu, 'German agricultural power: the impact on France and Britain', *The World Today*, Nov. 1979, pp. 453–61.

[6] Everling, *loc. cit.*, p. 226. See also the chapters on competition policy (by David Allen) and on industrial policy (by Michael Hodges) in Helen Wallace, William Wallace and Carole Webb (eds.) *Policy-making in the European Communities* (Wiley, London, 1977).

In the important field of *energy policy*, the Federal Republic again sees the role of the Community as being to supplement and co-ordinate policies which are essentially the responsibility of national governments. The Coal and Steel Community was welcomed by Germany in the 1960s as a framework for the running-down of coal production which was then thought to be necessary, and Germany's development of nuclear energy capacity has been achieved in part through her membership of Euratom. Since the radical change in Europe's energy situation which followed the Middle East crisis of 1973, the Federal Republic has made strenuous efforts to secure its supplies of imported oil. This has been done partly through direct bilateral agreements with oil-producing countries, but in connection with such agreements Bonn has stressed the principle of market forces more strongly than either London, Paris, or Rome: Germany's strong economic position has allowed her to pay the vastly increased price for imported oil with less difficulty than her Community partners, and she is also relatively better prepared to accept the general principle that the economic price for energy will rise in proportion to its scarcity. In the Community's energy policy discussions of the late 1970s, Germany has sought to win support for her view that North Sea energy should be made available to Britain's Community partners on preferential terms, and that they should have easier access to its exploration and extraction than hitherto.[7]

German attitudes to the Community's *regional and social policies* have varied, like those of other member states, according to the prevailing composition of the national government. In the period after 1969 the centre-left administration of Willy Brandt (Germany's first Social Democratic Chancellor since 1930) made a special effort to upgrade the social policy of the Community, in an attempt to emphasize that European integration was directly important to the man in the street. It was largely on Brandt's insistence that ambitious plans for an expanded Community social policy were included in the commitments agreed to in the Paris summit conference of October 1972: their realization was of course prevented by the economic crisis which hit Europe the following year.

Regional policy, as distinct from social policy, was accepted by the Brandt Government as an integral component of the plans for EMU set out in the Werner Report. In its general approach to the establishment of EMU, which was clearly in the interests of the Federal Republic, the German Government accepted the argument that too great a disparity between the economic levels of the Community's component parts would make 'the planned union unworkable, and that a substantial regional policy was needed to counteract this. There was even some support in Bonn for the further argument, put forward by Britain and Italy as the largest peripheral members of the Community, that the establishment of EMU would tend to draw economic activity from the periphery towards the centre, and that

[7] On the background, see the chapter by Robert Black, *ibid.*

the balance must be redressed by a regional development fund so designed as to redress the balance in favour of the peripheral areas.

By the time the details of the agreed regional development fund were debated in 1973–74, much had changed. EMU in its original form had proved abortive, and Britain had dropped out of the currency snake. Moreover, the energy crisis of 1973 had driven Britain and Germany apart, with Germany accusing Britain of unwillingness to co-operate in creating a joint Community policy. These factors, together with the toughening of German attitudes towards public spending after Schmidt replaced Brandt, meant that the Regional Development Fund set up by the Community in 1975 was on a much smaller scale than that envisaged by the Heath Government, and by George Thomson as the Commissioner responsible for this area, in 1973.[8]

The Federal Republic continues to accept that a Community regional development policy can do at least something to promote the convergence of member states' economies, and thus to keep the common market open, but the emphasis placed by the Schmidt administration has been on selective aid for specific regions or projects, rather than the more general approach envisaged in earlier years.

Finally, in this survey of Germany's specific interests in the development of Community policies, some attention must be given to two aspects of the Community's external affairs: firstly, *North–South relations* and secondly, *East–West relations*. On the first of these issues, German policy towards the series of EEC agreements with less developed countries, the Yaoundé Conventions of the 1960s and the Lomé Conventions of the 1970s, has been influenced by the pervasive economic policy of neo-liberalism and also by the fact that the developing countries concerned were mostly special protégés of France (and later of Britain). The non-interventionist basis of German economic policy has meant that throughout the long series of conferences of the late 1970s, attempting to establish a 'new international economic order', Germany has pressed her Community partners to adopt only a modest degree of interventionism as far as the prices of primary commodities are concerned. Although the Federal Republic agreed, at a European Council meeting in March 1977, that a common fund for commodity price stabilization should be set up, the German negotiators took a minimalist position, in strong contrast to that of France and Holland, as far as its size was concerned. A further reason for West German reticence in relation to EEC development aid for Africa and elsewhere is that Germany had no historic links with most of the developing countries concerned. Germany's record of contributions to development, both through the EEC and through the United Nations agencies, stands up well in comparison with that of some other industrial countries (notably the United States and Japan), but this is not an area of Community policy where the Federal Republic is

[8] See Helen Wallace, 'The Establishment of the Regional Development Fund', *ibid.*

likely to take major initiatives in the future, any more than in the past.[9]

In *East–West relations*, by contrast, Bonn naturally has a much more active interest, mainly because of the division of Germany into two states and the special position of Berlin. In defining its attitude towards the EEC's Common Commercial Policy, as applied to the state trading economies of Eastern Europe, the Federal Republic is partly influenced, as usual, by its overall philosophy of economic liberalism, which implies that international economic policy should essentially be limited to trade liberalization. This is one reason why the Federal Republic is reluctant to see the scope of the Common Commercial Policy extended from trade matters to cover economic co-operation agreements, which it prefers to keep on a bilateral basis (another reason for this is the profitability of such agreements for the Federal Republic, especially in its relations with the Soviet Union). In general, however, in its dealings with the Soviet bloc, the Federal Republic sees many advantages in acting in concert with its partners in the Community, now that Brandt's *Ostpolitik* of the early 1970s has removed some of the special obstacles which set Germany apart from these partners; for instance her non-recognition of the GDR or of the German–Polish frontier. Both in economic dealings (with the above qualifications) and in political, strategic, and human rights issues, the Federal Republic sees the benefits of dealing with Eastern Europe as a member of the EEC, rather than as an isolated West German state which might be suspected of still harbouring 'revenge-seeking' policies aiming at national reunification.

On two specific East–West points concerning her national interests, West Germany has been able to use the EEC to promote her policies. Firstly, in relation to the East German state, Bonn has won the agreement of her Community partners, ever since the Rome Treaty was signed, to a special protocol by which trade between the two Germanies is regarded by the whole Community not as external trade but as intra-Community trade, and thus not subject to the Common External Tariff. This arrangement not only gives West Germany the economic advantage of extensive dealings with the GDR (though, to be precise, the West German taxpayer heavily subsidizes this one-sided trade, whose direct beneficiaries are the individual firms which do the exporting), but also support for her political aim of keeping alive 'the substance of the German nation' which might one day, in a changed East–West context, provide a basis for reunification. Secondly, in relation to the vital question of the Federal Republic's links with Berlin, Germany's negotiators also gained the agreement of the whole Community that the 'area of application' of the Treaty of Rome should include not only the Federal Republic but also West Berlin. Thus, even though the Western allies do not regard West Berlin as part of the Federal Republic, and the Quadripartite Agreement of 1971 (between the United States, Britain, France and the Soviet Union) confirms that Berlin 'may not be ruled' from

[9] Morgan, *West Germany's Foreign Policy Agenda*, op. cit. pp. 58–69.

Bonn, the principle that West Berlin belongs to the Community has been used by the Federal Republic to strengthen its own links with the city. For instance, this purpose is served by the installing of certain Community institutions in West Berlin (the EEC research centre on youth unemployment and a section of its Patent Office), by the frequent holdings of EEC ministerial and parliamentary meetings there, and by the presence of three West Berliners – even though they are elected by the Berlin city Parliament and not directly by the voters – in the European Parliament. The Federal Republic's ability to insist that every Community agreement with an external partner includes an 'area of application clause' (meaning that it covers Berlin) gives further support to the German goal of maintaining links with Berlin: in recent years this doctrine has been applied to many agreements for which the Community's external partners were willing to pay the price of accepting these links, for instance the EEC–Maghreb economic agreement and the Community's fisheries agreement with the Soviet Union.[10]

4. Dissent in Germany on the Community and German Views on its Future Development

It will be clear from what has been said that there is very little dissent among West German political circles, or in public opinion generally, about the advantages Germany has gained from her membership of the Community. It is true that there was a phase in the early period of its history when the Social Democratic opposition strongly criticized Adenauer's policy of tying West Germany into a right-wing Community (indeed a Christian Democratic and clerical one), and in the late 1970s, conversely, there were signs that the Christian Democrats in Germany had some reservations about increasing their country's involvement in a Community which they saw as over-influenced by the philosophy of state intervention, by left-wing forces in Britain, Italy, and potentially France, and by the likely addition of further left-wing elements in Spain and Portugal. However, these reservations now appear as transient, and much less significant than the general commitment of all German political forces to the maintenance of the Community and of Germany's membership of it. Only among very limited circles on the extreme left of German opinion has the view been expressed that the Community is a capitalist organization, dominated by multinational companies and subservient to the United States, and that Germany's interests required distancing from it.[11]

Even the fundamental point of criticism raised by the SPD in earlier years, that the Federal Republic's integration in a West European Community would compromise the goal of national reunification, appears

---

[10] This section draws on the author's study (in progress) of 'The EEC and Berlin'.
[11] For this view see Gerhard Kade, *Die deutsche Herausforderung: 'Modell Deutschland' für Europa?* (Pahl-Rugenstein, Cologne, 1979).

without relevance to the affairs of Germany and Europe as they have actually developed. On the one hand, the prospects for the political reunification of Germany are generally agreed to be very remote (this was accepted even by the SPD when it fundamentally revised its foreign policy at the start of the 1960s);[12] on the other hand, the European Community has visibly developed into something very different from the kind of European superstate which might have exerted sovereign power over its constituent parts. It is hard to see that the Community, as it has actually developed and appears likely to develop in future, would stand in the way of any kind of association of the two German states which now or prospectively seems feasible.

The general state of German thinking about the future of the Community, and of Germany's place in it, has become clear in the course of the discussion during the late 1970s on the admission of Greece, Spain and Portugal. The main emphasis in this discussion, inside Germany, has confirmed the continuity of the fundamental attitudes to the Community analysed above. All influential circles in the Federal Republic support the admission of the three Mediterranean countries to a Community which will serve the same purposes as in the past, and will be organized along the same lines as at present. Enlarging the Community will contribute both to the economic goal of maintaining the prosperity of Germany and her partners, through a larger market for trade and investment, and to the political purposes of enhancing Germany's and Europe's security.

The attitudes of Germany's political parties and interest groups to the problem of enlargement indicate that there are limits to the price which the Federal Republic is prepared to pay for these desirable objectives. Although the SPD has adopted the general idea of a Community 'Marshall Plan' for the economic development of Southern Europe, there must obviously be a limit on the amount of resources which could be devoted to it. More generally, German representatives have made it clear that the agricultural, regional and social policies of the existing Community could not automatically be extended to a Europe of twelve members.[13]

Institutionally, the prospect of enlargement in the 1980s will strengthen the other factors which make the Federal Republic accept the essentially intergovernmental Community which is the legacy of the 1960s and 1970s. The degree of integration now achieved, both economic and institutional, has served German interests very well, and will continue to do so. The

---

[12] See William E. Paterson, *The SPD and European Integration* (Saxon House, Farnborough, 1974); and Juliet Lodge, *The European Policy of the SPD* (Sage, London, 1976).

[13] See Beate Kohler, 'Germany and the Further Enlargement of the European Community', *The World Economy*, May 1979, pp. 199–211; and Christian Deubner, 'The southern enlargement of the European Community', *Journal of Common Market Studies*, Mar. 1980, pp. 229–45. On German thinking about the Community and its policies, see Wilfrid Kohl and Giorgio Basevi (eds.), *West Germany: a European and Global Power* (Lexington Books, Lexington, Mass., 1981).

Federal Republic, as well as emerging more distinctly as an economic and political power on the international scene outside Europe, will without doubt continue to give the degree of priority to the European Community which it has given under Willy Brandt and Helmut Schmidt, and to play the same leading role in the Community's gradual development.

FURTHER READING

Peter A. Busch, 'Germany in the European Community: Theory and Case Study', *Canadian Journal of Political Science*, Vol. II, No. 3, 1978, pp. 545–73.

Ralf Dahrendorf, *Plädoyer für die Europäische Union* (Piper, Munich, 1973).

Deutsche Gesellschaft für Auswärtige Politik, *Regionale Verflechtung der Bundesrepublik Deutschland* (Oldenbourg, Munich, 1973).

Alfred Grosser, *The Western Alliance* (Macmillan, London, 1980).

Yao-Su Hu, 'German Agricultural Power: the Impact on France and Britain', *The World Today*, Nov. 1979, pp. 453–61.

Chris Hull, 'The Implications of Direct Elections for European Community Regional Policy', *Journal of Common Market Studies*, June 1979, pp. 332–49.

Gerhard Kade, *Die deutsche Herausforderung: 'Modell Deutschland' für Europa?* (Pahl-Rugenstein, Cologne, 1979).

Wilfrid L. Kohl and Giorgio Basevi (eds.), *West Germany: A European and Global Power* (Farnborough, Lexington, 1981).

Michael Leigh, 'Germany's Changing Role in the EEC', *The World Today*, Dec. 1975, pp. 488–97.

Roger Morgan, *West Germany's Foreign Policy Agenda* (Sage, Beverly Hills/London, 1978).

Hermann Müller-Roschach, *Die deutsche Europa-Politik 1949–1977* (Europa-Union Verlag, Bonn, 1980).

Robert Picht (ed.), *Deutschland, Frankreich, Europa: Bilanz einer schwierigen Partnerschaft* (Piper, Munich, 1978).

Geoffrey Pridham, 'The European Policy of Franz Josef Strauss', *Journal of Common Market Studies*, Vol. XVIII, No. 4, June 1980, pp. 313–32.

Eberhard Schulz (ed.), *Die Ostbeziehungen der Europäischen Gemeinschaft* (Oldenbourg, Munich, 1977).

Hans-Peter Schwarz (ed.), *Handbuch der deutschen Aussenpolitik* (Piper, Munich, 1975).

Hans von der Groeben and Hans Möller (eds.), *Die Europäische Union als Prozess* (Nomos, Baden-Baden, 1980).

IV

Italy

Geoffrey Pridham*

How should the role of a member state in the European Community generally be assessed? A comprehensive survey needs of course to include an historical angle, which both covers the original motivation for the member state's participation in the integration process and identifies broad patterns of continuity or otherwise in the pursuit of its European policy. At the same time, a thematic approach is essential for evaluating the specific features and priorities of that policy while paying attention to the variety of interlocking or separate factors which have conditioned its formulation. These latter should refer, for instance, to the current or changing political and economic situation of the country in question together with its own definition of national interests; the internal structure of policy-making and the extent to which integration activity is regarded as one particular area or as having a growing applicability to other policies both external and domestic; how far European policy is subject to consensus or division among political parties, interest groups and the public; and, not least, the influence of Community activity itself with regard to new and old areas of common policy as well as bilateral and multilateral relations with other EC states. In other words, an examination of a member country's role in the Community has to take into account not merely its European policy content and action but also different determinants and motives affecting that policy and operating in both the national and European contexts.

Just as the historical angle provides perspective so the thematic approach encourages an awareness of the complexity of policy-making. Both methods are particularly necessary in the case of Italy, one of the original six EC States, whose role has lacked any full interpretative study even by Italian

* A special thanks is given to Pippa Pridham for her helpful editorial comments on the original draft of this chapter.

writers[1] or has been assessed on the basis of short-term and sometimes superficial assumptions. Thus, one of the most commonly held judgements of Italy's participation in European integration places much emphasis on the gap if not contradiction between the prevalence of pro-integrationist rhetoric in Italian political circles and their marked inability or unwillingness to translate this into policy action. Criticism of Italy's 'verbal Europeanism', apparent among academic studies and political commentators alike, is in fact broadly justified, and notably with regard to her position in the 1970s, underlines the degree to which a member state's economic weakness fundamentally restrains its political role in the EC, but such a judgement by itself can be one-dimensional and verges on being moralistic.

Firstly, it is necessary to look at specific causes of Italian policy behaviour on integration matters – as suggested by the thematic approach – for these may vary over time and on examination may indicate a less simplistic picture of the country's role. Here, it is useful for example to ask how much European policy might be dictated by short-term considerations or motivated by a longer-term strategy; or, if Italian performance is so ineffective what is the relative impact on it of political instability, institutional or bureaucratic inefficiency, or simply economic constraints and pressures.

Secondly, it is helpful to note from a comparative standpoint that, as Christoph Sasse remarks in a survey of national European policy-making in the various states, 'the gap between proclaimed aims and real progress is comparatively more noticeable than it is in domestic politics'.[2] In other words, Italy differs from other member states more as a matter of degree rather than principle in this respect. The historical angle offers here the wider context in which to explain the merits and demerits of national European policies. During the decade of the 1970s, for example, the Italian role in the EC has been much criticized for a high record of violating Community regulations, an absence of political weight and initiative, and generally an inability to keep pace with the integration process. This has resulted in Italy being regarded as an obvious candidate for 'second-tier' status in the EC and in speculation that she might be 'drifting away' from the Community.[3] However, Italian policy can only fully be explained by

[1] For a discussion of some recent Italian literature on the subject, see Geoffrey Pridham, 'Concepts of Italy's approach to the European Community', *Journal of Common Market Studies*, Oct. 1980. F. Roy Willis, *Italy chooses Europe* (Oxford University Press, New York, 1971), is an historical rather than interpretative study and does not of course include discussion of the 1970s.

[2] Christoph Sasse *et al.*, *Decision-Making in the European Community* (Praeger, New York, 1977), p. 67.

[3] See the round-table discussion of Italian politicians in 'The Italian presence in the European Community', *Lo Spettatore Internazionale*, Apr.-June 1973. This concern surfaced intermittently in the Italian press from the early 1970s, e.g. leader in *Corriere della Sera*, 26 Mar. 1972, 'Fra Italia ed Europa: il fossato si allarga'; and also in the press of other EC states, e.g. *Süddeutsche Zeitung*, 17–18 Mar. 1973, 'Ist Italien für Europa verloren?'. Speculation about Italy 'drifting away' from the EC notably arose at the time of her trade restrictions in 1974.

considering broader developments at both European and national levels. In the former case, the growing scope of EC common policy activity has not only embarked on areas where Italy was evidently vulnerable (as with monetary integration), but also where an Italian commitment has been more forthright, such as the decision to implement direct elections to the European Parliament providing as this did an occasion for reaffirming strong Italian support for political union. At the same time, the greater importance of the Mediterranean basin during this decade for strategic, political and economic reasons meant that interest elsewhere in the EC in Italy's role intensified and tended to dwell on causes for concern. Looking at the national level, the most relevant occurrence has been the rise of the Communist Party (PCI) and its emergence as a possible governing party. While strengthening the domestic consensus on European integration, this development has raised the prospect of some modification of Italian European policy although in the meantime it produced further political deadlock at home.

At second glance, therefore, Italy affords an interesting and important example of the nature rather than merely the outcome of the integration process. Certain palpable observations may be made about her role and factors influencing it as an EC partner – weaknesses of economic structure and performance, a general lack of political weight at least compared with the two leading member states of France and West Germany, and overriding domestic problems – but they do demand closer scrutiny in order to avoid a platitudinous assessment. The need for a discriminating approach to Italian European policy is illustrated moreover by looking at the principal interpretative theme developed so far concerning its purpose – that is, Italy as an example of a 'penetrated system', where domestic and international factors interrelate closely with two-way effects – for this has sometimes been applied one-sidedly.

In his study of Italian foreign policy published in 1963, Norman Kogan selected as the key objective of that policy 'to protect the domestic social structure from internal dangers',[4] namely through the basic association of a distinct pro-Western orientation through NATO and European unification with the maintenance of a capitalist economic system and in particular the Christian Democratic Party's (DC) position of power. This close inter-relationship between external and internal political considerations was most noticeably evident during the Cold War years, and while remaining the principal leitmotiv of the Government's European policy, since then it has however been subject to changing emphasis due to different national party alliances at home as well as new developments in international affairs, such as the growth of détente and the less harmonious relationship between the EC and the United States during the 1970s. For this reason, Primo Vannicelli in one of the few interpretative studies of Italian European policy (1974) is one-sided in his insistence on the exclusive 'internalization' of

[4] Norman Kogan, *The Politics of Italian Foreign Policy* (Pall Mall Press, London, 1963), p. 136.

European issues or as he comments, 'in an unstable system with stalemating tendencies, frequent government crises and constant political manoeuvring within and among parties, exploitation of foreign policy for internal purposes is almost inevitable'.[5] Little or no attention is paid to actual cases where Italy has played a more active role in EC affairs – notably when specific national interests are at stake in common policy formulation, over the question of strengthening Community institutions and to some extent as a diplomatic intermediary – or to the converse impact of the integration process on Italian party policies, such as helping to convince the PCI to change its attitude towards the Community from the early 1960s and later adopt a European strategy. The point here is that the cardinal feature of policy-making in the EC is the two-way interlinkage between the national and European levels, especially when applied to individual cases of member states.

The intention of this brief survey is, following both historical and thematic approaches, to look at the form and context of Italian European policy. In doing so, the discussion will concentrate on three lines of enquiry: the origins of Italy's participation in European integration and the motivation behind her European policy; the pursuit of this policy and the effects of EC membership for Italy; and the evolving positions of the various Italian political forces towards the Community. This last aspect merits special and separate attention because the central role played by political parties in the functioning of Italy's political system means they have acted as the essential filter in both the definition of and the priority accorded that country's policy on European integration.

1. The Origins and Motivation of Italian European Policy

Without resorting here to detailed historical discussion of Italy's early European policy[6] – the basis of which was laid with the Marshall Aid programme of 1947, participation in NATO in 1949, and her founder-member role in the ECSC agreed in 1951 and later the EEC and Euratom in 1957 – it is important to clarify the essential features of this policy as the requisite starting-point for analysing subsequent policy behaviour as a member state and identifying its main patterns. How much was Italy's original participation in the integration process motivated by strategic or short-term considerations or by both? What was the relationship between the European and other policy areas, both foreign and domestic? And, in looking at the course of Italian European policy, is it possible or indeed valid to distinguish between different phases? The answers to these questions will provide some intimation as to how far official pro-integrationist options

---

[5] Primo Vannicelli, *Italy, NATO and the European Community: the interplay of foreign policy and domestic politics* (Harvard University, 1974), p. 22.
[6] On this see F. Roy Willis, op cit., chapters 2 and 3.

have been ideologically motivated in the sense of adherence to Europeanist positions or whether they were more a grandiose cover for particular political incentives or economic interests.

In the case of the first question, Giuseppe Petrilli, himself a prominent pro-integrationist,[7] was correct in asserting that 'Italy's European choice did not originate solely in an advanced maturing of its cultural Europeanism, but above all in the absence of other viable alternatives'.[8] European federalist ideas were undeniably present after the Second World War among political elites in government at the time Italy's European policy was first conceived; nevertheless, a more useful angle for assessing the full motivation behind this policy is to identify the specific considerations and reasoning of policy-makers in the context of the situation at the time. The existence of a federalist outlook did of course mean that projects for European integration were from the start viewed sympathetically in official circles; and indeed, the post-war Italian constitution reflected this outlook in its provision under *Basic Principles*: 'Italy ... agrees, on conditions of equality with other states, to such limitation of sovereignty as may be necessary for a system calculated to ensure peace and justice between nations; it promotes and encourages international organizations having such ends in view' (article 11). Furthermore, the decision to participate in European integration did entail some longer-term thinking, as outlined in the Schuman Plan of 1950 and indicated in the broad aims specified by the Treaties of Paris 1951 and Rome 1957, while Italy (like West Germany) needed to re-establish international credibility in the post-Fascist period and therefore replace her previous search for prestige and influence as a European power after national unification in 1870 with a new orientation and context for achieving national aims. However, policy strategy does imply an active pursuit of a long-term purpose to be implemented in successive stages, and based on a preference of one basic policy alternative over another, rather than merely an open support for vague aims. Did therefore the lack of a real alternative for Italy in her post-war assessment of her own actual and potential international role suggest that initial European policy was conceived by default or possibly in reaction to current events more than as a consequence of strategic choice?

From the party-political standpoint, an alternative was presented in that the political Left challenged in a fundamentalist way official policy from the time of Marshall Aid. Their preference for 'peace' and 'neutrality' was clearly dictated by (anti-capitalist) ideological and (philo-Soviet) strategic considerations, where the PSI and PCI in alliance adopted broadly similar positions;[9] but the domestic polarization which ensued from the 1948

[7] Giuseppe Petrilli, head of the state corporation IRI, was also president of the Italian Council for the European Movement.
[8] Giuseppe Petrilli, 'L'Italie et l'Europe', *Les Problèmes de l'Europe*, no. 66, 1974, p. 21.
[9] Richard Walker, *Dal confronto al consenso: i partiti politici italiani e l'integrazione europea* (Il Mulino, Bologna, 1976), p. 43.

Italian general election and the decision of 1949 to join NATO was itself a crucial factor in explaining the espousal by DC-led centre-Right governments (after the cross-party coalition including the PCI collapsed in 1947) of the Western alliance and proposals for European integration. During the first post-war years, governmental attention under the leadership of Alcide De Gasperi had inevitably concentrated on the immediate task of national economic reconstruction and political re-establishment to overcome the disruption of the War.[10] By 1947, the international context was crystallizing with the advent of the Cold War and therefore for Italy the pressing need to define her international role. At this point, the key external determinant of the Italian position was United States' pressure on Rome to accord with Western defence interests and maintain and strengthen a stable democratic system, which, interpreted, meant one freed of influence from the political Left.[11] This fundamental association of Western international security with internal stability, underlined as in the preamble to the North Atlantic Treaty,[12] was the vital premise underlying the beginnings of Italian European policy and remained an essential leitmotiv of the government position thereafter. The attitude of P. E. Taviani, a political colleague of De Gasperi's, that the ECSC could provide 'a united front against the spread of Soviet totalitarianism' illustrated the same official line of thinking over integration projects proper. In short, Italy's European policy owed its stimulus and adoption to the Cold War environment and the uncertainties of the Italian domestic situation, and became a major doctrinal ingredient in the governing parties' desire to maintain their power position at home. Atlanticism and European integration were the two principal themes of post-war Italy's external relations.

This policy evolution, with long-term implications, in response to the then prevailing political circumstances is confirmed by taking account of the attitudes of its two principal architects – Alcide De Gasperi (Prime Minister 1945–53) and Carlo Sforza (Foreign Minister 1947–51). Of the two, Sforza was the more open in the immediate aftermath of the War to ideas of European unification, and in a little-known article published in 1943 attacking the vices of national sovereignty had been prescient about the gradual and concrete path that integration would eventually take.[13] Sforza's own original suggestion was that such a process should be initiated by Franco-Italian co-operation, a theme that he was later to repeat following the Marshall Plan with his negotiation of an abortive Franco-Italian customs

[10] F. Roy Willis, op. cit., pp. 13 ff.

[11] *Ibid.*, pp. 18–19.

[12] This preamble stated that member countries sought 'to promote stability and well-being in the North Atlantic area'.

[13] Carlo Sforza, 'Italy and her neighbours after the War', *Foreign Affairs*, Oct. 1943, p. 107: 'Europe will not move toward unity at the wave of a magician's wand ... It is wiser to begin in a smaller way. One accomplished fact is more significant than a hundred theories or a thousand exhortations. What is needed in Europe is a concrete example of unity between nations, in one part of the Continent.'

union in 1947. Nevertheless, despite Sforza's own federalist sympathies, what really counted in launching Italy's actual European policy together with her pro-Western alliance decision was East–West confrontation. De Gasperi's conversion to European integration in the light of this development underlined the exact reasoning behind this policy. The Prime Minister's earlier position indicated no significant support for European federalism *per se*, even though this attracted favourable views among some sections of his own party, for his interest in integration which began around 1948 derived more pragmatically from his evaluation of the developing international and domestic political situation.[14]

This was not to deny that other motives were present in the Italian decision to engage in the integration process. The country's response to the Schuman Plan of 1950, which initially aimed at Franco-German reconciliation, soon attracted the active participation of other West European states, notably Italy which displayed some concern over the future German role in post-war Europe while at the same time keen to prevent any Franco-German hegemony in a European arrangement[15] (a preoccupation that was to reappear at different moments in the later history of Italian European policy). So far as (European) federalist motives were concerned, their existence[16] was more important in a secondary way in providing an attitudinal or even ideological backing to European integration among the ruling political elites rather than acting as a primary pressure for policy implementation. The experience of Fascism had naturally discredited the role of nation-state power and with it the concept of national sovereignty in Italian eyes;[17] although the specific idea that the European integrative framework was necessary for solving the country's particular economic, social and political problems was really a somewhat later addition to the conceptual arguments for Italian participation and acquired as it did increasing weight because of the ineffective performance of the post-war Italian state.[18] Altogether, therefore, Italy's original support for European integration derived from various short-term motives and long-term considerations, for it was unrealistic to separate the two from each other since the first stimulated the second.

The answer to the second question raised at the beginning of this section as to the relationship between the European and other policy areas, both

[14] R. Walker, op. cit., pp. 29 and 35.
[15] F. Roy Willis, op. cit., pp. 32–3.
[16] According to *ibid.*, p. 31, 100 senators and 235 deputies in the Italian Parliament belonged to the federalist Parliamentary Group for European Union.
[17] This point is made strongly by Altiero Spinelli, a European federalist, in 'European Union in the Resistance', *Government and Opposition*, vol. 2, no. 3.
[18] This theme first appeared during debates over the ECSC Treaty in 1951–52; see Ernst B. Haas, *The Uniting of Europe: political, social and economic forces, 1950–57* (Stanford University Press, 1958), p. 141.

foreign and domestic, follows from the preceding discussion. The essentially political – international security combined with internal stability – motive behind Italy's European policy position meant not only was it constituted as a central part of that country's foreign relations but also that from the start there was much scope for the 'internalization' of that policy as, in the words of Andrea Chiti-Batelli, a prominent official of the Italian Parliament:[19] 'European integration was not conceived as an appendix of national policy – a sort of sector, more or less removed, of the foreign policy or foreign trade of our country – but as an integrated part and priority of national policy, and first of all of the domestic sphere.' All the same, even against this background of a strong interconnection with other policy areas it is relevant for this study to establish the exact priority accorded European affairs.

A necessary precondition for such a priority within a country's overall external policy was the withdrawal from a wider independent role in international relations and abandonment of world-power ambitions, a position forced on Italy by the collapse of Fascism and the loss of her colonial territories after the War. As already seen, there was initially an intimate relationship between the Atlanticist and pro-integrationist themes of Italian post-war foreign policy. So far as the development of external policy is concerned, what arises is the changing priority between these two policy lines in relation to differing circumstances and the way in which this dual orientation was interpreted by Italian policy-makers. The party-political dimension, which revealed much variation on the Atlanticist and European themes from Right to Left including within the ruling DC, will be discussed below in the final section.

The first few years from the later 1940s, in which the basis of Italian foreign policy was laid, witnessed as a result of the Cold War situation a greater emphasis on the Atlanticist over the Europeanist option in the sense that the former prejudged the decision on the latter.[20] While 'Atlantic fidelity' remained a constant in Italian policy, for the aforementioned reasons of international security and United States influence as well as the desire to maintain DC dominance internally, the increasing envelopment in the integration process together with the EC's growing international weight by the 1970s, broadly promoted an overriding tendency to consider European affairs on their own merits and lend them prior attention. This qualitative evolution is most evident in Italy's case in the new focus given her traditional 'Mediterranean vocation', which had been largely subsumed within both the Atlanticist and European options during the 1950s and 1960s, either by reinterpreting the former (as among the DC Left) in a 'neo-Atlanticist'

---

[19] Chiti-Batelli, formerly, as an official of the Italian Senate, secretary to the Italian delegations to European assemblies, in *Dalle elezioni alla federazione europea?* (Le Monnier, Florence, 1979), pp. 43–4.

[20] P. Vannicelli, op. cit., pp. 5–9; and F. Roy Willis, op. cit., chapter 2.

direction[21] or subordinating this 'vocation' to the dictates of integration which then was a concern mainly of the non-Mediterranean area of Western Europe. Events in the 1970s – the growing strategic importance of the Mediterranean, the energy crisis from 1973 and of course the post-dictatorial applications for EC membership from Greece, Spain and Portugal – have shifted the balance of geographical interest in Community affairs more to southern Europe and consequently highlighted Italy's role as the most 'Mediterranean' of the original Six and enlarged Nine. It is significant that Italy has strongly supported further EC enlargement for the 1980s, despite the economic risks entailed by prospective competition from farming products in the three countries concerned subject to the terms of their entry, because of the desire to alter this pro-northern imbalance within the EC, not to mention strengthening the new and possibly fragile democratic systems, a consideration to which Italy is sensitized by her own history of instability.

With regard to the interrelationship between the European and domestic policy areas, the same point must be made as earlier that the distinctly political reasons relating to domestic stability for originally participating in the integration process preconditioned internal perspectives towards Italy's membership of the Community. The European framework has been viewed at the governmental level not only for its relevance to DC policies but also more broadly as an institutional and political safety-net to guarantee continuity and stability in the post-war Italian parliamentary system. In accordance with this outlook, there was some merit in accepting membership of the ECSC and EEC in the 1950s despite certain economic problems in adapting to the new competitive framework. As Italy had a very protected economy and a relatively young steel industry, business interests were opposed to the creation of the ECSC;[22] while Italian agriculture with its backward structural condition was concerned over the establishment of the EEC.[23] However, such was the Government's commitment to the Schuman Plan, for instance, that it both applied pressure on business through its control over steel financing and instructed its negotiators to demand special concessions to Italian interests in the Paris Treaty.[24]

In fact, whereas Italian European policy was from the start regarded by political elites as first and foremost a foreign policy or diplomatic exercise, national interest promotion became in the course of time a regular feature of this policy once integration activity developed further. This approach in Italy's role as a member state is seen most clearly with regard to the different

---

[21] 'Neo-Atlanticism' emphasized the Atlantic Alliance as an association for economic and political co-operation rather than a military alliance under American leadership and favoured links with the Mediterranean and, in particular Arab, countries. In short, it involved Italy playing a more independent line vis-à-vis the United States.

[22] E. B. Haas, op. cit., pp. 199–200.

[23] F. Roy Willis, op. cit., pp. 69–70.

[24] E. B. Haas, op. cit., p. 200; and F. Roy Willis, op. cit., pp. 35–6.

common policies which evolved. Thus, over the CAP Italy has attempted unsuccessfully to promote its structural aims as against the EC's concentration on pricing policy, as the former aspect would be more beneficial for rectifying the particular deficiencies of Italian agriculture,[25] while Italian interest inevitably came to focus on the need for a full-scale EC regional policy both as a result of discontent with the priorities of the CAP and in relation to other developing common policy areas, such as the industrial and monetary.[26] Similarly, successive Italian cabinets in the 1970s were insistent on a more dynamic approach at the EC level towards the question of unemployment because of the country's own severe problems here.[27] Generally, it could be said that Italy's promotion of a fuller and broader scope for European integration, particularly in the light of her own aggravated socio-economic and political problems in the 1970s, came to be actuated by material as well as political considerations, including the country's support for the aim of political union; her inability, as distinct from her motivation, to meet the necessary requirements for achieving new areas of integration activity is another matter and will be discussed below in the next section.

The third and final question about the possibility or validity of identifying different phases in Italian European policy has already in part been answered. From the foregoing survey, it is evident that this policy underwent some changes of emphasis and acquired an increasing priority within the context of the widening scope of European integration. Taking this point further, some direct assessment of the continuity of Italian policy here and how far and why it has been subject to varying patterns is worthwhile. There are several features of a consistent approach, notably in the persistent adherence by DC-led governments to the Atlanticist connections and to the aim of European political union to an extent that it has lent a certain static quality to the Italian position.[28] This is perhaps inevitable because of the uninterrupted rule of the DC ever since 1945 and its control, with some temporary exceptions, over all relevant areas of European policy-making. The DC has of course been required to compromise with different coalition partners, ranging from the Centre-Right in the 1950s, and the Centre-Left in the 1960s to policy co-operation with the PCI in the later 1970s; but it is more pertinent here to stress how the parties of the Left moved towards

[25] B. M. de Gennaro, 'Italian Agriculture and international policy in 1971', *Lo Spettatore Internazionale*, July-Dec. 1972, pp. 117–19.

[26] H. Wallace, W. Wallace and C. Webb (eds.), *Policy-Making in the European Communities* (John Wiley, London, 1977), pp. 123 and 141.

[27] *Ibid.*, p. 38; see also G. Bonvicini and S. Solari (eds.), *I partiti e le elezioni del Parlamento Europeo: interessi nazionali ed europei a confronto* (Il Mulino, Bologna, 1979), pp. 37–9.

[28] Donald Sassoon makes this point in his 'The making of Italian foreign policy', in W. Wallace and W. Paterson (eds.), *Foreign policy making in Western Europe* (Saxon House, Farnborough, 1978).

the DC's European and Atlanticist positions as a precondition for any alliance. This at least in very general terms has been the overall picture at the level of proclaimed aims of policy.

Continuity is less apparent when it comes to examining the effectiveness of Italian policy. In historical retrospect, the period of De Gasperi continues to be conspicuous as the highpoint of an activist Italian policy towards integration. This was due partly to De Gasperi's own unequalled authority as leader, reflected as this was particularly in the foreign/European policy sphere,[29] but also, it must not be forgotten, as a consequence of the fact that this period was in any case a notably dynamic one in the history of integration. Italian European experts have concurred self-critically in this distinction between the initial dynamic phase and the stagnant decades since. Bino Olivi has argued that since De Gasperi Italian governments have only used the Community instrumentally, even negatively, for pursuing particular interests and for reasons of partisan publicity;[30] while Altiero Spinelli has gone so far as to claim that 'Italy from the time of De Gasperi has no longer had a European policy', a factor which he attributed above all to her preoccupation with domestic and economic difficulties.[31] His reasoning is correct, though not his conclusion, for the 1970s may be viewed as a different phase from preceding decades in Italy's role as an EC member state because of the turnabout in her economic performance from the late 1960s with slower and more unstable growth, increasing balance-of-payments difficulties and the calamitous effects on Italy of world inflation and the rise in oil prices. All these adverse developments have acted as fundamental constraints on Italian European policy, as shown by her hesitation over entry to the European Monetary System inaugurated in 1978, but notwithstanding it cannot be said that Italy has lacked coherence in her approach to the EC.

Italy's 'passive' role in the EC must be seen in relative terms, for it should be juxtaposed with the main factor which has usually conditioned progress or the lack of it in European integration – the Franco-German relationship. In the face of this, Italy's influence as a single member state has unquestionably been limited as far as initiating new departures. This problem was a principal motive behind Italian pressure for the inclusion of the United Kingdom as an EEC member state, or as one Italian leader remarked succinctly in 1972: 'Thanks to Britain's entry it will be possible to overcome the situation prevailing so far in which, because of the narrower number of member countries and the relatively great weight of Germany and France, disagreement between these two countries has been sufficient to inhibit all chances of a common stand.'[32] No triangular relationship or counterbalancing

---

[29] N. Kogan, op. cit., p. 69.
[30] In his *Da un'Europa all'altra* (Milan, 1973).
[31] Quoted in *Corriere della Sera*, 17 Mar. 1973.
[32] Giuseppe Saragat, PSDI leader and former Italian President, in *The Times*, 4 Feb. 1972.

bilateral one between Rome and London has in fact emerged, not least because of Britain's particular reservations over integration as well as her own economic problems, although a common Anglo-Italian interest was important in the launching of a more comprehensive EC regional policy in the mid-1970s.

In conclusion, it may be said that Italy's original membership of the European Community, readiness to engage in further projects, and strong rhetorical support for the integration process, derived not so much from Europeanist ideology as such, but rather from a set of political assumptions which arose out of the aftermath of the War and have continued to underlie government policy over the past three decades. Conceptually, the Italian ruling elites had no fundamental objection to the ultimate objectives of European integration, and indeed espoused them; politically, they had a strong interest in promoting this process for external and internal reasons; although, economically, their decision to proceed with integrative projects was by no means so clear-cut in terms of their advantages. However, the changed circumstances in which the Community has proceeded and in which Italy has found herself have on balance tended to reinforce rather than challenge her own role as a member state.

2. The Pursuit of European Policy and the Effects of Italy's Membership

It is already clear therefore that Italy's role in the EC was conditioned both relatively with respect to the weight and influence of other member states and intrinsically as a result of her own economic weaknesses. The latter problem, although it came to the fore most of all in the 1970s, was potentially present before then, even if in the first years after the founding of the EEC Italy experienced an unprecedented though temporary boom with the impetus this gave to her exports.[33] Such factors explain Italian European policy, however, in only very general terms, for it is necessary to deal with more specific determinants of performance in this area and this above all refers in the Italian case to the political and institutional context in which European policy has been formulated. P. Vannicelli in his 1974 study placed much emphasis on this aspect, as summarized in his conclusion that 'a weak political system like that of Italy can substantially minimize the effect of integrative pressures because of the dynamics generated by its own precariousness, and despite the leaders' commitment to integration', and went so far as to insist on the overwhelming importance of 'the Italian Government's inability to formulate and implement a coherent European policy and to play a positive role at the Community level'.[34] Again, speaking

[33] K. Allen and A. Stevenson, *An Introduction to the Italian Economy* (Martin Robertson, London, 1974), pp. 62–3.
[34] P. Vannicelli, op. cit., pp. 52 and 22.

generally, this is probably no surprise considering the commonly recognized ineffectiveness of the post-war Italian state, but this judgement cannot be simply repeated without identifying the particular way in which European policy-making has been constrained or inhibited and noting any variation in its conduct.

This more differentiated approach is useful, for instance, when estimating the impact of executive instability of European policy. Italy was ruled by as many as 36 successive governments in the three-and-a-half decades from the end of the Second World War to the end of the 1970s, but the consequence of this was not so much any discontinuity of policy line as inconsistency or ineffectiveness in the pursuit of policy aims. Some cabinets have evidenced a variation of outlook – the Andreotti centre-Right government of 1972–73 was more Atlanticist in its postures than the centre-Left ones which preceded it – but throughout the whole post-war period the European policy area has been almost exclusively controlled by DC leaders: the Prime Ministership, the Foreign Ministry (though a Liberal held it during the Rome Treaty negotiations in the mid–1950s, while Saragat (PSDI) and Nenni (PSI) briefly controlled it during the 1960s), Agriculture, the Treasury and Trade and Industry. Performance has been adversely affected by the disproportionate extent to which individual governments have not been free to pursue an active and uninterrupted policy without the time and energy constraints imposed by regular coalitional manoeuvring and lengthy cabinet formations. It is here that Italy has most contrasted with the French Fifth Republic, where the relative longevity in office of the presidents, who have directed French European policy, has been an important factor of strength in the latter's role as a member state.

These limitations on policy performance dictated by executive instability are certainly severe, although they can be exaggerated when drawing conclusions about Italy's 'weak' political role in the EC. For example, a member country's chairing of Community institutions every so many years – as Italy did in 1965, 1971, 1975 and 1980 – is an occasion when its role comes under closer scrutiny, for not only does this function entail more assiduous attention to and preparation of EC affairs but the chairmanship's growth in importance from the 1960s has led to higher expectations as to achievement.[35] Bearing in mind that other EC states have performed this role disappointingly, for 'success' depends very much on the current trend of Community progress, Italian presidencies have not been undistinguished. In fact, on the first of the above occasions Italy played a crucial mediating role, for in the second half of 1965 her chairmanship coincided with the 'constitutional crisis' of the French boycott of EC institutions, when she managed to give coherence to the efforts of the other Five in responding to de Gaulle's defiance, an accomplishment which owed much to the personal

[35] See H. Wallace and G. Edwards, 'European Community: the evolving role of the Presidency of the Council', *International Affairs*, October 1976, pp. 535–50.

Community expertise and negotiating skill of Emilio Colombo.[36] One feature tempering the negative effects of Italian government instability has been a frequency of personnel continuity in relevant key ministries – Colombo, one of the country's foremost European experts, held the Treasury portfolio continuously through several cabinets from 1963–70 until he became Prime Minister (1970–72), after which he again for a while became Treasury Minister under Aldo Moro. There was also the coincidental fact that none of the aforementioned examples of an Italian chairmanship occurred during a governmental interregnum in Rome. The assumption of the Council presidency by Italy early in 1980 was beset with rumours of the impending collapse of the Cossiga Government, but this did not transpire immediately and the Italian Prime Minister acted as a useful background mediator over the vexatious problem of Britain's contribution to the Community budget. Italy in the person of Emilio Colombo, her Foreign Minister, played a crucial part in the final negotation of this problem in May 1980.

The foregoing role may be described as one of diplomatic activity, but how does this relate to Italy's general lack of political weight in the EC? This possible contradiction is explained more clearly by looking at the same problem in the light of the development of Community summits, which have been institutionalized as the European Council during the 1970s. It has been observed that Italian prime ministers at these meetings, lacking the same degree of authority as most of their colleagues, have not been invested with a clear role of leadership.[37] This is most evident if one compares them with the roles of the French President and the West German Chancellor – as Pompidou and Brandt at the 1969 and 1972 summits, and Giscard d'Estaing and Schmidt from 1974. Italy has sometimes been represented by a caretaker prime minister (as in March 1979), or by one whose domestic position is in doubt (as in April 1976 when Moro was on the point of calling an early national election). However, by contrast, Italian personnel continuity was once more underlined by the fact that at the December 1974 summit of all those present at the original summit in 1969 at The Hague, only the Italian leaders Moro, Rumor and Colombo were left.[38] Concerning her political influence in the European Council, Italy while not demonstrating any major pioneering force has been able to apply a significant pressure sometimes for a policy decision as most notably over the creation of the European Regional Development Fund during the

---

[36] John Newhouse, *Collision in Brussels: the Common Market crisis of 30 June 1965* (Faber and Faber, London, 1967), pp. 132–3 and 141. It is worth noting that with the simultaneous breakdown of the Franco-German relationship, Italy could more easily perform her desired role of mediator between these two countries.

[37] Annette Morgan, *From Summit to Council: evolution in the EEC* (Chatham House, PEP, London, 1976), p. 34.

[38] *Frankfurter Allgemeine*, 9 Dec. 1974. Moro was Foreign Minister in 1969 and Prime Minister in 1974; Rumor Prime Minister in 1969 and Foreign Minister in 1974; and Colombo Treasury Minister on both occasions.

1974–75 consultations over this. In other words, it is feasible at the EC institutional level to distinguish between a country's diplomatic–intermediary and political-initiative roles, where the former, although perhaps secondary, is by no means inconsiderable.

Despite this evidence of Italy's diplomatic influence, the effectiveness of her overall performance as a member state has suffered considerably from the problems of government management. This is not merely a question of overwhelming domestic difficulties which distract from the pursuit of European policy, an aspect usually emphasized by Italian political leaders themselves[39] and which often leads to highly self-critical appraisals in the Italian press;[40] the problem has arisen more consistently from the pronounced deficiencies of political co-ordination in the country's European policy-making. This may rightly be described as fragmented or, as one survey of national European policies noted, it is by no means clear who is 'at the wheel' of Italian policy towards the EC.[41] This diffuse state of affairs is a result of the general structure of Italian cabinets, whereby the Prime Minister is not 'prime ministerial' in the sense of enjoying an overriding authority in policy-making[42] and interministerial rivalry is encouraged by the existence of overlapping portfolios in key policy areas (notably economic and financial) and has been further strengthened by coalition and intra-DC factional interests.

The principal locus of European policy-making has been the Foreign Ministry in the sense of leading government spokesman in this area rather than active policy co-ordinator, for any assertion of the latter role would encounter the jealous and entrenched autonomy of other ministries.[43] In principle, this problem demonstrates the extent to which EC affairs have increasingly overlapped between traditional external and domestic policy concerns, although the structural confusion in Italy over the division of ministerial responsibilities has exaggerated the conflictual effects of this development. This is most apparent in the allocation of economic and financial matters among as many as six ministries (Treasury, Budget, Finance, Industry, Foreign Trade and State Corporations), which inevitably

---

[39] For example, interview with Andreotti, Prime Minister, on Italy's role in the EC against the background of domestic troubles, *The Times*, 2 Apr. 1973.

[40] Criticism of the lack of progress in European integration and Italy's contribution to this through her weak role was a frequent theme in the Italian press during the 1970s and revealed a certain sensitivity to foreign opinion, e.g. articles in *Corriere della Sera*, 12 June 1971, 16 June 1971, and 17 June 1971. This theme tended to reappear over cases where Italy found difficulties in adjusting to EC policy decisions, as over her delay in implementing VAT in the early 1970s and again over her import controls in 1974 and 1976. Politicians echoed this theme as did La Malfa, PRI leader, in his comments on Italy as the 'weak partner' of the EC (*Corriere della Sera*, 3 Mar. 1973 and 15 Mar. 1973).

[41] C. Sasse, op. cit., p. 69.

[42] With respect to foreign policy-making, see N. Kogan, op. cit., pp. 69–70.

[43] C. Sasse, op. cit., p. 21.

hinders any clear approach to EC affairs.[44] Rivalry has ensued, such as between the Treasury (a DC monopoly) and the Budget Ministry (invariably held by the PSI in the centre-Left governments) with deleterious repercussions on European policy-making;[45] while centrifugal institutional procedures have marked relationships between these portfolios and the Foreign Ministry, notably in the case of the Treasury whose special role in the EC area lies in the constitutional requirement that this ministry has to approve any expenditure outside the budget and hence with respect to implementing Community measures.[46] It is therefore no surprise that efforts to tighten up the mechanism of decision-making, such as through the Inter-Ministerial Committee for Economic Programming (CIPE, formed in 1967), have failed to overcome this diffusion of authority.[47]

A principal consequence of the institutional deadlock in Italian European policy formulation, not to mention other policy areas, is that some influence if not control has devolved elsewhere to other policy-making agencies. Two in particular – the Bank of Italy[48] (whose long-time President Guido Carli was a strong critic of the lack of sufficient co-operation inside the EC over problems produced by the oil crisis), and the public or giant corporations – have carved out for themselves an important role in respectively financial and foreign-trade affairs and accordingly in these sectors of European policy. A measure of the way in which the growing complex area of EC policy has exacerbated the institutional conundrum of Italian European policy-making is the assertion by the regions, inaugurated generally throughout Italy in 1970, of their claim to influence in this field, among others, in their search for political legitimacy.[49] The central state has attempted to check this pressure from the regions, as for instance in the official circular of December 1972 which confirmed that all correspondence with the EC as with other international organizations had to be transmitted through the Foreign Ministry,[50] Rome being mistrustful of any regional initiative that might result in direct contact with European Community institutions. Formally, this has remained so but in practice there has developed more and more *de facto* consultation between the Italian regions and the European Commission and Parliament, especially with the growth of a common

[44] H. Wallace, *National Governments and the European Communities* (Chatham House/PEP, London, 1973), p. 23.
[45] Interview with Signor Morelli, secretary to the monetary committee, European Commission, Brussels, Dec. 1975.
[46] C. Sasse, op. cit., p. 22.
[47] *Ibid.*, pp. 20–21; and H. Wallace, op. cit., p. 25.
[48] Its role was emphasized in interviews with Signor Morelli and Ugo Mosca, Director-General DG II, European Commission, Brussels, Dec. 1975.
[49] See articles by Gianfranco Martini, 'European presence of Italian regions and local official bodies', *Lo Spettatore Internazionale*, Jan.-Mar. 1975, p. 27–49; and Alfonso Zardi, 'Comunità europee, funzionalità dell'ordinamento regionale, "europeismo" delle politiche regionali in Italia, 1972-1977', *Comuni d'Europa*, Rome, Feb. 1979, pp. 5–10.
[50] G. Martini, op. cit., pp. 31–2.

regional policy not to mention over agricultural directives.[51] Regional authorities administered by the PCI have been noticeably persistent in this respect, challenging that EC funds should no longer be handled in the traditional way (as through the Cassa per il Mezzogiorno) but rather with the regions playing the key decisional part in their application.[52] Many regional governments have arranged conferences on their relations with the EC in order to publicize their potential role here. This demand for a voice in the formulation of Italian European policy, particularly with regard to certain common policy activities, is likely to remain if not grow, especially since further direct powers were transferred from the Italian state to the regions over economic development and social services in 1977.

The other consequence of deficient political co-ordination in the Italian approach to EC affairs is that as a result a greater onus has been placed on the need for systematization of policy at the bureaucratic level, but this has been largely missing. To some extent there has been more mutual co-ordination within the civil service as a substitute for the absence of clear political direction, although over large negotiating issues, bureaucratic channels (such as the institutionalized meetings of directors-general) cannot provide the requisite guidance.[53] European policy does of course suffer as any other policy area from the Byzantine character, lethargy, and unpreparedness of the Italian bureaucracy, as well as its relatively low status nationally. A certain lack of awareness of EC affairs has been a contributory factor to this general condition, as for instance in the shortage of integration specialists in the Foreign Ministry itself. According to one Italian enquiry in the early 1970s, 'European positions come very low in the aspirations and priorities of our diplomats or future diplomats'.[54] In fact, at this time, the Farnesina's (Foreign Ministry's) limited resources were more than stretched with only half-a-dozen administrative grade officials specializing in EC matters,[55] although some efforts have since been made to rectify this deficiency.

[51] *Ibid.*, pp. 32–3.
[52] For example, the case of Emilia-Romagna, whose president Guido Fanti (PCI) pressed strongly for this change: 'It must be absolutely avoided that the distribution of EC funds take place through channels like the Cassa per il Mezzogiorno which in the past have shown to be inadequate'. (*Corriere della Sera*, 21 Oct. 1975).
[53] C. Sasse, op. cit., pp. 21–2.
[54] Survey of the Istituto Affari Internazionali, Rome; see Cesare Merlini, 'Italy in the European Community and the Atlantic Alliance', *The World Today*, Apr. 1975, p. 163.
[55] H. Wallace, op. cit., pp. 45–6. For instance, in summer 1978 the Foreign Ministry appointed Renato Ruggiero, formerly the Commission's chief spokesman in Brussels with wide experience in Community affairs, to take charge of the administration of EC policy in Rome. As of early 1980, EC affairs were handled in the Foreign Ministry (as before) mainly by the General Directorate of Economic Affairs. This consisted of two departments for EC affairs: one dealing with internal EC matters and containing 16 personnel, including 7 senior clerks; the other covering EC external relations and containing 9 personnel, including 4 senior clerks. The Foreign Ministry's General

These personnel inadequacies have probably had more effect (adversely) on Italian policy-making than the (positive) fact that, at least as indicated by an opinion survey of 1973, Italian civil servants have been more favourably inclined towards the integration process than those of other member states.[56] Italy has gained a strong reputation, in contrast notably with France, for a poor personnel strategy in servicing her representation in EC institutions. From the establishment of the EEC in the late 1950s, Italy was either remarkably slow in making such appointments or tended with some exceptions not to send her best administrators to Brussels, with the lack of official incentives to those interrupting their national bureaucratic careers.[57] This shortage of Italian administrative quality has been particularly apparent in the higher reaches of the European Commission, so that choice has more often than not settled on ageing politicians or younger men with no obvious political prospects.[58] In the view of one study on this particular subject, 'for reasons which are closely tied to the unsure development of the Italian political world, our ruling class have always regarded a Community appointment with reticence; this is especially so for those who would be particularly suited to fill the post of Commissioner – the choice has often been long and arduous'.[59] This personal deficiency, although certainly not confined to Italy among member states, was illustrated by the problems in nominating an Italian to fill the post of European Commission President in 1970 and dramatized by Franco Maria Malfatti's premature retirement from that post in March 1972 in a blatant preference for furthering his national political career, a decision prompted by the early Italian general elections called for a few months later. This was regarded as something of a scandal and in the words of one Italian public figure as a 'symptom of the Italian lack of engagement in Community problems and obligations'[60] with the result that the Brussels correspondent of a prominent Italian daily newspaper felt that the Malfatti affair had hardly contributed 'towards the growth of prestige and political weight of Italy within the Community's institutions.'[61]

Directorate for Political Affairs also had a department taking care of political co-operation among the member states as well as following some other Community matters (Information supplied by Mario Quagliotti, First Counsellor, Italian Embassy in London, letter to the author, 7 Mar. 1980).

[56] See W. J. Feld and J. K. Wildgen, 'Italy and European unification: some preliminary comments on elite attitudes', *Il Politico*, no. 2, 1974, pp. 334–48.

[57] P. Vannicelli, op. cit., p. 33; and interviews with Italian officials in Brussels, Dec. 1975.

[58] N. Kogan, op. cit., p. 147.

[59] Wilma du Marteau, 'Italian presence in Community organisms in Brussels', *Lo Spettatore Internazionale*, Jan.-Mar. 1975, p. 58.

[60] Comment by the president of Confagricoltura, the Italian agriculturalists' federation, quoted in *L'Italia nella politica internazionale*, Rome, Jan.-Apr. 1972, p. 54.

[61] *Corriere della Sera*, 20 Mar. 1972. Malfatti later became Italian Minister of Education in several cabinets and briefly Foreign Minister in 1979.

Italian self-criticism again tended to highlight this personnel weakness with respect to the European policy field, but in fact these and other institutional difficulties were partly compensated for by the consequent weight acquired by Italy's Permanent Representation in Brussels not only because of insufficient co-ordination in Rome, but also of the mere distance between Brussels and the Italian capital. For this reason, Italy's Permanent Representation was one of the largest among the member states with the greater need to service committees directly from its own staff as opposed to that in Rome and prepare negotiating positions on location.[62] Its personnel was dominated by officials from the Foreign Ministry,[63] reflecting the extent to which the latter formally controlled this policy area, with a relatively high average length of service of four or five years. This allowed Italian personnel in this organ the chance to gather expertise in Community affairs, a factor notably illustrated by the case of Giorgio Bombassei who held the post of Italian permanent representative for as long as nine years from 1967–76. Consequently, the Permanent Representation became institution-ally 'the almost exclusive channel through which the Commission deals with the Italian administration and vice versa',[64] although it should not be forgotten that COREPER, the institution combining these national organs, has generally gained greater authority in preparing if not helping to formulate EC policy decisions in the course of time.

The final two interrelated questions which remain to be answered in this examination of Italy's policy role in the EC are: how much has her relative lack of political weight, due to executive instability and bureaucratic inefficiency as well as the basic problem of her weak economic structure and performance, affected Italy's influence in common policy making?; and what have been the benefits or drawbacks for Italy of her participation in the integration process? It is of course difficult if not almost impossible to measure exactly and comprehensively the effects of Community membership as a separate factor, but there are sufficient pointers to make this investigation worthwhile.

As to the first question, a useful distinction may be made between the initial negotiating stage and the application of decisions and routine attention to further procedures in common policy activity. In the former instance, the Italian record is not without significant achievement as shown by the part played in the Rome Treaty negotiations of 1955–57 in linking the EEC to Euratom against French reservations about the former,[65] in helping to overcome French reluctance about British entry negotiations in 1971 together

---

[62] H. Wallace, op. cit., pp. 62–3.
[63] 12 out of 23 and 17 out of 31 Permanent Representation officials were from the Foreign Ministry in 1968 and 1972 respectively; see H. Wallace, op. cit., p. 62.
[64] W. du Marteau, op. cit., p. 53.
[65] M. Camps, *Britain and the European Community, 1955–63* (Oxford University Press, London, 1964), p. 54.

with West German pressure,[66] and in sponsoring direct elections to the European Parliament, and the granting of new powers to the European Parliament,[67] as well as foreign policy co-ordination in 1970. Some Italian governments have also taken policy initiatives or insisted actively on special conditions in common policy formulation, though invariably such instances were explained either by external stimulus from elsewhere in the Community or by an unusual determination in Rome to push for particular national interests. The two most notable cases of this behaviour during the 1970s were over the reorganization of the European Social Fund (ESF) during 1970–71 and the establishment of the European Regional Development Fund (ERDF) during 1974–75.

With the ESF, Italy had a clear vested interest, having already obtained about 65 per cent of the Fund's small expenditure in the past,[68] and now pressed strongly and successfully for giving differential assistance to regions with special employment problems.[69] With the ERDF, the process was more complicated with the need to convince other EC governments to make a fresh commitment to expenditure, notably the German Federal Republic, although the energetic Italian role here amounted to a new departure from one of relative passivity apropos of the Community's rudimentary regional policy up to the 1970s. The ERDF case also showed that common policy progress depends heavily on a coalition among different EC states. Italy had negotiated a special protocol to the 1957 Rome Treaty promising EEC help with the Mezzogiorno, and between 1959–67 about 53 per cent of European Investment Bank loans were granted to Italy, mainly for southern development,[70] but in relative terms this involved only a small degree of Community capital investment. The problem was that since Italy was the only member state of the then Six with a clear-cut interest in regional policy, she remained isolated over this until the accession in 1973 of Britain and Ireland as other countries with distinct regional problems. Their combined negotiating weight was crucial in producing agreement on creating the ERDF, as a result of which Italy proved to be by far the main beneficiary (receiving 40 per cent of its share out of a total expenditure of 1,300 million units of account over three years).[71] The remarkable feature was the exceptional speed with which the Italian administrative follow-up produced the first list of relevant projects among

[66] Uwe Kitzinger, *Diplomacy and Persuasion* (Thames & Hudson, London, 1973), p. 36.
[67] During the 1960s the Italian Parliament voted four motions to introduce direct European parliamentary elections, see F. S. Baviera, 'Preparations for direct elections in Italy', *Common Market Law Review*, May 1978, p. 199.
[68] K. Allen and M. Maclennan, *Regional Problems and Policies in Italy and France* (Allen & Unwin, London, 1970), p. 335.
[69] For details, see R. E. M. Irving, 'Italy's Christian Democrats and European Integration', *International Affairs*, July 1976, pp. 410–11.
[70] K. Allen and M. Maclennan, op. cit., p. 334.
[71] H. Wallace, W. Wallace and C. Webb, op. cit., pp. 144–5.

the national applications. Apart from this negotiatory breakthrough, one factor which stimulated this uncharacteristic Italian official response was the conditions and deadlines imposed by Brussels on Rome as to guidelines for the co-ordination of regional aids. Nevertheless, this initiative in EC regional policy although significant for Italy, should not be judged out of the context of her haphazard traditional mechanism for regional policy, the Cassa established in 1950, and her background of limited effects in economic planning.[72]

Italian policy action in the predominant Community area of agriculture has been far less successful and illustrates more explicitly the political, bureaucratic and economic problems mentioned above. In general, the priority accorded the formulation of the CAP reflected French pertinacity and weight within the Community as well as the influence of the Franco-German relationship. Despite early doubts about CAP on the grounds of opening her backward agriculture to European competition, Italy tended in the first years of the EEC to accede to decisions taken, even if they were not particularly advantageous for her; however, from 1963 her governments began to modify their approach with more consistent emphasis being placed on a 'policy of interests', out of a growing concern over the dominance of the Paris–Bonn axis.[73] This more activist line characterized the Italian position from the mid-1960s up to the present time, producing some specific benefits like a reduction in the Italian contribution to the Agricultural Guidance and Guarantee Fund (FEOGA) and price support for certain Mediterranean products, but such concessions to Italy were few because her influence was restricted in the face of Franco-German direction and compromises in this area. According to an academic study of Italian policy on the CAP published in 1976:

> One cannot say that Italians influenced either the direction or development of the Common Agricultural Policy in the last fifteen years ... although Italian negotiators are not responsible for the balance of power in the Community, they are responsible for the Italian attitude in confronting this reality, that is, they are responsible for asking for exceptions rather than offering alternatives. The Italian position of the last fifteen years has been one of reacting rather than proposing. Even in sectors of vital interest such as fruit and vegetables, the Italians were able to add little to Commission proposals. This was true in regard to structural policy, which the Italians had recognized at the conference of Stresa as an area of vital concern. Yet for years they ignored this sector until it received the attention of the Commission. Thus, Italy may be judged as having lost the initiative in regard to the CAP.[74]

---

[72] On the operation of the Cassa per il Mezzogiorno, see K. Allen and A. Stevenson, *An Introduction to the Italian Economy* (Martin Robertson, London, 1974), chapter 6.

[73] R. Galli and S. Torcasio, 'The Italian participation in the negotiations of the Common Agricultural Policy', *Lo Spettatore Internazionale*, July-Sept. 1976, pp. 213-14.

[74] *Ibid.*, pp. 215-16. The Stresa conference of July 1958 initiated the first preparatory stage for the CAP after the establishment of the EEC.

It was not merely a question of asserting Italian interests, but also of implementing administratively the benefits gained. Indeed, one of the Italian weaknesses in Community negotiations, apart from the relative lack of political weight, has been insufficient or tardy preparation for negotiating positions such as in assembling necessary data that would strengthen Italy's bargaining hand. This bureaucratic dereliction characterized notoriously the failure to take advantage or malapplication of funds given to Italy under FEOGA. The examples of this administrative inefficiency were numerous. In one case, an EC directive on financing agricultural restructuring in 1972 was not followed by the required Italian demands for help with relevant projects until 1978.[75] Of the funds granted Italy for structural reform during the years 1965–74, only 15 per cent were effectively utilized up to the end of that period – a figure well behind those for other member states.[76] There were additional problems in that funds designated under FEOGA were misdirected to unneedy recipients, such as agricultural enterprises already modernized, reflecting among other things corrupt tendencies in Italian administration.[77] This amounted to an unqualified scandal, since Italian agriculture in general with its average size holding a third of that for the EC as a whole, sought to gain from the restructuring policy of the CAP, although the total importance of this policy should not be overrated as its possible benefits were relatively small compared with the immense undevelopment of this sector, especially in southern Italy.

Inept administrative backing for national policy positions has been a general feature of Italian participation in European integration. Where Italy has acted contrary to this trend, as over the ERDF and ESF, her behaviour has owed something to a particularly agile minister or been motivated by the visible chance of a quick negotiating move as opposed to the prospect of a hard bargaining slog; and also, significantly, because she has operated more freely without vested interests allied to the DC countering such a policy initiative. Even under the ECSC in the 1950s, Italy proved slow in applying for assistance under readaptation aid for steel-workers laid off by modernization, which neglect owed as much to the Government's reluctance to create a special group of 'privileged unemployed' among the high jobless total, as it did to bureaucratic inefficiency.[78] In more recent times, this pattern of inertia was again shown by Italy's failure based on 1978 figures, for instance, to make use of grants under the Social and Regional as well as Farm Guidance funds.[79]

[75] C. B. Carri *et al*, *Il mercato comune agricolo* (La Nuova Italia Editrice, Florence, 1979), p. 40.

[76] R. Galli and S. Torcasio, op. cit., p. 216.

[77] *Ibid.*, p. 217.

[78] E. B. Haas, op. cit., pp. 232 and 252.

[79] *The Economist*, 16 Feb. 1980, p. 57. According to German figures for 1978, Italy claimed only 30 million ecus from the European Social Fund although entitled to 209 million; 79 million ecus from the Regional Fund although entitled to 158 million; and 48 million from the Farm Guidance Fund although entitled to 242 million.

It was also largely bureaucratic lethargy or obstruction which accounted for the fact that Italy has achieved the highest record for belated or non-compliance with EC regulations. Italy's role is marked by a long history of such infringements, as for instance in 1969 when Italy was taken to the European Court of Justice concerning illegal tax rebates to her mechanical engineering industry on exports to countries outside the Common Market, a surcharge on imports into Italy of cotton yarn, and failing to abolish or reduce customs duties on unwrought lead and zinc,[80] while there were analogous cases of infractions against the ECSC Treaty in the 1950s.[81] In the 1970s, violations of EC directives have increased, ranging from aid to textiles and breaking the rules of an olive oil deal with Tunisia to the non-registration of vineyards and the imposition of a duty on exports of works of art.[82] As these examples illustrate, it was not always a question of inefficiency pure and simple. Antiquated laws accompanied cumbrous procedures, but quite frequently behind lethargy lay obstruction. A poll conducted in 1973 among civil servants of EEC member states indicated that Italian ones, notably in the Agriculture Ministry, were among those most inclined to employ organizational pressures to circumvent EC decisions if attempts to modify them at the political level in the Council of Ministers had failed.[83] This pattern of non-compliance caused particular concern in Brussels because it was preceded usually by a lack of prior consultation by Rome.[84]

The most prominent instance of this behaviour during the 1970s was Italy's three-year delay in applying VAT, which demonstrated the dominant influence of both political and bureaucratic factors. Italy had supported the introduction of VAT at the EC level way back in 1964 and assented to a plan of action in 1967 for its initiation three years later, but her difficulty in executing this decision arose because it was linked to general fiscal reform at the national level. This in turn activated severe opposition domestically from heavy industry, small business and consumer groups, encouraged exploitation of the issue by the political Left and not surprisingly met reluctance from within the Finance Ministry over the prospect of administrative restructuring. In the face of this widespread hostility the already unstable Government opted for abandoning the EC commitment. There

---

[80] Such cases were well publicized in the quality press abroad, e.g. see list of Italian infringements of EC regulations for the 1960s in *Le Figaro*, 21–22 Feb. 1970, 'Les règles à l'italienne du jeu européen'.

[81] E. B. Haas, op. cit., pp. 251–2.

[82] See 'Italy the laggard as Six enforce treaty rules', *The Times*. 10 Jan. 1972.

[83] W. J. Feld and J. K. Wildgen, op. cit., pp. 346–7.

[84] According to a German official in Brussels: 'Never once have the representatives of the Italian Government come to Brussels to discuss in a preventive way those measures that could be partially or totally against Community agreements; except for rare exceptions, Italy has always presented the Community with a *fait accompli*'. (Rapporti Roma-CEE: 'l'Italia ha un nemico – l'Italia', *Tempo*, 14 Nov. 1976).

followed bargaining between the European Commission and Rome over several postponements until Italy finally brought VAT into operation in 1973, by which time opposition at home had ebbed.[85] The eventual solution did in fact involve the first major fiscal reform effected by Italy since the War, where evidently pressure from EC partners had been one crucial determinant in producing this change. An interesting feature was the way in which the Italian government in question made a political expedient domestically of the EC mandate for carrying out this change.

What about the effects on Italy's role of the other factor of her economic weakness and vulnerability, which have so dominated and constrained her participation in the Community through the 1970s especially? This problem has been highlighted by the EC's efforts to launch monetary integration, unsuccessfully in the early 1970s and then again with the establishment of the EMS towards the end of the decade. Italy's fundamental balance-of-payments difficulties, accelerated by the advent of the energy crisis from 1973, not to mention her relapse in economic growth, have made her a dubious candidate for full participation in and contribution to this new area of policy harmonization. This was amply demonstrated by the Italian Government's temporary recourse to import controls in 1974 and again in 1976 because of a massive payments deficit, which although allowed under Articles 108 and 109 of the Rome Treaty occasioned concern among other EC member states about Italy's ability to keep pace with the integration process.[86] In fact, the granting of short- and medium-term credits both bilaterally from West Germany and in a concerted way by the EC (as with a $1,900 million loan in December 1974 and $1,500 million in May 1978) became a new element in monetary activity within the Community, although it hardly provided Italy with more than a transient cushioning for her basic problem. This was clear when the EMS was formed late in 1978, for Italian entry to this was conditional on a promise to transfer to her economic resources from the EC, and was complicated by PCI reservations over this scheme, the latter being one motive for the collapse of the Andreotti Government early in 1979. However, such was the fragility of Italy's economic situation and her dependence on EC support that as Guido Carli, president of Confindustria, pointed out: 'Italy cannot afford to join this system, and she cannot allow herself to remain distant from it.'[87] This close interlinkage between Italian economic development and Community policy did indicate one possible by-effect of Italy's economic weakness as a member state with the consequent need for Community 'intervention' in national

---

[85] For a discussion of the Italian case in implementing VAT, see H. Wallace, W. Wallace and C. Webb, op. cit., pp. 261–3; and K. Allen and A. Stevenson, op. cit., pp. 150–1.

[86] For example, see articles in *Financial Times*, 2 May 1974 and *Die Zeit*, 10 May 1974. During negotiations for the EC loan in 1976–77, Italian ministers made a series of reassuring visits to European capitals, notably by Andreotti as Prime Minister to Bonn, to cultivate their 'active solidarity'.

[87] Quoted in *Europäische Zeitung*, Jan. 1979.

policy priorities. This question had arisen earlier in connection with the economic policy conditions attached to the EC loan in 1974 and again over the ERDF allocation in 1975,[88] but its prospects for promoting any new departure in the direction of Italian economic policy remained at best an open matter and in the light of experience aroused scepticism.

By way of concluding this section on Italian European policy-making, it is useful to summarize as far as possible the main effects of Community membership. It has to be emphasized that, however much Italian governments might be inclined to regard the EC as an economic and political guarantor of stability, the country's main problems – notably North/South economic dualism – have to be solved primarily by Rome and not Brussels. It is clear from the preceding analysis that any estimation of a member state's record of benefits and disadvantages from EC membership has to be based on a conjunction of political and economic factors, that is, how far its role in policy-making in the European area has brought any significant changes in its position and development.

It should not be forgotten that Italy at the start of the integration process was still largely an agricultural country (with over 40 per cent of the working population employed in this area in 1951) and that she has undergone a painfully rapid and uneven industrial transformation during the course of her EEC membership, with more than half of the agricultural force moving into industry and socially disruptive migration movements accompanying this change. At the same time, Italy's restricted internal market and hence strong reliance on exports has made her particularly vulnerable to fluctuations in international trade. Thus, although the inauguration of the EEC in 1958 and the subsequent liberalization of trade provided an opportunity for surplus industrial capacity and stimulated Italian exports creating thereby an 'economic miracle' for a time, the very different circumstances of the 1970s together with Italian industry's arrival at full capacity have seen a reversal of performance in many basic respects. So far as industry specifically has been concerned, membership of the Community undoubtedly hastened the process whereby Italy caught up on delayed development potential, although the beneficial effects arising from competitiveness varied enormously. The outcome was positive for some individual sectors (such as the domestic appliances industry) and less successful for others (e.g. textiles) because of the nature of demand and competition, but the greatest benefit was enjoyed by the large dynamic companies like Fiat (automobiles), Pirelli (rubber), Olivetti (typewriters and office machines) and Montecatini-Edison (chemicals), which took full advantage of the expanded market. This confounded the worst fears of

[88] Wilhelm Haferkamp, the European Commissioner for economic affairs, went further in 1976 by suggesting a 'Marshall plan' for Italy to enable her to carry out far-reaching economic, social and administrative reforms, for which it would be necessary to impose 'harsh conditions' on Italy if such an international or purely EC loan was to be granted (*The Guardian*, 23 June 1976).

business circles which had originally, in the early 1950s, been doubtful if not alarmed about European integration because of Italy's shortage of resources after the War and had only been compelled to adjust following the Government's decision to participate. The slowing of economic growth in the 1970s has, however, made EC membership appear less tangibly beneficial and this has led to some disillusionment.

The consequences of European integration for Italian agriculture have not been substantial. This is because Italy's deep-rooted structural backwardness, notably the continuing small size of farms, has not really been overcome despite post-war attempts at improvements. The main political cause of this has been the inability of Italian governments to implement a coherent agricultural policy at home, a failure reflected at the EC level in Italy's *ad hoc* approach to the CAP, while the latter's emphasis on short-term pricing support rather than long-term structural considerations has not in any case helped Italy's greatest potential needs in this sector. All the same, there has been a strict limit on the extent to which the Community can financially support or assist national economic development, as the special problem of Italy's regional imbalance has shown. Ultimately, of course, any EC resources depend for their effectiveness on their application by the national administrative machinery, and here Italy as seen has had its own additional problems of inefficiency.

The three factors of executive instability, bureaucratic obstruction and unresponsiveness, and economic weakness are therefore very closely inter-related, for the deficiencies of any one of them may exaggerate the negative effects of the others. Italy has suffered especially in the 1970s from serious difficulties of an inherently weak economic structure and poor economic performance, but the regular absence of any systematic approach by her governments to EC policy-making has both further weakened her role as a member state and made these three factors more of a European concern. There have, nevertheless, been some significant exceptions to the general picture of limited activity, and these may indicate possible future changes in Italy's position, bearing in mind that support for European integration has continuously remained remarkably strong. Italy's various difficulties have not called into question the fundamental principle of EC membership because her participation in the Community has long involved an important reorientation in the country's politics and development since the fall of Fascism, although any conclusion about the political rather than economic effects of membership cannot be formed without reference to the role of the various national political forces.

3. The Party-Political Dimension to Italian European Policy: from Polarization to Convergence

The role of Italian political parties requires separate attention since they provide the ultimate determinant of the content and dynamics of European policy, as of any other policy area in Italian politics. Italy being a prominent example in the EC of a 'party state', not only are all public assignments but also – more relevant from the point of view of this study – all positions assumed on policy issues in the full sense are above all conditioned by party-political considerations. For instance, in Italy, it is impossible to assess the attitudes of interest groups on given questions or for that matter of other agents expressing sectional views without taking account of their partisan affiliation. The party-political dimension therefore provides the essential medium through which Italian European policy must be judged compre-hensively and many of its key features already discussed or referred to – the discrepancy between political aims and political action (e.g. as conditioned by both inter- and intra-party relationships), the degree and form of interlinkage between EC and domestic matters and how far policy is dictated by long- or short-term motives (depending on the existence or not of party strategies) – finally fall into place.

The overriding characteristic of the party-political dimension of Italian European policy since it was first conceived in the late 1940s has been the evolutionary process from a state of polarization to one of convergence. 'Convergence' is a more applicable term than 'consensus' because the movement of the parties towards a common acceptance of the EC framework as a basis for policy action – that is, particularly of the PSI from the later 1950s and notably the PCI during the course of the 1960s – was accompanied by growing policy differentiation between them within that framework. Agreement on the fundamental value of European integration has by no means led to cohesive overlap as to the interpretation of its purpose and hence of priorities to be pursued. Thus, by the time of direct elections to the European Parliament in 1979, one foreign observer of the Italian scene based in Brussels, noting 'the traditional and universal declarations of European faith expressed across the Italian political spectrum', commented aptly though somewhat simplistically:

> ... Europe is a political concept which has something to offer everyone. For the hardline Right-wing, Europe is a bulwark against Communism; for the Right-of-centre parties it is a guarantee of a wider capitalist future for Italy; for the centre-Left, Europe represents the best chance of avoiding powerless isolation in an increasingly interdependent world; for the Communists it represents a forum in which to demonstrate simultaneously their Leftism and their pragmatic reformism.[89]

This summary, while pointing out this tableau of party-political differen-tiation over the aims of integration, is oversimplified in that it fails to take sufficient note of the fact that Italian party positions are invariably multi-faceted, at least more so than is often realized by outside commentators.

[89] John Palmer in *The Guardian*, 30 May 1979.

Namely, an evaluation of party positions or their changes on European policy has to consider many different factors: the ideological aspect, their roles in the Italian political system with reference to Government or Opposition and party alliances, electoral concerns and naturally the impact of European integration itself both internally in the sense of its influence on economic affairs and externally regarding the Community's importance as an emerging factor in a changing international environment. Foreign opinion, whether official or journalistic, has tended frequently to focus on the ideological aspect of the parties to the exclusion of the other factors, omitting to take account of the fact that it is the actual balance of harmony between them all which provides the most useful angle for understanding the party-political dimension. This dimension may be examined most conveniently for the purpose of this study by looking at the main parties in turn, but the intention here is not so much a detailed or chronological survey of their evolving positions on European policy, discussed more fully elsewhere,[90] as a brief attempt to explain the patterns and interlocking motives which have produced the overall movement from polarization to convergence.

As indicated earlier, the DC's approach to European policy was initially and subsequently motivated by concern for the preservation of the domestic socio-political status quo and the maintenance of European security. It is of course a truism to say 'it is impossible to disentangle the DC's European policy from that of the Italian government',[91] but it is more instructive to draw the consequences from this phenomenon. To what extent has the party as a whole, as distinct from its leaders in relevant ministries, at all determined the course of European policy?; or indeed, has the immediate burden of governmental responsibility meant that the DC has not evolved any deliberate strategy or engaged in new thinking on European integration, bearing in mind that the conceptual assumptions underlying its policy from the start indicated a 'conservative' position? The answer to these questions is not so clear-cut as might appear at first.

Firstly, intra-party relationships in the DC are such that any straightforward distinction between governmental leaders and party organization as conventionally employed in comparative political analysis is not realistic. Governmental leaders have certainly since De Gasperi interchanged regularly in national office, but the constant of their political careers has been their own internal party bases. Factionalism as channelled through the DC factions (*correnti*) has embraced the European as well as other policy areas affecting the national political game, as indicated by differences of outlook between these various groups over both European policy assumptions and

[90] See especially Richard Walker, *Dal confronto al consenso: i partiti politici italiani e l'integrazione europea* (Bologna, Il Mulino, 1976); also D. Sassoon, 'The Italian Communist Party's European Strategy', *Political Quarterly,* July 1976; and R. E. M. Irving, 'Italy's Christian Democrats and European Integration', *International Affairs,* July 1976.

[91] R. E. M. Irving, *ibid.*, p. 415.

foreign relations in general. These were evident in the relative emphasis accorded by them to EC and Atlanticist orientations, which on the whole combined comfortably in the first decade with the Cold War but came to diverge somewhat with the growing international weight of the Community, the emergence of some rivalry of commercial interest between the United States and Europe and greater autonomy on the latter's part and the new merger in the 1970s between the wider external concerns of the EC and the Mediterranean region as the object of a traditional 'vocation' by Italy. Thus, P. Vannicelli identifies varying outlooks on NATO within the party, ranging from a critical position on the DC Left to absolute 'Atlantic fidelity' on its Right,[92] while specifically on EC affairs a similar gamut of attitudes has been apparent with the Left's pan-European, Third World and Christian internationalist preferences and support for a more socially-conscious Community, the Right's defence of a liberal economic system in the context of European security interests and the Centre's less definable and doctrinaire line of support for integration on conventional political grounds to do with national interests benefiting from a closer European framework.[93]

Although such a variety of outlooks on European integration is broadly related to different conceptual approaches to policy issues and indeed there has been a certain consistency about them, they should not be taken as too rigid when it comes to policy action. The influence of different *correnti* has been identifiable in some respects in the European policy area, as N. Kogan noted with respect to political personnel appointments in the Foreign Ministry[94] and also in the principle of 'equilibrium' affecting the composition of DC delegations to the European Parliament and for transnational party activity;[95] but altogether factional adherence has had more to do with political placement and loyalty to individual party leaders than a determined policy approach. *Correnti* leaders, where they become involved in EC affairs whilst holding national office, might well modify their 'conceptual' stand as did Fanfani by the time he became Prime Minister in the early 1960s, having moved from a leftward to a more orthodox position on European integration.[96] However, the different outlooks of the *correnti* on integration should not be completely excluded as an influence or as one variable among several, even though this may be a question of rhetoric rather than political behaviour. So far as their different outlooks had any influence, this contributed to an immobilistic approach by the DC, although in practice the Government's policy had most in common initially with the Right and thenceforth with the Centre.

---

[92] See table in P. Vannicelli, op. cit., p. 27, which is based on information for 1968.
[93] R. E. M. Irving, op. cit., pp. 412–15; and F. Roy Willis, op. cit., p. 285.
[94] N. Kogan, op. cit., pp. 71, 115 and 118.
[95] Interview with Luigi Granelli, MEP and head of the DC's international office, in Brussels, Feb. 1979.
[96] R. E. M. Irving, op. cit., p. 413.

Secondly, the problem of delineating the DC's approach to European integration has depended not least on the priority given to this policy area by the Government. Following the strong attention to European affairs during the De Gasperi period, the DC leadership since his time has shown less intensive interest in them – a change which was not unassociated with the DC's loss of hegemony after the 1953 election[97] and eventually the party's increasing involvement in the quagmire of domestic politics. There were other constraints on the DC's European policy formulation, most notably the coalitiónal factor. Even though the DC generally controlled the relevant ministries and insisted on compliance with its own policy assumptions as a 'price' for any new alliance with other parties, EC affairs could not remain entirely unaffected by the need to adapt to certain pressures from alliance partners. The centre-Left coalitions with the PSI from 1963 produced nothing approaching the more active policy expected by some, although on various secondary matters – especially the belated renewal of the Italian delegation to the European Parliament in 1969 to include both the PSI and PCI for the first time – the DC was forced to modify its position. Furthermore, one other determinant of DC European policy has been its *clientela* relationship with specified interest groups, as in this respect the *Coldiretti's* promotion of the demands of small farmers through the Ministry of Agriculture and hence influence on the Italian position over the CAP in favour of the pricing policy.[98]

It is difficult to portray DC European policy in any comprehensive way for, while generally committed to a conventional interpretation of European integration arising out of its original support for it from the late 1940s, the party has in government been subject to short-term constraints and pressures and has hardly been innovative in its approach. Its absence of internal debate over European policy suggests a classic example of a political party bereft of new thinking after more than a generation in power, but it is more than just that. The post-war assumptions which motivated the DC's European policy have been somewhat called into question by changing international relations since the Cold War, but more particularly by domestic developments on the political Left, with the effect of putting the DC on the defensive; however, it is important that the ideological aspect of its position on integration should not be overrated because the DC is not first and foremost an ideological party. If the DC can be regarded as having any long-term approach to European integration, it has been primarily the defence of the status quo – a factor which helps to explain Italy's 'passive' role in the EC – where sectional and partisan interests have been granted special attention even though wider national requirements over integration have sometimes demanded change and innovation.

[97] R. Walker, op. cit., pp. 46–7.
[98] R. Galli and S. Torcasio, op. cit., pp. 220–1.

In short, it cannot be said that the DC has developed a clearly delineated European strategy with specific objectives and here it contrasts most obviously with the PCI, which has benefited from the freedom from governmental responsibility to develop new ideas and elaborate a systematic and long-term approach in this area. It is interesting to note that, despite the PCI's evident reluctance to dramatize or even emphasize its policy differences with the DC in its pursuit of the 'historic compromise' during the 1970s, it has chosen to do so over EC affairs. This is because the PCI has used this area as a central part of its own legitimation process by occupying the space in effect vacated by the DC here and advocating a more active policy within the EC framework in both the interests of Italy and further integration. There was a direct connection during the 1970s between the PCI's domestic strategy and its revised position favouring pro-integrationist activity. At the time Berlinguer first enunciated the 'historic compromise' strategy in 1973, the PCI began to emphasize that it was more Europeanist than the DC and to monopolize political discussion in Italy about the failure of progress in the Community, a position made easier for the party by the growth of self-criticism within the EC partly in the same vein (e.g. the need for 'democratization' in the EC and stronger attention to social questions) and movement for new initiatives as from the Hague summit of 1969. Thus, in the same year of 1973 an article in a party review attacked 'the lack of involvement of the governing class and, in the name of a conventional and superficial Europeanism, its disinterest in the construction of the Community and Italy's place in it',[99] while Giorgio Amendola, the PCI's chief spokesman on EC affairs, argued that 'the history of Italian participation in the EEC has become a long story of non-fulfilment of obligations agreed to, of wretched cunning, of glaring falsehoods, of unjustified absences . . .'[100] Polemics apart, it was a case of the PCI proffering a different policy line but distinctly from within the Community system. This differentiation was revitalized by the prospect of direct elections to the European Parliament, as when Amendola in a major policy speech on this event to the PCI's central committee in December 1978 remarked:

The real point of argument which leads the PCI to oppose the DC is our criticism, which it does not accept, that it has in the name of Italy gone along with a Community policy which has increased our country's detachment from the stronger member states and has covered up this subordinate position with Europeanist rhetoric and a series of flights of fancy. The DC has tried to claim a Europeanist superiority for itself and accuse the Communists of having little conviction, merely because we have always rejected Europeanist rhetorical posturings and sought to expose the real character of the institutions, subjected as they are through the Council of Ministers to the will of the stronger states.

[99] B. Ferrero, 'L'Italia nella CEE: posizioni deboli e contraddittorie', *Politica ed Economia*, no. 4, 1973.
[100] Article by Amendola in *Rinascita*, 25 May 1973.

It is the same factor which divides us from the federalist movement. We recognize the federalist movement as performing a useful propaganda and promotional role, but always by way of zealously setting forward-looking aims rather than compelling the Italian parties, above all the DC, to pursue a more modest path but one geared to solving the immediate and concrete problems encountered by the Community.[101]

Without looking in detail at the background and course of the PCI's embarcation on its European strategy,[102] it is worth recording briefly several main factors motivating its change of position, from regarding European integration in hostile ideological terms as a creation of the Cold War and an attempt to buttress American capitalist domination of Europe, to accepting its framework and using it to channel its own policy aims, a process of rethinking that began in the early 1960s. These interrelated factors indicate how much this change was multicausal in its motivation.

Firstly, the changing international situation with détente was a vital aspect in this process as shown by the coincidence of the establishment of the EEC in the later 1950s with some new orientation towards less rigid solidarity in the international Communist movement.[103] It must be emphasized here that: the eventual adoption by the PCI of a European strategy, which led not only to its utilization of the EC framework but also its acceptance in 1974 of Italian membership of NATO, dovetailed with the PCI's earlier pursuit from the mid-1950s of 'polycentrism' and hence underlined how much its new position was long-term and not merely tactical in approach; the importance of this changing international situation itself as a factor illustrated that the PCI's basic policy evolution was not simply a question of 'internalizing' European positions for domestic political motives.

Secondly, the thinking behind the 'historic compromise' indicated at the same time that domestic and European strategies were closely interlinked. Amendola recognized this when he said in 1971 that the PCI's 'European platform' could form the basis of a 'meeting-ground' with other political forces.[104] This effort to use its European policy to 'consecrate' its democratic legitimacy was highlighted by the PCI's adoption of Altiero Spinelli, a prestigious European figure and EC Commissioner, as one of its independent Left candidates for the national elections in 1976, a move which aroused considerable interest at home and in Europe.[105] Spinelli argued strongly in

[101] Giorgio Amendola, *I Comunisti Italiani e le elezioni europee*, relazione al C.C. del PCI del 4/5/6 dicembre 1978, segretariato del gruppo comunista e apparentati, Lussemburgo, p. 33.
[102] On which see D. Sassoon's article in *Political Quarterly*, July 1976.
[103] *Ibid.*, p. 253.
[104] *Corriere della Sera*, 7 Oct. 1971.
[105] See interviews with Spinelli in *Time* magazine, 21 June 1976; *Der Spiegel*, 24 May 1976; and *Die Zeit*, 21 May 1976. Also article on foreign concern over Spinelli's candidacy in *Neue Zürcher Zeitung*, 19 May 1976.

this election, which was dominated by the issue of a possible PCI participation in government, that the PCI had fundamentally changed and that in Italy's time of crisis its entry to national office would contribute stability.[106]

Thirdly, there were also economic grounds for the PCI's 'conversion' to European integration. In fact, Amendola's first major statement of the PCI's new evolving approach towards the European Community in 1962 dwelt on the beneficial effects of membership for Italian economic expansion and growth of living standards and on the need for co-operation between working forces in member states.[107] Entry to the European Parliament by the PCI in 1969 was among other things justified by the task of defending the interests of Italian workers, migrant workers and small farmers.[108] It was on the same economic grounds that the Communist-allied trade union federation, CGIL, had revealed a positive response to integration before the PCI as far back as the Rome Treaty debate in Italy in 1957.

There were two consequences relevant to this study of the PCI's adjustment to and utilization of the integration process. Following its participation for the first time in one of the major EC institutions, the European Parliament from 1969,[109] the PCI gave increasing priority to the European policy area, as reflected in regular articles outlining its position on general and specific EC issues in both its daily *L'Unità* and weekly review *Rinascita*[110] as well as in seminars and conferences held to discuss and publicize its thinking on Community policies,[111] not to mention the full use made by the PCI of the publicity services of the Communist group in the European Parliament. Its MEPs came to assume a special role when it came to formulating party European policy at the national level, not surprisingly since the PCI established the practice from the very start of sending fairly prominent and high-calibre party representatives to Stras-

[106] Interview with Spinelli in *Die Zeit*, 21 May 1976.
[107] D. Sassoon, op. cit., p. 255, quoting Amendola's statement at length.
[108] Amendola press statement in *L'Unità*, 22 Mar. 1969.
[109] In 1966 the PCI's representatives had joined the Economic and Social Committee of the European Community, while at home it joined various bodies such as the executive of the Italian Society for the Council of European Municipalities in 1971. There have not been PCI members of either the Commission or Council of Ministers, although in the former case the Left independent Spinelli was a Commissioner at the time he joined the PCI election list in 1976. In the latter case, membership depends on the PCI's direct role in an Italian government.
[110] e.g. in Apr. 1970 *L'Unità*, the PCI daily, published a series of articles on the PCI's strategy in the EC, see issues for 22 Apr. 1970, 25 Apr. 1970, 26 Apr. 1970 and 30 Apr. 1970. From 1972, EC affairs featured in almost every foreign relations article in the PCI weekly *Rinascita* (see D. Sassoon, op. cit., p. 263).
[111] One of the earliest of these, in Nov. 1971, attracted much attention in the international press; e.g. see *The Times*, 25 Nov. 1971. The PCI published in full the material of these *convegni*; e.g. see *Quale Europa? I Comunisti Italiani e le elezioni europee*, Rome, 1978, which contains the speeches and addresses at the *convegno* held by the PCI in Rome in Nov. 1978 on direct elections to the European Parliament.

bourg, including Amendola himself.[112] But there was a wider purpose than just the search for democratic legitimacy behind the PCI's pronounced emphasis on its participation at the EC institutional level. Amendola disclosed something of the party line of thinking in an article on direct elections, which the PCI had long advocated, in February 1977: 'Italy, whose weakness makes it the country most vulnerable to external pressure, needs European unity more than the other countries in order not to remain isolated and, together with other countries in a united Western Europe, to defend its independence.'[113] This position recalled Berlinguer's statement during the 1976 election that Italian membership of NATO would help the PCI pursue its own form of socialism without risking Soviet intervention, and owed as much to the party's assessment of the international situation as well as desire to make reassuring policy commitments at home.

The other consequence of the PCI's acceptance of the EC framework was that, as a result of its insistence on change and reform in both the institutional and programmatic development of the Community, it pressed continuously for a more active and broader pursuit of integration in the EC. Its particular policy demands are well known and include: the strengthening of the European Parliament's powers and general 'democratization' of the Community's institutional structure, support for further EC enlargement, reform of the CAP to take more active account of Italian interests, extension of the EC's scope in the social field, and generally the application of integration to new areas. This full-scale promotion of integrative activity was featured in the PCI's programme for European elections in 1979 which advocated an EC role in such areas as employment policy, the rights of migrant workers (a special Italian concern not confined to the PCI among the national parties), the use of EC financial instruments to alter the balance between the economically weak and strong member states, the position of women and youth in society and the defence of civil liberties, control of multinationals (a long-time priority of the party), energy and more active support for the Third World.

The PCI's European strategy completed the overall convergence of Italian parties across the political spectrum over European integration. The smaller forces of the centre and centre-Right had supported Italy's membership from the beginning – the PRI and PLI for traditional federalist reasons, while their post-war assessment of East/West relations brought them close to the 'conventional' outlook of the DC on European policy. The PSDI adopted a similar position following its split with the Socialists and alliance with the government side of the polarized divide in the late 1940s; while the PSI a decade later moved towards acceptance of the EC framework, although this did not amount to any absolute adoption of DC positions,

[112] John Fitzmaurice, *The Party Groups in the European Parliament* (Saxon House, Farnborough, 1975), pp. 131–2.
[113] *Rinascita*, 11 Feb. 1977.

seeing that it favoured for example more concentration on the social aspects of integration.[114] Freed from its subordinate role *vis-à-vis* the DC in the centre-Left governments as from the early 1970s, the PSI has chosen to accentuate its own profile on European policy – a tendency encouraged by the challenge to it from 'Eurocommunism', the prospect of further EC enlargement which would open the way for a greater presence of southern European Socialist parties in the Community and of course the party-political rivalry emanating from the move towards direct European parliamentary elections. In the light of this last event, even newly-emerging fringe parties began to formulate their own views on integration – notably the libertarian Radicals, who following their 'arrival' in Italian politics in the mid-1970s sought to project their line of protest against established authority on the European stage as well[115] – while other groups on the extreme Left (DP, PdUP-Manifesto) took a hostile line towards integration reminiscent of the PCI's in the 1950s[116] and therefore provided the one small exception to this overall convergence over European policy.

Direct elections to the European Parliament made the varied party-political approaches to integration more conspicuous, thus demonstrating how much policy differentiation had grown within the common acceptance of the EC framework. The fielding of prominent party figures as candidates for these elections by all the parties – Berlinguer, Pajetta and Amendola for the PCI; Zaccagnini, Colombo and Piccoli for the DC; Craxi for the PSI; Pannella for the Radicals; and Almirante for the MSI – emphasized the common significance they all attached to the EC. At the same time, as a factor linked to this, there was a perceptible desire among the parties to change the balance of electoral strength in their own favour. The fulfilment of this depended on the possibility that the Italian electorate, freed from the necessity of voting for or against a government, would be more flexible in its partisan affiliations. This very attitude among the parties illustrated their strong recognition of the interlinkage between European and domestic politics, which had of course been a central feature in their common acceptance of European integration in the first place. The PSI was the most transparent in its pursuit of an electoral breakthrough here, as part of its new 'Eurosocialist' line under Craxi aimed at revitalizing its chances for its domestic competition with the PCI. The same tendency was not surprisingly evident among the small parties. The Secretary-General of the PLI remarked at a conference of the European Liberal Federation in April 1979: 'The European vote must be distinguished from the internal political situation in Italy, dominated as it is by the prevailing power of the Christian Democrats and Communists . . . we shall therefore now be waging an

---

[114] P. Vannicelli, op. cit., pp. 34–5.
[115] See A. Chiti-Batelli, *L'ultra-sinistra italiana e l'Europa* (Lacaita editore, Manduria, 1979), chapter 5.
[116] *Ibid.*, chapters 1 and 2.

electoral campaign for Italy and for Europe: and we shall ask the electors to make the Liberals as strong in Italy as they are already in Europe.'[117] The small PSDI similarly exploited its transnational party link with the European Socialists, including giving prominence to a message it received from Willy Brandt. Direct elections spotlighted more than before the depth of electoral motivation which lay behind party-political positions on integration. The results did not in fact accord with expectations about voting flexibility, although compared with the Italian national elections of a week before the PLI gained relatively and the PSI acquired some marginal extra support. The most significant aspect of the results was the turnout, which in Italy at 85.5 per cent was far higher than in any other EC member state.

Such a turnout directed attention to a final question related to the electoral aspect of party European policies, namely the attitude of Italian public opinion towards integration. Various distinct trends have been apparent for a long time: a very strong approval among the public for integration generally and support for its further progress, including the idea of a federal Europe, on which questions Italy has invariably been among the most positive of the member states, if not always the highest in this respect;[118] simultaneously, a marked lack of information among the Italian public about the functioning and the specific activities of the EC, which reflected as much on the common problem of political illiteracy, especially in Italy, as it did on the difficulties of projecting the Community to the national publics.[119] Opinion surveys have also reflected the attitude of interlinkage between European and domestic politics already visible at the level of party elites. A poll conducted on behalf of the European Commission in 1973 put Italy at the head of those EC member states which favoured mutual help between them when one member country found itself in major economic difficulties (at 88 per cent),[120] an attitude certainly visible too among Italian political elites. Similarly, an opinion survey of EC member states at the time of direct elections to the European Parliament in 1979 put Italy well ahead among those who thought that MEP candidates' stands on domestic matters were more important than on European matters (respectively 65

---

[117] Valerio Zanone in European Liberals and Democrats (ELD), *Meeting, Luxembourg, April 1979*, p. 19.

[118] This has been a distinct trend in the regular Eurobarometer soundings conducted on behalf of European Commission, e.g. 69 per cent thought EC membership was 'a good thing' in autumn 1973 and 78 per cent in spring 1979.

[119] R. Zariski, *Italy: the Politics of Uneven Development* (Hinsdale, Illinois, Dryden Press, 1972), p. 322. Italy has usually featured high among the 'don't knows' on particular EC issues; e.g. in 1972 as many as 84 per cent of Italians had never heard of the Mansholt Plan for CAP (*L'Italia nella politica internazionale*, Jan.-Apr. 1972, Rome, p. 54). For other poll evidence, see U. Kitzinger, op. cit., p. 33; and J. G. Blumler and A. D. Fox, *The European Voter* (Policy Studies Institute, London, 1980) for similar evidence on the Italian electorate's lack of information on the EC at the time of direct elections.

[120] *The Times*, 7 Dec. 1973.

per cent and 35 per cent, compared with the average for the eight countries investigated of respectively 43.9 per cent and 26.9 per cent).[121] What emerged from this was a stronger interest than elsewhere in the advantages for Italy of EC membership and some reflection of the provincial orientation in Italian political life, which combined with but did not necessarily contradict the pronounced 'conceptual' adherence to European union among the Italian public. The point was that the latter attitude derived foremost from political-cultural factors, while any paradox between provincialism and approval for the EC was explained in terms of the second being a passive viewpoint.

The relevance of these long-term trends of Italian opinion was that from the viewpoint of political parties these provided an added incentive to take pro-integrationist positions, for on balance it would be to their advantage to do so. The PSI had been encouraged by electoral considerations *inter alia* in abandoning its opposition to integration from the late 1950s,[122] and the same was no less a motive in the subsequent case of the PCI, for undoubtedly the search for party legitimacy cannot be divorced from electoral politics. The PCI has emerged from the overall process of party-political convergence over integration as having the most dynamic European policy, but did the party's greater prominence in Italian politics from the mid-1970s offer a real prospect of some redirection and reactivation of Italy's approach towards the Community? The PCI's definite views on the progress of European integration, its pressure for revising the Rome Treaty and more aggressive line on CAP reform may suggest a possible change, but there remain so many other variables and constraints that any clear-cut prediction about the effects of a PCI role in an Italian government is not possible. The experience of the party's programmatic and practical co-operation with the Andreotti Government of 1976–79 did not encourage strong chances for major change in the pursuit of Italian European policy, not to mention all the problems of persistent bureaucratic inefficiency, necessary compromise with the DC, other short-term pressures and above all Italy's economic weaknesses, as likely to restrain any new initiatives following a direct participation of the PCI in government at Rome.

An optimistic estimation is that any possible change of European policy behaviour would be in the distant future, depending most likely on policy success in other areas in the meantime. Spinelli indicated during the 1976 Italian general election that the PCI would seek control over important economic ministries, not external ones which give most direct management of EC affairs, upon entry to an Italian cabinet.[123] Undoubtedly, one reason for this preference was the party's desire not to provoke foreign opinion, which is more liable to attach a symbolic importance to the PCI directing

---

[121] See J. G. Blumler and A. D. Fox, op. cit. These figures excluded other categories of answer.

[122] R. Walker, op. cit., pp. 65–6.

[123] Interview with Spinelli in *Die Zeit*, 21 May 1976.

foreign, not to mention defence, affairs. European interest in the possibility of PCI participation in Italian government during the 1976 election revealed a foretaste of the nervousness that would surface in EC capitals in that event, even though the realistic probability of a new course in Italian European policy in at least the immediate and intermediate future would be minimal. Hence, foreign opinion, while conditioned primarily by ideological considerations, acts itself as a constraint on policy change in Rome.

4. Conclusions

This general convergence among the Italian political forces over European integration during the generation since De Gasperi with its consequences for internal stability is one of the salient features of Italy's role in the EC, as seen from the historical angle. It is a particularly significant development with two-way implications as Italy's participation in the integration process from its beginning was itself one decisive factor in promoting this convergence, both with the political Left's recognition of its positive economic effects and with their acceptance of the argument that Community membership was a necessary supportive framework for internal national stability. Other patterns concerning Italy's role in the EC which emerge from taking an historical perspective are her limited influence in directing the course of integration as a member state, certainly since the initial innovative period under De Gasperi; and, at the same time, the strongly pro-integrationist line pursued by Italy's many successive governments, at least in terms of policy aims if not always policy behaviour. These last two leitmotivs of Italy's role are not incompatible, for Italian awareness of the deficiencies of the national political system, not to mention of the country's serious problems of economic performance which have become more apparent in the 1970s than before, has tended to strengthen Italy's attachment to and reliance on European integration conceptually – even though in practice these very same factors have undermined her own ability to perform as an effective member state.

Such an overall picture would suggest a case of Italy playing a role in the EC that is 'passive', a characteristic commonly attributed to her in literature on the subject. It is here that the thematic approach is a useful corrective to any risk of over-simplified conclusions, for by focusing on specific determinants of policy behaviour as distinct from broad policy aims it allows a more differentiated interpretation. The European integration process has as a whole grown increasingly complex over time, so that a comprehensive evaluation of Italy's position as an EC member state has to take account of such factors as the relative influence of short- and long-term considerations in her European policy-making and the form and degree of interlinkage between the EC and other (both domestic and external) areas of policy. In the latter respect, Italian European policy has been strongly conditioned if not handicapped by many of the inhibiting factors which have determined effectiveness in other national policy areas, notably bureaucratic inefficiency and lethargy and executive political instability. In this diversified context, Italy's actual record of participation in the Community emerges as not so unimpressive as often considered despite these handicaps, especially at the diplomatic and negotiatory level, although her direction of policy formulation in the EC has been secondary to that exercised by France and West Germany with their long tendency towards active bilateral co-operation. The result of the thematic approach is to show that the role of Italy, as of any other member state in the European Community, has to be viewed multi-dimensionally.

FURTHER READING

K. Allen and A. Stevenson, *An Introduction to the Italian Economy* (Martin Robertson, London, 1974).

Rosemary Galli and Saverio Torcasio, 'The Italian participation in the negotiations of the Common Agricultural Policy', *Lo Spettatore Internazionale*, July-Sept. 1976, pp. 213-21.

Werner J. Feld and John K. Wildgen, 'Italy and European Unification: some preliminary comments on elite attitudes', *Il Politico*, no. 2, 1974, pp. 334-48.

R. E. M. Irving, 'Italy's Christian Democrats and European Integration', *International Affairs*, July 1976, pp. 400-16.

Norman Kogan, *The Politics of Italian Foreign Policy* (Pall Mall Press, London, 1963).

Cesare Merlini, 'Italy in the European Community and the Atlantic Alliance', *The World Today*, Apr. 1975, pp. 160-6.

Wilma du Marteau, 'Italian presence in Community organisms in Brussels', *Lo Spettatore Internazionale*, Jan.-Mar. 1975, pp. 51-67.

Geoffrey Pridham, 'Concepts of Italy's approach to the European Community', *Journal of Common Market Studies*, Vol. XIX, No. 1, Sept. 1980, pp. 77-83.

Natalino Ronzitti, 'Italian political parties and European Integration', *Lo Spettatore Internazionale*, Jan.-Mar. 1975, pp. 5-25.

Donald Sassoon, 'The Making of Italian Foreign Policy', in William Wallace and W. E. Paterson (eds.), *Foreign Policy Making in Western Europe* (Saxon House, Farnborough, 1978), pp. 83-105.

Donald Sassoon, 'The Italian Communist Party's European Strategy', *Political Quarterly*, July 1976, pp. 253-75.

Primo Vannicelli, *Italy, NATO and the European Community: the interplay of foreign policy and domestic politics* (Harvard Studies in International Affairs, no. 31, 1974).

Richard Walker, *Dal confronto al consenso: i partiti politici italiani e l'integrazione europea* (Il Mulino, Bologna, 1976).

F. Roy Willis, *Italy chooses Europe* (Oxford University Press, New York, 1971).

V

The Netherlands

Richard T. Griffiths*

This chapter will attempt to describe the implications for the Netherlands of membership of the European Communities from both political and economic standpoints. Because of limitations of space, it has proved necessary to restrict discussion on many items and, unfortunately, to omit others altogether. Thus it has proved impossible to say anything about the Dutch position on regional or social policy, on energy or development aid. The inclusion of such issues would undoubtedly have provided a more rounded picture of the Netherlands' role within the Communities but it would have been at the expense of what this author, at least, felt to have been more central concerns.

1. Towards the Treaty of Rome

The experience of the Depression and the Second World War had forced the Dutch to abandon policy positions that might otherwise have precluded participation in experiments at regional co-operation. Economically, the rising wall of protectionism of the late 1920s and 1930s led the Government to reverse its free trade policy, which had been held since the 1840s, and to protect vulnerable sectors of the economy. At the same time the Government tried, unsuccessfully, to co-operate with other nations in establishing havens of relative economic stability to which other countries might be drawn. In the political sphere, foreign policy since 1815 could be described as one of passive neutrality coupled with a belief in the efficacy of international law. This passivity was seen as the best way of avoiding conflicts potentially damaging to both trade and colonial interests. Faith in the

* The research for this chapter was undertaken in the Netherlands in the summer of 1979 and was made possible by a grant from the British Academy for which I would like to express my sincerest appreciation.

continued utility of such a policy did not long survive the landing of the first German paratroopers in May 1940.

During the War there was much soul-searching both inside and outside the Netherlands over the future world order and, more importantly, over the Dutch position within it.[1] Within the European context this led to an agreement, signed in September 1944, to form a Benelux customs union.[2] Although the Benelux initiative was soon to be overshadowed by developments of wider European significance, the experience yielded a number of important lessons. It demonstrated that, notwithstanding the relatively low level of existing tariffs and the complementarity of the two economies,[3] the stimulating effects on intra-area trade were far greater than originally anticipated. Moreover, it showed the economic dislocation expected to follow in the wake of tariff dismantling to be relatively slight. It also proved that trade liberalization could proceed without the necessity for complex arrangements for the co-ordination of economic policy. Finally, it demonstrated to the countries themselves that they could fruitfully co-operate at a political level, thus dispelling much of the mutual antipathy that existed before the war.[4] This co-operation was to lead later to a number of significant initiatives in the tortuous path towards closer European co-operation.

However, the Dutch did not view Benelux purely as an end in itself. With substantial trading links overseas and with the German hinterland, Dutch economic interests lay in co-operation in the widest possible field.[5] Thus in 1949 Foreign Minister Stikker (1948–52) proposed a plan for tariff reduction among members of the Organisation for European Economic Co-operation (OEEC), the establishment of a fund to help smooth out possible dislocation and provision for a higher measure of intergovernmental co-operation.[6] These proposals were rapidly overtaken by discussions on the

[1] H. Daalder, 'Nederland en de wereld, 1940–1945', *Tijdschrift voor Geschiedenis*, Vol. 61 (1953), pp. 170–200.
[2] Immediately after the War the agreement linking exchange rates came into effect. Because of problems of reconstruction, the Dutch dragged their feet over further progress so that it was not until January 1948 that the agreement to abolish tariffs on trade between the two areas was implemented. H. A. Schmitt, *The Path to European Unity. From Marshall Plan to Common Market* (Louisiana State University Press, Baton Rouge, 1962), pp. 29–30.
[3] Belgium and Luxembourg had already formed an economic union in 1921 and are, for convenience, treated as a single economic unit.
[4] F. Hartog, *Nederland en de Euromarkt* (H. E. Stenfert Kroese N.V., Leiden, 1971), pp. 10–19.
[5] This desire did not, however, prevent the Dutch torpedoing initiatives to extend the Benelux union to embrace France and Italy (christened FRITALUX by the French) or a later initiative to include Germany (GERBENELUX). Their rejections were motivated by fears that the new unions would be dominated by the larger partner(s).
[6] D. U. Stikker, *Memoires. Herinneringen uit de lange jaaren waarin ik betrokken was bij de voortdurende werelderisis* (Nijgh and Van Ditmar, Rotterdam, The Hague, 1966), pp. 161–6.

Schuman Plan to establish a European Coal and Steel Community (ECSC).

Whilst Dutch policy in the economic field represented a measure of continuity with the initiatives taken in the 1930s, politically there was a complete change of stance. Security was now perceived to lie not in an aloof independence but in the closest possible co-operation with other countries.[7] The practical expression of this policy lay in full-hearted support for the North Atlantic Treaty Organization (NATO) and, within NATO, unwavering support for the American nuclear monopoly.[8] Whilst it is outside the scope of this chapter to discuss it further, this 'Atlanticist' trend in Dutch foreign policy is vitally important in understanding Dutch attitudes towards European questions.

Thus Dutch policy after the War lay in encouraging the re-establishment of a stable economic and political order on the widest possible scale whilst fostering initiatives to that end in Europe in particular. Another policy consideration was how best to defend national interests within any new institutional framework which was to evolve. This last factor was to assume immediate importance in the negotiations for the ECSC which began in 1950. In the course of these Stikker proposed that a Council of Ministers be created to provide an intergovernmental check on the independence of the High Authority in order to avert the danger that sectoral policies on coal and steel might get out of step with general economic policy.[9] Interestingly, there is no sign, at this early stage, of the belief in supranationalism that was later to become the hallmark of the Dutch approach.

The Netherlands was rather less enthusiastic over the next steps towards European integration. It participated reluctantly in talks for a European Defence Community (EDC) only because it would serve to rehabilitate West Germany and it made it known that participation in a European Political Community (EPC) was contingent upon greater progress in the area of economic co-operation.[10] In September 1952, Beyen (1952–56), one

[7] S. Bodenheimer, *Political Union: A Microcosm of European Politics* (Sijthoff, Leiden, 1967), p. 166, has argued that this did not, in fact, imply a change in policy but a continuation of the same policy within a different context: '. . . membership in a western bloc dominated by one superpower has permitted a continuation of traditional Dutch neutrality within a new framework and has relieved them of the need to develop an ambitious foreign policy of their own'.

[8] R. W. Russell, 'The Atlantic Alliance in Dutch Foreign Policy', *Internationale Spectator*, Vol. 23, No. 13 (8 June 1969), pp. 1189–1208. See also J. J. C. Voorhoeve, *Peace, Profits and Principles. A Study of Dutch Foreign Policy* (Martinus Nijhoff, The Hague, 1979), pp. 101–9 *et seq.*

[9] W. Diebold, *The Schuman Plan. A Study in Economic Co-operation, 1950–1959* (Praeger, New York, 1959), pp. 61–3.

[10] I. Samkalden, 'A Dutch Retrospective View on European and Atlantic Co-operation', *Internationale Spectator*, Vol. 19, No. 7 (1965), pp. 634–7; and Voorhoeve, op. cit., pp. 110–12.

of two foreign ministers at the time,[11] proposed an all-embracing customs union among members of the ECSC but his suggestions were received with little enthusiasm. However, when the movement towards EDC and EPC came to grief, Beyen, together with the Belgian foreign minister Spaak, in a memorandum to other members in May 1955 relaunched proposals for a common market in trade, agriculture, energy and transport under the guidance of a communal authority. The intense co-operation among the Benelux countries in elaborating the proposals played no small part in securing their acceptance at the Messina Conference in June 1955.[12] The rest is history. Whereas earlier federalist approaches towards integration had failed, this broad-based functionalist initiative was to culminate in the signing of the Treaty of Rome in 1957.

Within the Netherlands there were certain apprehensions about ratifying the Treaty. There was uneasiness about the protectionist momentum which the upward revision of tariffs implied,[13] but against this the Government set advantages of trade security. There were also fears that the EEC might lead to the creation of antagonistic trade blocs, partly reflecting disappointment that the market was not wider in scope, and there were allied fears that it might weaken NATO. However, the ultimate defence of the Government was political – that the creation of a Common Market would terminate intra-European rivalry and promote the cause of peace and stability on the Continent. In the event the Treaty was ratified in the Second Chamber by an overwhelming majority.[14]

2. Shaping the European Communities: Policy Content

As we have seen, Dutch enthusiasm towards European integration was tempered by a preference for a wider and more liberal concept of economic relationships and, politically, by unswerving allegiance to the idea of Atlantic co-operation. Nearly three years after the signing of the Treaty of Rome, new initiatives were taken which appeared not only to undermine both of these principles but to threaten the effective representation of Dutch national

---

[11] Because of difficulties in allocating portfolios in the fourth Drees cabinet, two ministers of foreign affairs were appointed; J. W. Beyen in charge of European issues and J. M. A. H. Luns to take care of the rest. Once asked to explain the situation, Luns quipped, 'Because our country is so small, abroad is so large'.

[12] H. J. M. Aben, 'Plannen en werkelijkheid', in H. J. M. Aben (ed.), *Europa Onderweg: Ooggetuigen brengen verslag uit* (Elsevier, Amsterdam, 1967), pp. 20–6. This article was written in collaboration with ex-minister Beyen.

[13] Luns proposed that the external tariff of the EEC be cut by 20 per cent but this was opposed as serving to weaken the central discipline of the Common Market. A similar fate met his proposal that the EEC and the European Free Trade Association should extend their tariff cuts to all signatories of the GATT. See Voorhoeven, op. cit., p. 163.

[14] For a discussion on the trends of opinion within the Netherlands on the eve of the inception of the Common Market, see R. de Bruin, *Les Pays Bas et l'Intégration Européenne, 1957–1967*, Ph.D. Thesis (Paris, 1978), pp. 415–43.

interests at a European level as well. De Gaulle's proposals for 'political union' launched at the Rambouillet summit in July 1960 involved regular meetings of heads of government and foreign ministers backed up by a permanent secretariat. Four other permanent commissions were to be established to deal with foreign policy, defence, economic and cultural affairs and a European assembly was to be created with membership nominated by national parliaments. Throughout the so-called Fouchet negotiations which lasted from February 1961 to April 1962, the Dutch maintained an implacably hostile and often isolated opposition.[15]

It is difficult to unravel the exact logic behind the Dutch position but it would seem to rest on two basic objections. Firstly, there was a relative lack of interest in the Netherlands in developing a political community. More than the other nations, the Dutch interpreted their membership of the Community primarily in welfare terms and, thus, tended to adopt a more functionalist approach to questions of closer co-operation. Secondly, the Dutch were deeply suspicious of French motives since Franco-American relations were at a low ebb in this period. There was a very deep concern that in going along with de Gaulle's plans, the country would eventually be forced to choose between the Atlantic connection and closer European ties. Luns (Foreign Minister 1952–71) expressed both these sentiments in the following way, 'Europe is not and cannot be the Europe of the Six either economically or politically . . . I much prefer the outline of political integration in Europe which would be rather vague, including as many countries as possible, to an extremely elaborate political integration which would exclude other countries of Europe and which would be limited to the Six alone.'[16]

At first the Dutch tried to defuse the issue by urging that consultations on de Gaulle's proposals should take place in the wider forum of the Western European Union (WEU) of which Great Britain was a member. When this failed, the Dutch insisted outright that they would not proceed towards political union without British participation. Bodenheimer has argued that the Dutch commitment towards an open community was all along nothing more than a rationalization of a preference for British membership and that this, in turn, stems primarily 'from the Dutch perception of substantive British policy regarding the Atlantic alliance and the effect a British presence would have upon Europe's position within the Alliance'.[17] Other observers have commented that British membership was

---

[15] For an account of the Fouchet negotiations see Bodenheimer, *Political Union*, de Bruin, *Les Pays Bas et l'Intégration Européenne*, and A. Silj, *Europe's Political Puzzle: A Study of the Fouchet Negotiations and the 1963 Veto* (Harvard University Center for International Affairs, Harvard, 1967).

[16] Silj, *ibid.*, p. 57.

[17] Bodenheimer, op. cit., pp. 159–60.

viewed in terms of power politics, as a useful counter to the threat of Franco-German hegemony within an intergovernmental framework.[18]

Alongside the issue of British membership, a second policy stance was adopted by the Dutch Government. Given the distinctly cool attitude hitherto demonstrated towards the question of supranationalism,[19] it was ironic that the Dutch should now adopt the standpoint that they would be willing to participate in closer integration if existing supranational institutions were strengthened and if new supranational elements were introduced into the union.[20] Bodenheimer has interpreted Luns's conversion as a negotiating manoeuvre – knowing in advance that any such proposals would be unacceptable to the French, playing the supranational card was tantamount to saying 'no' to an intergovernmental Europe.[21] There was also a power-politics logic to the Dutch position in that strengthened Community institutions, which would be relatively free from nationalistic considerations and therefore more amenable to the force of rational (i.e. Dutch) arguments, would also serve to provide a counter to the danger of large power hegemony.[22] Whatever cynicism may have lain behind the Government's new-found enthusiasm for a policy of strengthening the position of supranational institutions, its conversion brought it into line with a significant stream of political feeling within the Dutch Parliament, which was to have important consequences later on.

The Fouchet negotiations were finally deadlocked in the spring of 1962 and well-meaning attempts by other nations to revive them floundered on the mutual intransigence of the French and Dutch. Whether it was good for Europe or not, the outcome represented a successful defence of Dutch interests. In the course of the negotiations, two new planks of European policy had emerged – a determination to secure British membership of the Communities and a desire to strengthen and democratize Community institutions. Progress in realizing the first of these aims received a temporary

---

[18] Russell, op. cit., p. 1204; and J. J. Schokking (ed.), *Nederland, Europa en de Wereld: ons buitenlands beleid in discussie* (Boom, Meppel, 1970), p. 71.

[19] Silj, op. cit., pp. 49–51; and Bodenheimer, op. cit., p. 161.

[20] During the negotiations concessions were made in this direction. In January 1962 the draft-treaty provided for a quasi-independent Secretary-General 'whose office would constitute a Community feature that could develop at later stages of the Union'. Later, in June 1962, Spaak proposed establishing a political commission to represent a 'Community interest'. The Dutch rejected both formulae (though the latter was also rejected by de Gaulle). See Bodenheimer, op. cit., p. 156.

[21] *Ibid.*, p. 159.

[22] 'A supranational co-operation can serve the interests of a small country, allowing it to throw the weight not of power, but of intellect, into a bigger whole'; see L. G. M. Jaquet, 'The Role of a Small State within Alliance Systems', in A. Schou and A. O. Brundtland (eds.), *Small States in International Relations* (Almqvist and Wiksell, Stockholm, 1971), p. 61. 'Supranational institutions preserve the sovereign equality of the smaller nations by artificially imposing constraints upon the larger countries roughly similar to those practical considerations which have always limited the actions of smaller nations'; see Bodenheimer, op. cit., p. 158.

setback with de Gaulle's veto of British entry in January 1963 and the announcement in 1964 by the British that they would not be making any new moves towards joining the Community. With the issue of British membership removed, albeit temporarily, from the political limelight, Dutch policy emphasis switched to the need to democratize the Communities and strengthen supranational elements in Europe.

The occasion for the manifestation of this new stance was the negotiations for a common agricultural policy (CAP). After much protracted discussion, punctuated by marathon sessions of the Council of Ministers, the Six had made quite considerable progress. In December 1963 the machinery for the CAP had been agreed and by December 1964 the common price levels had been accepted. The only issue remaining on the agenda, for June 1965, was to settle the financial regulation for the policy, under which it was envisaged that the Community would eventually receive its own revenues and would be exclusively responsible for administering the expenditure associated with the policy.

Within the Netherlands these negotiations coincided with an increasing resolve in Parliament to assert greater control over foreign policy and, in particular, to secure budgetary powers in favour of the European Parliament.[23] Sensing this change in mood, in December 1964, Luns signalled to the Council of Ministers, for the first time, the Dutch intention of strengthening the powers of the European Parliament.[24] The following February, the Dutch Parliament unanimously adopted a motion to accord the European Parliament a central position in the decision-making process of the European Communities.[25] In June 1965 Luns was forced to accept a motion, sponsored by all the major parties, to support the European Commission's proposals in the forthcoming negotiations,[26] effectively constraining his room for manoeuvre unless the Commission should change its position. The proposals contained, *inter alia*, provision for the Parliament to alter the budget by simple majority vote and that, if supported by the Commission, these amendments could only be altered by the Council of Ministers by a 5:1 majority.[27] The negotiations which took place in June 1965 eventually reached deadlock over the manner of financing the CAP, the timing of its introduction as well as the new decision-making structure. They culminated

---

[23] 'L'action du Parlement néerlandais n'est explicable que si l'on tient compte de la frustration qu'a provoquée la politique d'intérêt national menée par M. Luns depuis 1959. Durant six ans, les fédéralistes du Parlement ont eu l'impression d'être en face d'un Ministre habile, certes mais sans convictions européennes profondes; ils estiment aussi que le Parlement manque d'influence réelle sur la politique étrangère du gouvernement', de Bruin, op. cit., pp. 659–60.

[24] *Ibid.*, p. 673.

[25] *Ibid.*, pp. 694–7.

[26] *Ibid.*, pp. 708–16.

[27] J. Newhouse, *Collision in Brussels. The Common Market Crisis of 30 June 1965* (Faber and Faber, London, 1968), p. 61.

in the French walk-out and boycott of Community institutions. When the French returned to the fold, negotiations continued, though it was not until December 1969 that the final details of the package establishing the CAP were locked into place and when they were, precious little of the proposals for democratic control of the budget or qualified majority voting in the Council of Ministers remained. Given that there was little sympathy outside the Netherlands and Italy for such developments, progress in this direction was effectively blocked. In the Dutch Parliament, Luns reaffirmed the Government's commitment to democratization but that, given the political realities of the moment, it was unable to guarantee any positive outcome.[28]

One of the outcomes of the crisis into which the French walk-out plunged the Community was a renewed Dutch enthusiasm for the British candidature. When the application was finally made in May 1967 it received the full backing of the Dutch Government which, at the same time, declared itself opposed to further discussions on closer European integration until the issue of British membership had been settled.[29] The second French veto (November 1967) was greeted with open hostility in the Netherlands and, in concert with the other Benelux countries, the Dutch announced their intention of continuing the discussions outside the Community framework. For this to work, the Benelux plan required the adhesion of Italy and Germany but the Germans were anxious to avoid too open a confrontation with France. They were, however, willing to participate in discussions with Britain within the framework of the WEU on closer co-operation in foreign policy, technology, defence and monetary policy (France immediately boycotted these meetings).[30] The determination of the five EEC members, led by Benelux, not to allow the momentum of the second British application to peter out, coupled with the departure of de Gaulle in April 1969 helped to weaken French resolve. At the Hague summit in December 1969 it was decided to reopen negotiations with Britain and the other candidates; negotiations which were to culminate successfully in the signing of the Treaty of Accession in Brussels in January 1972.

The resolution of the issue of British membership removed Dutch objections to participating in discussions towards closer integration. The Hague summit had witnessed agreement not only on the question of enlargement but also on the need to accelerate progress towards economic and monetary union (EMU) and European political co-operation (EPC). It is convenient to examine these two issues separately.

The decision to proceed towards EMU had been taken in the absence of any consensus on the ultimate objectives of such a union or the mechanisms by which it would be attained. In the debate which followed, two basic schools of thought emerged. The Dutch standpoint initially coincided closely

[28] de Bruin, op. cit., pp. 774–5.
[29] Ibid., pp. 793–4.
[30] Voorhoeven, op. cit., p. 171.

with that of the Germans in what may be called the 'economist school'. They believed that closer policy co-ordination and convergent economic development should precede the tighter linking of currencies and the introduction of an element of supranational decision-making. The 'monetarist school', which embraced the Commission and the other member states, especially France, believed that exchange rates should be irrevocably fixed as soon as possible in order to provide the discipline to enforce policy co-ordination. They also believed that a supranational element should become important far earlier in the process.[31]

In 1971 the Six were able to agree on the Werner Plan which envisaged that EMU be attained by 1980. Its first phase was something of a compromise whereby permitted exchange rate fluctuations were to be confined to a narrow band (the famous 'snake'), the co-ordination of national budgets was to be achieved at the level of Council of Ministers and a Community Fund was to be set up to iron out exchange rate fluctuations. Only the first part of this package was ever implemented and by 1975 the shocks of unstable world currency markets, accelerating inflation and different national responses to the oil crisis had reduced even this to a total shambles. That same year a special advisory commission, set up by the Government to advise on the problem of European union, published its report (called the 'Spierenberg Report' after its chairman). At the heart of its advice was a 'monetarist' argument that 'the introduction of the monetary union can take place in accordance with a schedule . . . comprising a number of coercive stages'.[32] Surprisingly, the Government now did a complete volte-face, accepted the advice and declared its willingness to enter into binding commitments for the implementation of EMU.[33] Given the strong objections of other countries, notably Great Britain, to the surrender of sovereignty which EMU would imply, there was little that the Dutch could do to accelerate progress in the direction they desired. It was to take a Franco-German initiative in 1978, to strengthen the mechanism of exchange rate co-ordination, to establish the European Monetary System (EMS) and even this fell a long way short of what the Dutch would have wished.

Turning to the question of EPC, in 1970 the Belgian diplomat Davignon suggested that regular meetings of the foreign ministers be held to harmonize the European position on foreign policy issues. Dutch antipathy towards

---

[31] See L. Tsoukalis, *The Politics and Economics of European Monetary Integration* (George Allen and Unwin, London, 1977).

[32] D. P. Spierenberg, *Europese Unie: Rapport van de Adviescommissie Europese Unie* (Staatsuitgeverij, The Hague, 1975), p. 34. Spierenberg criticized the Tindemans Report published a little later for its belief that the Community would develop naturally towards closer co-operation and for its failure to suggest concrete measures to achieve EMU by 1980. See D. P. Spierenberg, 'Het Rapport-Tindemans. Een Kritische beschouwing', *Internationale Spectator*, Vol. 32, No. 3 (1976), p. 148.

[33] *Nota inzake de Europese Unie*, Handelingen van de Tweede Kamer der Staten-Generaal, Zitting 1975–1976, 13 426, No. 4.

the idea was strong. It reawakened all the fears apparent during the Fouchet negotiations that the standing of Community institutions would be diluted and that the integrity of NATO might be jeopardized. However, unlike the Fouchet negotiations, the Dutch did not block progress towards closer co-operation. In the first place, the participation of Great Britain appeared to ensure that the Atlanticist views would not be ignored. Secondly, the new arrangements did not automatically imply operating outside the Community institutions, although initially they did nothing to strengthen them.[34] However, Foreign Minister van den Stoel (1973–77) was able to extract some concessions in this direction which helped to reduce hostility to the idea.[35] It has also been suggested that, notwithstanding the constant Dutch insistence on supranationalism, intergovernmental processes (whether non-binding consultations in EPC or unanimous decision-making in the Council of Ministers) actually helped guarantee against small-power domination by larger partners.[36] Finally, whatever Dutch feelings about the course of developments, a 'yes', however reluctant, was better than a refusal which might have led to an even less acceptable alternative – bilateral co-operation between the larger powers.[37]

A final theme of Dutch policy has been continued pressure for a transfer of powers to supranational Community institutions and a strengthening of democratic control within the Community. In theory these policies represent the means towards the ultimate goal of a federal European state. In practice it is doubtful whether the Dutch are any more willing than other governments to countenance the massive transfer of powers which this would imply. Indeed, under the centre-left den Uyl cabinet (1973–77) there was some distancing from this concept.[38] In public statements on belief in a federal Europe it would appear that Dutch parliamentarians have become prisoners of their own success at having made the issue virtually a national religion.[39]

[34] See W. Wallace and D. Allen, 'Political Co-operation: Procedure as Substitute for Policy', in H. Wallace, W. Wallace and C. Webb (eds), *Policy-Making in the European Communities* (John Wiley and Sons, London, 1977), pp. 227–47.
[35] In 1973 it was agreed that political aspects of problems dealt with by the Community could be put on the EPC agenda, that the European Commission would be represented at meetings where discussions might impinge on Community work and that more meetings be held between EPC Ministers and the Political Commission of the European Parliament. See Voorhoeven, op. cit. p. 179.
[36] J. Boehmer, *Het Nederlandse beleid met betrekking tot de Europese samenwerking, 1971–1975,* Ph.D. Thesis, Leiden, 1976, p. 100.
[37] *Ibid.,* p. 120.
[38] In October 1973 den Uyl stated 'the question of what sort of society we wish to create in the Community is more important than the tempo at which the process of European unity is completed'. The statement caused much consternation in the Netherlands at the time since no Premier before him had so openly distanced himself from the concept of integration as such. See W. J. Veenstra, 'De Partij van den Arbeid en Europa', *Internationale Spectator*, Vol. 33, No. 4 (1977), p. 249.
[39] Boehmer, op. cit., pp. 103–5.

If one accepts that Dutch policy objectives are somewhat less ambitious than they often appear, pressure from the Netherlands has had some limited success. In December 1974 agreement was reached on a democratically elected European Parliament (elections for which were held in June 1979) and in 1975 it was agreed that the European Parliament have the final say over the adoption of the budget. Beyond that very little progress has been made and the focus of the struggle for democratic control has now shifted to the Parliament itself.

3. Shaping the European Communities: Policy-Making Process

Membership of a large international organization, whose range of competences embraced many areas of economic and social interest hitherto the preserve of domestic rather than foreign policy, created new problems for Dutch policy-makers. At the highest level the problem of policy co-ordination was complicated by the system of coalition government. Problems of coalition-balancing tend to give individual ministers a large measure of personal responsibility for policy and it was rare for the portfolios for major departments to be held by members of the same political party. The problem of interdepartmental co-operation was further accentuated by the relatively weak position to which the Foreign Ministry had been reduced after the War. During the 1930s, the intense diplomatic activity over economic questions meant that the implementation of foreign policy had devolved increasingly to the Ministry of Economic Affairs. After the War this position was reinforced by the fact that the newly-created Directorate General for Foreign Economic Affairs, BEB (*Directoraat-Generaal voor Buitenlandse Economische Betrekking*), intended to foster interdepartmental co-operation, was made responsible to the Economics Ministry. With negotiations for the EEC, the struggle for ministerial competence intensified.[40] In 1958 a new co-ordinating body was established under the Foreign Ministry, DGES (*Directoraat-Generaal voor Europese Samenwerking*), but BEB was still left in existence. Since there were now two ministerial co-ordinating bodies in existence a formal co-ordinating committee was set up, the CCEIA (*Coordinatie Commissie voor Europese Integratie en Associatie Problemen*), with a chairman supplied by BEB and the secretariat provided by DGES. Since, not surprisingly, conflicts still remained unresolved within the CCEIA, a cabinet committee was formed in 1961, the REZ (*Raad voor Europese Zaken*) under the chairmanship of the Prime Minister.[41] All this

[40] E. H. van der Beugel, *Nederland in de westelijke samenwerking. Enkele aspecten van Nederlandse beleidsvorming* (Brill, Leiden, 1966), pp. 16–19. Indicative of the relative ministerial importance at the time was the fact that negotiations for the formation of Benelux and the ECSC were conducted by the Economics Ministry.

[41] See H. Wallace, *National Governments and the European Communities* (Chatham House, London, 1973), pp. 33–5; and C. Sasse *et. al. Decision Making in the European Community* (Praeger, New York, 1977), pp. 24–7.

accomplished was to institutionalize the forum within which the struggle for ministerial competence between the Foreign Ministry and the so-called 'technical' ministries (especially the Economics Ministry) could play itself out.

Thus the ability of successive Dutch governments to formulate and present policy effectively at a European level has been hampered by this continuous tension between Departments. Valuable ministerial time has been wasted in resolving blistering interdepartmental rows over both policy content and departmental competence. Furthermore, in order to accommodate various departmental interests, the size of Dutch delegations at international negotiations has often proved large, unwieldly and cumbersome. Finally, and most importantly, the continuous squabbling has seriously weakened attempts to impart some unity to the overall direction of European policy.[42] The classic, oft-quoted, example was the occasion of the negotiations in 1964 over Nigeria's association with the EEC at which two rival delegations arrived, both claiming the right to represent the Dutch point of view.[43] More recently, the Agricultural Ministers agreed to a temporary ban on meat imports into the EEC from third world countries to which the Dutch minister assented (seeing it as a technical question) without considering whether his cabinet colleagues might not consider this action in conflict with Dutch policy on aid to less developed countries (a political question).[44]

In 1971 a government commission reported on the problem of interdepartmental responsibility and co-ordination (the van Veen Report). It rejected the possibility of a separate Ministry for European Affairs, arguing that it would carry too little political weight and that it would lack the necessary expertise for all the matters with which it would be confronted in Brussels. However, it did recommend that the position of the Ministry of Foreign Affairs as co-ordinator of European policy be strengthened.[45] In 1972 the Government acted to implement some of the recommendations of the van Veen Report. Although the delineation of ministerial responsibility still left room for a certain ambiguity,[46] ex-Secretary of State for Foreign Affairs, Professor Brinkhorst (1973–77) has claimed that the new arrangements have worked very well. He stresses the fact that the Secretary of State for Foreign Affairs took over the chairmanship of the CCEIA, which was pivotal to their success. As a political chairman of an interdepartmental committee of civil servants, he felt he had been able to influence policymaking at the preparatory stage before Departmental decisions had hard-

---

[42] van der Beugel, op. cit., pp. 21–2.

[43] de Bruin, op. cit., pp. 299–300.

[44] L. J. Brinkhorst, 'Coordinatie van Europees beleid in Nederland', *Sociaal-Economische Wetgeving*, Vol. 26, No. 12 (1978), p. 823.

[45] *Bestuurs-organisatie bij de Kabinets-formatie 1971. Rapport van de Commissie Interdepartementale Taakverdeling en Coordinatie* (Staatsuitgeverij, The Hague, 1971), pp. 33–4 and 75–8.

[46] Sasse, op. cit., pp. 22–3.

ened. He had been able to exercise his political authority to 'encourage' the settlement of interdepartmental differences and when unresolved differences were discussed at the REZ, his position amongst his colleagues was enhanced by his overall view of the issues and his practical experience in being able to advise on the feasibility of realizing different policy options in Brussels.[47] Whilst, as an outsider, this analysis seems a little too perfect, one must accept Professor Brinkhorst's statement that the practical results of the new arrangements have proved encouraging.

4. The Economics of the Common Market: Trade

We have already suggested that part of the Dutch reluctance to support proposals for closer political co-operation within the Community stemmed from a tendency to view the potential benefits of membership primarily in welfare terms. In this section we shall examine some of the more tangible economic benefits of community membership, starting with trade. In July 1960 the EEC took the first step towards the abolition of tariffs on intra-area trade and the erection of a common external tariff and it completed the process in July 1968. As a nation highly dependent on foreign trade, the Netherlands was among one of the most enthusiastic proponents of this policy.

At first sight the figures would seem to confirm the expectation that trade within an area in which tariffs were being eliminated would grow faster than trade with the rest of the world, where progress in this direction was more modest. Between 1958 and 1972 the value of Dutch exports to other EEC states increased at a rate of 14.8 per cent per annum compared with a rate of 7.6 per cent for exports to the rest of the world (the corresponding figures for imports were 12.0 and 7.6 respectively).[48] The question arises how far this difference was attributable to EEC tariff policies as opposed to other factors, such as the relatively faster growth of continental European markets or changes in the structure of trade in favour of manufactured goods, both of which would have served to deflect Dutch trade towards EEC member states without the extra fillip of tariff reduction.

It is necessary then, to attempt to isolate the 'EEC-effect' in promoting intra-area trade. A recent Dutch survey has claimed that between 1956 and 1969, Dutch exports of manufactured goods to member states were 80 per cent higher than they would have been in the absence of the EEC (the corresponding figure for imports was 26–35 per cent).[49] Leaving aside the

---

[47] Brinkhorst, 'Coordinatie van Europees beleid', op. cit., pp. 815–28.

[48] G. M. Taber, *Patterns and Prospects of Common Market Trade* (Peter Owen European Library, London, 1974), p. 54.

[49] See P. J. Verdoorn, 'Economische gevolgen der handelspolitiek integratie binnen de EEG 1956–1970'; and Spierenberg, *Europese Unie*, op. cit., pp. 121–27. These findings receive confirmation from another study which attempts to measure the trend development of trade intensities; see M. Lefeldt and A. Schneider, 'Structural Changes in EC Trade Intensities', *Intereconomics*, Hamburg, Vol. 12, No. 11/12 (1977), pp. 293–6.

problem of the accuracy of these calculations, another question arises as to how far this increase in Dutch intra-area trade has been at the expense of trade with the rest of the world. It might be that as a result of the common external tariff, the Netherlands switched its source of imports from low cost countries outside the EEC to higher cost countries within it. Far from benefiting either the economy or the consumer, this situation would penalize them. This is known as 'trade diversion'. On the other hand, the elimination of intra-area tariffs may well have promoted trade where previously none had been possible, in which case the effect will be beneficial. This is known as 'trade creation'. It would seem likely that the 'EEC-effect' observed above contains elements of both 'trade creation' and 'trade diversion' and, as can be imagined, the exercise of distinguishing between the two is fraught with difficulties.

Before we progress, a word of caution is appropriate. One economist, surveying the techniques for measuring trade creation and trade diversion, concluded that, 'all estimates of trade creation and diversion by the EEC which have been presented in the empirical literature are so much affected by *ceteris paribus* assumptions, by the choice of the length of pre- and post-integration periods, by the choice of benchmark year (or years), by the methods to compute income elasticities, changes in trade matrices and relative shares and by structural changes not attributable to the EEC but which occurred during the pre- and post-integration periods . . . *that the magnitude of no single estimate should be taken too seriously*'[50] (author's italics). Very few of the studies on this problem disaggregate their findings by individual countries and, of those that do, even fewer present their findings in comparable form. Two studies which do, come to apparently contradictory conclusions. The calculations in the study by Verdoorn and Schwartz are based on trade in manufactured goods only for the years 1956–69. Their most favourable estimate is that the Netherlands experienced net trade creation equivalent to 16.9 per cent of the 'normal' value of imports in 1969 (i.e. the level of imports in the absence of integration). Their less favourable estimate reduces this figure to 1.1 per cent.[51] Prewo's calculations cover all physical trade over the period 1959–70. He estimates that the Dutch economy experienced net trade diversion equivalent to 8 per cent of the 'normal' value of imports in 1970.[52] Both studies are in complete agreement, however, that the Netherlands benefited less than any of the other member states from the net trade creation effect of EEC tariff policies.

[50] W. Sellekaerts, 'How Meaningful are Empirical Studies on Trade Creation and Diversion?', *Weltwirtschaftliches Archiv*, Kiel, Vol. 109, No. 4 (1973), pp. 519–48.
[51] P. J. Verdoorn and A. R. N. Schwartz, 'Two Alternative Estimates of the Effects of EEC and EFTA on Patterns of Trade', *European Economic Review*, Vol. 3, No. 3 (1972), pp. 291–335.
[52] E. W. Prewo, 'Integration Effects in the EEC', *European Economic Review*, Vol. 5, No. 4 (1974), pp. 379–405.

The reasons for this relative failure to gain from the Community tariff policy are not hard to find. Because the Dutch had a relatively low tariff level in 1959, on the eve of the creation of the EEC, their economy stood to gain relatively less from the trade creating effects of mutual tariff reduction. Similarly, the high degree of openness of the economy prior to 1959 suggests that the Netherlands had already achieved a high degree of international specialization to meet the needs of foreign markets. On the other hand, the fact that the common external tariff implied an upward revision of Dutch levels of protection, accentuated the trade diverting effect on the economy. Finally, the fact that the trade preferences agreed within Benelux had to be extended to other members meant that the Dutch lost ground in that market – a case of negative trade creation or 'trade erosion'.[53] It is perhaps too easy to allow these econometric studies to shape our appreciation of what would have been the case had no integration occurred. This, of course, was not a realistic policy option. What the calculations do not tell us is what would have happened had the EEC been formed and the Netherlands left outside it![54]

5. The Economics of the Common Market: Transport

As the only net exporter of any significance in intra-Community transport services, one would have expected the Netherlands to have a vested interest in seeing the abolition of national discrimination in transport policies and the establishment of a common Community market. Yet progress to this end has proved painfully slow, due in no small measure to Dutch intransigence towards the proposals of other member states (particularly West Germany) and even towards those of the European Commission. It was not that the Dutch were against a common policy *per se* but against the form of policy that was being suggested.

As a long-established provider of European transport services it was natural that the Netherlands should expect to fare well in a relatively free and uncontrolled market which would give free rein to their competitive advantage. Indeed, it was argued that if logic demanded the abolition of restrictions on trade as being in the interests of the development of the Community as a whole, then the same considerations should apply to the transport of those goods. In opposition to those other states which emphasized the social or strategic position of transport, the Dutch pressed for the

---

[53] *Ibid.*, pp. 396–7.

[54] It is too early yet for detailed studies to have been published on the effects of the enlargement of 1973 on patterns of Dutch trade. An exception is W. F. Smits, 'De Nederlandse concurrentiepositie binnen de EG', *Economisch-Statistisch Berichten*, 9 May 1979, pp. 457–61, which suggests that the Dutch market share of the new member states declined between 1974 and 1977. Since his calculations, however, exclude trade in energy and agriculture some care should be taken in drawing any conclusions.

adoption of a relatively liberal policy. In particular, they strenuously opposed suggestions for the compulsory publication of freight rates and the imposition of national quotas on Community transport licences, both of which, it was felt, would serve to stifle free competition and lead to the sub-optimal utilization of resources.[55]

Dutch opposition towards regulation in the transport sector was rewarded in 1960 when the European Court ruled against the interpretation of the High Authority of the ECSC that freight rates should indeed be published. However, this minor success was short-lived for in 1962 the decision was reversed.[56] The same year the Commission published its Action Plan envisaging that countries adopt a so-called 'fork-rate system' (i.e. published minimum and maximum freight rates between which competition would occur) and that a system of quotas be established for Community licences. Both of these proposals were bitterly rejected by the Dutch for the next three years but eventually internal division within the Netherlands and the increasingly isolated negotiating position undermined the Government's stance. In 1964 agreement was reached on the principle of quotas and in 1965, after the French boycott made it even more difficult, politically, for the Dutch to resist the pressures of the other parties in the negotiations, the Government was forced to agree to the implementation of a fork-rate system. Both of these were seen as 'temporary' measures. Even then their introduction was to be delayed until 1968 whilst the ramifications of these agreements were worked out.[57]

The Dutch attitude towards a common transport policy is revealing because it further demonstrates that the Government is perfectly capable of a tenacious defence of national interests in the face of the opposition of other member states and even of the European Commission. Although eventually forced to compromise, the Dutch have succeeded in stalling progress towards a co-ordinated and comprehensive policy in this sphere. It is also interesting that this defence is structured not in terms of national self-interest but in an appeal to a higher principle – that a relatively free and liberal policy is economically more efficient than a highly regulated regime. Perhaps in terms of neo-classical economics the Dutch position has much to recommend it but it is instructive to reflect that when it comes to discussions on agriculture this principle does not seem to apply!

6. The Economics of the Common Market: Agriculture

In agriculture, as in transport, the Netherlands possessed a sector of the economy which provided an important share of national income (in 1968

[55] Hartog, op. cit., pp. 113–17. See also C. J. Oort, 'Het vervoer in de Europese Gemeen-schappen. Algemene Inleiding', in C. J. Oort *et al*, *Het vervoer in de Europese Gemeenschappen* (Kluwer, Deventer, 1969), pp. 9–39.
[56] K. Vonk, 'The Transport Sector. A Struggle for Balance and Mobility', *Internationale Spectator*, Vol. 19, No. 7 (1965), pp. 611–12.
[57] de Bruin, op. cit., pp. 829–88.

agriculture comprised 7.2 per cent of national income, transport 10.2 per cent) and a significant surplus contribution to the balance of payments (in 1968 agriculture had a net export surplus of 2,700 million guilders, transport 1,500 million).[58] In contrast with transport, however, the Dutch had little difficulty in agreeing to a common policy in agriculture, the CAP. Indeed, the system of artificially-supported, high domestic prices, coupled with export rebates and intervention buying, bore a close resemblance to the schemes already operating within the Netherlands before the inception of the CAP. When this national system of market regulation was applied at a Community level, it could be expected to confer extra benefits both on the agricultural sector and on the economy as a whole.

The most obvious observation to make is that it seems probable that the sheer magnitude of the costs of administering such a policy at a purely national level would have prohibited such a generous measure of protectionism. Under the CAP these costs were reduced. Firstly, the policy was funded at a Community level and because of the methods by which the funds were collected and dispersed, this placed less of a strain on the exchequer than would have been the case with a national policy (as illustrated below). Secondly, the costs of the policy itself were reduced because, since the high European Community price level prevails throughout the EEC for national production and traded produce alike, there is no necessity for export rebates on Dutch exports to member states to make Dutch produce competitive with world prices.[59] This second point leads to a benefit or cost for the balance of payments in so far as exports to member states will earn more foreign exchange than those to the rest of the world (ROW), because of the differences in prices, though, conversely, imports from within the Community will cost more. Whether this works out as a gain or a loss depends on the net trade flows inside and outside the EEC and the structure of the export and import packages. Finally, the fact that there is an element in the CAP expenditure to finance improvement schemes, it could be expected to contribute towards increasing levels of agricultural efficiency.

With the increasing isolation of the Community market from world competition and the attraction of relatively high prices within the EEC, it is not surprising to see Dutch agricultural exports (and, at a lower level, imports) concentrated increasingly on other member states. This is clearly shown in Table 5.1. This table also demonstrates that the Dutch earned growing surpluses on their agricultural trade with the EEC which more than offset increasing deficits with the ROW, yielding an ever growing surplus contribution to the balance of payments as a whole. It is impossible

---

[58] Hartog, op. cit., p. 113.

[59] The widespread incidence of 'green currencies' and MCA's in the 1970s does not fundamentally affect this premise since, for virtually the entire decade, prices within the EEC remained firmly above world prices.

to say just how far privileged access to Community markets was responsible for this 'balance of payments effect' since it must be noted that this trend was already apparent before the CAP began. It is possible, however, to measure a specific 'food gain' contribution to the surplus which derives from the way in which agriculture was protected. Thus the Dutch balance of payments benefited because, on balance, agricultural produce was sold on markets at which the high Community price prevailed whilst, on balance, agricultural purchases were obtained at lower world prices. This 'food gain' (the difference between Dutch agricultural trade with the EEC measured at Community and at world prices) has been estimated for 1978 at between £312 million[60] and £441 million.[61] At a rate of 4.2 guilders=£1 this would represent a not inconsiderable contribution to the balance of payments of between 1,300 and 1,800 million guilders.

Table 5.1   Value of Dutch Trade in Agricultural Products (annual averages, '000 million guilders)

	1956–59	1960–63	1964–67	1968–71	1976–8*
Exports to EEC	2.0	2.8	4.2	7.3	21.0
Imports from EEC	0.5	0.7	1.2	2.4	7.8
Balance	+1.5	+2.1	+3.0	+4.0	+13.2
Exports to ROW	2.2	2.4	2.8	3.5	6.0
Imports from ROW	3.3	3.6	4.6	5.7	12.4
Balance	−1.1	−1.2	−1.8	−2.2	−6.4
Overall Balance	+0.4	+0.9	+1.2	+2.7	+6.8

*EEC of 9 members

Source: Figures 1956–59 to 1968–71. J. de Hoog, *De gemeenschappelijke landbouwmarkt en de Nederlandse economie* (Jaarverslag Landbouw-Economisch Instituut, Den Haag, 1975), p. 12.
Figures 1976–78 calculated from Landbouw-Economisch Bericht, 1979, pp. 82–83.

It is difficult to establish precisely what the implications of guaranteed access to high price markets were for Dutch agricultural production partly because agriculture is a sector of the economy rarely characterized by dramatic changes in direction and partly because it is impossible to state how it would have developed outside the CAP. The average annual rate of increase in the volume of gross agricultural production improved marginally from 4.3 per cent per annum in 1960–70 to 4.4 per cent per annum in 1970–75. In terms of net production (gross production minus inputs of

[60] *The Economist*, Vol. 270, No. 7074, 31 Mar.–6 Apr. 1979, p. 38.
[61] *Ibid.*, Vol. 270, No. 7080, 12–18 May 1979, p. 63.

goods and services) the tempo of improvement certainly increased from an average growth of 2.7 per cent per annum in the 60s to 4.4 per cent per annum in the first half of the 1970s.[62] This increase in production was accompanied by a shift in the structure of production away from arable produce towards animal products. In 1962–64 the ratio between the two was 35:65 whereas by 1973–74 it stood at 32:68.[63] Whilst this change in the pattern of production undoubtedly confirmed the Dutch natural advantage in intensive production given the relative scarcity of land, it might feasibly have been reinforced by the fact that levels of protection in animal products such as butter and milk (where EEC prices were as much as five times the world price) were higher than for grains (where EEC prices were between one-and-a-half and two times world prices).[64] Although one cannot state exactly how far these developments were attributable to the CAP, an intuitive guess can be made as to the alternative of life outside the CAP when one looks at Danish agriculture which presents a picture of relative stagnation from the mid-1960s to her entry in 1973.[65]

When one comes to examining the impact of the CAP on levels of agricultural efficiency, the discussion becomes even more difficult. The tempo of improvement in productivity accelerated in the period 1970–75 compared with the previous decade with the average annual increase in net productivity (the relationship between net production and the costs of land, labour and capital) improving from 5.2 per cent per annum to 7.1 per cent per annum.[66] One factor within the CAP which might have contributed to this improvement is the structural shift in the pattern of output observed in the previous paragraph but only in so far that this shift in the concentration of production towards areas in which the Dutch were relatively more efficient was caused by differential prices within the EEC.

Another factor one could isolate is the funds for improvement received from the Guidance Section of the European Agricultural Guidance and Guarantee Fund (EAGGF). However, Table 5.2 shows that until 1975 the sums received from this source were small compared with the outlays of the Dutch Government itself. On the other hand, opponents of the CAP would argue that agricultural improvements were in spite of, and not because of, the policy and that indiscriminate protection is likely to deter rather than foster a climate of innovation and improvement. They would attribute the increase in productivity in agriculture more to the relatively greater attraction of non-agricultural forms of employment 'pulling' labour from the

---

[62] *Landbouwverkenning* (Ministerie van Landbouw en Visserij, The Hague, 1977), pp. 20–21.

[63] *Ibid.*, p. 18.

[64] Commissie, Europese Economische Gemeenschap, *De toestand van de landbouw in de Gemeenschap* (Verslag 1979, Brussels and Luxembourg, 1980), pp. 222–3.

[65] J. de Hoogh, 'De gemeenschappelijke landbouwmarkt on de Nederlandse economie', *Jaarverslag, Landbouw-Economisch Instituut*, The Hague, 1975, pp. 15–17.

[66] *Landbouwverkenning*, op. cit. p. 21.

Table 5.2 Expenditure on Projects for Agricultural Improvement in the Netherlands 1968–1978 (million guilders)

	National Government	Community Funds
1968	227	2
1969	218	7
1970	240	15
1971	241	10
1972	246	30
1973	209	40
1974	181	60
1975	260	100
1976	315	80
1977	218	100
1978	263	120

Source: National Government – Data supplied by Directoraat-Generaal voor de Landbouw en de Voedselvoorziening afdl. Landinrichtingsdienst, Utrecht. Community Funds – Data supplied by Centraal Bureau voor de Statistiek, afdl. National Rekening, Ref. no. 07317-79-E8; 18-10-79.

land, the outlays by national governments, and the general improvements in the economic infrastructure of the country.

There can be little doubt that the CAP has served Dutch national interests both in its contribution to the balance of payments and in funding a sectoral/social policy intended to ensure those working in agriculture a reasonable standard of living. Whether it has actually benefited the development of the agricultural sector, or even whether the economy might not have gained more with fewer resources tied into agriculture, are both open questions. It will be interesting to see how the Netherlands fares as the new EEC members challenge for agricultural markets and what position the Government will take when the whole question of agricultural protectionism is re-examined in the light of the current unwillingness to countenance unlimited expansion in the Community budget.

7. The Economics of the Common Market: Budgetary Transfers

It is appropriate to conclude this discussion on the economic benefits of Community membership with a brief reference to the net transfer of funds through the Community budget. In almost complete contrast with Great Britain, where this question has proved a burning political issue, virtually nothing has been publicized in the Netherlands on the matter. As an official

Table 5.3 Outlays and Receipts of the Dutch Government to and from the European Communities (million guilders)

	1968	1969	1970	1971	1972	1973
Outlays	164	130	248	950	1,150	1,580
Receipts	131	243	518	1,350	1,440	2,250
Balance	−33	+113	+270	+400	+290	+670

	1974	1975	1976	1977	1978
Outlays	1,410	2,340	2,550	3,090	3,450
Receipts	1,690	2,000	2,870	3,450	3,760
Balance	+280	−340	+320	+360	+310

Source: Centraal Bureau voor de Statistiek, afdl. Nationaal Rekening. Ref. no. 07317-79-E8; 18-10-79.

at the Ministry of Finance said to me, 'When one feels one is doing well out of a thing, then one does not look too hard.'

The main component in Dutch outlays to the Community in recent years has been the taxes and levies on production and imports (the ECSC levy, customs duties, levies on agricultural imports, MCAs levied on exports and imports, sugar production and storage levies and the coresponsibility levy on milk). In 1978 this category accounted for 68.7 per cent of government outlays to the Community. Most of the remainder (30.14 per cent) is accounted for by the Dutch contribution for financing that part of expenditure not covered by the Community's own resources and funds to cover expenditure under the EAGGF Guidance Section. The residual is made up of the contribution to the European Development Fund. Turning to receipts from the Communities, the lion's share (95.5 per cent in 1978) is made up of intervention and refund payments from the Guarantee Section of the EAGGF and the MCAs granted on imports and exports. The remainder is accounted for by transfers from the Social Fund, the Regional Development Fund and the Guidance Section of the EAGGF.

The figures in Table 5.3 confirm that the Netherlands has been an almost continuous beneficiary of the European Budget, the only exceptions being the years 1968 and 1975. Any attempt, however, to reform the CAP would almost certainly place this position in jeopardy.

8. The Future of the Common Market: The Dutch Vision

In July 1979 the first elections were held for membership of the European Parliament, elections in which most Dutch political parties took part. The occasion, therefore, provides an ideal opportunity for assessing the degree of agreement or disagreement within the Dutch body politic towards the future development of European integration.[67] The fact that the individual election programmes ranged over many issues outside the competence of the new European Parliament makes them useful documents for this purpose since they reflect party feeling over the entire spectrum of European Community affairs. Their utility in this direction is only marginally affected by the fact that the confessional parties, CDA (Christen Democratisch Appel) and the liberal VVD (Volkspartij voor Vrijheid en Democratie) both fought the elections on the platforms of their respective European Federations.

The most striking conclusion from a study of the election programmes is the remarkable consensus among the major political parties towards the central European issues. The only dissenting voices over the need for closer European co-operation were the minor parties of the extreme left and the extreme right which all laid stress, instead, on the need to defend national sovereignty (though, obviously, for different reasons). Among the major parties, the socialist PvdA (Partij van den Arbeid) were the coolest in their enthusiasm for closer co-operation, continuing the stance adopted by den Uyl in 1973. The party was willing to see closer co-operation at a European level only if Europe develops in a socialist/democratic character and does not compromise the socialist programme at a national level. At the other extreme the VVD sought the ultimate goal of a European government and in between the two were to be found the CDA and the important neo-liberal party D'66 (Democraten '66), whose programme as a whole was closer to the VVD's than that of the PvdA.

On the question of democratization of the Communities, the consensus among the major parties was even stronger. All four political parties were in favour of an extension of the European Parliament's budgetary powers and all were in agreement over the need to introduce majority decision-making into the Council of Ministers. All parties except the CDA stated explicitly in their programmes that the Parliament be given legislatory powers whilst D'66 aspired to the Parliament eventually becoming the centre of 'opinion-forming' within the Community. This consensus applied equally on the question of further enlargement with no dissenting voices to be heard over the desirability of further expansion of the Community.

Turning to economic policies, the CDA, VVD and D'66 all declared themselves in favour of economic and monetary union. The PvdA added an important caveat that closer monetary union was to be viewed as an end in itself and not as a motor for European integration. It was also emphasized

---

[67] The information for this section is derived from Y. H. Berghorst and P. M. Hommes, *Europese Verkiezingen. Programma's en analyse* (Martinus Nijhoff, The Hague, 1979); and from a study of the election programmes and information sheets of the individual Dutch political parties.

that member states should retain responsibility over their own economic policies. On the question of the CAP, it will come as no surprise that there was no discussion of wholesale reform of the policy although all the major parties were concerned to tackle the problems of surpluses and their implications for Third World trade.

It is difficult to ascertain from the results of the European parliamentary elections exactly what impact these appeals of the political parties had on Dutch voters. In the first instance the fact that the poll was disappointingly low (57.8 per cent as opposed to 87.5 per cent in the 1977 national parliamentary elections and 79.1 per cent in the 1978 provincial elections) may well have distorted the results since it was especially low in areas where the socialists might have expected to draw support. Secondly, it was impossible to have a poll on one sector of Dutch policy and not expect it to reflect, at least in part, the popularity of government and opposition parties. Of the major parties the PvdA and, to a lesser extent, the VVD lost support compared with the 1977 and 1978 elections whilst the CDA and D'66 increased their share of the vote. The latter showed a remarkable jump in popularity from 5.44 per cent of the poll in 1977, 5.20 per cent in 1978 to 9.03 per cent in 1979. Interesting also was the fact that the four 'rejectionist' parties that participated in the elections marginally increased their joint share of the vote from 5.74 per cent in 1977, 6.05 per cent in 1978 to 6.77 per cent in 1979, though this might say more about the voting behaviour of supporters of minority parties than anything about the attitude of voters as a whole. In the event, however, the most important election statistic was the 42 per cent abstentions.

The reason for the low turnout may well lie in boredom with the campaign, in the 'credibility gap' between the issues raised and the existing powers of the Parliament or in total bewilderment with the whole affair. There is evidence, however, that the politicians' view of Europe is not shared quite so fully by Dutch citizens. Although the European Commission's publication *Euro-barometer* has consistently shown that the overwhelming majority of Dutchmen questioned felt that membership of the EEC was 'good' for the country (in April 1979 84 per cent felt this way, in October 78 per cent; corresponding figures for those who felt it a 'bad' thing were 2 and 3 per cent respectively),[68] when asked more specific questions this enthusiasm begins to dissipate. A poll conducted for the Dutch news service in October 1978 showed that of those questioned only 46 per cent felt that further integration would be good for the economy (14 per cent, bad) and only 26 per cent that it would make the struggle against unemployment easier (33 per cent, more difficult).[69]

---

[68] Commission of the European Communities, *Euro-barometer. Public Opinion in the European Community*, Vols. 11 and 12 (1979). See also Voorhoeven, op. cit., pp. 184–6.
[69] N.O.S. *Publiek-en Programma- Onderzoek. Intern Bulletin. Nederlanders over Europa*, Oct. 1978.

9. The Future of the Common Market: The Dutch Role[70]

By any standards of comparison, against France, Germany and Italy, the Netherlands was, and still is, a small country. Yet it played a surprisingly large role in shaping the European Community of the Six. This was largely attributable to the fact that for much of the 1950s France was preoccupied by instability at home and decolonization problems abroad. As French self-confidence increased, the Germans proved reluctant to translate their growing economic power into political power and Great Britain, of course, remained outside the Community. It was in the circumstances of this relative vacuum that Dutch influence was able to express itself. Even at this time, however, our study has demonstrated the largely negative power of Dutch intervention – the ability, for example, to block French proposals during the Fouchet negotiations and to delay the implementation of the Commissions' plans for transport. Its positive influence, to move the Community in a direction it desired, could only succeed if the large powers were in agreement – as witnessed by progress towards mutual tariff reduction and the CAP and equally by the relative failure to move the other member states in the direction of democratization of the Communities.

By the 1970s, the Dutch were already being reduced to a smaller, though no less active, role within the EEC. On the one hand Germany began to play a larger role in the Community whilst, on the other hand, Britain's entry to the Community in 1973 decreased the relative role of the Netherlands in sustaining Atlanticist interests. However, the expectation that in Britain the Dutch would find a powerful ally for democratization within the EEC was soon rudely shattered. As the interplay between the larger powers assumed more importance, so the 'blocking-power' of the Dutch diminished. Indeed, as negotiations for the EPC demonstrated, reluctance to compromise might lead to the Netherlands being bypassed altogether. For the smaller powers this danger of being left out of limited bilateral contacts between the larger powers has assumed a very real dimension, as was almost the case at the Tokyo economic summit in 1979. Dutch policy must also take cognizance of the fact that without the agreement between the larger powers, further progress towards European integration will be impossible. Yet differences in interests between them make it extremely unlikely that any relatively permanent consensus will spontaneously be reached. If European co-operation is not to be blocked by total impasse, the smaller powers must attempt to participate in preparing the ground for consensus in a manner best exemplified by the Benelux co-operation in relaunching the Beyen Plan in 1955. The Europe of the 1980s, the Europe of ten, or even of twelve, will need such qualities of vision and political adroitness again if it is to overcome the economic, social and political problems confronting it.

[70] See L. J. Brinkhorst, 'Nederland in de Europese Gemeenschap: terugblik en vooruitzicht', *Internationale Spectator*, Vol. 38, No. 12 (1978), pp. 760–70.

FURTHER READING

H. J. M. Aben (ed.), *Europa onderweg. Ooggetuigen brengen verslag uit* (Elsevier, Amsterdam, 1967). Europe underway; Eyewitnesses publish a report.

Y. H. Berghorst and P. M. Hommes, *Europese verkiezingen. Programma's en analyse* (Martinus Nijhoff, The Hague, 1979). European Elections: Programmes and analysis.

S. J. Bodenheimer, *Political Union: A Microcosm of European Politics, 1960–1966* (Sijthoff, Leiden, 1967).

J. Boehmer, *Het Nederlandse beleid met betrekking tot de Europese samenwerking, 1971–1975* (Ph.D. Thesis, Leiden, 1976). Dutch policy with regard to European co-operation, 1971–75.

R. de Bruin, *Les Pays Bas et l'Intégration Européenne, 1957–1967* (Ph.D. Thesis, Paris, 1978). The Netherlands and European Integration 1957–67.

J. Deboutte and A. van Staden, 'High Politics in Low Countries: A study of foreign policy making in Belgium and The Netherlands', in W. Wallace and W. Paterson (eds.), *Foreign Policy Making in Western Europe* (Saxon House, Farnborough, 1977).

Europese Unie. Rapport van de adviescommissie Europese Unie (Staatsuitgeverij, The Hague, 1975). Report of the advisory commission on European Union.

F. Hartog, *Nederland en de Euromarkt* (Leiden, H. E. Stenfert Kroese, 1971). The Netherlands and the European Market.

J. de Hoogh, 'De gemeenschappelijke landbouwmarkt en de Nederlandse economie', in *Jaarverslag Landbouw Economisch Instituut Den Haag, 1975*. The Community agricultural market and the Dutch economy.

International Spectator, 8 Apr. 1965. Issue devoted to various aspects of Dutch interests within the EEC.

J. H. Leurdijk (ed.), *The Foreign Policy of The Netherlands* (Sijthoff en Noordhoff, Alphen aan den Rijn, 1978).

A. Silj, *Europe's Political Puzzle: A Study of the Fouchet Negotiations and the 1963 Veto* (Harvard, University Center for International Affairs, 1967).

J. J. C. Voorhoeve, *Peace, Profits and Principles. A Study of Dutch Foreign Policy* (Martinus Nijhoff, The Hague, 1979).

APPENDIX 5

Dutch Political Parties (from right to left of the political spectrum).

NPN – Nationale Partij Nederland	Racist
Boerenpartij	Farming Interests
GPV – Gereformeerd Politiek Verbond	Independent Protestant
SGP – Staatkundig Gereformeerde Partij	Parties
VVD – Volkspartij voor Vrijheid en Democratie	Liberals
KVP – Katholieke Volks Partij	
CHU – Christelijk Historische Unie	Christian Democrats
ARP – Anti Revolutionaire Partij	
CDA – Christen Democratisch Appel	The alliance of the three Christian Democrat parties
D '70 – Democraten '70	Conservative Socialists
D '66 – Democraten '66	Neo-Liberals
PPR – Politieke Partij Radicalen	Radicals
PvdA – Partij van de Arbeid	Socialists
PSP – Pacifistisch Socialistische Partij	Pacifist Socialists
CPN – Communistische Partij Nederland	Communists

VI

Belgium and Luxembourg

Adrian Poole

An old joke that has been circulating for several years in Brussels runs as follows: 'What are the characteristics of a typical European?' The reply comes: 'He will have the politeness of a Frenchman, the imagination of a German, the calmness of an Italian, the liveliness of a Dutchman, and an Englishman's flair for cuisine. In other words he'll be a Belgian.' Belgians are supposed to be typical Europeans in terms of general attitudes, habits, tastes and consumption patterns. On the other hand, if you ask the average Belgian whether he considers himself primarily a Belgian or a European, he will probably say he is a Fleming or a Walloon or that he hails from Antwerp or Namur. This parochialism does not prevent the Belgian attitude to European integration since the Second World War from being a positive one: indeed it might be described as uncritical. Belgium's attachment to the European ideal is of a fundamentally different nature from that of the other member states. As Leo Tindemans, the former Belgian Prime Minister, has said 'Being at the crossroads of Latin and German cultures, Belgium needs agreement and peace in Europe more than anyone else.' On a more practical level, as a free trade nation by tradition and by conviction, Belgium sees her relationship with Europe as 'a marriage of love and reason'.[1] Belgian historians are fond of referring to their country as a microcosm of Europe. To these various aspects of Belgium and its relationship with Europe we must now turn our attention.

1. Historical Background

To understand Belgium's attitude to Europe, it is necessary to sketch in briefly the history of the country. As a state, it only dates from 1830, when

---

[1] Heading of Chapter I (page 7) of *La Belgique et la Communauté Européenne*, Textes et Documents No. 317 (Brussels, Ministère des Affaires Etrangères du Commerce Extérieur et de la Coopération au Développement, 1979).

the Belgians achieved their independence from the Dutch. The two countries had been forced together by the great powers at the Congress of Vienna settlement in 1815, with King William of the Netherlands as the ruler of both. The uneasy marriage could not last and the 1830 revolution eventually brought a new ruler to the throne. Although a foreigner, who spoke French indifferently, Leopold of Saxe-Coburg-Saalfeld (Leopold I of Belgium) did much to assure the stability of the new state. The 1830 constitution, which even now remains substantially unaltered, served as a model for the rest of Europe and the 1848 upheavals had little impact in Belgium.

Peace between the Netherlands and Belgium was finally ratified by the Treaty of London in 1839, which proclaimed 'Belgium . . . will form an independent and perpetually neutral state. She will be bound to observe this same neutrality towards all other states.'[2] This was the famous 'scrap of paper' torn up in August 1914 when the Germans invaded Belgium; nevertheless this neutral status had assured that throughout the nineteenth century, Belgium was not involved in any European war, in spite of one or two uneasy moments.

After the shattering of illusions about their neutral status during the First World War, it is not surprising that the Belgians were willing to sign a defensive military agreement with France (29 June 1920), the details of which were to remain secret. This agreement was opposed by many Flemish circles, ever suspicious of anything that smacked of French hegemony. The final legal termination of Belgium's neutral status was to be found in the terms of the Treaty of Locarno (1 December 1925) signed by Britain, France, Italy and Belgium: it talked of the 'abrogation of the neutrality treaties of Belgium'[3] and gave a guarantee of the inviolability of the existing frontiers between Germany and Belgium and Germany and France.

However, Belgium's new status was only to last eleven years. In 1936 she returned to a policy of neutrality, or rather one that came to be called independence/neutrality. The reasons for this were manifold, both internal political (the growth of the Rexist movement and of Flemish nationalism) and external, as outlined much later by Paul-Henri Spaak, the Belgian Foreign Minister, in a speech to the House of Representatives on 16 March 1938. 'The policy of independence . . . is the daughter of two failures, the failure of Locarno, the failure of the League of Nations.' (He was referring to the German invasion of the Rhineland and Italy's invasion of Ethiopia.) He went on, 'We had to rid ourselves of preconceived ideas and draw inspiration from several indisputable facts: our geographical position, our relative strength, the existence on our territory of Walloons and Flemings.

[2] Quoted in *Documents d'Histoire de Belgique*, Tome II, *La Belgique Contemporaine de 1830 à nos jours*, Textes et Documents No 316 (Brussels, Ministère des Affaires Etrangères du Commerce Extérieur et de la Coopération au Développement, 1978).

[3] *Ibid.*, p. 186.

And above all we had to draw inspiration from one decisive element: in Western Europe, Belgium is an essential element of European equilibrium.'[4]

This speech has been quoted at some length as it demonstrates certain permanent key elements in Belgian foreign policy, notably its cornerstone role in any European arrangements.

The policy of independence/neutrality was steadfastly maintained right up to the German invasion of Belgium on 10 May 1940. Neither French nor British troops were allowed into Belgium until the country had actually been invaded. The '18 day war' and the split between King Leopold and his ministers are outside the scope of this study. What is significant for the development of Belgium's European policy was the period when the Belgian Government, along with others, was in exile in London. Wide-ranging discussions took place between the Belgian, Dutch and Luxembourg Governments which were eventually to lead to the Benelux agreement.

Throughout this period, it had become evident that the policy of independence/neutrality was dead and buried and Spaak, its progenitor, was far-sighted enough to see that in post-war Europe a radical change would be necessary. In a note written in 1941 to Miss Irene Ward, a Conservative MP (a note which appears to have been passed on to the Foreign Office), he said that a united or federated Europe under British leadership must be the nucleus of post-war policy and reconstruction. 'What has happened in Europe in the last twenty months proves that it is indispensable for the countries of Europe to unite.'[5]

On the other side of the Channel, in occupied Belgium, Hendrik de Man, the well-known socialist leader whose attitude to the Germans in 1940 was extremely equivocal, was working out his own version of the future of Europe in a book entitled *Réflexions sur la paix* (1942) which was confiscated by the German authorities as soon as it appeared. He maintained that larger economic units must be created – a modern Zollverein.[6] The great branches of production (coal, steel and oil) should be internationalized. A strong, united Europe was the prerequisite for a peaceful world. It would appear that he may even have coined the phrase, 'Europe will be socialist or it will not exist at all'.[7]

The Belgian Government which returned from exile in 1944 was therefore ready to begin the process of progressively abandoning the independence/neutrality policy. Subsequent governments have concentrated on improving Belgium's security and pursuing European integration. Hence a willingness to accept the implantation of the North Atlantic Treaty

[4] *Ibid.*, pp. 187–8.
[5] See P.-H. Spaak, *Combats Inachevés*, Vol. I, *de L'Indépendance à l'alliance* (Fayard, Paris, 1969), p. 148.
[6] It is interesting to note that Luxembourg was a member of this customs union of German states. She joined it in 1842 and left in 1918.
[7] This summary of de Man's views is taken from Jacques de Launay's *La Belgique à l'heure allemande* (Paul Legrain, Brussels, 1978), pp. 257–8.

Organization (NATO) and the Supreme Headquarters Allied Powers in Europe (SHAPE) on Belgian soil in 1966, in spite of some opposition from Spaak's own Socialist Party. It is also evident that the Belgian Government was more than happy that Brussels should be the capital of the European Economic Community.

Belgium has been willing to play the role of lubricant, mediator and persuader. For example, it was Spaak who kept the lines open in 1965 after the crisis within the EEC leading to the French refusal to participate in any Community committees. It was Pierre Harmel, the Belgian Foreign Minister, who in 1966 re-examined East–West relations and established contacts with Poland. So successful was he that in 1969 he was invited to the Soviet Union because they considered him an agent of mediation, someone who could transmit Russian views to the West and someone who knew what was feasible in NATO.[8] King Baudouin was invited to Moscow in 1975 and in a speech said 'A small country can address itself to states of world importance'[9] and went on to urge armaments reductions. Finally, it was Leo Tindemans, former Belgian Prime Minister, who was chosen by the EEC to produce a report on political union (1976). Indeed, his European reputation is probably greater than it is in his own country.

In all these matters, Belgium has been trusted because she has no particular axe to grind. An example of this can be seen in the attitude of Jozef van der Meulen, Belgian representative on the Committee of Permanent Representatives (COREPER) from 1959 until his retirement in 1979. He established a reputation as someone who could achieve compromises and someone who was listened to with respect. In the difficult period between 1965 and 1966 he succeeded in maintaining communications between France and the five other countries of the EEC. Two quotations will indicate his point of view. The first dates from 1975: 'The continuity of Belgian policy is essential if we wish Belgium to continue to play a conciliatory role between the great European powers. It is a natural role for us . . . This cast of mind has enabled us to organize compromises between the Six and we will continue in the Europe of the Nine. The point is that we are a country with a mixed, many-sided civilization, we have a certain propensity to conciliation because of our origins and our history.'[10] The second quotation dates from 1979 in an interview given just before his retirement: 'I am convinced that the salvation of Belgium is through Europe.'[11]

---

[8] A detailed study of Belgium's role in East–West negotiations is to be found in the *Courrier Hebdomadaire*, No. 707, dated 9 Jan. 1975, entitled *La Belgique et la Conférence sur la CSCE*, published by CRISP (Centre de Recherche des Institutions Sociales et Politiques) in Brussels.

[9] Quoted in *Le Soir* (Brussels daily), 3 July 1975.

[10] Quoted in Dossiers du CRISP No. 8, *La Belgique dans la Communauté Européenne* (Brussels Apr. 1975), p. 5.

[11] *Le Soir*, 17 July 1979.

Belgium's two tenures of the EEC Presidency in the 1970s were from January until June 1970 and from July to December 1977. During the first period, the Belgians worked actively to promote Britain's entry into the EEC. During the second, good progress was made on various issues. For example, negotiations for Greece's entry into the EEC began, the Spanish application was made and the European Commission gave its opinion on Portugal's entry. At the same time, there was a certain fear in Belgian circles that such enlargement could lead to a weakening of the Community's institutions. This has not, however, quenched Belgium's enthusiasm for enlargement. In May 1979, Wilfried Martens, Belgium's then Prime Minister, welcomed Greece as a new member with the words 'The accession of your country is a pledge of greater unity and reinforcement of democracy in Europe'.[12]

Furthermore, during this presidency, an attempt was made to improve relations with COMECON and to define the EEC's position with relation to South Africa. But perhaps the principal issue at stake was the direct elections for the European Parliament, for which the Belgians did their best to make the definitive arrangements.

Belgium's attitude to the EEC, then, has always been positive and constructive. Fortunately for her, high principles and self-interest have generally marched hand in hand. Brussels' status as the capital of Europe has increased the identification of Belgium with Europe and the loss of the Belgian Congo (now Zaire) has reinforced this tendency.

2. Attitudes of Belgian Political Parties to Europe

In marked contrast to the bitter controversy about Europe which has taken place in some countries, there has always been a general consensus amongst all Belgian political parties that European integration is a desirable goal. Indeed, it has been taken so much for granted that there have been few passionate parliamentary debates on the issue; other internal problems have loomed much larger. Nevertheless, it is instructive to examine the different nuances of opinion between the individual political parties (see Appendix 6.A for full titles of the various parties: in each case the Flemish abbreviation is given first. See also Appendix 6.B for details of various parliamentary votes on European treaties and Appendix 6.C for the European Election results 1979).

(A) CVP/PSC (SOCIAL CHRISTIANS)

This party is a descendant of the pre-war Catholic party. It changed its name in 1945 as an indication of its identification with similar parties in Western Europe. Its Flemish wing (the CVP), constitutes by far the

---

[12] *Le Soir*, 30 May 1979.

strongest party in Flanders and its President is Leo Tindemans. The party, which has participated in all governments since 1947 (except for the period 1954–58) has been probably the most enthusiastic of the Belgian political parties for the European idea, but there have been divergencies within its ranks, between those of a federalist turn of mind and those who have echoed General de Gaulle's views.

During the election campaign for the European Parliament in 1979, great stress was laid on the fact that Leo Tindemans had been elected President of the European People's Party (EPP). Voters were asked to vote 'for a real Europe', 'for a Europe in the service of mankind', 'for a Europe where men live in freedom'. They were reminded of the necessity of Europe being 'a strong voice in the international forum' and the benefits of reconciliation after centuries of war were emphasized, (this theme does not occur in the election propaganda of other parties). Other points drawn to voters' attention were the importance of more cultural contacts, e.g. European passport; the harmonization of social security; the fact that youth had a great role to play in the Europe of the future; Belgium's part as a link between northern and southern Europe; and the necessity of an early discussion of European defence.[13]

A good summing up of the CVP/PSC's attitude is to be found in a declaration made in February 1979 by Fernand Herman, a PSC member of the House of Representatives, 'We must construct a Europe of everyone, for everyone and by everyone. That is for us a Europe of the heart and of reason',[14] a declaration that is a nice blend of Lincoln and Pascal. In less lyrical vein M. C-F. Nothomb, President of the PSC, was quoted as saying, 'We refuse to make a myth of Europe as if it were the key to all our problems . . . but even less do we want a mythology of Europe as a nationalist or regionalist turning back on itself. Small countries, much more than large ones, need the European dimension to settle the problems of our type of industrial society. It is clear that only European action can offer Belgium a possible alternative in the struggle for employment and the return to growth.'[15] Thus the CVP/PSC have placed Belgium firmly in its European context, a theme often returned to by Wilfried Martens (the then CVP Prime Minister) in his speeches.

(B) BSP/PSB (SOCIALISTS)

This party was called the Socialist Workers' Party (Parti Ouvrier Belge) before the Second World War but changed its name to the Belgian Socialist Party in 1945, presumably to enhance its electoral appeal. It remained for

[13] *Le Soir*, 6 May 1979. Also election leaflets.
[14] *Le Soir*, 10 Feb. 1979.
[15] *Le Soir*, 23 May 1979.

a long time one of the few unitary parties in Belgium but inevitably it eventually split into two halves in October 1978, the Socialist Party in Wallonia and the Belgian Socialist Party in Flanders.

The BSP/PSB often formed part of coalition governments since 1945 and Spaak almost had a monopoly in the determining of Belgium's foreign policy. But his enthusiastic advocacy of European integration was not always whole-heartedly accepted by his party. There were reservations felt by some members: these were due to what has been described as 'international nostalgia', that is to say preferring a world forum rather than a European one; to a fear of excessive American domination in Europe, which was perhaps fostered by Spaak's keen advocacy of partnership with the United States; and to a feeling that European integration might represent a continuation of the Cold War. In addition, most of the European enthusiasts of the 1950s were men of the Right. To illustrate these reticences it should be noted that Spaak had difficulty in getting Socialist senators to vote for the treaty approving the European Coal and Steel Community (ECSC). The PSB's reservations about the installation of NATO and SHAPE in Belgium in 1966 have been noted above.[16]

However, this attitude tended to change after the signature of the Treaty of Rome and most members of the party shared Spaak's views of hostility to the policy of General de Gaulle, the importance of the enlargement of the EEC to include Great Britain, Denmark, Ireland and Norway, and a wish to see the powers of the European Parliament extended. This latter theme reappears in the 1979 European Parliament election programme of the PSB and BSP, along with other themes such as: 'It is not enough to talk about a united Europe – it is what sort of Europe it will be that matters'; 'The Europe of Strauss and Thatcher is rejected'; 'We must construct a Europe which is more human, more just, more democratic and shows more spirit of solidarity'; 'The Socialists constitute the strongest political group in the European Parliament'; 'A vote for Karel van Miert (President of the BSP) is a vote for Brandt.'[17]

The BSP's European Parliament election campaign seems to have been more dynamic than that of the PSB and inquests on the latter's relatively poor election performance have subsequently taken place. However, it should be noted that Ernest Glinne of the PSB has been elected President of the Socialist group in the European Parliament, and there is no doubt that the BSP/PSB will play an active role within the European Socialist parliamentary group.

---

[16] See G. Marchal-Van Belle, *Les Socialistes belges et l'intégration européenne* (Brussels, Editions de l'institut de Sociologie, Université Libre de Bruxelles, 1968) *passim*, and also CRISP dossier CH 433 by Nicole Loeb dated 28 Feb. 1963 and entitled 'Les trois grands partis politiques belges et l'intégration européenne'.

[17] These quotations are all from election leaflets, mostly BSP.

(C) PVV/PRL (LIBERALS)

The pre-war Liberal Party (Parti Libéral) changed its name to the Party for Liberty and Progress in 1961. In 1977 the Walloon section of the party combined with dissidents from the Walloon Rally (RW) to form the Party for Reform and Liberty in Wallonia (PRLW), only to change its name again just before the 1979 European Parliament elections to the Party for Reform and Liberty (PRL). The PVV's title has remained the same since 1961.

The Liberals have had a long tradition of anti-clericalism; much of this has disappeared since the War, but there has been little change in its generally conservative attitude towards economic and social matters, evidenced by such electoral slogans as 'less taxation, more freedom'. Its attitude towards Europe has always been slightly more lukewarm than that of the CVP/PSC and there has been conflict in the party between internationalists and integrationists. On the whole, however, its European policy has tended to stress the economic advantages of integration. This emphasis is understandable in view of the party's general adherence to liberal economic policy and the fact that many of its adherents are engaged in industry and commerce.

The formation of the European Liberal Democratic Party in Stuttgart in 1976, to which the various liberal groups in Belgium adhered, enabled the party to stress further its 'Europeanness'. During the 1978 legislative elections the PVV was one of the few parties even to mention Europe in its election propaganda. The favoured slogan was 'a modern Belgium in a united Europe'. In the 1979 European election campaign the PVV chose a squirrel in a yellow T-shirt for its emblem, 'a symbol of saving, of the ability to crack hard nuts and to advance in bounds'. In its propaganda the party emphasized that Europe was for the young, that the problem of youth unemployment was serious, that small- and medium-sized businesses should be encouraged and private initiative supported. Agriculture and horticulture were essential features of the EEC economy: the usual genuflections towards the protection of the environment and the urgency of an energy programme were also made. Two slogans were prominent 'Liberals aim at European co-operation with free men who want to make progress' and '20 million Liberals for a Europe with more work and less taxes'.[18] The Liberals have also tried to maintain their distance from what they see as futile domestic arguments. To quote Jean Gol, President of the PRL, 'Fanaticism and linguistic intolerance create conflicts unworthy of the European era we have just entered'.[19] As the liberals did not at that time form part of the coalition, such objectivity was easier to maintain.

[18] These quotations are from PVV election leaflets.
[19] *Le Soir*, 26 June 1979.

(D) COMMUNITY PARTIES (PARTIS COMMUNAUTAIRES)

These are thus named since they normally only present candidates in their own region. These parties are:

The Volksunie – VU (People's Union) in Flanders
The Vlaamse Volkspartij – VVP (Flemish People's Party) in Flanders
The Rassemblement Wallon – RW (Walloon Rally) in Wallonia
The Front Démocratique des Francophones – FDF (Democratic French Speakers' Front) in Brussels

The VU is the oldest of these formations (1954) – the other parties have formed as a reaction, the FDF in 1964 and the RW in 1968. The RW lost a great many of its supporters in 1977 to the PRLW (*vide supra*) but in the European elections it picked up some ground.

VU – Ever since its inception, the party has always stressed the federal aspect – a federated Europe of people and regions – but at the same time it has implicitly been suspicious of French hegemony. In its 1955 manifesto it warned the voters against 'the changes which European integration could cause to the Dutch integrity of the Flemish area'.[20] In foreign and military affairs it urged 'the pursuit of the union of the Low Countries within the framework of Benelux . . . and the encouragement of an independent Belgian policy in relation to the problems of European integration in the political, economic and military field'.[21]

This somewhat mistrustful attitude towards European integration faded away after Belgium's entry into the EEC and much more stress was laid on the importance of a federated Europe, composed of people and religions. The VU rejects the idea of Brussels being a separate region in Belgium and in the 1978 elections one of its spokesmen, Vic Anciaux, who is now its President, said 'We must make Brussels important, the capital of a federal country, the partner of a prosperous Flanders, the "heart of Europe".' In its European Parliament election manifesto in 1979 phrases such as the following occur: 'We want to be Europeans but to remain Flemings'; 'Unitary states must be dismantled'; 'We want a large Europe on a small scale' (E. F. Schumacher is quoted later in the manifesto); 'We do not want a Europe organized on unitary lines, based on a centralized Jacobin model'.[22] In the eyes of the VU a Europe of regions is not incompatible with European integration: it is the unitary states which cause the blockages.

VVP – This party made its first appearance on the electoral scene in December 1978 as a constituent part of the Flemish Block (Vlaams Blok), a conglomeration of some of the smaller Flemish groupings. It won one

[20] *Documents d'histoire de Belgique*, op. cit., p. 99.
[21] *Ibid.*, p. 101.
[22] These quotations are from election leaflets, in 1978 and 1979.

seat. However, for the European Parliament elections it presented itself as the VVP and won no seats. Its attitude is similar to the VU but more uncompromising: many of its members are ex-VU members who have left that party because they disapproved of its participation in government and what they saw as its unduly generous concessions to the French-speaking part of the country. It rejects completely the Egmont agreement (a 1977 regionalization project) and its slogans during the European elections were: 'less state, more Europe' and 'Flanders knows no boundaries'. One of its candidates foresaw a federal Benelux with Flemish and Romance districts.[23]

The VVP also drew attention to what it described as the very unfair allocation of seats to Flanders in the European Parliament (13 out of 24). In proportion to the population, the Flemings, they maintained, had a right to 62 per cent of the seats, i.e. 15 out of the 24 Belgian seats. As a gesture of generosity they would have been prepared to offer one of these 15 seats to the German-speaking minority, fellow sufferers from Walloon domination.[24]

The VU and the VVP both share the concept of a Europe of peoples (Volken), not a Europe of parties and stress the importance of the Dutch-speaking presence in Europe. In this connection, two interesting speeches were made at the fifty-second Ijzer pilgrimage celebrations on 1 July 1979 (Flemish nationalists meet annually to commemorate the heroism of Flemish soldiers in the First World War). One was made by a Dutchman who had worked in the EEC in Brussels for many years. He said: 'The newly-elected Dutch and Flemish members of the European parliament should speak Dutch in the Parliament. Thus the French dream of a Latin Europe will not materialise.' The other speech was made by the president of the organizing committee, who said: 'Flanders can assure its future in Europe and in the world without Belgium, on the basis of all peoples' right to autonomy.'[25]

There is therefore very little difference between the VU's and the VVP's attitude to Europe. Hostility to France, hostility to the Belgian state are shared attitudes, expressed more frankly and openly by the VVP.

RW/FDF – For the European Parliament elections the RW/FDF operated as a cartel, although the interests of Bruxellois and Walloons are certainly not identical. Therefore before looking at the European elections one must look at the two parties separately.

As might be expected, there are certain resemblances between the RW's attitude to Europe and that of the VU and VVP but there are important

[23] These quotations are from election leaflets.
[24] *Doorbraak* 22 May 1979 (bi-weekly organ of the Flemish People's Movement – VVB). The paper calculates that the existing system means there is one member for 445,434 electors in the Flemish electoral college, as against 367,888 in the French. A 14:10 split would modify the figures to 413,617 and 404,677 respectively.
[25] *Le Soir*, 3 July 1979.

differences. The RW is very hostile to any idea of an expansion of Benelux's powers. At its foundation congress in 1968, the Party declared 'The RW is determinedly in favour of a united and independent Europe, but rejects any attempt to create a political Benelux, of which our region would be the poor relation'.[26] On the other hand, like the VU and VVP, they consider there is much more hope for Wallonia in a European rather than a Belgian framework. But the reasons are economic, not political, as in the case of the Flemings. Wallonia, it is said, receives four times less financial aid than English regions with similar problems.[27]

The FDF was founded in 1964 and later attracted into its ranks no less a figure than Paul-Henri Spaak, who transferred his allegiance from the PSB just before his death in 1972. His daughter, Mme Antoinette Spaak, is the President of the FDF and now a member of the European Parliament. Being an exclusively Brussels party, it also wishes to see more power devolved to the regions.

The European election campaign for the two parties opened with a joint congress on 31 March 1979 at which Henri Mordant, President of the RW, stated 'One of the reasons why the Walloons wish to see Europe born is that they are not happy in present-day unitary Belgium. For us, what is at stake in these elections is that we can, as Walloons, have access at the European level; we can make ourselves heard there and can have a dialogue with Europe.'[28] He returned to this theme on two subsequent occasions. On 15 May 1979 he said 'We count on Europe to help us to suppress scandals like those of the Fourons or of the Brussels periphery. Walloons and Bruxellois both have an interest in disengaging themselves from the Belgian central power and drawing nearer to Europe.'[29] On 31 May 1979 he stated 'This country (i.e. Belgium) is hostile to us. Europe will be for us a less mean (*mesquin*) framework which will give us back our qualities as citizens.'[30]

The election posters of the FDF/RW showed the face of Mme Spaak with the slogan 'the voice of your region in Europe'. Stress was laid in their manifesto on 'a Europe of diversity, a pluralist Europe which respects and encourages regions and cultures'. What is more, 'the interests of Wallonia and Brussels must be defended at the European level. We shall place Brussels and Wallonia on the European map.'[31]

Whether all these aspirations can be achieved with only two members in the European Parliament remains to be seen.

---

[26] *Documents d'histoire de la Belgique*, op. cit., p. 105.

[27] *Le Soir*, 16 May 1979.

[28] *Le Soir*, 3 Apr. 1979.

[29] *Le Soir*, 16 May 1979. The Fourons (Voer) is an area in the Flemish province of Limburg with an active French-speaking population. The reference to Brussels is to the presence of French elements in the Brussels periphery in an area which is Flemish territory.

[30] *Le Soir*, 1 June 1979.

[31] *Le Soir*, 10 May 1979.

(E) OTHER POLITICAL PARTIES/GROUPS

The attitude to Europe of some of the smaller political parties and groups merits examination. Amongst these must be classified the Belgian Communist Party (KPB/PCB) which won four seats in the House of Representatives (and one in the Senate) in the 1978 elections and none in the European elections. In the past it ritually denounced the EEC as an instrument of the Cold War but with the progress of time this attitude has changed to one of enthusiasm. Part of its 1979 election manifesto stated that it stood for 'a democratic and peaceful Europe at the service of the workers and of its peoples. Belgium's belonging to Europe is a lasting and fundamental idea.' As far as enlargement of the EEC is concerned, the party adopts a very tolerant attitude. 'We recognize the right of all the peoples concerned to decide if they want to join.'[32]

Even the small Marxist group 'All power to the workers' (AMADA/TPT) showed themselves to be just as keen Europeans as the orthodox communists. In their manifesto they stated 'European unity is a necessity for the defence of world peace. The powers of the European Parliament must be increased so as to include the problems of foreign policy and defence.' Predictably, the manifesto goes on to urge the expropriation without compensation of all multinational businesses and banks.[33]

A further indication of the 'Europeanness' of left-wing thought in Belgium is provided by the publication (in late June 1979) by a group of Marxist economists of a 'Counter project for Europe'. In their view, the process of economic and political integration in Europe is an irreversible one and will continue. The group urges that 'the most progressive parts of the Treaty of Rome should be implemented and that a "Europeanization" of social struggles should take place'.[34]

There were only two groups during the elections which showed themselves actually hostile to Europe. These were the Trotskyite Revolutionary Workers' League (LRT/RAL) and a group called 'E-Non' (Europe-Non). In LRT's manifesto, Ernest Mandel, the well-known figure in the Fourth International, who headed the LRT's Flemish list (RAL), declared 'the party is against the Europe of the bosses and the multinational corporations. It is for a socialist United States of Europe. The governments of the member states (of the EEC) should break with the Common Market.'[35] E-Non was only active in Wallonia and obtained 1·1 per cent of the votes there. It was composed of six organizations but its electoral platform was the same as presented in the other countries of the EEC under the umbrella slogan 'Against the Europe of the bosses, for the unity of the workers'.

[32] These quotations are from its election leaflets.
[33] *Le Soir*, 30 May 1979.
[34] *Le Soir*, 11 July 1979.
[35] *Le Soir*, 26 May 1979.

All this quasi-unanimity about Europe evident in the election propaganda of the political parties may give a false impression of public enthusiasm for the European elections. In general, the public was largely indifferent. It was unfortunate that the European elections followed so soon after the legislative elections in December 1978, not to mention the previous legislative elections in April 1977. This indifference is partly due to a general lack of interest in politics, partly to an attitude which considers concrete and immediate realities, such as unemployment and linguistic problems. In an opinion poll taken in the spring of 1978 only 36 per cent of Belgians said they would vote in the European parliamentary elections. This is rather a strange figure when one remembers that the vote in Belgium (as in Luxembourg) is compulsory. In the autumn of 1978 a similar poll revealed that only 28 per cent had read or seen anything about direct elections (36 per cent said they would vote and 20 per cent said they would probably vote). On the other hand 66 per cent of those questioned considered that the EEC was good for their country.[36]

Some politicians were very conscious that they had not made sufficient effort to coax public opinion and that they had taken the EEC too much for granted. On 11 June 1979, Wilfried Martens, the Prime Minister, after expressing his satisfaction with the CVP results, was reported as saying 'As head of the Belgian Government, I am not so happy with the results.' In particular he was concerned with the increase in void and spoiled papers. Governments and European political parties, he said, should make public opinion more conscious of the question of European integration.[37] This point was reaffirmed by Mme Spaak in a speech on 16 June 1979 in which she said 'The larger traditional parties have not been able to make people understand the concrete importance of Europe'.[38] In fact, in spite of all the encomiums about Europe, the election was really a re-run of the 1978 national legislative elections, with the regional parties hoping to see their position enhanced through a weakening of the Belgian state and a strengthening of Europe.

3. Effects of the EEC on Belgium

One can now perhaps look at the effects of the EEC on Belgium. Economically, it is obvious that Belgium, a state entirely dependent on exports and overseas trade, stood to gain a great deal from access to a wider market than just the Benelux countries and to benefit from the lowering of tariff barriers. Although it is difficult to establish precisely how much the improvement in

---

[36] *Eurinfo*, No. 33, Nov. 1978 (Brussels, Bulletin mensuel du Bureau de Presse et d'Information pour la Belgique, Commission des Communautés Européennes), p. 2. Also *Eurinfo*, No. 36, Mar. 1974, p. 5.

[37] *Le Soir*, 12 June 1979.

[38] *Le Soir*, 17 June 1979.

the country's prosperity in the 1960s was due to EEC entry, the fact remains that in the period 1957 to 1966 exports increased by 8 per cent per year and imports by slightly more (8.1 per cent). Between 1958 and 1973 imports from EEC partners increased from 45 per cent to 70.7 per cent of total imports and exports to these partners from 45 per cent to 73.1 per cent of total exports.[39]

Belgium's entry into the ECSC caused some problems for her. Belgian miners' wages were high and coal was dearer than in the other ECSC countries. The general inefficiency of the coalfields in Wallonia forced the ECSC to treat the Belgian coalmining industry in isolation and to continue subsidies for five years. Nevertheless, the coal industry suffered a marked reduction in income. Many mines had to be closed, which led to strikes in the industry. In 1961 the ECSC offered 45 million Belgian francs (about £320,000 at the then rate of exchange) to help retrain 5,000 miners affected by pit closures. Over the years, even more pits have been closed. In 1964 the country had 58 pits, in 1974 15 (5 in Kempen, 7 in Hainault and 3 near Liège). Between 1956 and 1978 the ECSC and EEC helped in the retraining of 106,216 workers in the coal and steel sectors. Furthermore, Belgium gets more intervention support for her coal industry than any other EEC country, 135.50 EUAs (European Units of Account) per ton, as compared with 22 EUAs for France and 0.30 EUAs for Great Britain. Given the state of the Belgian coal industry the ECSC and EEC have probably done their best. 'It reflects great credit on the Government, the ECSC and the regional development associations that the switch from mining has been effected so smoothly.'[40]

The Belgian farm sector, although small (some 3 per cent of the working population in 1976) has benefited from the Common Agricultural Policy (CAP) in that agricultural productivity increased at a rate of about 8 per cent per annum between 1968 and 1975. There has also been a constant diminution in the number of farms in Belgium. In 1959 there were 174,163; by 1976 this figure had fallen to 88,697. This trend was characterized not only by a slow increase in the average size, but also by a general reduction in the area cultivated. In spite of this rationalization and modernization of agriculture the general standard of living of farmers is considered not to have kept up with that of the rest of the Community. In 1976 the remuneration of work in agriculture was estimated at only 78 per cent of what would be considered parity with other sectors. In this respect the CAP has perhaps not benefited Belgian farmers but one always retains a certain scepticism about such estimates.[41]

In spite of the protestations of successive Belgian Governments about

[39] Figures refer to BLEU as a whole and are from Dossier du CRISP, No. 8, op. cit.
[40] See R. C. Riley, *Belgium* (Hutchinson, 1978), p. 61. Statistics are from *Eurinfo*, No. 36, Mar. 1979.
[41] Statistics from *Eurinfo*, No. 33, Nov. 1978, op. cit.

their enthusiasm for the European ideal, skirmishes with the European Commission have taken place from time to time on the question of regional aid. In a law of 1951, the Belgian Government nominated certain areas as development regions. To be placed in this category an area had to satisfy certain criteria. A new law of 1966 extended the criteria so that in theory 679 communes (representing 33 per cent of the Belgian population) became eligible. A further law of 1970 envisaged aid to investment in various development regions. These last two laws were criticized by the European Commission who said they were partially incompatible with the Treaty of Rome because they were much too general and imprecise and also because the form that some of this aid took was unacceptable. Various long, drawn-out discussions between the Commission and the Belgian Government have since taken place. In 1972 the Commission specified certain districts (arrondissements) in which aid was justified and asked the Belgian Government to produce new proposals. Discussion still continued but there has been no solution so far.[42]

The impact of the free movement of workers has been that workers from other EEC countries now constitute 4.8 per cent of the total work force in Belgium (foreign workers as a whole constitute 8.1 per cent). Foreign nationals form 11 per cent of Belgium's population; of these, the largest single group being the Italians (30 per cent). As in the case of Luxembourg (see below) many Italians worked in Belgium before 1957 but Belgium's membership of the EEC has undoubtedly encouraged the influx of many more. Unfortunately, their unemployment rate is high. In September 1978 foreign workers represented more than 15 per cent of those unemployed and 45.5 per cent of these were Italians.[43]

The economic effects of the EEC must overall be rated as favourable to Belgium's economy. When one turns to the political scene, it is probably true to say that membership of the EEC has led to Belgium being *less* united internally than before. Paradoxically, greater European unity has increased internal dissensions. W. Verkade, in his book on *Democratic Parties in the Low Countries and Germany*, draws attention to 'the petrification of national party bulwarks' in Belgium and asks 'is this caused by the fact that the raison d'être of Belgian unity was always based on its necessity in a European balance of power and on its economic unity and that both these necessities are now disappearing in the perspective of European unity in the field of economic life and international politics?'[44] This explains the inordinate enthusiasm of the regional parties for Europe and the overall results of the first European Parliamentary elections were, for example, greeted with approbation by the anti-Egmont committee (a

[42] *Eurinfo*, No. 36, Mar. 1979, op. cit.
[43] *Eurinfo*, No. 35, Jan./Feb. 1979, op. cit.
[44] W. Verkade, *Democratic parties in the Low Countries and Germany* (Universitaire Pers, Leiden, 1965), p. 224.

Flemish nationalist body). In a statement published in June, they hailed the elections as 'the beginning of the construction of a democratic Europe, based on the free choice of citizens and peoples. The reform of the structure of the Belgian state on the basis of a two-fold federalism fits perfectly with the desire to equip the EEC with smaller scale structures.'[45]

Let the last word on this issue be with the then Belgian Prime Minister, Wilfried Martens, in a speech made on 20 June 1979 in which he, placing Belgium in a European framework, pointed out that regionalizations and *communautarisation* (his word) were not incompatible with European integration. 'This double movement of integration at the European level and of regionalization or decentralization demonstrates and corrects a phenomenon common to all European countries: that of the inadequacy of nation states to resolve a series of contemporary challenges. They have become at the same time too small and too big to make a valid response to all present challenges. Europe is essential and so is decentralization.'[46]

4. Luxembourg

What has been said about Belgium's enthusiasm for the EEC applies even more forcibly to Luxembourg. There can be few countries which are more European-minded and more keen to see integration strengthened. It should be made clear that this applies to the political leaders, not necessarily to the mass of the people. It is indeed obvious that a country with a population of 363,700 (1979) cannot stand in splendid isolation from its neighbours. The Grand Duchy's links with Belgium through BLEU (Belgo-Luxembourg Economic Union) and Benelux are dealt with below.

Its two chief political leaders in the last decade, Pierre Werner and Gaston Thorn, from the Social Christian and Democratic (liberal) parties respectively, have carved themselves out European reputations, Werner for the plan on economic and monetary union in 1970 and Thorn for his aggressive advocacy of European integration. At one time M. Thorn displayed distinctly *Pooh-Bah* characteristics, being simultaneously Prime Minister, Minister of Foreign Affairs, Minister of Commerce, Minister of Sport *and* President of the United Nations General Assembly. He became President of the Federation of European Liberal Democrats, and is now President of the European Commission itself.

M. Thorn has been criticized in his own country for his flamboyant style, his penchant for political tourism and his often aggressive attitude towards France. He has never wavered in his enthusiasm for European integration, save on one occasion when Luxembourg's national interests were seriously threatened. This was in 1978 when there was talk of moving the European

[45] *Le Soir*, 15 June 1979. The Egmont pact of 1977 envisaged three regions (Flanders, Wallonia and Brussels) but for many Flemings, Brussels is not acceptable as a separate region.
[46] *Le Soir*, 23 June 1979.

Parliament out of Luxembourg. M. Thorn reacted strongly and even spoke of boycotting the European elections if such a step were contemplated. In general, however, his views are well summarized in an article entitled 'Europe: Valmy or Waterloo?' published in the Belgian daily *Le Soir* on 7 June 1979. The title refers to differing opinions about the European elections. For some they represent Valmy, 'the happy defeat of an out-of-date and baneful nationalism'. For others they are the Waterloo of the nation state and 'the shameful victory of the party of the foreigner'. He castigates 'sacrosanct national sovereignty' and blames governments for not having outlined the contours of a future Europe during the election campaign. Europe is making no progress: all states are confronted with the problems of inflation, unemployment and energy. It has become the scapegoat for errors in national policy. But there are no credible national solutions. What is required is a new regional policy, a European monetary system. The CAP needs to be rearranged but he points out that it has given European farmers a degree of security they have not known for centuries. He goes on to urge a European policy in the fields of computers and research.

As to what sort of Europe he envisages, he presents a somewhat hazy picture. He rejects a confederal Europe 'which will be nothing more than a continuation of the haggling and present tensions between member states who jealously preserve their sovereignty'. On the other hand federalism 'the delight of theorists, increases the confusion of public opinion'. The solution is to bring back Europe to realities and rediscover its necessity. The right of veto must go.

In spite of its lame conclusion, the article contains all the essentials of M. Thorn's political views on Europe. Like Spaak in Belgium, these views have dominated Luxembourg's foreign policy and there would be few Luxembourg politicians to disagree with him: however, as in Belgium, there has hardly been any debate in the Grand Duchy on the nature of the EEC or its future: it has all been taken very much as part of the landscape. Even during the elections to the European Parliament, European issues were blurred by local ones because parliamentary elections took place on the same day. And this in spite of the lavish allocation of seats in the European Parliament to Luxembourg (six seats, representing one seat for 60,000 electors).

One of the major benefits of the EEC to Luxembourg has been the location of so many EEC institutions in the country, many of them on the Kirchberg plateau outside Luxembourg city. The Grand Duchy houses the Secretariat of the European Parliament, the European Court of Justice, the European Investment Bank, the Calculation Centre, the Office of Publication and Statistics, the Audit Office, the services of the European Monetary Agreement, not to mention a non-EEC organization, *Eurocontrol*. It is estimated that some 4,000 civil servants are employed in these organizations. There is clearly some unease in Luxembourg lest the European Parliament's permanent home should be transferred to Brussels or Strasbourg, instead of its present nomadic existence. However, the Government is probably confident that differences within the Council of Ministers will postpone any decision on this issue for some time.

The banking sector has also increased by leaps and bounds over the last few years. In 1955 there were 13 banks with 996 employees, whereas in 1976 there were 84 banks with 5,921 employees. The trend is still upwards (108 banks in 1978, with 7,000 employees). In 1960 3 per cent of workers in banks were foreigners: by 1976 this figure had risen to 28 per cent. The banking sector employs nearly 5 per cent of the national work force. It is of course difficult to say how much of this expansion is due to Luxembourg's membership of the EEC, but it is perhaps significant that West German banks account for 50 per cent of the banking business and provide the largest single source of tax revenue for the Luxembourg Finance Ministry.[47] Foreigners constituted an estimated 84,000 out of a total population of 355,400 (about 24 per cent) in 1977. In 1949 there were 7,600 Italians in the country: there are now 22,000. The figures for French and Belgians have risen from 3,700 to 10,000 and 3,600 to 7,500 respectively. Other significant nationalities are 19,000 Portuguese, 8,500 Germans and 3,000 Spanish. Much of this influx of labour must be ascribed to Luxembourg's membership of the EEC.

Luxembourg's dependence on the EEC for her trade is strikingly illustrated by the fact that in 1977 more than 75 per cent of her exports went to the other countries of the Nine and more than 90 per cent of her imports came from these sources. Somewhat naturally her main markets are Belgium and Germany (34.8 per cent and 36.3 per cent of imports, and 22.8 per cent and 27.9 per cent of exports in 1976).[48]

This short summary should be sufficient to show Luxembourg's entire dependence on the EEC. In this connection there are two main problems – a declining steel industry and a declining birth rate amongst Luxembourgers. It is estimated that if present trends continue, by the year 2,000 Luxembourgers will only constitute 65.8 per cent of the population (as against 81.6 per cent in 1970).[49]

5. Benelux

The genesis of Benelux has been briefly mentioned above, but in order to understand more about the position of Belgium and Luxembourg in Europe,

[47] See 'Banking and Finance in Luxembourg', *Financial Times Survey*, 28 Sept. 1979. There are over 27 German banks in Luxembourg: the next largest group being the Scandinavians (14).

[48] See Georges Als, *Luxembourg – Historic, Geographic and Economic Profile* (Grand Duchy of Luxembourg Government Information and Press Service, 1978), *passim*. See also *The Grand Duchy of Luxembourg in Figures* (Ministère de l'Economie Nationale 1978); and Financial Times, *Survey of Luxembourg*, 18 Apr. 1978.

[49] Als, op. cit., p. 41.

it must now be treated in more detail. It would be a mistake to think that collaboration between Belgium, Holland and Luxembourg in the economic field was a measure undertaken only under wartime conditions. The germs of such an agreement are already to be found in BLEU which dates back to 1922. This abolished tariff barriers between the two countries and established parity between the Belgian and Luxembourg franc. It also provided for a common gold reserve, joint negotiations of trade agreements, a common pool for the receipt of customs and excise duties and unified trade statistics. In spite of its title, it remained merely a customs union.

Nor was this the only move towards economic co-operation. In 1930 the Netherlands, Belgium and Luxembourg together with Norway, Sweden, Finland and Denmark, signed the Oslo Convention which stated they were ready to lower tariffs between them. And in 1932, BLEU and the Netherlands signed the Ouchy Convention, under the terms of which they agreed reciprocally not to increase tariffs and to try and eliminate existing commercial restrictions. Although both these conventions remained a dead letter because of opposition from the great powers, they do represent a preliminary indication of the desire of these small states to work together.

In September 1944 the three Benelux countries signed a convention to establish a customs union which would eventually become a full economic union. All the countries agreed that the exile governments, when they returned, should already have signed the convention, otherwise it would be subject to endless delays by parliaments and pressure groups. Even so, the customs union did not come into operation until 1948. The next stage in the treaty for economic union was signed in 1958 and came into force in 1960. It provided for the free circulation of goods, capital and workers, for common policies for prices, wages and currency and for common commercial agreements with other countries. Benelux would no doubt have made much greater progress if EEC negotiations had not been taking place at the same time; there was also talk in 1949 of a Franco-Italian-Benelux agreement with the elegant title of FRITALUX or FINEBEL. The significance of Benelux is that it showed that the lowerings of tariff barriers *was* possible and that the dire predictions of ruin and disaster were not fulfilled. As Spaak said in a speech in the Chamber recommending ratification of the treaty 'I believe that this agreement between Belgium, Holland and Luxembourg is a good thing for our country and an example to the world'. In the Messina negotiations in 1955, leading to the formation of the EEC, it was the Benelux ministers who acted as the spur.

Benelux was not very successful in the matter of harmonizing agricultural prices: it had to be left to the EEC to resolve this particular problem. In addition, not much progress has been made in the harmonization of VAT or excise duties in the three countries. Benelux is not a supranational organization and political union does not come into consideration. The Walloon mistrust of any extension of the powers of Benelux would in any case hamper any further moves towards political union. Walloons are much

happier in an EEC framework, rather than being a minority in an
organization dominated by Dutch speakers. Furthermore, Benelux has been
overshadowed by its big brother, the EEC, and any progress in the future
must surely be within this framework.

6. Conclusions

Belgium and Luxembourg form the kernel of the EEC and, along with the
Netherlands are probably its most enthusiastic members. The Belgians want
no more Ramillies, Waterloos or Passchendaeles fought out on their soil.
They are tired of being the cockpit of Europe and wish their good
communications to be used for peaceful purposes. Hence the EEC as a
force of peace is in the minds of many Belgians (witness the CVP/PSC
election propaganda quoted above). It is also probably true to say that the
absurdity of national frontiers is more evident in this area than anywhere
else in Europe.

The problem has been that the self-evident 'rightness' of EEC membership
has led to public apathy and indifference on the issue: it is not a burning
question, like the economic crisis or linguistic quarrels. No doubt hopes are
cherished that the EEC will somehow resolve Fleming/Walloon tensions.
And yet ironically Brussels, the capital of Europe, is a predominantly
French-speaking town in Flemish territory and consequently the battle-
ground on which Teuton and Gaul meet. This conflict may be solved at
European level, but predictions are dangerous.

FURTHER READING

Henri Bernard, *Terre Commune: histoire des pays de Benelux, microcosme de
l'Europe* (Brepols, Brussels, 1962).
Henri Dorchy, *Histoire des belges* (Editions A. de Boeck, Brussels, 1975).
Christian Franck, 'La politique extérieure de la Belgique en 1977', *Res Publica*,
No. 2, 1978, pp. 357–65.
Paul Hatry, *Le marché commun et la Belgique* (Editions du Centre Paul Hymans,
Brussels, 1957).
Jonathan E. Helmreich, *Belgium and Europe: a study in small power diplomacy*
(The Hague, 1976).
D. O. Kieft, *Belgium's return to neutrality: an essay in the frustrations of small
power diplomacy* (Oxford, 1972).
Ernst Heinrich Kossmann, *The Low Countries 1780–1940* (Clarendon Press,
Oxford, 1978).

Theo Luykx, *Politieke geschiedenis van België, Vol 2, van 1944–1977* (Elsevier, Amsterdam, 1978).

R. C. Riley and G. J. Ashworth, *Benelux: an economic geography of Belgium, the Netherlands and Luxembourg* (Constable, 1975).

Septentrion, *Revue de la culture néerlandaise*, No. 1/79, 'Les partis politiques flamands et les élections européennes', pp. 78–80.

Synthèses, *Bruxelles, Carrefour de l'Europe* (Brussels, 1970).

Vormingscentrum Lodewijk Dosfel, *Vlaamse Beweging in Europa* (Ghent, 1979).

APPENDIX 6.A

Belgian political parties

CVP	Christelijke Vlaamse Volkspartij	} Social Christians
PSC	Parti Social Chrétien	
BSP	Belgische Socialistische Partij	
PSB	Parti Socialiste belge	} Socialists
PS	Parti Socialiste (since October 1978)	
PVV	Partij voor Vrijheid en Vooruitgang	
PRLW	Parti pour la réforme et la liberté wallonnes	} Liberals (LIB)
PRL	Partie de la Réforme et de la Liberté	
PL	Parti Libéral (Brussels only)	
VU	Volksunie (Flanders)	
VVP	Vlaamse Volkspartij (Flanders)	
RW	Rassemblement Wallon (Wallonia)	} Community parties (i.e. regional)
FDF	Front démocratique des francophones (Brussels)	
KPB	Kommunistische Partij van België	} Communists
PCB	Parti communiste belge	
RAL	Revolutionaire Arbeidersliga	} Trotskyites
LRT	Ligne Révolutionnaire des travailleurs	
AMADA	Alle macht aan de arbeiders	} Maoists
TPT	Tout le pouvoir aux travailleurs	

APPENDIX 6.B

Belgian Parliamentary Votes on European Treaties (1948–72)

	House of Representatives			Senate		
	For	Against	Abstentions	For	Against	Abstentions
Council of Europe 1949–50	150	4	2	140	6	0
ECSC Treaty of Paris 1951	165	13 2 PSC 5 PSB 1 LIB 5 PCB	13 7 PSC 6 PSB	102	4 3 PCB 1 PSC	58 1 PSC 1 Indep. All Socialist Group
European Defence Community 1953 and 1954	148	49 9 PSC 30 PSB 4 LIB 6 PCB	3 1 PSC 1 PSB 1 LIB	125	40 10 PSC 26 PSB 3 PCB 1 Indep.	2 1 PSC 1 PSB
Treaties of Rome, EEC and Euratom, 1957	174	4 PCB	2 1 PSC 1 Flem' nat.	134	2 PCB	2 1 PSB 1 Indep.
Treaty of Enlargement of EEC 1972	164	5 PCB	0	138	0	1 PCB

Source: La Belgique dans la Communauté Européenne, Dossier du CRISP, No. 8, April 1975, pp. 3 and 4.

For abbreviations see Appendix 6.A.
The terms PSC and PSB in this table refer to Flanders as well as Wallonia.

APPENDIX 6.C

European Election Results 1979, Belgium and Luxembourg

BELGIUM	3 constituencies	Flanders Wallonia Brussels
	2 electoral colleges	13 Dutch-speaking members
		11 French-speaking members
	(Brussels electors belong to one of these two colleges)	

Dutch-speaking
College (13)

7 CVP (including Leo Tindemans)
3 BSP (including Karel van Miert)
2 PVV
1 VU

French-speaking
College (11)

4 PS
3 PSC
2 PRL
2 FDF/RW (including Mme Spaak)

LUXEMBOURG One constituency with 6 members
3 Social Christians
2 Liberals
1 Socialist

VII

Denmark

Clive Archer

In many ways Denmark sits at the crossroads of Europe[1] – it straddles Scandinavia and the European continent, the Baltic and the North Sea and, with Greenland and the Faeroe Islands still part of the Danish kingdom, has ties to the North Atlantic. Denmark's attitude to post-war integration has been moulded by conflicting pressures from its neighbours. Dependent to a great extent on foreign trade, the Danes have seen the countries that provide their major markets – the United Kingdom, the rest of Scandinavia, West Germany – adopt different approaches to European integration from the 1950s to the early 1970s. The extension of the European Communities in 1973 partially helped to solve this problem by bringing together the United Kingdom, West Germany and Denmark in a market arrangement linked by free trade agreements with the other Nordic states. The Danish people voted in October 1972 to follow Britain into the Communities but the years leading to this decision, the referendum debate and events since have demonstrated the reservations that many Danes, and, in some cases, the Danish Government, have had about the European Communities. The Danes remain, together with the British, the most sceptical members of the Communities.

1. Denmark's Decision to Join the European Communities

Finding a suitable institutional framework for her immediate post-war trade policy was a major dilemma for Denmark. The country depended greatly on trade, had low tariffs and exported mainly agricultural goods. Denmark's

---

[1] Perhaps the most thorough investigation in English into Denmark's European policy is Gunnar P. Nielsson's *Denmark and European Integration: A small country at the crossroads* (Ph.D. dissertation – University of California at Los Angeles; University Microfilms, Ann Arbor, Michigan, 1966).

major market was the United Kingdom though the West European continent and the rest of Scandinavia were becoming important outlets. Whilst the Organisation for European Economic Co-operation (OEEC) provided an excellent instrument of co-operation for the West European economies, it did not successfully tackle the tariff question. Denmark of the late 1940s had few natural resources apart from its agriculture and the skill of its people, and Danish exports faced a continuing threat from other countries' tariffs.

From the end of the war Danish ministers sought schemes that would bring Denmark into a grouping with her major trading partners with no, or few, barriers to trade. Up to the end of the 1950s there were basically three sets of plans that interested Danish governments: those involving a Nordic trade arrangement; the plans for a customs union of the members of the European Economic Community; and those including all the OEEC countries in a West European-wide free trade area.

(A) NORDIC PLANS

In the wake of the Marshall Plan and the expressed American desire that the West Europeans should pool their resources, Nordic ministers meeting in Oslo in February 1948 established a Joint Nordic Committee for Economic Co-operation to examine four major areas – a common external tariff; the reduction and removal of intra-Nordic non-tariff barriers; the Nordic division of labour and industrial production; and the co-ordination of Danish, Norwegian and Swedish foreign trade policies. Whilst the Committee, which produced an interim report in early 1950,[2] generally considered that the creation of a Scandinavian market would be of great benefit, a Norwegian minority report outlined their reservations: Norway had been more deeply affected by the war than Denmark and Sweden, it still needed to concentrate on recovery and consequently was not ready to subject its industries to Swedish and Danish competition or allow resources to be switched from vital rebuilding. After four more years' investigation, the Norwegians once again decided that most of their industry still had to be protected.[3] At this stage, the newly-formed Nordic Council took a hand. A proposal that the governments should try to negotiate a limited union was taken up by Danish, Norwegian and Swedish ministers in October 1954 when they established a Committee of Ministers of Economic Co-operation and a Nordic Economic Co-operation Committee (NECC) composed of civil servants.[4] The NECC completed a massive study in 1957 with a detailed examination of the Nordic market, the possibilities for a

[2] *Ibid.*, pp. 250–4.
[3] *Ibid.*, pp. 256–60.
[4] *Ibid.*, p. 264. Finland joined these negotiations in 1956.

customs union and assorted questions[5] but this did little to persuade the Norwegians to risk entering a Nordic Customs Union.

(B) THE COMMUNITY IDEA

Whilst the tedious process of Nordic committees continued throughout the 1950s, two other developments in trade matters directly affected Denmark. The first of these stemmed from the 'Community Approach' of 'the Six' to trade and economic problems and led to the formation of the European Economic Community, consisting most noticeably of a common market, a common external tariff, a common agricultural policy, and supranational institutions. The Danish response to the Schuman Plan and the ECSC had been one of disinterest as Denmark had no coal and steel industry but the establishment of the Spaak Committee after the Messina meeting of 'the Six' (June 1955) promised to touch their interests more closely. A common external tariff to the south of their border boded ill for Denmark's exports and a common agricultural policy for 'the Six' presented a threat to Danish agriculture unless a satisfactory arrangement could be made with the Community countries.

(C) OEEC DEVELOPMENT

As a result of the Messina meeting and an initiative by Denmark and other low-tariff countries, the OEEC established a working party to examine the possibility of the customs union of 'the Six' existing within a wider Western European free trade area. This was deemed to be 'technically possible' and further OEEC working parties tackled the prospect in detail. The ratifications of the Treaties of Rome in the summer of 1957 made a solution more urgent and in October 1957 the OEEC established a ministerial committee (the Maudling Committee) to negotiate a free trade agreement. During these negotiations it became clear that there was a sharp division between the British, who wanted industrial free trade between the EEC and other OEEC states, weak intergovernmental institutions to control these arrangements, no common external tariffs for the OEEC and the exclusion of agricultural trade from any agreement, and the French who placed emphasis on the establishment of the EEC's common external tariff and considered that any OEEC-wide trade arrangement should include the harmonization of external tariffs, economic and social policies, should include agricultural trade and be controlled by strong institutions. Denmark, together with the Benelux countries and West Germany, attempted to bridge this gap. The Danes were generally sympathetic to the United Kingdom's stance – as a low-tariff country they welcomed free trade, they had no love for supranational institutions and were wary of harmonizing social and economic policies with 'the Six'. However, Denmark did want

[5] *Ibid.*, p. 319.

agricultural trade included in any free trade scheme and, in this, they found themselves in opposition to the British Government. Efforts to reach a compromise between the French and the British failed and the intransigence of both sides became apparent at the Maudling Committee meeting of 13–14 November 1958: Mr Maudling adjourned the Committee early in 1959.[6]

This move presented the Danish Government with a dilemma. Their desired settlement had been some sort of low-tariff Nordic Customs Union working within a wider West European free trade area with agricultural trade included in the plans. Compromise in the working parties on the full inclusion of agriculture and unfruitful Nordic discussions were followed in July 1958 by a 'Shock Report' of a Danish government commission warning of the possible deleterious effects for almost 40 per cent of Danish industry of exposure to a wider West European free trade area or the EEC. The breakdown of the Maudling Committee negotiations represented the collapse of Danish trade policy strategy and in early 1959 the Danish Government was confronted with the prospect of trying to save its existing exports by bilateral arrangements with the evolving trade bloc to the south.

(D) THE ADVENT OF EFTA

After the November 1958 meeting of the Maudling Committee, representatives of the Scandinavian, British, Swiss and Austrian Governments and their industry and agriculture started examining proposals for a new approach to trade matters. Failing a response from the EEC on interim trade arrangements, they drew up plans for a free trade association between themselves. Representatives from the Outer Seven – Portugal had joined the group – negotiated the details of an industrial free trade area in Stockholm in the summer of 1959. The plan was for the creation of a free trade zone over a period of ten years, keeping in step with the EEC's tariff reductions. Agricultural and fisheries trade would not be included though the most industrialized countries indicated that special agreements could be made with Denmark, Norway and Portugal.

During May and June 1959 the Danish Government had been pursuing plans for a 'bridge' between 'the Six' and 'the Seven'. When it became clear that the EEC was not interested in such arrangements and after a meeting of the Nordic prime ministers in July 1959 had buried any prospect of a Nordic Customs Union, the Danes turned their attention to the Stockholm negotiations. Denmark failed to get agricultural and industrial trade treated alike but they did negotiate bilateral agricultural trade agreements with Britain and Sweden. By March 1960 the Stockholm Convention establishing

---

[6] Miriam Camps, *Britain and the European Community 1955–63* (Oxford University Press, London, 1964) pp. 153–84.

the European Free Trade Association had been ratified and EFTA started functioning in May 1960.[7]

For almost another thirteen years EFTA remained the major framework for Danish trade. During this period four major strands were apparent. First, the pattern of Danish exports changed from being heavily agricultural to being more industrial in nature and Denmark's markets became more varied, a process undoubtedly helped by free trade within EFTA.

Table 7.1: Danish Trade Developments 1960–1970[8]

	Percentage of total exports	
	1960	*1970*
Agricultural exports	42	35
Industrial exports	58	65
To: United Kingdom	27	19
EEC	28	22
Nordic Area	16	27
Others	29	32

The figures in Table 7.1 underline another trend in the 1960s – Denmark's important EEC outlet was becoming increasingly threatened by Community protectionism. Danish governments hoped that the formation of EFTA would lead to an early multilateral settlement of the market division of Western Europe and that in the meantime their sales of agricultural products to Western Germany would not be affected. It came as some disappointment in the first year of EFTA's existence that the EEC refused to regard EFTA as an equal bargaining partner and it seemed that Denmark would be faced with decreasing export returns from two major areas: the British market was in decline and Danish products were being locked out of the Community. This prospect fired Danish governments throughout the 1960s to pursue the aim of a united Western European market.

The third strand in Danish trade was that of growth of the Nordic market helped by common membership of EFTA. The rising importance of this market meant that it had to be given serious consideration in Danish market plans – it would be no use entering the EEC at the cost of losing free access to Scandinavian markets. A final point is that though Denmark's sizeable agricultural exports helped to finance the industrialization process

[7] T. C. Archer, 'EFTA and the Nordic Council', in K. J. Twitchett (ed.), *European Co-operation Today* (Europa Publications, London, 1980).
[8] Danish Ministry of Foreign Affairs: Committee on Denmark's relations with the European Communities, *Danmark og de Europaeiske Faellesskaber*, 3 supplerende redegørelse (Copenhagen, Ministry of Foreign Affairs, 1971), p. 64.

that took place in Denmark in the 1960s, it could not supply all the money needed – the rest was made up by an increasing external debt.

(E) DENMARK'S APPLICATIONS TO THE COMMUNITIES

During the years of Danish EFTA membership, the Government made three attempts to join the EEC and also participated in an effort to create a Nordic Economic Union ('Nordek').

Following the United Kingdom's decision in July 1961 to apply for membership of the EEC, the Danish Government took a similar line. In the subsequent parliamentary debate, Foreign Minister J. O. Krag stressed other EFTA members' support of the British and Danish initiative, the need to maintain Scandinavian co-operation and the increasing importance of national governments (as opposed to supranational institutions) within the Communities.[9] The Danish Parliament (Folketing) sustained the Government's decision to open negotiations with the EEC by 152 votes to 11, with only the left-wing Socialist People's Party against. Denmark's application for membership was submitted to the Council of Ministers on 10 August 1961 and the Danes started the presentation of their case on 26 October 1961. They had consulted closely with the United Kingdom beforehand and their approach mirrored that of Britain. They wanted full membership; they accepted the Treaty of Rome and did not consider that their membership would warrant it being changed as any special problems could be solved by protocols and other arrangements; they were willing to join in any political co-operation based on the Bonn Declaration of July 1961; they also applied for membership of the Coal and Steel Community and Euratom. The 'special problems' included a request for the Nordic Common Labour Market to be maintained, exceptional treatment for capital transfers and harmonization of social policies and special arrangements on agriculture.[10] The last point was of importance for the Community. The Danish Government wanted to participate in the formulation of the EEC's Common Agricultural Policy, they wanted Denmark included in the British-EEC agricultural negotiations and they desired Danish agricultural exports to the Community to be maintained throughout the negotiating period by a quota arrangement. None of these Danish requests for special treatment for their agriculture were granted.[11] During 1962 the momentum went out of Denmark's EEC negotiations as they became increasingly overshadowed by the British case and as issues such as the Nordic Labour Market were shelved because they were not of immediate concern. The signing of the Helsinki Convention in March 1962 by the five Nordic states codified Nordic co-operation and reminded Denmark of her Nordic obligations but,

[9] *Folketingstidende 112 Aargang 1960–1*, cols. 4674–87.
[10] *Folketingets Markedsudvalg Beretning No. 1.*, pp. 2–8. Details of these and other Danish requirements can be found in G. Nielsson, op. cit., pp. 565–81.
[11] *Ibid.*, pp. 579–80.

soon after, discussion of the labour market question with the EEC was postponed as Norway had by then applied for Community membership and it was thought that the subject could be dealt with in multilateral talks at a later stage.[12]

President de Gaulle's press conference of 14 January 1963, at which he effectively vetoed British membership of the EEC, shocked the Danish negotiators who for a while considered that their own approach might not be affected.[13] When it became clear that Denmark was to be excluded with Britain, Norway and Ireland, the Danish Government returned to its pre-1961 policy of trying to build bridges between EFTA and the EEC and also attempting to obtain concessions from the EEC for Danish agricultural trade. Danish fears of the falling away of their EEC market were somewhat fulfilled though the move towards free trade within EFTA opened up the Nordic market – especially that of Sweden – for them. In 1967 Denmark again joined the United Kingdom in renewing its membership application to the EEC. With the growth in her Nordic trade Denmark was anxious that any solution should include the other Nordic countries as well as the United Kingdom but serious negotiations were not even started before President de Gaulle delivered the second French veto on the extension of the Community in December 1967.

(F) NORDEK

Denmark's newly-elected Liberal-Radical-Conservative coalition government responded to this rebuff in early 1968 by proposing a Nordic Economic Union which included a customs union and a central fund. Negotiations between four of the Nordic states (Iceland was excluded) took place during much of 1968 and 1969 but in March 1970 the Finnish Government announced its unwillingness to sign the Nordek Treaty which it considered had become associated by then too closely with the question of the extension of the European Communities.[14]

(G) EXTENSION

The meeting of the heads of government of the EEC at The Hague in December 1969 provided the requiem for Nordek but a clarion call for those awaiting extension of the European Community. Once more the United Kingdom, followed by Denmark, started membership negotiations and by the time it came to make its opening statement on the subject, the Danish Government was well prepared for its task. The failure of Nordek

[12] *Ibid.*, pp. 575–7.
[13] *Ibid.*, pp. 590–8.
[14] T. C. Archer, 'Nordek: Shadow or Substance?', *Integration*, 1971, No. 2, pp. 108–16; C. Wiklund, 'The Zig-Zag Course of the Nordek Negotiations', *Scandinavian Political Studies* (Old Series), Vol. 5, 1970, pp. 307–35.

had deflated those within Denmark who had preferred a Nordic trade link to EEC membership and the work of a special committee on Denmark and the European Community from 1968 onwards provided a close study of most of the potential problems that could arise in negotiations.[15]

(H) THE NEGOTIATIONS

The Danish side opened these negotiations by accepting the treaties establishing the three Communities, the Communities legislation adopted since their foundation, plans for the further development of the Communities and their political goals. The Danes requested certain transitional arrangements and brought up a few practical questions of particular interest to Denmark but these were dealt with during negotiations without much trouble. The whole negotiating process between the Applicants and the Communities was dominated by the case of the United Kingdom and, to a lesser extent, that of Norway. Since the 'Shock Report' of July 1958 Danish industry and agriculture had become better prepared for competition with the EEC countries and they had been provided with a useful training ground in EFTA. So by 1970 the Danes were ready to accept full membership without a transitional period, but this was ruled out by the requirement that all the new members should have the same transition period. So, along with the other applicants, Denmark agreed on a five-year changeover during which time tariffs with the Community countries would be lowered and the Common External Tariff adopted by 1 July 1977.

Two areas were of particular interest for Denmark during the 1970–71 membership negotiations. The first was peculiarly Danish: the position of the Faeroe Islands and of Greenland in relation to the EEC. Both territories were part of the Danish kingdom and each sent two members to the Danish Parliament but both were culturally and economically, as well as geographically, separate from metropolitan Denmark. Furthermore Greenland had a minister in charge of its affairs who had a seat in the Danish Cabinet whilst the Faeroese elected their own local parliament to deal with internal Faeroese affairs, questions of common interest to the islands and mainland Denmark being dealt with by the Prime Minister's Office.

The main concern of both Greenland and the Faeroes during membership negotiations was that of fisheries. The EEC's adoption of an outline Common Fisheries Policy in June 1970 meant that eventually all fishing vessels of the Community countries would be able to fish within the fishing limits of their fellow members. The United Kingdom, Denmark and Norway succeeded in obtaining an interim settlement which allowed them to retain twelve-mile national limits for special parts of their coastline until either a new policy was agreed or until 1982 when Community members would revert to the doctrine of the June 1970 policy. The coast of Greenland was

[15] Danish Ministry of Foreign Affairs: Committee on Denmark's relations with the European Communities, op. cit.

accorded special treatment and an interim twelve-mile national limit. The Faeroese, being so dependent on fishing, were not satisfied with such a settlement, especially as they were hoping for a 50-mile, or even a 200-mile, Faeroese fishing limit. The Danish Government obtained for them a three-year period in which they would decide finally whether to join the EEC. Meanwhile, the Faeroe Islands would continue their traditional customs union with the Danish mainland and would have a free trade agreement with the rest of the Community.[16]

The second major area of interest for Denmark during the negotiations was the relationship of the non-applicant member states with the expanded EEC. The acceptance by the Six of a network of free trade arrangements between the Communities and the remaining EFTA states solved this problem and meant that Denmark would be able to maintain the free trade relationship with the other Nordic states that had been built up through EFTA.[17]

After these successful negotiations the Danish Prime Minister, J. O. Krag, signed the Treaty of Accession on 22 January 1972. What remained to be completed before Denmark became a full member of the European Community on 1 January 1973 was the ratification of that signature.

(I) RATIFICATION

Paragraph 20, section I, of the Danish Constitution states that the powers of the realm may be delegated to international authorities established by mutual agreement with other states in order to promote international law and co-operation. However, section 2 of paragraph 20 requires that a Bill allowing such a transfer must have a majority of five-sixths of the members of the Folketing or, failing that, needs to be passed by a simple majority and then submitted by the Government for approval by the electorate in a referendum. Paragraph 42 of the Constitution requires that for a referendum result to be negative in such a case, there must be a plurality of votes against, representing at least 30 per cent of the electorate. Otherwise the measure stands.

Votes in the Folketing on the EEC issue on 11 November 1970 and 18 May 1971 showed that opponents there could not obtain the blocking one-sixth needed to be sure of a referendum.[18] During early 1971 public opinion in Denmark seemed to be swinging heavily against Danish membership of the EEC – opposition rose to about 30 per cent and support dropped under the 40 per cent level in the opinion polls. The Social Democrats, in

---

[16] Danish Ministry of Foreign Affairs: Committee on Denmark's relations with the European Communities, *Forslag til lov om Danmarks tiltraedelse af De Europaeiske Faellesskaber*, Tillaeg 1 (Copenhagen, Ministry of Foreign Affairs, 1972), p. 39.

[17] *EFTA Bulletin*, Nov. 1972, June 1973, pp. 7–9, and Nov. 1973, pp. 4–6.

[18] N. Petersen and J. Elklit, 'Denmark Enters the European Communities', *Scandinavian Political Studies* (Old Series), Vol. 8, 1973, p. 200.

opposition since 1968, found that their supporters were particularly vulnerable to this swing. Rather than face the election due for winter 1971/72 with a voting force susceptible to defection to left-wing parties on the European Community membership issue, the leadership of the party chose to announce on 3 May 1971 that there should be a mandatory referendum on the membership bill whether or not it obtained the necessary five-sixths vote in the Folketing.[19] The Radicals on the government side, who had their own doubts about the EEC, agreed with this cautionary move and eventually the other two government parties, the Liberals and Conservatives, followed suit. Although this effectively removed the membership issue from the election in September 1971, it was noticeable that in the new Folketing both the Social Democrat and Radical parties had MPs who were staunch opponents of the EEC. The new Social Democrat minority Government later decided that the referendum should be held a week after the Norwegian one – a move considered a tactical victory for the opponents of Danish entry who thought that should the strong opposition to Norwegian membership of the EEC manifest itself in Norway's vote then the Danish electorate might follow this lead.

The battle over Danish membership was conducted at two levels during the period before 2 October 1972 – the date of the referendum. There was the parliamentary debate which had as its main aim the enacting of legislation concerning Danish membership of the European Community. This was done on 8 September 1972 when the necessary laws were passed by 141 votes to 34 with two abstentions and two absentees. All the Conservative and Liberal MPs voted *for* as did the majority of Social Democrats and Radicals. However, a dozen Social Democrats, four Radicals and a Greenland MP joined all 17 of the Socialist People's Party in opposition and the two Faeroese MPs abstained. (It can be seen that the opposition vote cleared the one-sixth hurdle needed to require a referendum on the legislation.) The second part of the battle was carried out amongst the electorate and to some extent reflected the division within parliament. The importance of this campaign for Denmark's later posture in the EEC should not be underestimated.

(J) THE REFERENDUM

The campaign in the six months before the referendum did little to shift those who had already expressed support or opposition to membership in early 1972. However, it does seem to have produced a majority of two to one for membership amongst the near-third of the electorate who were 'don't knows' in April 1972. Such a move was of particular importance for

[19] Paragraph 42, section 1 of the Danish Constitution allows for a referendum on a law if a third of the membership of the Folketing demands it. The Social Democrats alone made up more than a third even before the 1971 election.

the Social Democratic party – it turned a potential small majority against membership into a small majority in favour.[20]

Those groups in favour of Denmark joining the EEC were the Conservative and Liberal parties with few defections from their ranks; the Social Democrats and Radicals with a noticeable minority in their ranks against; the LO (Danish TUC) by a small majority; and the organizations representing trade, industry and agriculture. This broad section of the Danish political and economic establishment carried out an expensive and effective campaign which stressed two aspects in particular: the people who mattered in Danish society were for membership and Denmark could not afford to stay out of the EEC. The large majority in parliament for joining the EEC was emphasized and a range of people from resistance heroes to past prime ministers were advertised as supporters in a campaign co-ordinated by an umbrella organization called the Committee for Danish Membership of the EEC. The business, farming and trade union interests of this Committee were demonstrated in a number of articles outlining the effects of a 20 per cent devaluation assumed necessary if membership were rejected and the unemployment that would result from firms leaving a Denmark outside the EEC.

The opponents had an anti-establishment air about them. They included the Socialist People's Party, the Communist Party and other groups left of the Social Democrats, a number of Social Democrats and trade unionists, some Radical MPs and the Young Radicals, the Justice Party (free trade followers of Henry George) and a host of smaller parties, groups, fronts and forums. Most of these were organized – after a fashion – into the People's Movement against the European Community. The People's Movement lacked the money and methods of its opponents but nevertheless ran a spirited campaign. Its emphasis was on the loss of Danish sovereignty should Denmark join the EEC, although it spent much of its time refuting the pro-Marketeers' arguments. The Social Democrats against the European Community produced a newspaper advertisement with a full page photograph of Peter Shore – then spokesman on EEC matters for the British Labour Party – and headed 'Labour says no' in an effort to persuade its adherents that they were not alone.

The Norwegian people's rejection of membership in their referendum of 28 September 1972 added a twist to the tale of the campaign. The People's Movement urged Denmark to follow their Nordic brethren whilst those for membership pointed out that Norway needed a trade agreement with the EEC and Denmark could ease her path from within the Community.

(K) THE RESULT

The turn-out in the 2 October referendum was a record for Danish elections and referenda: 90.1 per cent. Of the registered voters 56.7 per cent (63.3

[20] P. Hansen, M. Small and K. Siune, 'The Structure of the Debate in the Danish EC Campaign', *Journal of Common Market Studies*, Vol. XV, 1976, pp. 103–6.

per cent of those who voted) said *yes* and 32.9 per cent (36.7 per cent of those voting) said *no*, so the membership legislation was clearly accepted. Four noticeable areas voted no – the Southern and Eastern constituencies of Greater Copenhagen, North Aarhus and Greenland. The Greenlanders voted 70.3 per cent *against* and 29.4 per cent *for* but had to enter the EEC with mainland Denmark. Jutland was the most pro-Market part of the country. Support for EEC membership tended to be highest in rural areas and in the upper social classes, lowest amongst the working class and inner city areas.[21] Surveys showed that Yes-voters were strongly motivated by economic arguments whilst No-voters were primarily concerned with questions of integration and loss of sovereignty. There was low support for federalism and European integration, even among EEC supporters: 'The Danish politicians did not obtain any mandate for a federalist or integrationist EC policy in the 1972 referendum – but neither did they seek one'.[22] Another researcher concluded of Danish opinion that 'The Common Market is supported by some men, but least by "the common man" '.[23] So despite the apparently overwhelming positive vote for membership of the European Community the Danish electorate was by no means writing a blank cheque for its politicians to cash in at Brussels.

(L) ASSESSMENT

Why did Denmark join the EEC? It is important to remember that Denmark has never sought unconditional membership of the Community – simultaneous British membership was always a precondition. As Gunnar Nielsson has written: 'Ever since the Six was formed, the Danes have faced the predicament of having a too significant economic interest in the Common Market to ignore it but too many restraining factors to join alone.'[24] Dr Nielsson's work has also shown that Danish governmental support of the political aims of the Community was somewhat sporadic and opportunist[25] and the author of a study already cited states that, 'Denmark had originally applied for membership almost entirely on economic grounds'.[26] Professor Peter Hansen has posed the problem of Danish European policy as being 'how to cope effectively with change in the external environment, and its effects upon internal economic and societal structures'. The view of the

[21] N. Petersen & J. Elklit, op. cit., pp. 210-2.
[22] N. Petersen, 'Attitudes towards European Integration and the Danish Common Market Referendum', *Scandinavian Political Studies* (New Series), No. 1, 1978, p. 41.
[23] Hans Jørgen Nielsen, 'Attitudes Towards EC in Denmark 1971-75', Paper prepared for workshop on 'Mass/Elite Attitudes towards Europe', ECPR Joint Sessions of Workshops, London 7-12 Apr. 1975, p. 14.
[24] G. Nielsson, op. cit., p. 614.
[25] Ibid., pp. 587-9 and 600; P. Hansen, 'Adaptive Behaviour of Small States. The Case of Denmark and the European Community', *Sage International Yearbook of Foreign Policy Studies*, Vol. 15, 1976, p. 158.
[26] N. Petersen, op. cit., p. 24.

Danish Government and economic establishment was that it was increasingly difficult to maintain national, autonomous controls of these structures and that Denmark should try 'to utilize the opportunities for influencing the environment' by joining the enlarged Community.[27] Certainly the potential benefits of such a step increased enormously once the United Kingdom decided on membership, once Danish industry was restructured after the 'Shock Report' and over a decade of competition within EFTA, and once the Communities had agreed on free trade arrangements for the EFTA non-applicants. Furthermore, the potential political costs were decreased in the 1960s as Community institutions became less supranational and more susceptible to the wishes of the individual member governments.

2. Denmark in the Communities

What stance has Denmark taken on Community policies and objectives since joining on 1 January 1973? On the whole, Danish governments have tended to be cautiously co-operative on EEC matters. Their policy has been neatly encapsulated in the following terms: 'Denmark's official EC policy most resembles that of France, Denmark has always had reservations about the suggestion to increase the "level of integration" whilst she welcomes an increase in "the scope of integration", including fisheries policy, agricultural policy, protection to the environment, regional policy, monetary policy, economic policy, industrial and trade policy.'[28]

The increase in 'the scope of integration' has allowed Danish governments a chance to affect through the Community the external factors which impinge on the whole range of domestic as well as foreign policies of a small country. Danish ministers have therefore tended to support effective action in these areas by the Community. On the other hand, the Government in Denmark has felt itself constrained, not least by a public unenthusiastic about European integration, in accepting any deepening of 'the level of integration' – for example any change in the member governments' right to veto in the Council of Ministers issues that they consider against their national interest. Danish attitudes to the direct election of the European Parliament can be seen in this light.

Among all the policies undertaken by the European Community Denmark has had a particular interest in the following:

(A) CAP

One of the first groups in Denmark to call for Danish membership of the European Economic Community was the farmers' organizations (excluding the smallholders). Denmark has had much to gain from the Common

[27] P. Hansen, op. cit., pp. 172–3.
[28] S. Auken, J . Buksti and C. L. Sørensen, 'Denmark Joins Europe', *Journal of Common Market Studies*, Vol. XV, 1976, p. 2.

Agricultural Policy (CAP) both in terms of safeguarding its farmers' markets and in financial support from the intervention fund (FEOGA). Since membership, the CAP has helped Danish balance of payments by some £300 million a year and in 1973–76 Danish agriculture received Community payments worth about £1,200 million. It is therefore not surprising that all the Danish governments that have been in power since January 1973 – Social Democrat, Liberal or a coalition of the two parties – have had as a cornerstone of their market policy the unfailing support of the principles of the CAP. Whilst they consider that minor adjustments could, and should, be made to it, Danish governments, unlike their British counterparts, have always believed that no major reform of the CAP is necessary. One Danish official has written 'that higher and more reasonable prices for agricultural products (from Denmark) are "the cost" of free access for industrial products to the Danish market'.[29] Any attempt to change the CAP radically will meet fierce resistance from the Danes.

(B) TRADE

The Danes have continued to argue against the creation of barriers to trade. They have advocated the expansion of the Community's market for industrial goods and have encouraged the EEC to take a liberal line in GATT, UNCTAD and Lomé Agreement negotiations. Restrictionism has always been a fear of Danish industry and agriculture and whilst the Common External Tariff and the CAP provide some protection for them, they are not anxious to provoke other countries – in particular the United States – into retaliatory action against Community, including Danish, products.

(C) INDUSTRY AND EMPLOYMENT

Denmark has supported the harmonization of production standards, and the ending of technical obstructions to industrial trade and also rules of competition that will hinder the misuse of monopoly power. Denmark has given support to the idea of a legal framework for 'European companies'. At the same time the Danish Government has concerned itself with common regulations for working conditions and has placed heavy emphasis on Community action against unemployment – the Danes support an enlargement of the Social Fund for this purpose. In particular, Danish Social Democrat governments have pressed for a Community interest in 'participation' at work and industrial democracy.

(D) EUROPEAN MONETARY SYSTEM

Denmark has been always ready to re-establish fixed currencies within the EEC; 'a common unit of account in all areas of co-operation . . . a gradual

---

[29] Ambassador Jens Christensen, 'Are the Danes Good Europeans?', *Danish Journal*, No. 1, 1976, p. 3.

pooling of the foreign exchange reserves of Member States and to conduct a common monetary policy to third countries'.[30] The Danes have therefore joined the European Monetary System (EMS) and have on several occasions adjusted their currency value – especially in relation to the Deutschmark – to other countries in the System. In particular, Denmark has wanted access to the capital markets of the Community, especially to finance their balance of payments deficit.

(E) REGIONAL POLICY

Certain countries such as Ireland and Italy have seen the expansion of the Regional Development Fund as a *sine qua non* for their adoption of the EMS. The Danes have opposed a large increase in this Fund. The major part of the Danish receipt from the Fund goes to Greenland.

(F) FISHERIES

The Greenlanders are also concerned about the development of a Community Common Fisheries Policy (CFP). In this they have a different interest to that of mainland Denmark. Greenland, like Iceland and Faeroes, is heavily dependent on fishing but unlike these other two communities has not yet developed its full fishing potential. Greenland thus has a large fishing zone (the fishing limits were extended out to 200 miles or the median line in January 1977 in all the Community states with coastlines) but a little fleet of small boats. The Greenlanders are anxious that quota agreements made for them by Denmark through the European Community should not allow both other EEC members or third countries too great an access to their waters. The Community has provided money not only for the development of the Greenlandic fleet but also for a better fishery protection service in Greenland waters.

The fishermen from mainland Denmark face a different problem. Most of them look forward to the full adoption of CFP that will open the fisheries zones of all Community members to their boats. The temporary adjustments to the CFP made at the time of the first extension of Community membership allowed for exclusive national fisheries zones up to a limit of 12 miles around members' coasts until 1982. With the general extension of limits in 1977, much larger nationally-controlled fisheries zones were created. It has been the European Commission's intention that not only should there be common marketing arrangements for fish – something accepted by Community members – but that the division into national zones should be ended and that arrangements should be made to divide up the benefits of the new EEC fisheries zone between the fleets of the member states. Denmark has

---

[30] *Ibid.*, p. 3.

a small national zone and a large fleet.[31] The Danish fishermen would therefore be likely to benefit from the creation of a Community zone and their Government has pressed for the adoption of such a policy and an end to national controls. In this, they have been strongly opposed by the British Government whose national sector would be a major contributor to a Community zone and who have insisted on strict conservation measures, many of which have adversely affected Danish North Sea fishermen.[32]

(G) ENERGY, RESEARCH, ETC.

The Danes are prepared to see Community money put into research projects particularly in such areas as energy, health, environment, transport, which the individual member states would find difficult to undertake by themselves. Denmark has also been in favour of energy-saving proposals, although these are usually carried out under the International Energy Agency's auspices, and has welcomed co-operation through the EEC on anti-pollution measures. As well as taking these policy stands, the Danish Government has taken a cautious view of institutional developments within the Community. They have been conservative in preserving veto rights in the Council of Ministers and in opposing plans for a 'directorate' of two or three leading Community countries. Official comment has been rather wary about further powers for the European Parliament, which might make EEC decision-making even more difficult.[33] Direct elections to the Parliament were greeted with a certain amount of suspicion – not just among the EEC opponents.

3. The EEC and Danish Interests

Danish membership of the EEC can be seen in Peter Hansen's terms, that is as an attempt by the country to influence its political and economic environment. This view means that Community institutions are identified as instruments available to a small country to further its interests. Danish market interests are normally seen as securing its trade outlets and sources of raw materials and its economic aims are primarily those of keeping confidence in the kroner and thereby extending Denmark's borrowing ability. This view of Danish interests adopts the traditional notion of them being a conglomeration of the wishes of the major economic interest groups – both sides of industry, agriculture and fisheries. These interests emerge at their strongest where the demands of these groups overlap and are

[31] Denmark in 1976 had 11,218 full-time fishermen (compared to the United Kingdom's 16,830) (*ICES Bulletin Statistique* Vol. 61), in 1974 had 7,310 motor fishing boats and the United Kingdom had 6,874, (*Ibid.* Vol. 59). The Danish North Sea Zone covers 56,000 square km, the United Kingdom's 244,000 square km.
[32] C. M. Mason (ed.), *The Effective Management of Resources* (Frances Pinter, London, 1979), pp. 142 and 149.
[33] Jens Christensen, op. cit.

affected by conflict between, say, industry and the agricultural sector.

Clearly, membership of the EEC has served both Danish industry and agriculture well in providing market accessibility – the hope of the 1950s of bringing together the German and British markets has been fulfilled. However, membership has coincided with the general depression in world trade and the massive rise in oil prices. A country like Denmark, so dependent on its foreign trade and on energy imports,[34] was bound to suffer. As a result Denmark has experienced inflation, the subsequent devaluations of its currency, large balance of payments deficits and record unemployment – all the things that the pro-Marketeers predicted would happen if Denmark stayed out of the Community. Even traditional occupations such as fishing have been hit, with EEC policies bringing little relief as yet. Attacks on the CAP, especially by the British who benefited from cheap Danish farm products for so long, are seen as attempts to undermine the one Community policy which has substantially benefited an important sector of the Danish economy, agriculture, and a powerful interest group in Danish politics, the farmers. Despite the realization that Denmark's present economic ills are not caused mainly by their EEC membership, the Danes have little reason to be very enthusiastic about the Community.

Rather than seeing Danish EEC membership as providing *the* answer for Danish interests, it is more useful to see it as the best available answer, given that these interests are primarily economic. Attempts to form a Nordic Customs Union failed in the late forties, in the 1950s and in 1968–70, all at times when the European Community alternative was not really open for Denmark. Maybe membership of a Nordic Customs Union linked to the European Community by a free trade agreement (resembling those given the EFTA non-applicant countries in 1973) could have provided an alternative trade strategy for Denmark, but this would have left Danish agriculture outside the CAP and Danish industrial products would have had to trade in the Community under conditions over which Denmark had no control.

If Danish interests are interpreted not just in economic terms but in a broader fashion, Danish EEC membership becomes more questionable. It is true that Denmark has much to contribute to the Community in social and cultural affairs, but in selfish terms the protection of the values represented in Danish social and cultural policies may be better secured within a Nordic context and may be harmed by further exposure to the brash commercialism of certain EEC countries. Those who would want the Danes to develop an 'alternative' society to the economism and bureaucratic organization of the EEC do not see Community membership as conducive to Danish national interests, let alone the interests of individual Danes.

---

[34] Denmark imports about 90 per cent of its energy needs. Its exports are just over 40 per cent Danish Gross Domestic Product.

4. Danish Opinion and the Communities

In October 1972 the Danish electorate clearly accepted membership of the European Community though, as noted, this was accompanied by a certain underlying reserve. Since joining the EEC, Danish governmental attitudes have reflected this caution, particularly with reference to any deepening of the level of integration within the Community. Facing the disappointments of membership, the Danish public has, on the whole, moved from support to indifference about EEC membership and from caution over to opposition to certain Community activities.

(A) THE DANISH PARLIAMENT

Of the present members of the European Community Denmark has the most developed system of parliamentary scrutiny of EEC activities. This reflects Danish concern over integration and also encourages a certain political wariness in EEC matters. First, it should be noted that the Danish political system as reflected in their parliament (the Folketing) has become very complex. By the end of the 1960s there were five major parties represented in the Folketing – the Conservatives and the Liberals worked closely together, the Social Democrats had formed most of the post-war governments, many of which were minority ones, the Radicals switched their allegiance between the Social Democrats and the Conservative-Liberal group, whilst the Socialist People's Party was to the left of the Social Democrats and sometimes sustained Social Democrat governments. The 'protest election' of December 1973 added another five parties – the anti-direct tax Progress Party of Mr Glistrup became the second largest parliamentary party from a standing start, the Centre Democrats, who had broken away from the right-wing of the Social Democrats, entered the Folketing for the first time as did the Christian People's Party, whilst the free-trade Justice Party and the Communist Party both re-entered parliament after a thirteen-year absence. After the most recent election (in October 1979) there are still ten parties in the Folketing though the Communists have had their place taken by the Left Socialists (a 'New Left' party). This fragmentation has meant that a broad consensus has to be obtained between a number of parties if immobilism is to be avoided. Such a consensus is normally built on a fairly low common denominator and quite often separate agreements are built up between different coalitions of parties on different issues – for example defence, foreign affairs, housing policy, economic affairs. This means that although the attitude of each party towards the European Community is fairly well known (see section l.J), the constellation of support for any one of the Community policy proposals will depend on the area covered – whether it be agriculture, participation in industry, the Lomé Convention or customs harmonization.

The system of scrutiny which allows Danish parliamentarians to voice their opinion on Community activity consists not only of the occasional debate on the floor of the Folketing but also of the continual monitoring by a specialist committee. Given that many Community directives require national legislation for implementation and that financial contributions to Community coffers have had to be agreed by national legislatures, Danish Governments have been anxious to maintain a parliamentary majority on Community questions. Likewise individual parliamentarians, especially those opposing or sceptical about the EEC, have wanted to keep political control over what the Government agrees at Brussels.

The Folketing's Market Relations Committee (MRC) has been used as both a sounding board and a means of control. The MRC has seventeen ordinary members who are elected to represent the relative strength of the parties in the Folketing. The committee has attracted senior party members including some party leaders and ex-ministers. Originally it was established in 1961 when Denmark first applied for entry to the EEC but it has really come alive since Danish membership in 1973. It was then given the right to be briefed by the Government on all the EEC Council's binding decisions. After a crisis in February 1973 when the Danish Minister of Agriculture accepted an agreement in Brussels much less favourable than expected by most of the parties, the MRC's powers were strengthened to give it greater control over government action in EEC matters. The relevant minister has to obtain a mandate from the MRC on issues to be decided in Brussels and ministers are obliged to keep in touch with the MRC as negotiations develop and as new or revised mandates are needed. This is not such a draconian constitutional control on the executive as it may seem. The MRC does not vote as such – party representatives voice their opinions – and ministers are not bound to follow its advice. They do so from a sense of survival – they know that MRC views reflect party opinions in the Folketing as a whole, and it is there that the Government will have to cobble together a majority. Furthermore the MRC has a basically pro-Market bias in its membership – again reflecting the views of the political parties. However, its existence spells out for ministers the political constraints on EEC policies which are expected by the parties and ultimately by the voters.[35]

(B) THE POLITICAL PARTIES

The views of the political parties about Danish membership of the EEC were clarified during the referendum debate. Since then the parties have been able to express their opinions in Parliament and at national elections and have also been provided with an extra forum during the direct elections to the European Parliament held in Denmark on 7 June 1979.

[35] The role of the Market Relations Committee is explained in detail in J. Fitzmaurice, 'The Danish System of Parliamentary Control over European Community Policy', in V. Herman and R. van Schendelen (eds.), *The European Parliament and National Parliaments* (Saxon House, Farnborough, 1979).

One commentator has divided Danish political parties into three groups on the EEC issue – the federalist, the pragmatic pro-Europeans and the anti-integrationists. Among the first group – whose espousal of federalism is mostly rather weak – are included the Conservatives, the Liberals and the Centre Democrats. The second description is used to cover the Social Democrats, the Christian People's Party, the Radicals and the Progress Party and hides a variety of attitudes including the anti-bureaucratic crusade of Mr Glistrup and the Social Democrats' wish to use the EEC to extend social reform. The last group includes the Justice Party with its free trade criticism of the EEC, the Socialist People's Party, the Left Socialists and the Communists, all of which perceive the Community as being 'a capitalistic set-up'.[36]

(C) THE DIRECT ELECTIONS

The direct elections to the European Parliament allowed the Danish political parties to define their attitudes towards the EEC more sharply and the Danish voters to voice their opinion on both these attitudes and on Danish membership of the Community generally. The elections also saw the revival of the People's Movement against the European Community which had campaigned for a *no* vote during the 1972 referendum. The People's Movement wanted Denmark out of the Community and, meanwhile, they wanted a halt to any advance towards political and economic union. After the referendum they had been eclipsed, especially when the British referendum vote seemed to suggest that the question of membership would not be re-opened, but the prospect of direct elections at a time when Denmark was suffering economically revived their fortunes. Denmark returned sixteen members to the European Parliament. Greenland elected one MEP and the other fifteen were chosen under proportional representation by mainland Denmark. All the parties mentioned above – except the Communists – ran lists and the People's Movement ran its own list. The Conservatives, Liberals, Centre Democratic and Christian People's Party had a technical electoral agreement which allowed them to maximize their number of seats. The Communists decided not to run their own list but to fight under the People's Movement banner and the Justice, Socialist People's and Left Socialist Parties had a technical electoral alliance with the People's Movement. Of the twenty People's Movement candidates, three were Social Democrats; two were Radicals; two Conservatives; two Communists; and four others came from the Liberals, Justice Party, Left Socialists and Socialist People's Party. The election itself was a victory for the 'sofa' voters. The turnout of 46.8 per cent was about 40 per cent less than that in the general election five months later. The other noticeable victor was the People's Movement which returned four MEPs. These joined together with

[36] C. L. Sørensen, 'Danish Party Policies on European and Nordic Cooperation', *Co-operation and Conflict*, XIV, 1979, pp. 171–91.

other assorted MEPs such as the Italian Radicals and Walloon nationalists to form the Technical Co-ordination Group at the European Parliament in order to get the benefits of a recognized group. This was despite the mixed political nature of the four People's Movement MEPs – a Radical, a Communist, a Social Democrat and an independent. The Liberals, with three MEPs and the Conservatives with two, improved their position from the 1977 general election. The Centre Democrats, with their leader elected, and the Radicals with none of their candidates returned, held their share of the vote. The Social Democrats, with three MEPs, dropped about 15 per cent, the Progress Party (one MEP) lost almost 9 per cent of its share of the vote, and the Christian People's Party lost about half its 1977 percentage vote. The Socialist People's Party returned one MEP, and he was joined on the left-wing benches in the European Parliament by the Greenlandic representative – a former Catholic priest.

(D) PUBLIC OPINION

The 7 June 1979 election demonstrated public scepticism about the EEC. In particular Social Democrat voters, faced with the party's pro-EEC candidates, felt cross-pressured and many of them stayed at home. The views of the Danish public, demonstrated in opinion polls, underline general wariness about developments in the EEC. Asked if they were for or against the unification of Western Europe, a sample of Danish voters replied: 15 per cent very much for (the smallest figure for the nine Community countries), 33 per cent were to some extent for, 15 per cent were to some extent against it, whilst 15 per cent were very much against unification. The EEC weighted average for this last group was 4 per cent. Only 12 per cent of those asked thought that European unification should be accelerated, whilst 27 per cent thought it should be slowed down, and 25 per cent thought membership of the EEC was a bad thing – 36 per cent thought positively of it. 25 per cent thought that the Community should go much further than it had towards economic and political union, whilst 45 per cent disagreed.[37]

(E) THE FUTURE

Given the parliamentary situation in Denmark, the views of the political parties and the mood of the voting public, it is unlikely that any Danish Government will support any move towards increased supranationality in the Community. Present EEC policies – especially the CAP – will be upheld and others, such as a Common Fisheries Policy, encouraged. Extension of the Community to include Greece, Portugal and Spain will be welcomed, but any review of the institutions that might diminish the Danish

[37] 'Eurobarometer', *Bulletin of the European Communities Commission*, No. 1, 1979, pp. 108–30.

voice in EEC decision-making will be stoutly resisted. The European Community may provide Denmark with the mechanism to adapt to international conditions but the Danes are anxious not to be swallowed up in this machinery.

FURTHER READING

N. Amstrup and C. Lehman Sørensen, 'Denmark: Bridge between the Nordic countries and the European Communities?', *Co-operation and Conflict*, Vol. X, nos. 1–2 (1975), pp. 21–32.

T. C. Archer, 'The Danish and Norwegian Applications, *The World Today*, Vol. 27 (1971), no. 10, pp. 448–56.

T. C. Archer, 'Norway's "No" and Denmark's "Yes"', *The World Today*, Vol. 28 (1972), no. 11, pp. 467–70.

S. Auken, J. Buksti and C. Lehman Sørensen, 'Denmark joins Europe: Patterns of Adaptation in the Danish Political and Administrative Processes as a result of Membership of the European Communities', *Journal of Common Market Studies*, Volume XV (1976), pp. 93–129.

E. Bjøl, 'Le Danemark et la Communauté Européenne', *Journal of European Integration* (Canada), 1978, Vol. II, no. 1, pp. 25–48.

Jacob A. Buksti, 'Corporate Structures in Danish EC Policy: Patterns of Organisation, Participation and Adaptation', *Journal of Common Market Studies*, Vol. XIX (1980), pp. 140–59.

J. Fitzmaurice, 'The national parliaments and European policy making: the case of Denmark,' *Parliamentary Affairs*, Vol. 29 (1976), pp. 310–26.

G. Gage, 'Denmark's Road to the European Communities', *Scandinavian Studies*, Vol. 46, no. 4, 1974, pp. 331–51.

P. Hansen, 'Adaptive Behavior of Small States. The Case of Denmark and the European Community', *Sage International Yearbook of Foreign Policy Studies*, Vol. 2, 1974, pp. 143–74.

P. Hansen, M. Small and K. Siune, 'The Structure of the Debate in the Danish EC Campaign: a study of an opinion-policy relationship', *Journal of Common Market Studies*, Vol. XV (1976) pp. 93–129.

S. Henig (ed.), *Political Parties in the European Community* (George Allen and Unwin Ltd., London, 1979), Chapter 3, 'Denmark' by John Fitzmaurice.

P. M. Leslie, 'Interest Groups and Political Integration: the 1972 EEC Decisions in Norway and Denmark', *American Political Science Review*, Vol. LXIX, 1975, pp. 68–75.

T. Miljan, *The Reluctant Europeans* (C. Hurst, London, 1977).

N. Petersen, 'Attitudes towards European Integration and the Danish Common Market Referendum', *Scandinavian Political Studies*, Vol. 1 (New Series), 1978, pp. 23–42.

N. Petersen and J. Elklit, 'Denmark enters the European Communities', *Scandinavian Political Studies*, Vol. 8, 1973, pp. 198–213.

C. Lehman Sørensen, 'Danish Elite Attitudes towards European Integration', *Co-operation and Conflict*, Vol. XI, 1976, pp. 259–79.

A. H. Thomas, 'Danish Social Democracy and the European Community', *Journal of Common Market Studies*, Vol. XIII (1975), pp. 454–68.

W. Wallace and W. E. Paterson (eds.), *Foreign Policy Making in Western Europe* (Saxon House, Farnborough, 1978), Chapter 5, 'Foreign Policy Making in Scandinavia' by Ib Faurby.

VIII

Ireland

Trevor C. Salmon

1. Pre-Hague Background

Irish interest in and attitudes to developments in post-war Europe underwent a radical transformation in the years 1958 to 1961. Previously, although a founding member of both the Organisation for European Economic Co-operation and the Council of Europe, Ireland had been somewhat outside the mainstream of events. Although Irish isolation can be over-emphasized, Ireland had long experienced a certain insularity from international affairs.[1] Neutrality in the Second World War symbolized the distinctive Irish approach. Neutrality, partition, irredentism and the relative youth of independence profoundly influenced Irish perceptions in the post-war period. Even those who believed in the spirit of the Hague Congress of 1948 and wanted Ireland to play a role believed 'Partition nullifies usefulness of our efforts'.[2] Irish participation in the OEEC and Council of Europe was marked by the 'sore thumb' policy of raising partition on every possible occasion. The focus was upon partition and this led to non-participation in the North Atlantic Treaty.

The Irish paid lip-service to the European idea but adopted a minimalist position with respect to structures and powers. Essentially, as Eamon de Valera observed, they felt 'it would have been most unwise for our people to enter into a political federation which would mean that you had a European Parliament deciding the economic circumstances, for example, of our life here ... We did not strive to get out of that domination of our affairs by outside force or we did not get out of that position to get into a

---

[1] A good account of the historical background of the Irish in international affairs is to be found in P. Keatinge, *A Place Among Nations: Issues in Irish Foreign Policy* (Dublin, Institute of Public Administration, 1978).
[2] Sean MacBride, Minister of External Affairs 1948–51, *Dail Debates* Vol. 112: column 903.

worse one'.[3] Moreover, the key consideration was the British attitude, since in the 1948–60 period over 75 per cent of Irish exports went to Britain and about 50 per cent of Irish imports were from Britain.[4] Irish independence was thus circumscribed by its economic dependence upon Britain. Consequently, no real interest was shown in economic integration in the decade after the war, although proposals relating to agriculture generated some interest.

Internal and external factors combined to change Irish policy. Internally it became apparent that 'The policies hitherto followed . . . have not resulted in a viable economy'.[5] Emigration and unemployment were high, and between 1949 and 1956 the rate of growth of Irish GNP was well below both the United Kingdom and OEEC average. Externally, the OEEC discussions on a free trade area profoundly worried the Irish. They sought a 30-year transitional period, identifying with other countries in the course of economic development, and the inclusion of agriculture.[6] Although some progress was made on matters of concern to the Irish, they breathed a sigh of relief when the negotiations collapsed for reasons outside their control. Nonetheless, it was clear the issue of free trade would not disappear, whilst the negotiations led the Government to the view that free trade was not necessarily the ogre it had appeared. The evident failure of previous policy and the prospect of freer trade in Europe led to a fundamental re-appraisal of economic policy which was crystallized in the White Paper 'Economic Development' in the autumn of 1958. The conclusion was reached 'that, sooner or later, protection will have to go and the challenge of free trade be accepted. There is really no other choice for a country working to keep pace materially with the rest of Europe.'[7] This was a crucial change of policy.

The first tariff reductions by the Six in January 1959 and British plans for an industrial free trade area meant there could be no turning back for the Irish despite the breakdown in the OEEC negotiations. They felt unable, however, to accept the obligations of European Community membership given their state of development and the non-participation by their largest customer. Moreover, Britain effectively excluded Ireland from the negotiations leading to the European Free Trade Association arguing (a) the new arrangement was for developed countries only and would involve no special development fund and (b) no question of agriculture being included. Ireland had sought both in the OEEC negotiations. To minimize the consequences

---

[3] Eamon de Valera, *Dail Debates* 152: 548 ff.

[4] B. Chubb, *The Government and Politics of Ireland* (Oxford University Press, London, 1974), p. 330.

[5] The White Paper, *Economic Development* (Stationery Office, Dublin, Pr 4803, 1958), p. 2 ff.

[6] For a discussion of Irish policy at this time see, G. FitzGerald, 'Ireland and the Free Trade Area', *Studies* 1957 (Vol. 46) pp. 19–26.

[7] *Economic Development*, op. cit., p. 2.

of exclusion from both, Ireland sought informal partial interim agreements with the Six and Seven but to no avail.

Doors that appeared firmly closed opened suddenly for the Irish with the shift in British attitudes. Given this, the basic Irish decision was not difficult, it being vitally important for them to avoid any action which might jeopardize their trading relations with the United Kingdom. More generally they recognized that 'if all the countries of Europe with which we are trading . . . join together in an economic union, we cannot be outside it . . . no economic future for this country if it were to be cut off by a uniform tariff applying to both agricultural and industrial projects from all our European markets'.[8] It confirmed the ending of protectionism and the need for Irish industry to adapt to new conditions, whilst hopefully providing Ireland with some compensating advantages. The pursuit of such advantages led the Irish to move from an initial preference for association to seeking full membership. Only it would provide 'a voice in the formulation of policies and ensure access on a footing of equality to a large and growing market . . . render possible recourse to sources of assistance'.[9] Moreover, participation in the Common Agricultural Policy offered assured and remunerative outlets for Irish agricultural produce, ending Irish suffering at the hands of the British cheap food policy. Agricultural considerations are important in a country where 25 per cent of the national income came from agriculture, and 36 per cent of employment.[10] It was acknowledged that 'membership on the basis only of full obligations . . . would create a critical situation',[11] but they did not seek a particularly long transitional period. The primarily economic motivation for the 1961 application was evidenced by the leading role played in the decision by the economic departments.

Political changes occurred too. Exclusion from European developments worried the Irish, whilst partition became relatively less of a live issue. Rather than it determining attitudes to other policies, it was now made to fit into the European plans of Sean Lemass. Similarly, neutrality was somewhat de-sanctified with the acknowledgement that Ireland could not be indifferent to the outcome of the struggle between communism and democracy;[12] that 'there is no neutrality and we are not neutral';[13] and that 'NATO is necessary for the defence of the countries of Western Europe, including this country'.[14] Ireland had not been invited to the conferences of the non-aligned. By 1961 integration was portrayed not as curtailing

---

[8] S. Lemass, Taoiseach, *Dail Debates* 191: 264.
[9] *European Economic Community* (Stationery Office, Dublin, Pr 6106, 1961), pp. 34–5.
[10] Chubb, op. cit., p. 327 and p. 329.
[11] S. Lemass, *Dail Debates* 191: 264.
[12] S. Lemass, *Irish Times*, 20 Aug. 1960.
[13] S. Lemass, *Dail Debates* 191: 525.
[14] S. Lemass, *ibid* 193: 4 ff.

sovereignty, but rather the sharing of sovereignty involved an 'extension of our freedom not the reverse'.[15]

The Government recognized membership would make painful adjustments necessary. Fears existed about the impact of tariff dismantlement; possible dumping; and about the ending of the Irish incentive schemes to attract industrial investment.[16] Such issues were seized upon by the opponents of entry, as were the perceived threats to Irish sovereignty and neutrality, and the concomitant threat of NATO membership. Initially, however, opposition was negligible given the perception that 'Common Market may not be all we wish, but not much choice' given the British application.[17]

A delay in the acceptance of the Irish application for negotiation caused fears that the United Kingdom might enter the Community before Ireland, resulting in a severe dislocation in Anglo-Irish trade. The Community was concerned with the Irish ability to accept all the obligations of membership, particularly given their case during the OEEC free trade negotiations, and an initial memorandum submitted by Dublin in the summer of 1961 seeking many concessions.[18] Doubts also existed concerning the genuineness of the Irish political commitment. No real negotiations took place before de Gaulle's 1963 veto, and Ireland failed to gain entry for non-Irish reasons, although there were doubts about Irish preparedness. A kite flown earlier to convince Europeans of Irish commitment, namely possible Irish membership without Britain, was quickly grounded and the emphasis upon the primordial importance of Anglo-Irish trade reasserted itself. The Government remained convinced, however, that 'the historical forces making for unity are so strong that they must eventually prevail . . . [and therefore we] will continue to plan and prepare our entry'.[19] As a reflection of this conviction, measures already planned in contemplation of free trade in the Community by 1970 were introduced; for example, two unilateral tariff reductions of 10 per cent were made in 1963–64.

An interim agreement with the Community was also sought but it was quickly concluded there was 'nothing specific Ireland could do in the existing situation to further her interests under the heading of full membership, association or an item by item agreement'.[20] Given this stalemate the Government turned to a trade agreement with Britain. The Anglo-Irish Free Trade Area which came into existence in 1966 'allowed for the

---

[15] S. Lemass, *ibid* 191: 2571 ff.
[16] Statement by Sean Lemass to Council of Ministers, Brussels 18 Jan. 1962, reproduced in *European Economic Community: Developments Subsequent to White Paper* of 30 June 1961 (Stationery Office, Dublin, Pr. 6613, 1962), pp. 63–4.
[17] Barry Desmond, *Dail Debates* 191: 596.
[18] For a review of the response of the Six, and a critique of the Irish Government's approach see G. FitzGerald, *Seanad Debates* Vol. 61, Col. 1833 ff.
[19] S. Lemass, *Dail Debates*, 199: 617 ff.
[20] F. Aiken, Minister of External Affairs, *Seanad Debates* 61: 1873 ff.

complete phasing out of the industrial tariffs over a ten-year period; Ireland, still in the mid-sixties one of the most highly protected economies in Western Europe, was to be exposed to the rigours of international competition by the mid-seventies'.[21] Membership of EFTA was also contemplated.

The Irish application for Community membership was briefly revived in 1967 following the British lead. Given the British move, the Irish again felt they had little choice, whilst by 1967 the CAP was developing in a manner very attractive to the Irish. The motivation was still primarily economic, but there was a greater awareness of the political dimensions and aspirations of the Community by 1967. It was now perceived that instead of emphasizing the concessions Ireland required, it must demonstrate positive commitment. This perception has remained influential. Even after the December 1967 failure by the Council of Ministers to agree on opening negotiations, again for non-Irish reasons, most people in Ireland continued to believe that membership was inevitable.

2. Post-Hague (December 1969): Negotiations for Entry

The Hague summit led to serious negotiations for the first time on an Irish application for EEC membership. With the Department of External Affairs playing a more central role than previously, its Minister, Dr Patrick Hillery, formally opened negotiations in June 1970.[22] Great stress was placed upon Ireland's commitment to the objectives of the Treaties of Rome and others, the development and political objectives of the Community, and upon Irish acceptance of the economic obligations of membership. Only after emphasizing this background of commitment did the Irish raise the specific points they wished to negotiate, namely:-

(a) potential problems for certain sensitive industries, protection against dumping, and the question of incentive schemes to attract industrial investment.
(b) transitional arrangements for Anglo-Irish trade, still involving 70 per cent of Irish exports and 50 per cent of Irish imports. It was essential to Ireland that this trade continue with the least possible disturbance during the transition.
(c) potential problems on plant and animal health regulations, and future arrangements for fisheries.
(d) the need for parallelism in the negotiations with each applicant and the crucial requirement of simultaneous accession. This reflected concern over proposals for a Community of Seven as an initial step towards enlargement.

---

[21] P. Keatinge, op. cit., p. 141.
[22] Details relating to the negotiations and the official view of the outcome can be found in *Keesing's Contemporary Archives* (Keynsham: Keesing's Publications Ltd.), 1971 (XVIII), pp. 24533-4 and 25205-6; *The Accession of Ireland to the European Communities* (Dublin, Stationery Office, Prl. 2064), 1972; *Bulletin of the European Communities*, Supplement 1/72, *The Enlarged Community: Outcome of the Negotiations with the applicant states*; and *The Treaty of Accession* (London: HMSO, Cmnd. 4862-1, 1972).

Most of these issues were resolved to Ireland's satisfaction during the negotiations:

(a) although the Irish had to drop their request for special tariff treatment for the jute industry, they considered the agreement on their motor assembly industry a major achievement. This allowed for the continuance for 12 years after accession of the special arrangements existing for the industry, albeit with minor modifications.

Given the small size of their home market and production units they obtained permission to use their own anti-dumping legislation in urgent cases, subject to 'post factum' approval by the European Commission. Ireland also obtained permission to continue granting export tax reliefs to new firms beginning manufacturing for export in Ireland. They had to concede that after accession the European Commission would examine the whole structure of state aids throughout the European Community, although if the reliefs went, an alternative scheme would be introduced, to be equally effective in promoting industrial development in Ireland. The Irish felt the agreement would permit Ireland to maintain an advantage over other areas of the Community until 1990.

(b) Ireland only marginally achieved a preference for a longer transitional period for industry than for agriculture, five years being agreed for industry and four and a half years for agriculture. Ireland accepted a five-year transition for Irish tariffs to the common external tariff. Five years were to pass before free movement of workers, services and capital were effected. Crucially, the Irish rights under the Anglo-Irish Free Trade Area were to continue during the transitional period.

(c) Little difficulty was experienced on agricultural issues once the transitional arrangements were agreed and assurances given regarding immediate Irish access to Community funds for agricultural finance, saving Ireland £30 million in export subsidies. Whilst not entirely satisfied with the animal and plant health arrangements, the real disquiet arose over fisheries, especially the question of equal access to the waters of EEC member states. Ultimately agreement was reached that until the end of 1982 member states would be able to restrict fishing within their waters within a six-mile limit to those who traditionally fished the waters and vessels from ports in the local geographical area. Final arrangements would reflect the objectives of the common fisheries policy and a report by the European Commission on the economic and social development of coastal areas and the state of fish stocks. The Irish felt the agreement protected 92 per cent of their national catch, and placed great hope upon the Commission report. None the less, for many, fishing arrangements were the least satisfactory of the terms.

(d) Ireland emphasized its serious social and economic imbalances of a regional nature stressing that such imbalances must be removed if a degree of harmonization consonant with Treaty objectives, particularly economic and monetary union, was to be achieved. To the Irish a major achievement was the negotiation of Protocol No. 30 of the Irish Accession Treaty whereby 'THE HIGH CONTRACTING PARTIES, DESIRING to settle certain special problems of concern to Ireland and HAVING AGREED the following provisions, RECALL that the fundamental objectives of the European Economic Community include the steady improvement of the living standards and working conditions of the peoples of the Member States, and the harmonious development of their economies by reducing the differences existing between the various regions and the backwardness of the less favoured regions; TAKE NOTE of the fact that the Irish Government has embarked upon the implementation of a policy of industrialization and economic development designed to align the standards of living in Ireland with those of the other European nations and to eliminate under-employment while progressively evening out regional differences in levels of development; RECOGNIZE it to be in their common interest that the objectives of this policy be so attained; AGREE to recommend to this end that the Community institutions implement all the means and procedures laid down by the EEC Treaty, particularly by making adequate use of the Community resources intended for the realization of the Community's above-mentioned objectives; RECOGNIZE in particular that, in the application of Articles 92 and 93 of the EEC Treaty, it will be necessary to take into account the objectives of economic expansion and the raising of the standard of living of the population.'[23]

The Irish regarded this as a commitment that Community resources would be available to assist them, particularly a far-reaching regional policy.

3. The Debate and Referendum

The Irish pro-market campaign benefited enormously from Fine Gael support. For years they had desired entry, although they might have opposed membership on the terms negotiated. Whilst criticizing the terms, especially the fishery arrangements, their overall enthusiasm meant such criticisms were muted during the referendum campaign. Fine Gael support was assured when their version of the proposed constitutional amendment was accepted by the Fianna Fáil Government. Objecting to the wide nature of the government proposal, Fine Gael's amendment limited Irish commitments to those 'necessitated by the obligations of membership'. The constitutional amendment was limited to the existing European Communities and did not

[23] *Treaty of Accession, ibid.*

authorize the transfer of power to any future Community. It was designed
partly to remove doubts concerning Irish neutrality.[24]

Pro-marketeers believed British membership meant Irish options did not
lie between the status quo and joining, but rather joining or putting in
jeopardy the special trading relationship with Britain. Moreover, membership would provide a large and assured market, with higher guaranteed
prices, for Irish agricultural products, and less dependence on the low prices
of the British market. A White Paper noted that prices paid to Irish farmers
for most major products would progressively rise to the common price levels
of the Community during the transition, with cattle, beef, milk and dairy
products (60 per cent of Irish agricultural output) benefiting in particular.
It predicted that 'on the basis of prices and costs obtaining in the Community
in 1970/71 ... the volume of gross agricultural output will increase by
about one-third by 1978 and, allowing for the higher EEC price levels, the
increase in the value of output will be over 75 per cent'.[25] It estimated that
family farm incomes would more than double, given a continued decline in
numbers. These increased incomes would benefit the whole Irish community
given the multiplier effect.

In the industrial sector the issue was less clear-cut, although pro-
marketeers believed increased unemployment would not be a problem. Since
1961 Irish industry had become more widely based, had experienced freer
trade and involvement in the Anglo-Irish Free Trade Area. Where difficulties arose, it was felt, they would probably have arisen anyway. There
would be no net redundancy. Although increased competition would pose
problems for traditional industries, the enhanced prospects for developing
export-oriented industry would more than compensate. Ireland would
become attractive to foreign investors from other Community countries and
to those outside the Community seeking an entry to its market. Total net
employment would actually increase.[26]

Whilst longer-term trends favoured entry, advocates of entry were conscious of probable short-term difficulties. One answer was foreign investment. Another revolved around the hopes attached to Protocol No. 30 and
regional policy. Stress was laid on the potential role of European Community
funds; for example, the Agricultural Guidance and the Social Funds. It was
expected the latter would provide financial assistance to help overcome
employment difficulties caused by Community membership. In addition,
safeguard provisions existed enabling the Government, with Commission
approval, to deal with problems in particular sectors.[27] A genuine expectation

[24] For the debate on the nature of the constitutional amendment see *Dail Debates* 257:
1095–1142, 1286–1555, 1720–32 and 258: 393–484, 519–621. See also, John Temple
Lang, 'Legal and Constitutional Implications for Ireland of Adhesion to the EEC Treaty',
Common Market Law Review 1972(9), pp. 167–78.
[25] *The Accession of Ireland to the European Communities*, op. cit., p. 40.
[26] *Ibid.*, pp. 49–50.
[27] *Ibid.*, p. 16.

existed of a transfer of resources from the wealthier central core of the European Community to the periphery.

It was expected that membership would aid the task of securing real independence from Britain, and end alleged British exploitation of Ireland. Whilst the Irish would lose some of their sovereignty, 'sovereignty which we have no effective power to exercise ... Britain will also lose the sovereignty she exercises at our expense'.[28] No state was really independent in the modern world, and Ireland would be foolish to cut itself off from the countries around it. Non-participation might lead to exploitation by the European Community member states, and would certainly mean the lack of an Irish voice in decisions which affected it. Ireland, it was argued, must participate in such decisions.

It was contended that membership would ease Ireland's partition by making the border less relevant. The CAP would remove major economic differences, whilst the vesting of economic power in Brussels would make the debate over government from Dublin or London less real. North and South were expected to perceive certain common interests within the Community. On the often related issue of neutrality, pro-marketeers emphasized the formal position that the Community did not involve defence. None the less it was acknowledged that 'when we become a member ... and it is intended that the unity of Europe be sought within that Community, in that circumstance we would defend Europe if the defence of Europe became necessary ... It is not a matter of our neutrality. It is a matter of defending Europe if we are part of Europe.'[29]

Pro-marketeers also had to contend with fears of land sales to foreign nationals (historically a sensitive issue), of free immigration and fears concerning the fishing industry.[30] To a certain extent the negotiated terms neutralized these fears. Control of land sales was to remain in Irish hands for at least the transitional period, whilst free movement of labour was postponed until the end of the transition. Awkward choices about fishing were to be postponed until 1982.

The Irish Council of the European Movement, having previously generated government attention and favourable predisposition towards Europe, was the umbrella organization for the pro-market campaign. It produced a number of pamphlets examining both general and specific issues e.g. land purchases, Northern Ireland, neutrality, employment and the alternatives. The campaign was well financed. Fianna Fáil and Fine Gael were both active, although the latter believed primary responsibility rested with the government party and so were less active in holding grass-root briefing

[28] G. FitzGerald, *Dail Debates* 241: 2009.
[29] Dr P. Hillery, Minister of External Affairs, *ibid.*, 246: 1372.
[30] An examination of the referendum is contained in E. Wistrich 'Referenda: The Lessons for Britain', *New Europe*, Winter 1974/5 (Vol. 3 No. 1), pp. 7–14. See also P. Keatinge, *The Formulation of Irish Foreign Policy* (Institute of Public Administration, Dublin, 1973) pp. 167–8 and 257–60.

meetings etc. The agricultural community generally favoured membership, although small farmers in the West were worried about their future. Despite some fears, industry also generally favoured entry.

Its discordant composition badly affected the anti-market campaign. Parliamentary opposition was provided by the Irish Labour Party, which campaigned against the terms negotiated and the very nature of the European Community. Previously the party had reluctantly accepted membership, believing there was no real alternative. Its 1971 annual conference, however, voted against membership, preferring associate status. This change partly reflected the affiliation of the party and the Irish Congress of Trade Unions in 1967, which gave Labour a more sectional economic pre-occupation.[31] The Common Market Study Group, launched early in 1971, included a number of republicans, intellectuals, and representatives of small farmers and small firms. The discordant component was Official and Provisional Sinn Fein. Their contribution caused the Labour Party to spend time explaining how its opposition differed from theirs.[32]

Opposing entry the Labour Party moved an amendment in the spring of 1972 to a formal government motion asking the Dáil to take note of the January 1972 White Paper. Labour sought to add 'and deplores the inadequacy of the negotiations described therein and rejects the terms set out'.[33] Fine Gael abstained on this amendment. In particular, Labour attacked what they regarded as Patrick Hillery's undertaking on Irish preparedness to enter into military commitments. This, it was argued, 'advertised the fact . . . that this Government was and are willing to accept any terms whatever in order to get into the Common Market . . . That was done very early on . . . and prejudiced the whole subsequent course of the negotiations . . . If in entering . . . we present ourselves as a doormat acquiescing in advance to anything that comes to us, we shall be treated precisely in that way.'[34] It was also claimed Ireland had tied itself too closely to the United Kingdom during the negotiations, when common cause with Norway, especially over fishing, might have been more profitable.

Opponents made much of the neutrality issue, arguing neutrality was a valuable asset not to be thrown away lightly. They pointed to the Swedish decision to negotiate a trade agreement rather than seek membership, and the non-participation of Austria and Finland. Anti-marketeers wished Ireland to return to its position at the United Nations in the late 1950s and early 1960s. They complained that whilst Ireland might retain the legal right to avoid participation in future Community defence arrangements, it would have lost the real power to say no, given its economic commitment.

[31] P. Keatinge, *The Formulation of Irish Foreign Policy*, ibid., pp. 276–7.
[32] As Conor Cruise O'Brien expressed it, 'I disliked our "allies" more than I disliked even either set of adversaries'. See Conor Cruise O'Brien, *States of Ireland* (Hutchinson, London, 1972), p. 292.
[33] *Dail Debates* 259: 1926.
[34] *Ibid.*, 259: 2206.

Indeed, Ireland would suffer a diminution of power to decide anything.

The possibility of the subordination of the Irish economy to Brussels and multinational corporations provoked concern, partly because of Irish history and partly because of the alleged disastrous economic effects of membership. The fact that the Community was 'slavishly based on the principles of free trade. Its rules are designed to achieve the allocation of labour and capital through the operation of market forces'[35] would create problems for traditional Irish industries. The Labour Party claimed to accept the principle of European unity 'but not on the basis of a capitalist free-for-all untempered by even a modicum of planning'.[36] Anti-marketeers did not believe that the promised new employment opportunities would materialize, since all previous government planning forecasts had 'consistently envisaged increases in the total work force, which has in fact declined in all cases'.[37] They were also sceptical about the prospect of redistribution, highlighting the absence of adequate regional and social policies. Pro-Europeans were guilty of a basic error of judgement in seeing the Community 'as in some way a philanthropic body . . . The leopard of capitalism has not changed its spots . . . it has not suddenly become benevolent, altruistic.'[38]

A Common Market Study Group analysis disputed the alleged agricultural gains to be made from EEC membership. It argued that agricultural output could fall and that the Mansholt Plan and other factors might reduce agricultural employment by 66 per cent in 1980 compared to what would otherwise have been the case. The rate of decline in the agricultural population would not slow, and employment in agriculture-related industries would also fall, adding to the problems caused by increasing unemployment in other sectors. It argued that the gap between EEC and world prices would narrow anyway. Any benefits from membership would go predominantly to the richer, larger farmers.[39] The Mansholt Plan, in any case, worried the small farmers of the West with its emphasis on reducing farmland acreage, guaranteed prices and markets, whilst encouraging movement off the land and increasing the average size of landholdings. The recurring Irish nightmare of emigration and rural depopulation, and the spectre of being a peripheral area of the Community were powerful arguments in the anti-marketeers' campaign. To small farmers in the West and the potentially unemployed, the portrayal of the Community as a rich man's club appeared to contain an element of truth.

---

[35] Labour Party Annual Conference, Galway, 1971; see *Ireland and the European Community: The Labour Party European Elections 1979 Policy Statements* (The Labour Party, Dublin, 1979), pp. 11–12.
[36] loc. cit.
[37] R. Crotty, *Ireland and the Common Market: An Economic Analysis of the Effects of Membership* (Common Market Study Group, Dublin, 1971), p. 42. This contains a thorough-going critique of the economic arguments for Irish entry.
[38] Justin Keating, *Dail Debates* 248: 687.
[39] Crotty, op. cit., pp. 1–29.

Anti-marketeers questioned the fiction that membership would in some way end partition. Given the above, plus an increased cost of living, fear of immigration, the land sales and fisheries problems, it was argued that the price of membership was too great for any of the benefits involved. Alternatives were not only available but even preferable given the damage membership would do the Irish economy and sovereignty. Anti-marketeers believed Ireland could negotiate a trade agreement with the Community, given the Swedish and other precedents, and that alternative markets were available for Irish agricultural output. In addition, Britain could insist on continued access to their market for Irish exports. Outside the Community, Ireland would control its fisheries and would be free to take appropriate measures to develop the Irish economy. Hard work might be necessary but alternatives existed which allowed Ireland to control its own destiny.

More extreme opponents focused on emotional calls not to 'let your children fight side by side with the British paras in NATO',[40] this a few weeks after 'Bloody Sunday' in Londonderry, and put up posters picturing gangster-faced cigar-smoking Germans proclaiming, 'I want your daughter in the Ruhr'.[41]

The disparate anti-market elements found it difficult to establish a comparable umbrella organization to the Irish Council of the European Movement, although in an effort to mobilize all elements of opposition the Common Market Study Group launched in July 1971 the Common Market Defence Campaign. It produced pamphlets on the economic consequences of membership, the alternatives, prices, agriculture and sovereignty, etc. Other publications were issued by trade unions, the Labour Party and both wings of Sinn Fein. The campaign suffered from a lack of finance and organization. Labour's efforts were somewhat muted, although it provided a certain legitimacy to the anti-market campaign, in addition to some articulate speakers. The campaign was damaged by the irredentist issue, and tarred with the IRA brush.

The Irish people found many reasons for voting 'Yes' on 10 May 1972. Although 'The vote has variously been interpreted as a massive rejection of the IRA physical force movement, a turning away from autarkic Gaelic nationalism, and as an acceptance of European perspectives. Perhaps it is better interpreted as a reflection of not only the economic, but also the political facts of life in Irish society.'[42] All constituencies voted heavily in favour. The north and west generally having a higher *Yes* vote than the east and Dublin. Much of the *No* vote came from Labour supporters. In a turnout of 71 per cent, high for an Irish referendum, 83 per cent (1,041,880) voted *Yes* and 17 per cent (211,888) *No*.

[40] Quoted by Michael O'Higgins, *Seanad Debates*, 72: 799.
[41] Quoted by E. Wistrich, op. cit., p. 12.
[42] Tom Garvin and Anthony Parker, 'Party Loyalty and Irish Voters: The EEC Referendum as a Case-Study', *Economic and Social Review*, Oct. 1972 (Vol. 4. No. 1), pp. 35-9.

4. Irish Attitudes within the Community

(A) POLITICAL ASPECTS

Ironically having pursued Irish entry into the European Community for over a decade, the Fianna Fáil Government lost a general election weeks after entry, although the Community was not an election issue. The incoming Coalition Government comprised Fine Gael and Labour, who had fought on opposite sides during the referendum campaign. Labour, however, had accepted the referendum result as decisive. Deciding Irish entry must be wholehearted, it dropped its outright opposition, becoming a constructive critic, seeking to improve the Community and promote Irish interests. Garret FitzGerald of Fine Gael, a committed European of long standing, was appointed Minister of Foreign Affairs. This ensured that the coalition would be at least as pro-European as the previous government. Until the end of the first Irish presidency of the Council in June 1975, FitzGerald set the tone and style of the Coalition's European policy, enthusiastic and *communautaire*. Although, even initially, a certain duality was evident in the Irish approach to the Community.

This stemmed from the tension between maximizing specifically Irish interests and support for Community solutions and objectives. Initially, this tension was obscured as being *communautaire* for the most part happily coincided with Irish interests. The Irish perceived that 'If it's a real Community with solidarity, then the regions will have to be brought up to the level of everywhere else, and that requires massive transfer of resources . . . Ireland cannot lose by sticking to ideals – the worst share-out will give you more than you put in . . . we don't have to keep asking for money if we get the principle of solidarity applied.'[43] Moreover, given that Ireland would be 'to a remarkable degree a net beneficiary of Community policies . . . Ireland must be careful not to appear too much in the role of constant "demandeur" . . . Ireland must seek to compensate for this by playing a positive and constructive role in the present running and future development of the Community.'[44] This role would be expressed by support for Community-orientated institutions and policies. Happily, these would, in themselves, safeguard and advance the interests of a small member, such as Ireland. If Community and Irish interests were, however, to clash, the Irish would, and did, pursue the latter.

The duality in the Irish approach was reflected in their attitudes to:-

[43] Dr P. Hillery, Ireland's first Commissioner, in an interview in the *Irish Times*, 13 Nov. 1973.
[44] Dr Garret FitzGerald in a very important speech, 'Irish Foreign Policy within the Context of the EEC', to the Royal Irish Academy, 10 Nov. 1975. In this speech Dr FitzGerald outlined his approach to the Community.

(i) The European Commission:

As early as May 1973 FitzGerald expressed concern about the increasing 'politicisation of the Commission along national lines'.[45] The Irish objected to this, perceiving that the Commission's exclusive power of initiative, so crucial to the small states, depended upon the degree of independence the Commission enjoyed *vis à vis* member states. To make Commissioners less dependent upon national governments, the Irish in 1975 proposed enhancing the powers of the President-Designate of the Commission to allow him to propose other members of the Commission, and making the Commission genuinely responsible to the European Parliament.

Yet Coalition ministers launched major attacks on the independence and integrity of the Commission when it refused to meet specifically Irish interests, such as the request for a derogation from the equal pay directive in 1976. This refusal, in fact, involved the Commission, in a modest way, displaying the very independence enjoined upon it by the Irish. In addition, the choice of the Irish Commissioner, Richard Burke, in 1976 reflected more concern with loyalty to the Taoiseach, ideology and political patronage than with the Community. As Liam Cosgrave noted 'There is no Fianna Fáil applicant anyway.'[46]

(ii) The European Parliament:

Initially Ireland worked to increase the powers of the European Parliament. Supporting direct elections as desirable in their own right, the Irish believed that the consequent greater authority of the Parliament would justify transferring greater powers to it. None the less they held up agreement on direct elections over the issue of the number of Irish seats, believing the proportion should remain as negotiated before entry and that Ireland would be hard-pressed to man important committees adequately if that proportion was reduced. More recently, a certain wariness regarding increasing Parliament's powers has been evident from Fianna Fáil. There is concern at the possibility of the Parliament being dominated by urban considerations, and hostility to the CAP. Fianna Fáil argued in 1979 that 'to grant the Assembly wide-ranging legislative power, as Fine Gael suggest, would be to rob us of the means to pursue our vital national interest in the Community. We can ill-afford to have a crucial matter of national interest decided by a Parliament where Ireland would only have . . . 15 members out of 410.'[47] Fianna Fáil are, of course, allied with the Gaullists in the European Progressive Democrat grouping within the Parliament.

[45] This was contained in his first policy statement to the Dail as Minister. *Dail Debates* 265: 742–70.
[46] Quoted in *The Irish Times*, 24 Nov. 1976.
[47] *Irish Times*, 22 Jan. 1979.

(iii) The unanimity principle:

Garret FitzGerald believed that 'the interests of Ireland are best served by minimizing the use of the unanimity principle and, by extending the range of decisions taken by majority vote'.[48] Belief in the veto assumed that Irish interests were best served by stopping decisions rather than moving to a system facilitating decisions and preventing obstruction by one other country. In fact, Ireland was more likely to suffer through the use of the veto by others, for example, by a veto on raising agricultural prices. In any case, he argued, it is harder for a small country to use the veto. A veto should, FitzGerald believed, only be used in the interests of national survival. During the first Irish Presidency he built upon the December 1974 Paris Summit decision to lessen the dependence upon unanimity.

None the less, in practice the Irish recognized the need to retain and use the veto. Most importantly they threatened to veto the 1974 Paris Summit unless guaranteed that there would be progress on the regional fund. The veto was brought into play by both governments during the negotiations on a common fisheries policy. Essentially, the Irish position has become that of not advocating change until Ireland was convinced 'majority voting will promote our interests and Community interests'.[49]

More generally on political questions, Ireland has been concerned at the tendency of France and Germany, and other larger countries, to attempt to decide matters amongst themselves. This concern surfaced, for example, when they felt inadequately briefed in advance of the Bremen European Council in 1978 on Franco-German plans for a European Monetary System. They objected to suggestions of a two-tier Community, and to the lack of specifically Community representation at the international economic summits. The Irish fear the emergence of a directory which would undermine the Commission's right of initiative. Ireland played a part in securing Community participation in economic summits. Its pique at the larger states' behaviour led to an abortive attempt to develop a small nation action group which would stand together against the larger states' inclination to take action on an anti-Community basis and to offer a measure of protection against the politics of scale. The Irish have increasingly accepted bilateralism as an accepted part of Community negotiations, if Ireland is involved. For example, in the winter of 1977–78, Ireland concluded a bilateral agreement with the French over access to the Paris sheep market in defiance of the wishes of the Commission.

In attitudes to enlargement, external relations and political co-operation, Ireland has generally been Community-minded. Enlargement is supported, provided that there is a *pro rata* increase in the Community's financial resources, adequate resource transfers to Ireland, and improved Community

---

[48] Speech to Royal Irish Academy, op. cit.
[49] Michael O'Kennedy, *Dail Debates* 269: 698 ff.

decision-making mechanisms, i.e. that existing members, particularly Ireland did not suffer as a result. The Irish believe their past experience and state of development helped ease the negotiations leading to the Lomé Convention. Irish neutrality, anti-colonialism, and attitudes to disarmament are seen as making a special contribution to Community political co-operation. This involves pressure on the more 'conservative' countries to adopt a more 'progressive' stance, and shifting the centre of gravity of the Nine in a 'progressive' direction. The Irish have breached Community solidarity in political co-operation. Particularly marked was the refusal to withdraw their ambassador from Madrid in protest against the execution of Basque separatists. Coming immediately after the successful first Irish Presidency of the Council, it caused comparisons to be made between Irish calls for solidarity with respect to redistribution within the Community and its refusal to show solidarity with its partners with respect to conditions in Spain. Ireland has also deviated from Community positions at the United Nations, particularly on decolonization and southern Africa.[50]

Since 1973 Fianna Fáil have been less enthusiastic about the Community than Fine Gael. Both major Irish parties in opposition focused upon apparent weaknesses in the handling of negotiations and apparent lack of success in certain policy areas. Fianna Fail's more guarded approach has been evident after their return to power in 1977, with a slightly more nationalistic emphasis and greater firmness. None the less, the difference between the two parties when in government should not be exaggerated, since the Coalition was less enthusiastic in practice than in rhetoric, particularly after the end of the first Irish Presidency in June 1975. Having proved Irish loyalty, commitment and distinctiveness from perfidious Albion, more nationalistic orientations came to the fore, and the *communautaire* approach was less in evidence. Governments of all parties acted within the same broad parameters. Despite changes of government, there has been an Irish approach to the Community.

(B) ECONOMIC ASPECTS·

Ireland's attitude to the economic aspects of integration was revealed in the 1957 OEEC negotiations, when the Irish sought the inclusion of agriculture and aid for the economically weak and developing. Although since 1957 the Irish economy has been transformed, these concerns have persisted. The extent of Ireland's clear financial gain from membership is demonstrated in Tables 8.1, 8.2, and 8.3.

[50] See, for example, Rosemary Foot, 'The European Community's Voting Behaviour at the United Nations General Assembly', *Journal of Common Market Studies*, June 1979 (Vol. XVII, No. 4), pp. 350–60.

Table 8.1 Ireland's receipts from, and payment to, the European Community during the period 1973 to 1977

	1973	1974	1975	1976	1977
(a) *Receipts by way of grants and subsidies*	£m	£m	£m	£m	£m
EAGGF – Guarantee Section	36.6	63.8	104.3	102.0[1]	244.5[1]
Guidance Section	—	—	0.4	3.0	7.3
European Social Fund	—	3.6	4.0	4.6	8.2
European Regional Development Fund	—	—	1.8	8.5	8.5
Regional studies jointly financed by Ireland and the Communities					
Pilot projects and studies to combat poverty					
Research and Investment projects	—	0.2	0.4	0.5	1.1[2]
Projects in the hydrocarbons sector					
Monies for miscellaneous surveys and studies carried out by Irish agencies for the Commission					
Total[3]	36.6	67.6	110.9	118.6	269.6
(b) *Payments to the European Communities and other contributions arising as a result of membership*	£m	£m	£m	£m	£m
Contribution to the budget of the European Communities	5.3	6.7	9.8	13.4	22.1
Contribution to the EIB	0.8	0.8	0.4	0.2	0.2
Contribution to the ECSC					
Contribution to Euratom research programmes	—	0.3	0.5	1.3	1.6
Miscellaneous contributions					
Total	6.1	7.8	10.7	14.9	23.9
Net receipts [4], i.e. differences between Totals at (a) and (b)	30.5	59.8	100.2	103.7	245.7

Notes

[1] Receipts under the Guarantee Section include amounts of £24m in 1976 and £128m in 1977 for the UK and Italian MCA import subsidies which have been administered by Ireland in respect of Irish exports to the UK and Italy since 17 May 1976.

[2] This figure includes £0.59m in respect of amounts approved for projects relating to hydrocarbons and uranium in 1977.

[3] In addition to the receipts figures shown in the table, receipts also arise as a result of Community regulations on social security for migrant workers. Ireland's receipts under this heading were £1.5m in 1973, £1.3m in 1974, £2.0m in 1975, £2.2m in 1976 and £3.3m in 1977.

[4] This refers to money actually received. Receipts in some areas may not be obtained until several years after the commitment of expenditure.

Source: European Parliament Directorate-General for Research and Documentation (PE 43.006/rev.), *The effects on Ireland of Membership of the European Communities* (June 1979), p.23.

Table 8.2 Irish net receipts from Community (minus MCA subsidies paid to Ireland for agricultural exports to the United Kingdom and Italy)

1973:   £30.5m
1974:   £59.8m
1975:   £100.2m
1976:   £79.7m
1977:   £117.7m

Source: Ibid, p. 24.

Table 8.3 Community loans to Ireland, 1973–77

£m	1973	1974	1975	1976	1977
EIB	11.1	24.8	22.0	35.4	52.1
ECSC	0.2	–	1.2	–	–
Community loans	–	–	–	156.0	–
Total	11.3	24.8	23.2	191.4	52.1

Source: Ibid., p. 25.

Aid granted by the Community 'represents 6–7 per cent of the Irish current expenditure budget, after deduction of the MCA subsidies paid to Ireland for exports to the United Kingdom and Italy. It is about 11 per cent if MCAs are included.'[51] None the less, the Irish have been severely disappointed by the poor level of redistribution achieved by the Regional and Social Funds, and the Community's failure to live up to the Treaty obligations and Protocol No. 30. In the EMS debate, Ireland sought to convince the Community that resource transfers for 1976 to Ireland only amounted to a staggeringly low 0.3 per cent of Irish GDP. This figure was arrived at by excluding most of the CAP payments. The Irish argued any redistribution achieved by the price support function was largely by chance and should be ignored. They also complained that the relative impoverishment of the less prosperous member countries had increased. In 1970, for example, Irish per capita GNP was 54 per cent of the Community average, but only 48 per cent in 1975.[52] With the emergence of the economic crisis of the 1970s and the inadequate Community response, the Irish complained bitterly that they had given up substantial economic powers to the European Community, and yet those powers were not being effectively used for the

[51] European Parliament Directorate-General for Research and Documentation (PE 43.006/rev.), *The Effects on Ireland of Membership of the European Communities* (June 1979), p. 25.
[52] Michael O'Kennedy, Minister of Foreign Affairs, in a speech 7 Jan. 1978, to Athlone Fianna Fail Comhairle Ceanntair.

Community benefit. Protectionism had been given up, but the Community's *laissez-faire* approach meant it did not act firmly enough to defend its members. Irish disappointment has been all the more severe since redistribution was one of the juicier carrots held out during the referendum campaign. Ireland has been upset that greater emphasis has not been placed upon the areas of greatest need.

The Irish have found Council of Minister cuts in Commission proposals with respect to the Social Fund 'absolutely incomprehensible', believing the resources allocated to be totally inadequate.[53] Given their dissatisfaction with these policies, with unemployment rising to 12 per cent during the recession and job creation in the first five years achieving only 5 per cent of target, the Irish have sought a Community employment fund. From an Irish perspective the problem with the Community budget is not the size of CAP but rather the inadequacy of industrial, regional and social policies.

The potential gains for Irish agriculture were the major positive economic argument in favour of Irish Community membership. Not surprisingly Ireland has consistently opposed any tampering with the principles of CAP. They have resisted proposals to shift the burden of financing agriculture on to national governments or to the producers of surplus commodities. In the first six years of membership Irish agriculture received a total of £20 million from FEOGA Guidance Section, and £600 million from the Guarantee Section (excluding MCAs). The significance of these amounts emerges by comparison with the receipts from other policies. Irish farmers have also benefited from increased price levels and better market access. Virtually every sector of Irish agriculture has benefited, although some more than others. The transformation of Irish agriculture from being generally weak and backward to becoming dynamic and forward-looking can be attributed primarily to Community membership.[54] The whole economy has benefited from this transformation, although the rapid rise in prosperity for the farmers has not been achieved without social strains appearing, particularly in the area of taxation.

Attitudes to redistribution and CAP heavily influenced the Irish approach to both EMS and EMU. They clearly perceived that the CAP gains for Ireland had 'been put at risk by the economic divergences and consequent monetary chaos of the last few years . . . We must be prepared to contribute to the restoration of order in the economic and monetary affairs of the Community, even if this creates some temporary difficulties for us – because the cost to us of failure in this matter would be so great.'[55] Ireland also

[53] Richie Ryan, Minister of Finance, *Irish Times*, 30 Sept. 1975.
[54] The transformation and its impact are discussed in E. Attwood, 'New Prosperity for Irish Farming', *Ireland Today*, 15 July 1979 (No. 954), pp. 6–7. See also E. Attwood, 'The Consequences of Participation in the CAP to the Irish Economy', in M. Whitby (ed.), *The Net Cost and Benefit of EEC Membership* (Wye College, Ashford, 1979), pp. 47–64.
[55] FitzGerald speech 8 Apr. 1976 to Seminar on Regional Development in Letterkenny.

perceived a linkage between moves towards EMU and the development of comprehensive regional and social policies. Initially the Irish thought this linkage was widely accepted and were caught somewhat off balance when this proved not to be the case in the EMS negotiations in the autumn of 1978. Irish support for EMS was conditional upon Community policies being applied with due regard to the different impact between central and peripheral regions. They proposed a series of measures designed to strengthen the economies of the less prosperous participants within the proposed EMS. Ireland sought up to £650 million in extra aid over five years to soften the blow of participation, with more being necessary if the United Kingdom did not participate. A problem was the general expectation, which proved erroneous in 1979, that Irish participation in EMS would lead to a revaluation of the punt against the pound, affecting Irish exports to the United Kingdom. The actual performance of the punt against the pound was a blow to Irish pride, particularly since breaking the link with sterling had a profound nationalist dimension. It had been seen as marking the real assertion of Irish independence from Britain. The euphoria was also punctured by the confusion arising over the terms offered to Ireland at the Brussels European Council in December 1978 to induce her to participate in the EMS. A general feeling developed that Ireland had been let down, and had been led to expect too much, either by its own leaders or by some of its continental partners.

The attempt to create a common fisheries policy has caused the Irish further disquiet. On this issue Ireland has faced a real test of its attitude to the Community, for, on fisheries, the obligations of membership began to hit home. On this issue Ireland, on occasion, has been more isolated than on any other. Three of its Community partners (France, the Netherlands, and West Germany) made diplomatic protests, it upset its closest allies, and was taken to the European Court of Justice for failing to fulfil its obligations under the Rome Treaty. These events followed the Irish introduction of interim unilateral measures for fish conservation in the spring of 1977, and the arrest of 10 Dutch skippers. The Court decided the measures were discriminatory. The fisheries issue showed the Irish were capable of great jingoism when they perceived their interests to be threatened. It marked a sad end to the Fine Gael and Labour Coalition's European policy and saw an almost xenophobic campaign in the country by Fianna Fáil and the Irish Fishermen's Organisation. In the country at large, indignation was rife that the Community should expect access to an Irish resource, with no apparent appreciation of Irish pursuit of access to the resources of others for years!

The fisheries issue illustrated that the limits of Irish enthusiasm for the Community were narrower than the rhetoric sometimes suggested. On occasion, there has been a reluctance to face up to the responsibilities and obligations of membership. The real Irish position with regard to the Community was expressed by Garret FitzGerald at a party conference in

1975. 'At times . . . the Community appears a cockpit of infighting . . . it is our job to make sure that when such infighting occurs, we are in there with the best, defending our national interest. But it should never be overlooked that these conflicts of national interest are always resolved within an overall framework of European solidarity.'[56] It is this balance which the Irish themselves have tried to achieve and maintain, with their performance reflecting concern for both national and Community interests.

5. The Community and the Furtherance of Irish Interests

Given the level of economic development in Ireland, the Irish have sought special consideration on a number of issues. They have stressed the need for redistributive policies; special loans under the EMS; growth in the Irish fishing industry; and the implementation of Protocol No. 30. In addition, they have been staunch defenders of the CAP. Underlying these specific issues, however, more basic concerns of the Irish can be identified.

(A) THE BRITISH CONNECTION

The former unequal bilateral relationship with Britain has been transformed within the multilateral Community context. This context makes it somewhat easier for the Irish to defend their interests *vis-à-vis* Britain. Prior to 1973, the Irish perceived that any trade agreement with Britain was bound to be to Ireland's disadvantage. Post 1973 they have been able, in the field of agriculture, for example, with the support of others, to resist attempts to change the system to their disadvantage.

Irish dependence upon Britain has been reduced. Between 1972 and 1978 the proportion of Irish exports going to the British market fell from 61 per cent to 47 per cent, and Irish trade with Britain declined from 55 per cent to 48 per cent of total Irish trade.[57] The proportion of imports from the United Kingdom has remained steady. Increasingly divergences in economic interests have emerged, as evidenced by Irish attitudes to British renegotiation in 1974–75, and EMS. It is a measure of the impact of Community membership that by 1975 there was a general feeling that Ireland should attempt to stay in whatever Britain did, although they hoped fervently the question would not arise. Prior to 1973 few had suggested membership without Britain but by 1975 there was almost equal unanimity the other way. The importance of this reaction should not be underestimated. It was one thing to argue during the referendum campaign that EEC membership offered the best chance of lessening economic dependence upon Britain and quite another to contemplate a trade barrier between Ireland and Britain,

[56] G. FitzGerald, Fine Gael Ard Fheis, Mar. 1975.
[57] *The Effects on Ireland of Membership of the European Communities* (1979), op. cit., pp. 129–31.

particularly since avoidance of such a barrier was a major argument for entry. The emergence from the British shadow was critically important to the Irish.

(B) ECONOMIC INDEPENDENCE AND DEVELOPMENT

It is arguable that participation in EMS marked the final stage of the Irish independence struggle. In addition, Community membership has contributed significantly to the economic growth, development and well-being of the country. Agriculture has played a crucial role in this progress, the 1970s being a momentous decade for that sector. Better prices and markets generated confidence and prosperity. Between 1970 and 1978 farm output increased 35 per cent in volume, and farm incomes by 75 per cent in real terms.[58] The multiplier effect has brought prosperity to other areas. Since 1972 the rate of economic progress has shown a marked acceleration, with annual growth (in real terms) of 3 per cent. In both 1977 and 1978 Ireland had the fastest growth in the Community.

Despite such progress, the beneficial impact of membership has not been readily appreciated by the Irish people, because it has been obscured by the world economic crisis. Moreover, specific problems and issues have attracted a good deal of attention, for example, the problems of a number of older, traditional industries leading to redundancies. It sometimes appears that the Community does least for those most adversely affected by the consequences of membership. There is little overt recognition that several of these difficulties would have arisen with or without membership. Overall, however, membership has led to great strides in Irish economic independence and development.

(C) IDENTITY

The Irish have long been sensitive to the apparent lack of awareness by foreigners of Irish independence and distinctiveness from the United Kingdom. Since 1973, to dispel any remaining doubts about Ireland being a British satellite, they have self-consciously emphasized the distinctions between their attitudes to the Community and those of Britain. This has been reflected in both their general approach and rhetoric towards the Community and in specific policy areas, such as CAP and EMS.

In addition, Community membership and participation in political co-operation have enormously widened the range of Irish concerns. For example, within two years of membership, Ireland had opened five new embassies, to take the total to 26, whilst there were 14 new non-resident accreditations. The Irish have become involved with the ACP countries, the Euro-Arab dialogue and have, of course, represented the Community when holding the Presidency of the Council. Some have argued Ireland now has

[58] E. Attwood, *Ireland Today*, op. cit., p. 6.

less influence and a less separate identity since involvement in political co-operation eroded its non-aligned position. Irish governments believe, how-ever, that Irish influence has been enhanced, arguing Ireland now has opportunities to press its views more widely and meaningfully than was possible for a small country acting in isolation. Ireland's special contribution, resulting from Irish history, under-development and non-alignment, is seen as enhancing Irish prestige and as modifying the image of Ireland generated by a decade of strife in Ulster. For a comparatively young state 'identity' is important and the Irish are conscious of it.

(D) THE QUESTION OF ULSTER AND A UNITED IRELAND

'The national territory consists of the whole island of Ireland, its islands and the territorial seas.'[59] The effort to give meaning to this article of the Irish Constitution is perceived by many as *the* national interest. The Irish Government has claimed the 'right to speak in relation to events that happen throughout the whole country'.[60] Several debates in the European Parliament have been enlivened by Anglo-Irish disputes over this claimed right. After the first direct elections to the European Parliament, Neil Blaney, an Independent MEP, tried to get all 18 MEPs from the island to meet informally and to work together in the interests of the whole country. Although this attempt failed, there are frequent references in the south to the '18 Irish MEPs'. Dublin welcomed the fact that all the people of Ireland elected their representatives to the European Parliament on the same day, using the same electoral system.

The Irish Government has long advanced the view that 'there is an essential community of interests on the island', particularly given the importance of agriculture to both economies. For example, with respect to Community agricultural prices negotiations, Irish ministers have argued that 'the attitude of the Irish representatives in Brussels more closely reflects the interests of Northern farmers than British representatives can'.[61] Michael O'Kennedy believed the same was true with respect to regional policy and aspects of the Community's external trade policy, particularly textile imports. The Irish Government believes that, 'In the long-term, economic interests determine the actions of States and, while at the moment other interests will be uppermost in Northern Ireland minds, these economic considerations will determine things',[62] this process being aided by Irish economic development.

In the short-term there has been an effort to involve the Community in the problem. Addressing the European Parliament in June 1979, the Irish

---

[59] The famous Article 2 of *Bunreacht Na hEireann* (Constitution of Ireland).
[60] J. Lynch in BBC interview, 1 Mar. 1971.
[61] Michael O'Kennedy speech, 15 Nov. 1977.
[62] G. FitzGerald, 30 May 1978, *Irish Times*.

Prime Minister, Jack Lynch observed that, 'For as long as conflict and confrontation remain in any part of the countries that comprise the Community, so long will our hopes and ideals be overshadowed.'[63] He asked members 'to combine in a common effort to remove the causes of division and to support measures for the advancement of peace and harmony in places where these most essential of qualities do not exist ... must never forget that it was to avoid the recurrence of bloodshed and devastation that the Community [was] ... devised'.[64]

Ireland has also sought to take advantage of that feature of the regional policy which allows special aid for projects in border areas whose economies are disrupted by frontiers. Although they have been somewhat frustrated by British recalcitrance on the issue, some cross-border studies and projects have been undertaken.

The effort to lessen significance of the border has suffered, however, with the emergence of two separately valued currencies on the island, which resulted from Irish participation in EMS and the break of the link with sterling. In the short-term this has further entrenched the border, particularly given the devaluation of the punt relative to sterling. The Irish Government, however, believes that in the long-term the break with an ailing, declining British economy will further the most basic of Irish concerns, especially if the southern economy continues to develop rapidly.

6. Opposition to Membership

Despite having grown since 1972, opposition to Community membership is not significant in Ireland. The real debate is not between opponents and supporters of Community membership, but concerns the most appropriate methods of pursuing and maximizing Irish interests and benefits. Parliamentary opposition parties have sought to outbid the incumbent governments as the real champions of Irish interests, bemoaning government handling of specific negotiations. Criticism rather than opposition characterizes the attitude of the three major parties. Most criticism has come from Labour, which has maintained that its 1972 forecasts were closer to the mark than the 'alluring prospect, held out by Fianna Fáil, of tens of thousands of extra jobs and stable prices'.[65] In particular, it has complained that the Nine have failed to respond as a Community to the employment crisis. Leading trade unionists have also focused on this crisis, believing that the doctrinaire, free enterprise basis of the Treaty of Rome is inadequate to deal with the social and economic problems faced by the EEC's 40 million trade unionists, and especially with some seven million unemployed in the Community as a whole. Moreover, given the *laissez-faire* economic ethos of the Community,

[63] J. Lynch, Statements and Speeches 9/79, *Ireland Today*, 1 Sept. 1979 (No. 955).
[64] loc. cit.
[65] *Labour Party, Ireland and the European Community*, op. cit., p. 12.

the hopes of redistribution and the harmonious development of regions were 'at best a piece of romantic nonsense'.[66] Increased prices, unequal benefits to rural and urban areas, attacks on Irish fisheries, the apparent threat to Irish neutrality and the apparent lack of concern for the small and weak have all come under attack. Such criticisms are not confined to Labour and trade union circles, although other critics use different phraseology. In the Irish parliamentary parties there is no question of withdrawal or even of less than whole-hearted membership, but rather a genuine desire to be constructive and to bring about changes to the benefit of both Ireland and the Community.

Outright opposition to membership is expressed by the Irish Sovereignty Movement, socialist groups and Provisional Sinn Fein, all of which are numerically small. The ISM is an outgrowth of the Common Market Study Group. After the referendum defeat, many of those opposed to membership transformed themselves into this new nationalist and radical ginger group. They have asked 'Where are the benefits?' They claim increased prices and unemployment are a result of membership, and that the Community offers nothing to the urban working man. Essentially, ISM seeks to defend Irish neutrality and sovereignty and to retain powers to shape the Irish economy and politics to maximize the public welfare. They believe that the larger Community countries want the advantages of open trading relationships but none of the responsibilities. Rather than entry into EMS being a sign of independence, it merely meant subordination to West Germany. The ISM argues it is not necessary to accept the defeatism implied by Community membership. Several small European states have managed to go their own way, securing trade agreements with the EEC while upholding their national independence and neutrality. ISM sought an abstentionist policy regarding the first direct elections to the European Parliament, believing participation would encourage the myth that the Common Market could be fundamentally democratized and reformed. This plea was unsuccessful, as the turnout in June 1979 was 63.6 per cent. Whilst not high by Irish standards, it was the fourth highest in the Community overall.

Provisional Sinn Fein also abstained from the direct elections. They, too, have focused upon sovereignty and neutrality, in addition to attacking the capitalist nature of the EEC, the theft of Irish mineral wealth and fish, and phasing out small farms. Others of a republican predisposition took solace from the fact that on 7 June 1979, for the first time since 1918, all Irishmen voted for the same parliament.

7. Conclusions

Despite particular problems, the critics and opponents, Ireland has benefited enormously from Community membership. The delay in gaining entry

[66] J. Keating, 24 July 1975, *Irish Times*.

between 1961 and 1973 in the long-run proved to be to Ireland's advantage. By 1973 it was better prepared to cope with the problems membership brought and to take advantage of the opportunities it offered. For some, the 1970s were a bonanza. Ireland has changed considerably since the depression of the late fifties, and few question the correctness of the referendum decision. Towards the end of 1979, however, a certain apprehension developed about the future, particularly with respect to the outlook for CAP and Irish agriculture, the centre-pieces of Irish membership. The end of the decade also saw the disappointing second Irish Presidency of the Council, which fizzled out in some disarray with the changes in the Fianna Fáil leadership at the end of 1979.

Although slightly apprehensive about the 1980s, there is little doubt the Irish would rather face the future within the Community than without.

FURTHER READING

Brigid Burns and Trevor C. Salmon, 'Policy-making coordination in Ireland on European Community questions', *Journal of Common Market Studies*, June 1977, pp. 272–87.

J. Cooney, *EEC in Crisis* (Dublin University Press, Dublin, 1979).

A. Coughlan, *The Common Market: Why Ireland should not join* (Common Market Study Group, Dublin, 1970).

R. Crotty, *Ireland and the Common Market* (Common Market Study Group, Dublin, 1971).

B. Dowling and J. Durkan (eds.), *Irish Economic Policy* (Economic and Social Research Institute, Dublin, 1978).

Patrick Keatinge, *The formulation of Irish foreign policy* (Institute of Public Administration, Dublin, 1973).

Patrick Keatinge, *A Place among Nations: Issues in Irish Foreign Policy* (Institute of Public Administration, Dublin, 1978).

Patrick Keatinge, 'Odd man out? Irish neutrality and European security', *International Affairs*, July 1972, pp. 438–49.

Patrick Keatinge, 'Foreign Policy of the Irish Coalition Government', *The World Today*, August 1973, pp. 343–51.

D. McAleese, 'Ireland in the Enlarged EEC: Economic Consequences and Prospects', in J. Vaisez (ed.)., *Economic Sovereignty and Regional Policy* (Gill and Macmillan, Dublin, 1975).

E. Moxon-Browne, 'Ireland in the EEC', *The World Today*, Oct. 1975, pp. 424–32.

E. Moxon-Browne, 'The relationship between the Irish Parliament and the European Parliament: 1973–77', in V. Hermann and R. van Schendelen (eds.), *The European Parliament and the national parliaments* (Saxon House, Farnborough, 1979).

Conor Cruise O'Brien, 'Ireland in International Affairs', in O. Dudley Edwards (ed.), *Conor Cruise O'Brien Introduces Ireland* (Deutsch, London, 1969).

Mary T. Robinson, 'Irish Parliamentary Scrutiny of European Community Legislation', *Common Market Law Review*, 1979, pp. 9–40.

Trevor C. Salmon, 'The Changing Nature of Irish Defence Policy', *The World
Today*, Nov. 1979, pp. 462–70.

IX

The Future Challenge: New and Potential Members

Geoffrey Edwards

There was a certain irony in the submission of three applications for membership of the Community between 1975 and 1977. The existing member states appeared beset by seemingly intractable problems. Despite (or perhaps because of) the United Kingdom's commitment by referendum to continued membership, for example, progress towards further integration appeared impossible. The quiet shelving of the Tindemans Report on European Union was to many symptomatic of the Community's malaise and stagnation. The applications, from Greece in June 1975, Portugal in March 1977 and Spain in July 1977, were therefore greeted with enthusiasm, albeit on the wane by July 1977. Roy Jenkins, President of the Commission, declared 'The Community can take pride in the fact that there are applicants at the Community's door, and that this is a sign that the Community is a rallying point for both democracy and economic advance.'[1] Pride was thus combined with an acute awareness of the political importance to the applicants of an enthusiastic welcome. Each had applied soon after holding the first democratic elections after periods of dictatorship, and when the stability of their new systems was still in question. A rejection by the Community was therefore considered out of the question by member governments (with the encouragement of the applicant governments) on the grounds that damage might be caused not only to the Community's image but to the new democratic governments themselves and so to the security balance in Western Europe.

Political and strategic considerations were therefore paramount in the Community's initial response to the three applications. They continued to

---

[1] Quoted by G. Contogeorgis, 'The Greek View of the Community and Greece's Approach to Membership', in W. Wallace and I. Herreman (eds.), *A Community of Twelve? The Impact of Further Enlargement on the European Communities* (College of Europe, Bruges, 1978), pp. 26–7.

be dominant for some time. It was only gradually that there was any attempt to come to grips with the possible problems of further enlargement, though the Commission in its Opinion on the Greek application advocated caution.[2] Doubts tended to be expressed in terms of the apparent irreconcilable processes of enlarging the Community and deepening its content, as had been the case in the first round of enlargement. Even so most member governments, though for different reasons, were prepared to endorse Anthony Crosland's conclusion that 'because quite simply the political benefits of enlargement outweigh the practical difficulties, enlargement is an investment in the democratic future of Europe and in the long run the benefits will far outweigh the costs'.[3] Given the circumstances in which the three applications were made, few, initially, were prepared to emphasize possible material costs and benefits.

Of course, in 1975–76, only Greece had formally laid its application on the table. With a population of only nine million, Greek membership was not considered likely to be particularly burdensome, even if, as the Commission pointed out, there were some potential agricultural and regional problems.[4] The Commission's caution in posing such problems provided the Greeks with something of a shock. But for some time the Commission appeared alone in its attitude. It was only when the sedate pace of the Greek negotiations became overtaken by the Portuguese and Spanish applications that the potential costs of further enlargement became more readily apparent. In the southern regions of France, in particular, opposition to Spanish agricultural competition grew in strength, gathering with it support from both Gaullists and Communists. In consequence, the Greeks received a further shock as the Community's position on entering into substantive negotiations became increasingly tough. Negotiations that were already difficult, in part because of a certain slowness on the part of the Greeks to appreciate the full implications of membership, became all the more so as the Community's awareness of the possible precedents it was creating for Portugal and Spain became more acute. The resulting tardiness on the part of the Community and the threat of the 'globalization' of enlargement negotiations caused the Greeks a concern that led to some energetic lobbying by the Greek Prime Minister, Mr Karamanlis, in Community capitals.

The tendency to globalize enlargement issues was due both to the nature of the three applicants and to the likely impact of their combined membership

---

[2] Commission of the European Communities, *Bulletin of the European Communities*, Supplement 2/76, Jan. 1976. Among the first studies of the problems of enlargement was that prepared by the Federal Trust for Education and Research; see G. Edwards and W. Wallace, *A Wider European Community: Issues and Problems of Further Enlargement* (Federal Trust, 1976).

[3] Quoted by G. Contegeorgis, op. cit., p. 26.

[4] European Commission, Supplement 2/76. See also its Supplement 3/78, *Enlargement of the European Community, Economic and Sectoral Aspects*.

on the Community. Common to all three applicants had been the desire to return to the European comity of nations after varying periods of isolation because of their dictatorial regimes and with their democratized systems still in their infancy. Their acceptance by the Community, even if only in principle, provided a significant psychological impact. It conferred recognition on their democratic credentials thereby lending an important additional legitimacy both to the systems themselves and, though of less lasting importance perhaps, to the parties in government. It also reconfirmed their Western European orientation, signalling their re-entry into the mainstream of European political and social development and their rejection of other options, whether real or imaginary. But in addition, and despite the many declarations in all three applicant countries that they wished to adhere to a political and not merely an economic community, economic considerations were also of the greatest significance. All three are, for example, heavily dependent on trade with the Community. Although the level of their economic development varies considerably, they continue to be in Community terms developing countries, relying heavily on relatively backward agricultural sectors and with severe regional problems. Each, though especially Portugal, has therefore expected membership to bring substantial assistance for modernization and development through Community funds and the European Investment Bank and a greater attractiveness to large-scale foreign investors. Such expectations will inevitably create an important shift of emphasis within the Community – not least through creating added weight to existing demands of Mediterranean agricultural producers.

But the globalization of the enlargement issue masked, as the Greeks frequently and determinedly pointed out, an equally important range of differences among the three countries. While their interests will coincide on a number of issues, they are the product of sometimes radically different traditions and circumstances. Their past relationships with the Community have, for example, been on very different bases. Greece had signed an Association Agreement in 1962. Its commitment to ultimate integration with the Community goes back therefore to 1959–60, even if it proved insufficient to bring about the harmonization of Greek agricultural, industrial and other policies with those of the Community envisaged under the Agreement (and for which the so-called freeze in relations during the period of the Colonels' regime cannot be wholly blamed). None the less, the Greeks continually emphasized that membership was always a long-term aim and that they merely wished to accelerate a process towards possible membership that was in any case due to be negotiated in 1984.

Portugal's relations with the Community have been closely linked with those of Britain; once the United Kingdom joined the Community it became imperative for the Portuguese along with other EFTA members to reach a better understanding with the Nine. While Portugal's free trade agreement was similar in most respects to those signed by the other members of EFTA it also included additional agricultural provisions in recognition of the significance and backwardness of Portuguese agriculture. But so long as Portugal was ruled by a right-wing dictatorship committed to the maintenance of its African empire by force, its relations with Europe were too strained for the question of Portuguese membership to arise.

Before 1975 Spain was in many ways more isolated from the Community than its fellow applicants, despite the sometime sympathy of the French Government for closer relations. Although the Franco Government had sought Associate status in preparation for future membership as early as 1962 and (in the absence of any Community response) had repeated the initiative in 1964, Spain's relations with the Community were governed by only a preferential trade agreement which, at the Community's insistence, covered industrial but not agricultural trade. Hostility to the Franco regime prevented any closer relations. Political considerations continued to dominate Community relations with Spain; as late as 1975 negotiations on a renewal of the preferential trade agreement were broken off following the execution of five alleged terrorists in Spain.

Such differences among the three countries have inevitably had an important bearing on the approaches adopted towards Community membership and accession negotiations. In the case of Greece, the application was justified both domestically and internationally as the logical outcome of the commitment of 1961 which was merely being reaffirmed after the brief interruption of the Colonels. Considerable resentment was therefore aroused when the Community appeared to view the Greek application less in terms of a positive commitment to a Europe that, in the words of Mr Karamanlis, 'once united will become a power capable of influencing the progress of humanity', than as an element in Greek relations with Turkey and the United States.[5] As one Greek supporter of membership put it, 'It can hardly be expected that a country such as Greece which, as early as 1961 when other countries were toying with the idea of a free trade area, had sought links with the Community leading to accession by 1984, would enter the Community in order to demonstrate ill-will in the field of political co-operation.'[6] Portugal and Spain have not yet reached the stage for such rhetoric, largely because so far the Community plays a different role. Rodríguez Inciarte, the then General Secretary for Spanish relations with the Community, declared, 'For a whole generation of Spaniards Europe has signified the image of economic progress and political balance from which we were systematically alienated due to the existence of a regime of an autocratic character.'[7] Vitor Constancio, at one time responsible for Portugal's relations with the Community, echoed the sentiment when he

[5] *The Times*, 27 Sept. 1976.
[6] A. Chloros, 'A Contribution and an Agonizing Reappraisal', in Loukas Tsoukalis (ed.), *Greece and the European Community* (Saxon House, Teakfield Ltd., 1979), p. 19.
[7] R. Inciarte, 'Spain and the European Community: Past, Present and Future', in *Spain, Portugal and the European Community* (UACES, 1979).

221

portrayed the Community as 'a reference point from which we could compare our situation. And that was important in creating a European consciousness among many intellectual groups in Portugal before 1974. Officialdom at that time tended to look towards Africa and, as a reaction, we looked towards Europe.'[8]

1. Portugal

This division in Portugal – which has a parallel in Greece if not in Spain – has persisted since the Revolution. The left-wing military, especially within the Revolutionary Council whose role has remained influential, have tended to favour a Third World, pro-African orientation for Portugal. The parties of the centre-right, which now make up the Democratic Alliance, and the socialists have had strong ideological, and financial, links with other Western European parties, particularly those of West Germany.[9] However, their ability to translate their commitment to Community membership into practical policies has been patchy. Domestic considerations, especially the economy, have effectively impeded any consistent approach. The Socialist leadership despite its own commitment to membership has at times been obliged to try to straddle the pro-European and pro-African elements within the party's ranks. The inability of the political parties to work together to form a parliamentary majority in order to tackle the economic consequences of the Revolution allowed President Eanes considerable latitude in the exercise of his constitutional powers, including the appointment of non-party technocratic governments such as that of Maria de Lurdes Pintassilgo, which reflected his own somewhat ambivalent attitudes towards Europe. With considerable support from the left and the military he sought closer links with the former Portuguese colonies in Africa, in part at least as a first step towards presenting Portugal as a bridge between the industrialized North and the developing South.

Moreover, political uncertainties and organizational difficulties meant that delays in formulating negotiating positions were endemic. A further complicating factor has been the Communist Party's opposition to Portuguese membership and preference for a Third World policy. The party remains a highly-structured organization that has had little truck with the 'reformist' Euro-Communists of Spain and Italy. However, since the failure of anything substantial to emerge from its advocacy of closer links with the Soviet Union and COMECON, the Communist Party appears to be biding its time. Although the parliamentary elections of 1979 and 1980 showed a

[8] *Financial Times*, 14 Nov. 1978.
[9] Professor Beata Kohler of the Technische Universität, Darmstadt, has done extensive work on relations between West German parties and their counterparts in the applicant countries which, it is hoped, will be published in the near future. Some of her preliminary findings were presented to the UACES Conference on New Approaches to the Study of European Integration, 2–4 Jan. 1980.

continuing swing to the right, the Communist party retained over 16 per cent of the vote and could still play a crucial role once the terms of membership are known, particularly through its domination of the trade union movement.

While the issue of Community membership played little direct part in either parliamentary elections, the success of the Democratic Alliance has resulted in the membership negotiations being pursued with much more determination. The overwhelming majority in Parliament favours membership. Many reflect the position of the Socialist leader, Mario Soares, that, 'We Portuguese, unlike some British and Danes, do not wonder whether or not we are Europeans – we have never accepted the idea that Africa began at the Pyrenees. Anyway, what conceivable alternative do we have – to join the Third World without oil or massive natural wealth?'[10] But the issue of membership has been present in a more indirect way. It has, for example, been used by the Democratic Alliance and its supporters as an element in their campaign to revise the 1976 Constitution in the interests of private enterprise. Under the Constitution and subsequent legislation the armaments, oil-refining, iron and steel, base petrochemicals, fertilizer and cement industries, banking and insurance are reserved to the State. Because of the central role played by the banks in industry, something like 2,000 companies were removed from the private sector on their nationalization. The reaction of the remaining private sector has been predictable and their use of the prospect of membership of an organization based essentially on a free market economy to further their cause unsurprising. As one member of the Portuguese Confederation of Industry was reported as saying, 'Once our application has been accepted, the government will have to start obeying EEC rules, socialist constitution or no.'[11] The European Commission has attempted to counter such a position in several public utterances, notably that of the Commissioner for Industrial Policy, Vicomte Davignon, who pointed to the extent of state intervention in France and Italy.[12] None the less, the private sector continues to regard Community membership as in its interests. In addition to constitutional revision, membership is expected to bring about substantial Community aid and an influx of foreign capital which together will weigh against the likely consequences of opening Portuguese industry up to full Community competition. However, expectations of aid and foreign private investment may prove over-optimistic. It remains the case that for both the industrial and agricultural sectors it is often easier to point to the potential problems of membership than to real benefits. Reliance on, for example, the expansion of established sectors such as textiles and iron and steel, in which existing member states already have severe difficulties, may complicate negotiations. Benefits in the agricultural

[10] *The Guardian*, 5 June 1978.
[11] *The Guardian*, 14 Nov. 1977.
[12] *Financial Times*, 16 Jan. 1979.

sector could also prove to be illusory despite higher prices for domestic produce and possible structural aid because Portugal is a net importer of food. Portugal could thus find itself in a position not wholly dissimilar from that of Britain as a net contributor to the Community's budget.[13] However, in resolving the problem of Britain's budgetary contributions, EEC member states appear to have accepted the need for greater equity and the avoidance of resource transfers from poorer to richer members of the Community. The additional pressures to reform the Community's budget and the common agricultural policy created by the British settlement may be such that the problem will not arise for Portugal, though there are likely to be delays and difficulties in negotiations. But the position is made worse for the Portuguese by the close interrelationship between the problem of the backwardness of its agriculture and the outstanding political question of land ownership in the south.

High expectations of substantial economic assistance are matched or even exceeded by socio-political considerations. Among many groups EEC membership is looked on as a crucially important step in transforming Portugal, its administration, tax laws, social welfare system and so on, into a modern society. And if elections provide any guidelines the majority support the aim of EEC membership. In the 1980 elections, the Democratic Alliance and the Socialists received some 75 per cent of the popular vote; and although the Democratic Alliance failed to secure the victory of its candidate in the 1980 Presidential elections, President Eanes is not opposed to Community membership even if some of his supporters are. But as one somewhat cynical observer noted, 'Most people think it (i.e. Community membership) will be good for them because they have been told so by the politicians they vote for.'[14] There are doubts as to whether, as yet at least, knowledge of the issues extends further than the newspaper reading élite, although the influence of the 600,000 and more Portuguese migrant workers should not be underestimated. The Government has yet to undertake the important task of preparing the public for membership. At the same time it has to tackle the still severe problems within the domestic economy, including the thorny question of the decollectivization of agriculture, within the framework established by the constitution and upheld by the Revolutionary Council. The emphasis on domestic issues was inevitably reinforced during 1980 with both Parliamentary and Presidential elections and it is likely to be continued for some time in view of the continued determination of the Democratic Alliance under the new leadership of Francisco Pinto Balsemao to reform the constitution. Continued public support for EEC membership will, inevitably, depend on the course of the negotiations and the final terms obtained. There remains a belief that Portugal deserves an easy passage both as a developing country and a newly democratic one. If

[13] Edwards and Wallace, op. cit., p. 32.
[14] *The Guardian*, 14 Nov. 1977.

the negotiations do prove difficult an increasing number may question the need to go beyond the ties derived from membership of EFTA from which Portugal has already received substantial benefits. Whether or not there remains a residual hostility born of the Salazar years towards the industrialized countries of Europe, severe problems in the negotiations could aggravate continuing domestic difficulties and create a highly sensitive political situation.

2. Spain

Support in Spain for membership is as yet even more widespread than in Portugal. The political and economic orientation of the country is almost wholly towards Europe and the Community despite its greater isolation from the mainstream of European developments during the Franco era. Links with central and southern America while strong (Spain has observer status at meetings of the Andean Pact) are, for the most part, cultural or even romantic. There is little economic underpinning to them; trade with South America is little more than that with the United States. And although there remain close links with several Arab countries, their significance lies more in the security of energy supplies. Such extra-European links as in Portugal create a sense of being an intermediary in the North-South dialogue, a sense that found expression in Spain's attendance as an observer at the Havana Conference of Non-aligned Countries in 1979. However, most Spaniards see such links as a potentially useful adjunct to the Community's existing policies rather than as an alternative to Community membership (though some modification of Spanish policies might be called for, such as those towards Israel).

Spain's isolation under Franco has created attitudes and practices that will inevitably have important repercussions on the Spanish approach to substantive negotiations and to fulfilling the demands of membership. Isolation encouraged, often with official support in the past, a strong attachment to the concept of sovereignty. Reaction to the Commission's extremely cautious Opinion on Spanish membership published in November 1978[15] was received with as much anger as surprise that so much emphasis should be placed on the problems of assimilating Spain for the Community. Since the application and the initial response of the member states had in essence been politically motivated, many Spaniards had expected a more politically sensitive treatment of the difficulties and problems facing Spain in moving from dictatorship to democracy in adverse economic conditions. During 1978 with, for example, the outburst of M. Chirac, the French Gaullist leader, it became clear that Spain's application was not universally welcome. Resentment and the frustrations aroused by slow Community

---

[15] Commission of the European Communities, *Bulletin of the European Communities*, Supplement 9/78, Nov. 1978.

procedures were to some extent assuaged immediately before the 1979 elections, in large part through the active diplomacy of Sr Suárez. But they were rearoused in June 1980 by President Giscard d'Estaing's call for a delay in the process of further enlargement and are likely to grow if negotiations prove to be unduly protracted because of French domestic politics. Difficult Community negotiations, if combined with the persistence of economic problems and regional unrest and terrorism, pose a challenge to the maintenance of a political system that, as the attempted military coup in February 1981 showed, cannot be taken wholly for granted.

So far, however, there remains a wide consensus in favour of membership among political parties and the public. Despite the various internal difficulties and tensions within the Union of Centre Democrats, the party formed by Sr Suárez in 1977 from the disparate groups of the centre-right, it has followed a consistently pro-EEC policy. Significantly, Sr Calvo Sotelo, who became Prime Minister in February 1981, was Spain's Minister for relations with the European Community from 1978 to September 1980 and is a convinced European. The PSOE, for its part, under the leadership of Felipe González, has swung towards a relatively coherent social democrat platform, encouraged by the support of the Community's Confederation of Socialist Parties. The Spanish Communist Party, in sharp contrast to its Portuguese counterpart, is firmly committed both to Community membership and to the gradualist path towards communism adopted by the Italian party. Although the PCE gained only 9 per cent of the vote in the 1979 elections it remains an influential force because of the strength of the well-organized Workers' Commissions which command the support of almost 50 per cent of Spanish trade unionists (though it should be added that the level of unionization remains relatively low). Several regional parties, looking perhaps towards a Community of the future in which regional representation is as significant as present national representations, are also generally favourable to membership. The commitment of the parties leaves as the main imponderable therefore the extent to which public opinion becomes mobilized on particular issues. The hostility of the French farming lobby notwithstanding, public opinion remains largely indifferent; for many the issue has already been decided by the Government with the agreement of the opposition parties and is therefore not generally questioned. The government-sponsored opinion poll in the autumn of 1979 underlined the point, for whereas 67 per cent were reported to be in favour of membership and only 7 per cent against, only 10 per cent could name the existing member states of the Community and 30 per cent confessed to know nothing at all about it.[16]

Continued support will therefore rest heavily not merely on the continued commitment of the Government and the opposition parties but on their ability to prepare the public for the practical effects of membership.

[16] *Financial Times*, 4 Oct. 1979.

Throughout Spanish-Community relations the EEC has pushed hard for industrial free trade while maintaining restrictions on Spanish agricultural produce. It continued to do so during the membership negotiations, favouring a short transitional period for industrial goods and a longer period for agriculture. The Spanish proposed an across-the-board transitional period of between 5 and 10 years. The desire of the Spanish farming lobby to gain full access to the Community market and the potential benefits of the CAP as quickly as possible is strong – with the exception of Galician beef and dairy producers who fear being swamped by Community competition. The Spanish lobby therefore viewed the Community's reluctance to envisage an across-the-board transitional period with an alarm that was reinforced by its relative lack of strength *vis-à-vis* the Government when compared with either the industrial lobby or the French agricultural lobby. Moreover, while Spanish industry has maintained a surplus in trade with the Community in recent years, reports suggest that once tariffs are removed and Community regulations on taxation, subsidies etc. are enforced, several important sectors will face severe difficulties in coping with Community competition. Herr Schmidt, the German Chancellor, is reported as warning Spanish industry that 'when the customs barriers are removed, the powerful and big companies are going to invade the Spanish market and compete hard, often leaving Spanish companies on the sidelines'.[17] Others have suggested that there is a vital need for Spanish industry to improve its productivity and to concentrate more on high technology sectors, but that other sectors, including steel, textiles and chemicals and petrochemicals, will be able to maintain an effective competitive position. Greater difficulties will be faced by sectors such as fisheries, shipbuilding and the motor industry, presenting further problems of unemployment which is already running at over 9 per cent.[18] In addition, as the Greeks have found, the Community in the interests of its own workers can take a tough stance on the question of migrant labour, whether it arises from agricultural reforms or industrial stagnation. Nor, in present circumstances, are the Guidance Section of the EAGGF, the Regional Fund or the Social Fund likely to meet Spain's high expectations. Political considerations remain sufficient to preclude the reversal of the decision to accept Spanish membership but economic considerations with substantial political clout within the Community will make the negotiations protracted and difficult for the Spanish. However, the events of February 1981 reinforced the political dimension of Spain's application and increased the determination of both government and opposition to achieve a successful outcome to the negotiations in the shortest possible time.

[17] *The Guardian*, 11 Jan. 1980.
[18] European Research Associates, *Spanish Industry and the Impact of Membership of the European Community*, prepared for the European Commission and quoted by the *Financial Times*, 11 Jan. 1980. The OECD figure for unemployment in Spain was 9·3 per cent in 1979.

3. Greece

Some five and a half years after submitting its application Greece became the tenth member of the European Community on 1 January 1981. The practical effects of membership therefore are soon to be felt. Yet the possible economic impact of membership has always been subordinate to political considerations in the approach of most pro-European groups and of the Greek Government under Mr Karamanlis. As George Mavros, the former leader of the Centre Union Party, now the Union of the Democratic Centre, declared, 'Full integration offers economic opportunities but it also guarantees Greece's international position and prestige and enables it to defend effectively its interests and the free institutions.'[19] The whole issue of early membership was also intimately bound up with the political prestige of the then Prime Minister and now President, Mr Karamanlis, who 'whenever the negotiations appeared to be dragging . . . was always ready to lobby in the capitals of Europe and his persistence has paid off handsomely'.[20] Mr Karamanlis was able to avoid the pitfalls and difficulties of the globalization of enlargement negotiations and to achieve membership for Greece three or four years in advance of the date envisaged under the 1961 Association Agreement.

Greece shared many of the political motives of Portugal and Spain in applying for Community membership. Beyond these, however, were several factors peculiar to Greece, some of which caused no little concern to the existing member states. One of the foremost characteristics of Greek politics since the collapse of the Colonels has been the widespread intense hostility to the United States. It arose in part because the United States too often appeared to condone or even prop up the Colonels' regime and in part because of American links with Turkey after the Turkish invasion of Cyprus (though at the insistence of the United States Congress an embargo was imposed in 1975 on some military aid and assistance). The Government's decision to withdraw from the integrated military structure of NATO in 1974 was therefore extremely popular. Turkey's continued presence in Cyprus and its actions in the Aegean and over the Greek Government's attempts to return to NATO have sustained strong nationalist feelings. These have also inhibited the Government's dealings with the United States. The socialist party, PASOK, under the leadership of Andreas Papandreou was quick to exploit such difficulties.[21] But whereas PASOK has regarded the Community as merely the economic extension of NATO, many Greeks have looked to the Community as the only alternative to continued dependence on America. Although the Community's attempts to deal even-handedly

[19] *The Times*, 27 Sept. 1976.
[20] R. Clogg, 'Greece Joins Europe', *World Today*, Vol. 35, No. 7, July 1979, p. 273.
[21] In July 1976, for example, Mr Papandreou declared, 'Our armed forces, with the whole-hearted support of the people, will give the necessary reply to whoever should dare to violate our national space'. See *The Times*, 19 July 1976.

with the Greeks and the Turks have provoked problems for the Greek Government (without satisfying the Turks either), the Community has at least been given the credit for both condemning the Colonels and imposing restrictions on the working of the Association Agreement, even if these did not add up to a 'freeze' as so often claimed.[22] Continued tensions in the Eastern Mediterranean in Greek relations with Turkey and the uncertainties over Yugoslavia after Tito's death caused an anxiety in Western capitals which proved a useful bargaining instrument for the Greek Government in the accession negotiations.

The upsurge of nationalism in Greece proved to be an important factor in the 1977 elections in which PASOK increased its support from 14 to 25 per cent. Most political commentators had expected a substantial rise in PASOK's support given the circumstances of the 1974 elections when Mr Karamanlis appeared to be the only alternative to the Colonels, but many were surprised by the extent of the increase. It was, in addition, significant for Greece's relations with the Community for PASOK has in general, though with varying degrees of hostility, been opposed to Greek membership of both the Community and NATO. Apart from suggesting certain parallels with the British Labour Party, PASOK's stance in the 1977 elections may yet prove to be important if adaption to membership proves more difficult than the Government has predicted. The 1977 manifesto stated firmly that Greek accession 'will consolidate the peripheral role of the country as a satellite of the capitalist system; will render national planning impossible; will seriously threaten Greek industry; and will lead to the extinction of Greek farmers ... We must restructure relations with the EEC on the basis of a special agreement (of the Norwegian type) which will allow for Greek control over the national economy and the movement of capital goods ... In any event PASOK believes that the crucial matter of our accession to the EEC cannot be decided without ... a fair referendum ... The policies of Europe must not aim at the creation of a new superpower but at closer co-operation of countries with a common cultural tradition which will eventually lead to the creation of a federal socialist state.'[23] Together with the Communist Party (KKE), PASOK boycotted the parliamentary vote on the ratification of the Treaty of Accession in June 1979.

The great majority of Greeks were and remain in favour of membership. None the less, Mr Papandreou reflects some of the doubts held in certain quarters that Community membership will create more serious problems than merely those of adaptation. The Greek economy has developed rapidly since the 1950s, the average income per capita rising from 31 per cent of that of the Community in 1955 to 55 per cent in 1976.[24] But economic

[22] See, for example, G. Yannopoulos, *Greece and the European Economic Communities: the first decade of a troubled association* (London, 1975).
[23] *Greece*, No. 74, 4 Nov. 1977, Greek Press and Information Office, London.
[24] *The Times*, 11 Dec. 1979.

development slowed down during the period of the Colonels with the Junta leaving a legacy of rising unemployment and inflation, lack of investment, high defence expenditure and extensive corruption. And while the Government under Mr Karamanlis began to tackle many of these problems with some success, not only do important structural problems remain but the process of development has inevitably been affected by the general economic recession. In its Economic Survey for 1978 the OECD suggested that Greek industrial capacity had 'not expanded at a rate normally expected in a developing country'.[25] There has, for example, been a tendency, born of political and economic uncertainties, for investment to be directed more towards property and housing than towards more productive uses. Much of Greek industry is still in the hands of small and medium-sized family concerns with relatively low productivity and insufficient capital for expansion. PASOK in expressing their fears of Community competition has thereby gathered support. Similarly, within the relatively inefficient agricultural sector, change and pressures for reform may undermine the widely hoped for benefits accruing from higher prices, especially, but not exclusively, in the livestock sector which faces higher grain prices. Although inflation in Greece has brought prices closer to those at present prevailing in the Community, adjustments to the latter also create further problems for the consumer.[26] Even among the sectors expected to benefit from Community membership – or at least to be able to cope with accession – such as larger companies and shipping companies, there have been signs of increasing doubts about the consequences of adhering to Community regulations and the gradual erosion of competitiveness due to rising wage levels. Among regulations likely to have important repercussions on the still highly protected Greek economy are those relating to state aids and the phasing out of export subsidies at a time of sluggish domestic demand and when adjustment has to be made to the common commercial policy. The problems of adaptation may well be 'larger than the Greeks expect or are prepared to admit'.[27] Significantly, Greece concentrated on achieving the hitherto unglamorous transport portfolio in the Thorn Commission, clearly intent on protecting its shipping interests in particular.

The Government was widely criticized – by both pro-European groups as well as those opposed – for failing adequately to prepare the country for membership. It has remained, in public at least, seemingly convinced that the political benefits are overwhelming and that membership is an all-embracing panacea for Greece's problems. As in Portugal and Spain, the main economic motive has been the prospect of membership bringing with

[25] OECD, *Economic Survey* (Paris, 1978), p.30.
[26] For a discussion of the prospects for Greek agriculture, see the papers by J. Marsh and A. Pantelouri in Tsoukalis, op. cit., pp. 68–83.
[27] W. Hummel, *Greek Industry in the European Community: Prospects and Problems* (German Development Institute, Berlin, 1977).

it a large inflow of foreign capital to take advantage of as yet lower wage levels and other incentives – including those designed to attract industry away from the Greater Athens area in which more than 45 per cent of industrial workers now live. Legal protection for foreign investment is also guaranteed under the constitution as a further incentive. In his speech in the debate on the ratification of the Treaty of Accession, Mr Karamanlis recognized that considerable efforts would be required to modernize Greek industry and that structural reforms would be necessary in both the public and private sectors. But the thrust of his speech on that as on other occasions was directed towards the political benefits of returning to the Western European comity of nations and taking part in the development of the Community.[28] But the need for structural reforms has been an issue taken up by many other supporters of entry. There is a concern whether the 'ramshackle bureaucracy and inadequate educational system can stand up to the strains'.[29] As in Portugal and Spain great store is set by the potential for change brought about by membership to many sectors of society. Nor is it only among Greeks that membership is seen as creating new opportunities. One of the primary motives of the European Trades Union Confederation in accepting the membership of the weak and poorly-representative Greek trades union congress was to create sufficient pressures through increased contacts to bring about the end of the Government's domination of official trade unionism in Greece.

To speculate about the future balance between the forces making for change and those making for continuity in the new circumstances created by Community membership is obviously hazardous. Institutions and bureaucracies in general have an innate capacity to absorb new pressures and members with little outward change and it is doubtful if the Greek institutions will be an exception. Moreover, the capacity of several Greek political parties to survive the Junta and thereby perpetuate old habits and relationships has been remarked on by several commentators even if party labels have changed to reflect the greater awareness of democratic or social democratic forces.[30] Greek politics are also highly personalized. Mr Karamanlis held a seemingly unassailable position as national leader while Prime Minister and his influence is likely to continue to be extensive as President. It remains to be seen, however, whether his leadership of New Democracy (for the most part the pre-Junta National Radical Union) was indispensable to the Party's electoral success. Mr Papandreou is equally dominant in PASOK and has been able to impose his own somewhat idiosyncratic ideology on what is increasingly a mass party. This personalization of politics poses important questions not only about the future of

[28] *Greece*, No. 112, 4 July 1979.
[29] Clogg, op. cit., p. 273.
[30] See, for example, the discussion between R. Clogg and D. Dimitrakos in Tsoukalis, op. cit., pp. 103–35.

the individual parties but, in a Community context, about the interplay of Greek parties with those of the Community. Alignments with existing Community party groups have not posed simple choices. New Democracy, for example, with its aspirations to include the centre as well as the right, was reluctant to become too closely identified with either the Conservative or the Christian Democrat groups, regarding them both as too right-wing. Its links with the Liberal group, which arguably covers the broadest political spectrum from Italian neo-fascists, via the Giscardians to the Dutch radicals, have not been close (except perhaps at the highest level as far as the Giscardians are concerned). PASOK with its individual blend of nationalism and socialism has been described as more akin to Third World rather than European socialist parties.[31] Its links with European socialist groups have been extremely limited, in part because they were regarded as too reformist and in part because of PASOK's hostility both to the Community and to Greek membership. With the approach of accession, however, PASOK appeared to be adopting a more moderate line and, influenced perhaps by the fact that the Socialist Group in the European Parliament contains several British and Danish anti-Marketeers, had decided to join the Group. Spanish and Portuguese parties are for the most part likely to have an easier task in extending their already close links with their Community counterparts.

4. The Challenge of Enlargement

Much of the concern within the Nine over enlargement has arisen from fears that Community decision-making will grind to a halt in the face of yet further disparate demands. Notwithstanding the European Parliament's efforts to stake its claim in the decision-making process (to which enlargement adds only a marginally complicating factor), attention has focused on the Council of Ministers and the Commission. The Spierenburg Report and that of the Three Wise Men were direct responses to the problems posed by further enlargement.[32] Greek leaders, more familar with the capabilities of the Community's decision-making and aware of the concern of some existing member states, have been at pains to allay fears of stagnation. But some suggestions current in Greece for the development of the Community are themselves likely to raise problems. The close inter-relationship between security issues, relations with the United States and with Turkey (which has already proposed an accelerated programme for its eventual membership of the Community) has, for example, led several Greek pro-Marketeers to look to the Community for some sort of

---

[31] D. Dimitrakos in Tsoukalis, op. cit., p. 132.
[32] *Proposals for the Reform of the Commission of the European Communities and its Services* (The Spierenburg Report), Brussels, 24 Sept. 1979. The Report of the 'Three Wise Men' (Messrs Biesheuvel, Dell and Marjolin) on the European Institutions, prepared for the European Council of Oct. 1979 was published in 1980.

defence/security identity. Again notwithstanding the efforts of the European Parliament to place the issue of European defence co-operation on the Community agenda, opposition to any Community involvement in defence issues has been strong, not least from the French. Policies aimed at greater integration (which advance national interests at the same time) not infrequently lead to considerable frustration on the part of the proposer as well as creating further dissension among the other member states.

But national interests demand that all three countries pursue an active approach to the Community. Inevitably the greatest attention has been focused on the future of the CAP. All three are likely to lend their weight to that of Italy and France in the interests of greater protection for their Mediterranean produce. In view of the severe regional disequilibria in the three countries they are likely also to press for the enlargement of the Regional Fund along with Britain and Italy, and the introduction of a coherent industrial policy. Many of their demands, in other words, would result in a substantial increase in Community budgetary expenditures. But the expense of the CAP is already under attack. Britain in particular has long been critical of the proportion of the Budget devoted to agricultural support. West Germany, especially since the decision of June 1980 on Britain's budgetary contributions, has added its voice to the growing demands for reform. Without significant reforms, budgetary expenditures will soon outrun revenues irrespective of further enlargement. But reform will not be easy and negotiations are likely to be difficult and protracted. For Greece, accession thus occurs at a particularly opportune moment since it can participate in the negotiations. For Spain and Portugal, the outlook is one of delays and frustration as the member states seek to find a new *modus vivendi*.

Further enlargement creates additional complications in an already difficult situation within the Community. It poses further problems for a decision-making process that has become increasingly intergovernmental. Most of the smaller member states have traditionally emphasized the role of the Commission *vis-à-vis* the Council and the domination of the larger states and especially that of France and Germany. It remains to be seen whether the strength of nationalism in Greece will run counter to this tradition. But certainly the accession of one and later two more member states settles none of the existing problems of the Community and goes some way to reinforcing many of them. In such circumstances the *de facto* if not *de jure* loosening of the Community will be the major challenge of the 1980s.

FURTHER READING

Raymond Carr and Juan Pablo Fusi, *Spain: Dictatorship to Democracy* (Allen and Unwin, London, 1979).

Christian Deubner, 'The Southern Enlargement of the European Communities', *Journal of Common Market Studies*, Vol. XVIII, No. 3, March 1980, pp. 229–45.

Economic and Social Committee of the European Communities, *The Community's Relations with Spain* (Brussels, 1979).

Economic and Social Committee of the European Communities, *Enlargement of the European Community: Greece, Spain, Portugal* (Brussels, 1979).

G. Edwards and W. Wallace, *A Wider European Community? Issues and Problems of Further Enlargement* (Federal Trust for Education and Research, 1976).

Antonio da Silva Ferreira, 'The Economics of Enlargement: Trade Effects on the Applicant Countries', *Journal of Common Market Studies*, Vol. XVII, No. 2, Dec. 1978, pp. 120–42.

Robert Harvey, *Portugal: Birth of a Nation* (Macmillan, London, 1978).

A. Schlaim and G. N. Yannopoulos (eds.), *The EEC and the Mediterranean Countries* (Cambridge University Press, 1976).

J. W. Schneider (ed.), *From Nine to Twelve: Europe's Destiny* (Sijthoff & Noordhoff, Alphen aan den Rijn, The Netherlands, forthcoming).

Panos Tsakaloyannis, 'The European Community and the Greek-Turkish dispute', *Journal of Common Market Studies*, Vol. XIX, No. 1, Sept. 1980, pp. 35–54.

Loukas Tsoukalis, 'A Community of Twelve in Search of an Identity', *International Affairs*, July 1978, pp. 437–51.

Loukas Tsoukalis (ed.), *Greece and the European Community* (Saxon House, Teakfield Ltd, 1979).

Loukas Tsoukalis, *The European Community and its Mediterranean Enlargement* (Allen & Unwin, London, 1981).

UACES, *Spain, Portugal and European Community* (London, 1979).

W. Wallace and I. Herreman (eds.), *A Community of Twelve? The Impact of Further Enlargement on the European Communities* (College of Europe, Bruges, 1978).

Notes on Contributors

Clive Archer is a lecturer in International Relations at the University of Aberdeen, Secretary of its Centre for Nordic Studies, and former Secretary of the Scotland in World Affairs Study Group of the Scottish Branch of the Royal Institute of International Affairs. He has spent extended periods of study at universities and institutes in Stockholm, Oslo, Copenhagen, and Aarhus. He has written a number of articles and reports on Scandinavian politics and foreign relations. His doctoral thesis was on British-Scandinavian Relations in the context of EFTA, and he is the editor of *The Nordic Model* (with Stephen Maxwell), 1980.

Carol Cosgrove Twitchett is a Visiting Fellow at the University of Reading, and taught formerly at the London School of Economics and the Universities of Aberdeen and Surrey. She was a consultant to the African, Caribbean, and Pacific states in the Lomé II negotiations, and is Moderator in European Studies for the University of London GCE Board. Her publications include numerous articles on European and international affairs and the following books: *The New International Actors: The UN and the EEC* (with Ken Twitchett), 1970; *A Reader's Guide to Britain and the European Communities*, 1970; *Europe and Africa: From Association to Partnership*, 1978; *ACP Foreign Trade*, 1979; *Harmonisation in the EEC* (ed.), 1981; and *A Framework for Development: The EEC and the ACP*, 1981.

Geoffrey Edwards was awarded a Ph.D. in International Relations from the London School of Economics in 1973. After a period in the Research Department of the Foreign and Commonwealth Office, he joined the Federal Trust for Education and Research, becoming Deputy Director in 1978. He is the author of numerous articles on the European Communities and the following books: *A Wider European Community? Issues and Problems of Further Enlargement* (with William Wallace), 1976; *The Council of Ministers of the European Community and the President-in-Office* (with Helen Wallace), 1977; *Federal Solutions to European Issues* (co-editor), 1978; and *The Common Man's Guide to the Common Market* (co-editor), 1979.

Richard T. Griffiths is Professor of Social and Economic History at the Free University, Amsterdam. He was formerly Lecturer in European Studies at the Manchester University Institute of Science and Technology, and was awarded a

Ph.D. from Cambridge University for a study of Dutch industrial development in the nineteenth century. His publications to date have been primarily in the field of nineteenth- and twentieth-century Dutch economic development.

Annette Morgan is a lecturer in History and Politics at Brunel University, and a Visiting Lecturer for Stanford University in Britain. She previously taught at Sussex, Harvard, and Boston Universities, and was the National Secretary for France for American Field Service International Scholarships. She has published numerous articles on European and international affairs and *From Summit to Council: Evolution in the EEC*, 1976.

Roger Morgan is Head of the European Centre for Political Studies at the Policy Studies Institute, London. He has taught at a number of British and American Universities, was formerly Professor of European Politics at Loughborough University, and Deputy Director of Studies at the Royal Institute of International Affairs. He has published numerous articles on European and international affairs. His books include *The German Social Democrats and the First International, 1964–72*, 1965; *Modern Germany*, 1966; *Britain and West Germany: Changing Societies and the Future of Foreign Policy* (with Karl Kaiser), 1971; *West European Politics since 1945: The Shaping of the European Community*, 1972; *High Politics/Low Politics*, 1973; *The Unsettled Peace: A Study of the Cold War in Europe*, 1974; and *West Germany's Foreign Policy Agenda*, 1978.

Adrian Poole is a Principal Lecturer in European Studies at the Portsmouth Polytechnic. He has had a wide experience teaching European languages and history, and during the war was commissioned in the Royal Artillery, later transferring to the Intelligence Corps. His main research interests are centred on Belgian politics and the language question.

Geoffrey Pridham is a Lecturer in European Politics at the University of Bristol. He has undertaken extensive research and written numerous articles on German and Italian political parties and transnational formations in the European Community. His books include *Hitler's Rise to Power: The Nazi Movement in Bavaria, 1923–1933*, 1973; *Documents on Nazism, 1919–1945* (co-editor with Jeremy Noakes), 1974; *Christian Democracy in Western Germany: the CDU/CSU in Government and Opposition, 1945–1976*, 1977; *Transnational Party Co-operation and European Integration: the process towards direct elections* (with Pippa Pridham), 1981; and *Change and Continuity in the Italian Party System: the case of Tuscany in the 1970s*, 1980.

Trevor C. Salmon is a Lecturer in Politics at the University of St. Andrews. He undertook postgraduate work at the University of Aberdeen, and taught formerly at the National Institute for Higher Education, Limerick. His main research interests are Irish foreign and defence policy within the context of the European Community, and he has had several articles published on these topics in the *British Journal of International Studies*, the *Journal of Common Market Studies*, and *The World Today*.

Kenneth J. Twitchett has taught at a number of universities and other institutes of higher education. He has published numerous articles on international politics and European integration and the following books: *International Security: Reflections on Survival and Stability*, 1971; *The Evolving United Nations*, 1971; *Europe and the World: The External Relations of the Common Market* (ed.), 1976; and *European Co-operation Today* (ed.), 1980.

Select Bibliography

Compiled by Ken Twitchett

This bibliography is not comprehensive, and indicates only some of the publications illustrating the various aspects of co-operation in contemporary Europe. The classification of the literature is flexible and a reference placed in one section might also be relevant to another section. Throughout preference has been given to more recently published English-language books. For the most part it omits the more specialist references to particular EEC member states cited in the further reading lists at the end of Chapters II to IX. The bibliography itself is based on that contained in K. Twitchett (ed.), *European Co-operation Today* (Europa, 1980), pp. 260–72.

1. General and Historical

René Albrecht-Carrié, *The Unity of Europe* (London, 1966).

Berhanykun Andemicael, *Regionalism and the United Nations* (New York, 1979).

Carol Ann Cosgrove and Kenneth J. Twitchett, *The New International Actors: The UN and the EEC* (London, 1970).

Peggotty Freeman (ed.), *Europe Today and Tomorrow* (London, 1977).

Peter Hall, *Europe 2000* (London, 1977).

Walter Hallstein, *Europe in the Making* (London, 1973).

W. O. Henderson, *Zollverein* (Chicago, 2nd edn., 1959).

Wayland Kennet, *The Future of Europe* (London, 1976).

Walter Lipgens, 'European Federation in the Political Thought of Resistance Movements During World War II', *Central European History*, Vol. 1, No. 1, Mar. 1968, pp. 5–19.

R. W. G. MacKay, *Towards a United States of Europe: Analysis of Britain's Role in European Union* (London, 1961).

D. J. A. Mathew, *The Medieval European Community* (London, 1977).

Richard Mayne, *The Recovery of Europe* (London, 1970).

Richard Mayne (ed.), *Europe Tomorrow* (London, 1972).

Roy Mellor and E. Alistair Smith, *Europe, A Geographical Survey of the Continent* (London, 1979).

E. Monick, 'Occupation and Liberation, 1940–1944', *Three Banks Review*, Sept. 1976.

Kenneth J. Twitchett (ed.), *European Co-operation Today* (London, 1980).

Derek W. Urwin, *Western Europe Since 1945* (London, 2nd edn., 1972).

Richard Vaughan, *Post-War Integration in Europe* (London, 1976).

Richard Vaughan, *Twentieth Century Europe* (London, 1978).

Alan Watson, *Europe at Risk* (London, 1972).

F. R. Willis (ed.), *European Integration* (London, 1975).

Arnold Zurcher, *The Struggle to Unite Europe, 1940–1958* (New York, 1958).

2. The European Idea

Max Beloff, *Europe and the Europeans* (London, 1957).

Count Richard Coudenhove-Kalergi, *Europe Must Unite* (London, 1940).

Lord Gladwyn, *The European Idea* (London, 1966).

W. Ivor Jennings, *A Federation for Western Europe* (London, 1940).

Jaroslav Krejci and Vitezslav Velimsky, *Ethnic and Political Nations in Europe* (London, 1981).

Richard Mayne, *The Europeans: Who Are We?* (London, 1972).

Richard Mayne, 'The Role of Jean Monnet', *Government and Opposition*, Vol. 2, No. 3, Apr.–July 1967, pp. 349–71.

Jean Monnet, *Memoirs* (London, 1978).

Guido Piovene, *In Search of Europe: Portraits of the Non-Communist West* (London, 1976).

Denis de Rougemont, *The Meaning of Europe* (London, 1966).

Denis de Rougemont (ed.), *The State of the Union of Europe* (Oxford, 1979).

Anthony Sampson, *The New Europeans* (London, revised edn., 1971).

Meic Stevens, *Linguistic Minorities in Western Europe* (Llandysul, Dyfed, 1976).

3. The Atlantic Alliance

Margaret Ball, *NATO and the European Union Movement* (New York, 1959).

John Baylis (ed.), *British Defence Policy in a Changing World* (London, 1977).

James Chace and Earl C. Ravenal (eds.), *Atlantis Lost: United States-European Relations after the Cold War* (New York, 1976).

Lord Chalfont, 'SALT II and America's European Allies', *International Affairs*, Oct. 1979, pp. 559–64.

Julian Critchley, 'A Community Policy for Armaments', *NATO Review*, Vol. 27, No. 1, Feb. 1979, pp. 10–14.

G. K. Douglas (ed.), *The New Interdependence: The European Community and the United States* (Farnborough, 1980).

Ori Even-Tov, 'The NATO Conventional Defence: Back to Reality', *Orbis*, Vol. 23, No. 1, Spring 1979.

J. Freymond, 'An Atlanticist or European Europe', *The World Today*, May 1975.

John Garnett (ed.), *The Defence of Western Europe* (London, 1974).

C. Gasteyger (ed.), *Europe and America at the Cross Roads* (Paris, 1972).

Frans A. M. Alting von Geusau, *Uncertain Détente* (Leiden, 1979).

Theodore Geiger, *Transatlantic Relations in the prospect of an Enlarged European Community* (London, 1970).

J. Godson (ed.), *Transatlantic Crisis: Europe and America in the 70's* (London, 1974).

Alfred Grosser, 'Les Occidentaux: Western Europe and the United States since the Second World War', *West European Politics*, May 1980, pp. 158–65.

Alfred Grosser, *The Western Alliance* (London, 1980).

Walter F. Hahn and Robert Pfaltzgraff (eds.), *Atlantic Community in Crisis: A Redefinition of the Transatlantic Relationship* (New York, 1979).

Peter Hill Norton, *No Soft Options: The Politico-Military Realities of NATO* (London, 1978).

Karl Kaiser, *Europe and the United States: The Future of the Relationship* (Washington, D.C., 1973).

Karl Kaiser, 'Europe and America: A Critical Phase', *Foreign Affairs*, Vol. 52, No. 4, July 1974, pp. 725–41.

Karl Kaiser and Hans-Peter Schwartz (eds.), *America and Western Europe: Problems and Prospects* (Lexington, Mass., 1979).

Gavin Kennedy, *Burden Sharing in NATO* (London, 1979).

Sir John Killick, 'Is NATO relevant to the 1980s?', *The World Today*, January 1980, pp. 4–10.

Lawrence Laplan, 'NATO and the Nixon Doctrine: Ten Years Later', *Orbis*, Spring 1980.

Derek Léebaert (ed.), *European Security: Prospect for the 1980s* (Farnborough, 1980).

George Lichtheim, *Europe and America: The Future of the Atlantic Community* (London, 1963).

Gerhard Mally (ed.), *The New Europe and the United States: Partners or Rivals?* (Lexington, Mass., 1974).

Roy Mason, 'The Eurogroup', *NATO Review*, April 1975.

K. A. Myers, *NATO: The Next Thirty Years* (London, 1980).

NATO Information Service, *The Eurogroup* (Brussels, 1979).

Escott Reid, *Time of Fear and Hope* (Ontario, 1978).

J. Robert Schaetzel, *The Unhinged Alliance: America and the European Community* (New York, 1977).

Willem Scholten, 'The Eurogroup's First Ten Years', *NATO Review*, April 1978.

Simon Serfaty, *Fading Partnership: America and Europe after 30 Years* (East-bourne, 1979).

Michael Smith, 'From the "Year of Europe" to a Year of Carter: Continuing Patterns and Problems in Euro-American Relations', *Journal of Common Market Studies*, Vol. XVII, No. 1, Dec. 1978, pp. 26–42.

Gaston Thorn, 'Reflections on the Atlantic Alliance and on Europe', *NATO Review*, April 1975.

G. Tucker, *Towards Rationalizing Allied Weapons Production* (Paris, 1976).

Paul Wilkinson, *The Defence of the West* (London, 1980).

P. Windsor, 'NATO's Twenty-five Years', *The World Today*, May 1974.

P. Windsor, 'A Watershed for NATO', *The World Today*, Nov. 1977, pp. 409–16.

4. The European Communities

(i) *General*

H. Arbuthnott and Geoffrey Edwards (eds.), *A Common Man's Guide to the Common Market* (London, 1979).

Bernard Burrows, Geoffrey Denton and Geoffrey Edwards (eds.), *Federal Solutions to European Issues* (London, 1978).

European Commission, *Challenges Ahead: A Plan for Europe* (London, 1980).

European Commission, *The Community Today* (London, 1980).

European Commission, *Steps to European Unity: Community Progress to Date: A Chronology* (Luxembourg, 1980).

Henri Etienne, 'Community Integration: The External Environment', *Journal of Common Market Studies*, June 1980, pp. 289–312.

Ulrich Everling, 'Possibilities and limits of European Integration', *Journal of Common Market Studies*, March 1980, pp. 217–28.

Stuart Holland, *The Uncommon Market* (London, 1980).

Leon Hurwitz (ed.), *Contemporary Perspectives on European Integration: Attitudes, Non-Governmental Behaviour and Collective Decision Making* (London, 1980).

Anthony Kerr, *The Common Market and How it Works* (Oxford, 1977).

Pierre-Henri Laurent (ed.), 'The European Community After Twenty Years', the *Annals of the American Academy of Political and Social Science (Special Issue)*, Nov. 1978.

Juliet Lodge, 'Loyalty and the EEC: the limitations of the functionalist approach', *Political Studies*, Vol. 26, 1978, pp. 268–84.

G. N. Minshull, *The New Europe: An Economic Geography of the EEC* (London, 2nd edn., 1979).

Roger Morgan, *West European Politics since 1945: The Shaping of the European Community* (London, 1973).

Robin Mowat, *Creating the European Community* (London, 1973).

Emile Noel, *The European Community: How it Works* (London, 1979).

Michael Shanks, 'The EEC: A Community in Search of an Identity', *Three Banks Review*, Sept. 1977, pp. 52–66.

Ken Simmonds, *European Community Treaties* (London, 4th edn., 1980).

Lord MacKenzie Stuart, *The European Communities and the Rule of Law* (London, 1977).

Paul Taylor, 'Interdependence and Autonomy in the European Communities', *Journal of Common Market Studies*, June 1980, pp. 370–87.

John Usher, *European Community Law and National Law* (London, 1981).

Helen Wallace, 'The Impact of the European Communities on national policy making', *Government and Opposition*, Vol. 6, 1971, pp. 520–38.

Derrick Wyatt and Alan Dashwood, *The Substantive Law of the EEC* (London, 1980).

(ii) *The ECSC and the Schuman Plan*

Derek Curtis Bok, *The First Three Years of the Schuman Plan* (Princeton, N.J., 1955).

William Diebold, *The Schuman Plan: A Study in Economic Co-operation, 1950–59* (New York, 1959).

John Goormaghtigh, 'European Coal and Steel Community', *International Conciliation*, No. 503, 1955, 65pp.

I. P. Keane, 'The British Steel Industry and the European Coal and Steel Community', *Three Banks Review*, Dec. 1974.

Max Kohnstamm, 'The European Coal and Steel Community', *Recueil des Cours* (Leiden), Vol. 90, 1957.

Louis Lister, *Europe's Coal and Steel Community: An Experiment in Economic Union* (New York, 1960).

Henry L. Mason, *The European Coal and Steel Community: Experiment in Supranationalism* (The Hague, 1955).

R. T. Nichols, *The European Coal and Steel Community* (Santa Monica, California, 1962), 38pp.

André Philip, *The Schuman Plan: Nucleus of a European Community* (Brussels, 1951), 46pp.

Christopher Wilkinson, 'Recent Developments in European Coal and Steel Community Policies', *Three Banks Review*, Mar. 1977, pp. 56–76.

(iii) *Defence and Political Co-operation*

David Allen (ed.), *European Political Co-operation* (London, 1980).

Raymond Aron and Daniel Lerner (eds.), *France Defeats EDC* (New York, 1957).

Susan Bodenheimer, *Political Union: A Microcosm of European Politics, 1960–1966* (Leiden, 1967).

Abbot A. Brayton, 'Confidence-Building Measures in European Security', *The World Today*, Oct. 1980, pp. 382–91.

Bernard Burrows and Christopher Irwin, *The Security of Western Europe: Towards a Common Defence Policy* (London, 1972)

Michael D. Butler, *European Defence Problems in the 1970s: The Case for a New Defence Community* (Cambridge, Mass., 1971).

François Duchêne, 'A New European Defence Community', *Foreign Affairs*, Oct. 1971, pp. 69–82.

Federal Trust, *European Defence Co-operation* (London, 1979).

Edward Fursden, *The European Defence Community: A History* (London, 1980).

Lord Gladwyn, 'Western Europe's Collective Defence', *International Affairs*, Apr. 1975.

Stephen Kirkby, 'The Independent European Programme Group: The Failure of Low-Profile High-Politics', *Journal of Common Market Studies*, Dec. 1979, pp. 175–96.

Michael Palmer, *The Negotiations on Political Union* (London, 1962).

Alessandro Silh, *Europe's Political Puzzle: A Study of the Fouchet Negotiations and the 1963 Veto* (Cambridge, Mass., 1967).

(iv) *Institutions and Decision-making*

Bill Brecton, 'The European Parliament: a new Babel – Members very quickly learn not to tell jokes', *The Listener*, 19 Feb. 1981.

Neville Brown and Francis G. Jacobs, *The Court of Justice of the European Communities* (London, 1977).

David Butler and David Marquand, *European Elections and British Politics* (London, 1981).

David Coombes, *The Future of the European Parliament* (London, 1979).

David Coombes *et al, European Integration, Regional Devolution and National Parliaments* (London, 1979).

Mattei Dogan, *The Mandarins of Western Europe: The Political Role of Top Civil Servants* (Chichester, 1975).

Basil de Ferranti, *In Europe – one man's view of how Europe really works* (London, 1979).

John Fitzmaurice, *The European Parliament* (Farnborough, 1978).

Stanley Henig (ed.), *Political Parties in the European Community* (London, 1979).

Stanley Henig, *Power and Decision in Europe: The Political Institutions of the European Community* (London, 1980).

Valentine Herman and Juliet Lodge, *The European Parliament and the European Community* (London, 1978).

Valentine Herman and Juliet Lodge, 'Is the European Parliament, a Parliament?', *European Journal of Political Research*, Vol. 6, 1978, pp. 157–80.

Valentine Herman and Marinus van Schendeles (eds.), *The European Parliament and the National Parliaments* (Farnborough, 1979).

Journal of Common Market Studies (Special Issue), 'The Policy Implications of Direct Elections', June 1979.

R. H. Lauwaars, 'The European Council', *Common Market Law Review*, Vol. xix, No. 1, 1977, pp. 25–44.

Robert Lecourt, *The Community's Institutional Problems* (Brussels, 1978).

Juliet Lodge, 'Towards the European Political Community: EEC Summits and European Integration', *Orbis*, Vol. xix, 1975, pp. 626–51.

David Marquand, *Parliament for Europe* (London, 1979).

Hans J. Michelmann, *Organizational Effectiveness in a Multinational Bureaucracy* (Farnborough, 1978).

John Mitchell, 'The Sovereignty of Parliament and Community Law: The Stumbling-Block that Isn't There', *International Affairs*, Vol. 55, No. 1, Jan. 1979, pp. 33–46.

Annette Morgan, *From Summit to Council: Evolution in the EEC* (London, 1976).

Gregg Myles, *Court of Justice of the European Communities* (Belfast, 1978).

Emile Noel, 'The Coreper and the deepening of the European Community', *Government and Opposition*, Vol. 6, 1971, pp. 422–27.

Emile Noel, 'The Coreper and the deepening of the European Community', *Government and Opposition*, Vol. 6, 1971, pp. 422–7.

Emile Noel and H. Etienne, 'The Permanent Representatives Committee and the "Deepening" of the Communities', *Government and Opposition*, Vol. vi (1971), pp. 422–47.

Michael Palmer, *The European Parliament: What it is – What it does – How it works* (Oxford, 1981).

Trevor Parfitt, 'The Budget and the CAP: A Community Crisis Averted', *The World Today*, August 1980, pp. 313–18.

Geoffrey and Pippa Pridham, *Transnational Party Cooperation and European Integration* (London, 1981).

C.Sasse *et al., Decision-making in the European Community: A Reappraisal* (New York, 1977).

Avi Shlaim, 'The Role of Summitry in EEC Decision-making', *International Relations*, May 1974.

Altiero Spinelli, 'Reflections on the Institutional Crisis in the European Community', *West European Politics*, Vol. I, No. 1, 1978.

D. Strasser, *The Finances of Europe* (New York, 1977).

C.Tugendhat, 'Problems of Community budgeting', *The World Today*, August
1977.

Helen Wallace and Geoffrey Edwards, *The Council of Ministers of the European
Community and the President-in-Office* (London, 1977).

Helen Wallace, William Wallace and Carole Webb (eds.), *Policy-Making in the
European Communities* (Chichester, 1977).

Helen Wallace, *Budgetary Politics: The Finances of the European Communities*
(London, 1980).

(v) *Economic and Social Policies*

A. M. El-Agraa (ed.), *The Economics of the Common Market* (London, 1980).

Rosemarie Allen, 'Fishing for a Common Policy', *Journal of Common Market
Studies*, Vol. XIX, No. 2, Dec. 1980, pp. 123–39.

C. W. Bellamy and Graham D. Child, assisted by Anthony Morris, *Common
Market Law of Competition* (London, 2nd edn., 1978).

K. J. Button, 'Recent Developments in EEC Transport Policy', *Three Banks
Review*, Sept. 1979, pp. 52–73.

Alan Campbell, *EEC Competition Law* (Amsterdam, 1980).

George Close, 'Article 84, EEC – The Development of Transport Policy in the Sea
and Air Sectors, *European Law Review*, June 1980, pp. 188–207.

Peter Coffey (ed.), *Economic Policies of the Common Market* (London, 1979).

Doreen Collins, *The European Communities, Vol. 1: Social Policy of the European
Coal and Steel Community, 1951–1970*, and *Vol. 2: Social Policy of the European
Community, 1958–1972* (London, 1975).

Carol Cosgrove Twitchett (ed.), *Harmonization in the EEC* (London, 1981).

R. Churchill, 'Revision of the EEC's Common Fisheries Policy', *European Law
Review*, Apr. 1980, pp. 95–111.

André Danzin, *Science and the Second Renaissance of Europe* (Oxford, 1979).

Brian Davey, Tim Josling and Alister McFarquhar, *Agriculture and the State*
(London, 1976).

John Drew, *Doing Business in the European Community* (London, 1979).

Andrew Durand, 'European Citizenship', *European Law Review*, Vol. 4, No. 1,
Feb. 1979, pp. 3–14.

European Commission, *The Community and its Regions* (Luxembourg, 1980),
21 pp.

European Commission, *Transport Network for Europe: Outline of a Policy* (London,
1980).

Rosemary Fennell, *The Common Agricultural Policy of the European Community*
(London, 1979).

Michael Fogarty, *Work and Industrial Relations in the European Community*
(London, 1975).

Kenneth D. George and T. S. Ward, *The Structure of Industry in the EEC*
(London, 1975).

K. D. George and C. Joll, 'EEC Competition Policy', *Three Banks Review*, Mar.
1978.

Lyn Gray and Ian Waitt, 'Uncommon split on supranational training plan', *Times Higher Educational Supplement*, 23 May 1980.

Jack Hayward (ed.), 'Trade Unions and Politics in Western Europe', *West European Politics* (Special Issue), Jan. 1980.

T. Heidhues, T. Josling, C. Ritson and S. Tangerman, *Common Prices and Europe's Farm Policy* (London, 1978).

Stuart Holland, *The Regional Problem* (London, 1976).

John Holloway, *Social Policy Harmonisation in the European Community* (Farnborough, 1981).

G. Ionescu (ed.), *The European Alternatives: An Inquiry into the Policies of the European Community* (Alphen aan den Rijn, 1979).

F. G. Jacobs, 'The Free Movement of Persons within the EEC', *Current Legal Problems*, 1977.

Emil Joseph Kirchner, *Trade Unions as a Pressure Group in the European Community* (Farnborough, 1977).

Valentine Korah, *An Introductory Guide to EEC Competition Law and Practice* (Oxford, 1979).

Roger Lawson and Bruce Reed, *Social Security in the European Communities* (London, 1975).

Juliet Lodge, 'Towards a Human Union: EEC Social Policy and European Integration', *British Journal of International Studies*, Vol. iv (1978), pp. 47–74.

Nigel Lucas, *Energy and the European Communities* (London, 1977).

Robert Maclennan, 'Food Prices and the Common Agricultural Policy', *Three Banks Review*, Sept. 1978, pp. 58–71.

Roy Manley (ed.), *Creating a Caring Community* (Fabian Tract, London, 1979).

John Marsh, *UK Agricultural Policy Within the European Community* (London, 1978).

John Marsh and Pamela J. Swanney, *Agriculture and the European Community* (London, 1980).

Hanna Maull, *Europe's Quest for an International Energy Policy* (London, 1980).

Willem Molle, Bas van Holst, and Hans Smit, *Regional Disparity and Economic Development in the European Community* (Farnborough, 1980).

J. R. Nicholls, *The Impact of the EEC on the UK Food Industry* (Farnborough, 1978).

Michael Shanks, *European Social Policy, Today and Tomorrow* (Oxford, 1977).

Michael Shanks, *The Consumer in Europe* (Brussels, 1979).

Dennis Swann, *The Economics of the Common Market* (Harmsworth, 4th edn., 1978).

José de la Torre and Michel Bacchetta, 'The Uncommon Market: European Policies towards the Clothing Industry in the 1970s, *Journal of Common Market Studies*, Vol. XIX, No. 2, Dec. 1980, pp. 95–122.

Christopher Tugendhat, 'Europe and Industrial Policy', *International Affairs*, July 1979, Vol. 55, No. 3, pp. 402–8.

John Waller, 'Consumer Protection in Europe', *Local Government Studies*, July-Aug. 1980, Vol. 6, No. 4, pp. 57–62.

Philippa Watson, *Social Security Law in the European Communities* (London, 1980).

Roger Williams, *European Technology* (London, 1975).

Douglas Yuill, Kevin Allen, and Chris Hull, *Regional Policy in the European Community* (London, 1980).

(vi)   *External Relations* (including impact on the Third World).

David Allen, 'The Euro-Arab Dialogue', *Journal of Common Market Studies*, June 1978, pp. 323–42.
David Allen (ed.), *European Political Co-operation* (London, 1980).
Stephen J. Artner, 'The Middle East: A Chance for Europe', *International Affairs*, Summer 1980, pp. 420–42.
Peter Coffey, *The External Economic Relations of the EEC* (London, 1976).
Carol Cosgrove Twitchett, *Europe and Africa: From Association to Partnership* (Farnborough, 1978).
Carol Cosgrove Twitchett, *ACP Foreign Trade* (Brussels, 1979).
Carol Cosgrove Twitchett, (ed.), *Towards Lomé II: Europe and the Developing World* (London, 1979).
Carol Cosgrove Twitchett, 'Lomé 2 – a new ACP-EEC Partnership?', *The World Today*, Mar. 1980.
Carol Cosgrove Twitchett, *A Framework for Development: The EEC and the ACP* (London, 1981).
Michael Dolan, 'The Lomé Convention and Europe's Relationship with the Third World: A Critical Analysis', *Journal of European Integration*, Vol. 1, No. 3, May 1978.
Geoffrey Edwards and William Wallace, *A Wider European Community* (London, 1976).
European Commission, *The European Community, International Organisations and Multilateral Agreements*, (Luxembourg, 1980).
Rosemary Foot, 'The European Community's Voting Behaviour at the United Nations General Assembly', *Journal of Common Market Studies*, June 1979, pp. 350–560.
Geoffrey Goodwin, 'The External Relations of the European Community – Shadow and Substance', *British Journal of International Studies*, Apr. 1977, Vol. 3, No. 1.
M. Hanabusa, *Trade Problems Between Japan and Western Europe* (Farnborough, 1979).
Michael Hardy, 'The European Community and Japan: Agenda for Adjustment', *The World Today*, Nov. 1980, pp. 428–35.
Edward Heath, 'A World of Our Making', *New Europe*, Vol. 6, No. 3, Summer 1978, pp. 36–45.
Christopher Hill and William Wallace, 'Diplomatic Trends in the European Community', *International Affairs*, Vol. 55, No. 1, Jan. 1979, pp. 47–66.
Chihiro Hosoya, 'Relations between the European Communities and Japan', *Journal of Common Market Studies*, Vol. XVIII, No. 2, Dec. 1979, pp. 159–74.
Roy Jenkins, 'Europe and the Third World: The Political Economy of Interdependence', *Round Table*, Oct. 1978, pp. 304–14.
I. G. John (ed.), *EEC Policy Towards Eastern Europe* (Farnborough, 1975).
David Jones, *Food and Interdependence* (London, 1976).

Michael Leigh and Nicholas van Praag, *The Mediterranean Challenge* (Brighton, 1979).

Beate Lindemann, 'Europe and the Third World: The Nine at the United Nations', *The World Today*, July 1976, pp. 260–9.

Juliet Lodge, 'New Zealand and the Community', *The World Today*, Aug. 1978, pp. 303–10.

Juliet Lodge, 'Australia and the European Community', *The World Today*, July 1980, pp. 272–8.

Roger Morgan, *High Politics, Low Politics* (London, 1973).

Kathryn Morton and Peter Tulloch, *Trade and Developing Countries* (London, 1977).

Blanca Muñiz, 'EEC – Latin America: a relationship to be defined', *Journal of Common Market Studies*, Vol. XIX, No. 1, Sept. 1980, pp. 55–64.

John and Pauline Pinder, *The European Community's Policy Towards Eastern Europe* (London, 1975).

John Pinder, 'Integration in Western and Eastern Europe: Relations between the EEC and CMEA', *Journal of Common Market Studies*, Vol. XVIII, No. 2, Dec. 1979, pp. 114–34.

Antonino Pitrone, *EEC GSP Scheme* (Rome, revised edn., 1979).

Abby Rubin, *Lomé II: The Renegotiation of the Lomé Convention* (London, 1978).

Robin Sharp, *EEC/ACP: One More Time?* (Amsterdam, 1978).

Avi Shlaim and George Yannopoulos (eds.), *The European Economic Community and the Mediterranean Countries* (London, 1976).

Avi Shlaim and George Yannopoulos (eds.), *The EEC and Eastern Europe* (London, 1979).

Alan Taylor, 'The Euro-Arab Dialogue: Quest for an Inter-regional Partnership', *The Middle East Journal*, Autumn 1978.

Phillip Taylor, *When Europe Speaks With One Voice: The External Relations of the European Community* (London, 1979).

Alfred Tovias, *Tariff Preferences in Mediterranean Diplomacy* (London, 1977).

Kenneth J. Twitchett, *Europe and the World: The External Relations of the Common Market* (London, 1976).

Edmund Wellenstein, *Twenty-five Years of European Community External Relations* (London, 1979).

Wolfgang Wessels (ed.), *Europe and the North-South Dialogue* (Paris, 1978).

Ann Weston, 'How Sensitive is the EEC's Generalized System of Preferences', *ODI Review*, No. 1, 1980, pp. 11–29.

Ann Weston and Vincent Cable, *South Asia's Exports to the EEC: Obstacles and Opportunities* (London, 1979).

Ann Weston et al., *European Economic Community's System of Preferences: Evaluation and Recommendations for Change* (London, 1980).

Miguel Wionczek, 'The relations between the European Community and Latin America in the context of the international economic crisis', *Journal of Common Market Studies*, Vol. XIX, No. 2, Dec. 1980, pp. 160–74.

5. EFTA

N. D. Aitken, 'The Effect of the EEC and EFTA on European Trade: A Temporal Cross-Section Analysis', *American Economic Review*, Vol. 63, No. 5, 1973, pp. 881–92.

Clive Archer, 'Britain and Scandinavia: Their Relations within EFTA, 1960–1968', *Co-operation and Conflict*, Vol. xi, 1976, pp. 1–23.

H. Corbet and D. Robertson (eds.), *Europe's Free Trade Area Experiment* (Oxford, 1970).

Victoria Curzon *et al.*, *EFTA and the Crisis of European Integration* (London, 1968).

Victoria Curzon, *The Essentials of Economic Integration: Lessons of the EFTA Experience* (London, 1974).

Sir John Coulson, 'EFTA: Its Functions after the Abolition of Tariffs', *European Yearbook*, 1967, pp. 43–9.

P. Dreyer, *Scandinavia Faces Europe* (Paris, 1973).

EFTA Secretariat, *Convention Establishing the European Free Trade Association* (Geneva, 1967).

EFTA Secretariat, *The Trade Effects of EFTA and the EEC, 1959–1967* (Geneva, 1972).

EFTA Secretariat, 'The experience of the EFTA Countries since the Free Trade Arrangements were signed', *EFTA Bulletin*, July/Aug. 1977, pp. 10–21.

Frank Figgures, 'Legal Aspects of the European Free Trade Association', *International and Comparative Law Quarterly*, Oct. 1965, pp. 1079–88.

Neville March Hunnings, 'Enforceability of the EEC-EFTA Trade Agreements – a rejoinder', *European Law Review*, Vol. iii, No. 4, Aug. 1978, pp. 278–90.

J. Lambrinidis, *The Structure, Function and Law of a Free Trade Area* (London, 1965).

Gunnar Lange, 'The European Free Trade Association: Some Reflections on its Origins, Functions and Future', *European Yearbook*, 1963, pp. 3–21.

David Robertson, 'EFTA and the NAFTA proposal: an economic appraisal', *The World Today*, Vol. 25, No. 4, April 1969, pp. 145–58.

6. Nordic Co-operation

S. V. Anderson, *The Nordic Council: A Study in Scandinavian Regionalism* (London, 1967).

N. Andren, 'Nordic Integration', *Co-operation and Conflict*, Nos. 3–4, 1967, pp. 1–25.

Clive Archer (ed.), *Scandinavia and European Integration* (Aberdeen, 1971).

Clive Archer and Stephen Maxwell (eds.), *The Nordic Model* (Farnborough, 1980).

Barbara Heakel, *The Scandinavian Option* (Oslo, 1976).

Ingeborg Lyche, *Nordic Cultural Co-operation* (Oslo, 1974).

Toivo Miljan, *The Reluctant Europeans: The Attitudes of the Nordic Countries towards European Integration* (London, 1977).

Nordic Council, *Nordic Co-operation* (Stockholm, 1965).

Nordic Council, *Nordic Economic and Social Co-operation* (Stockholm, 1968).

Nordic Council, *Nordic Economic and Cultural Co-operation* (Stockholm, 1970).

Nordic Council, *The Role of the Nordic Countries in European Co-operation* (Stockholm, 1973).

Nordic Council, *Co-operation Agreements between the Nordic Countries* (Stockholm, 1978).

Nils Ørvik, 'Nordic Co-operation and High Politics', *International Organisation*, Vol. 28, No. 1, Winter 1974, pp. 61–88.

K. Skjelsbaek, 'The Nordic Countries in Nordic and More Encompassing International Organisations', *Co-operation and Conflict*, 1974, pp. 1–8.

V. Sletten, *Five Northern Countries Pull Together* (Copenhagen, 1967).

E. Solem, *The Nordic Council and Scandinavian Integration* (New York, 1977).

Bengt Sundelius and Claes Wiklung, 'The Nordic Community: The Ugly Duckling of Regional Co-operation', *Journal of Common Market Studies*, Vol. XVIII, No. 1, Sept. 1979, pp. 59–75.

Bengt Sundelius, 'Coping with Transnationalism in Northern Europe', *West European Politics*, May 1980, pp. 219–29.

Barry Turner and Gunilla Nordquist, *The Other European Community* (London, 1980).

F. Wendt, *The Nordic Council and Co-operation in Scandinavia* (Copenhagen, 1959).

C. Wiklund, 'The Zig-Zag Course of the Nordek Negotiations', *Scandinavian Political Studies*, 1970, pp. 307–35.

7. Co-operation in Socialist Europe

(i) *General*

Nils Andren and Karl Birnbaum (eds.), *Beyond Detente: Prospects for East-West Co-operation and Security in Europe* (Leiden, 1976).

Zbigniew Brzezinski, *The Soviet Bloc: Unity and Conflict* (Cambridge, Mass., 3rd edn., 1967).

Adam Bromke and Teresa Rakowska-Harmstone (eds.), *The Communist States in Disarray, 1965–1971* (Minneapolis, 1972).

Karen Dawisha and Philip Hanson (eds.), *Soviet-East European Dilemmas: Coercion, Competition and Consent* (London, 1981).

Charles Gati (ed.), *The International Politics of Eastern Europe* (New York, 1977).

Kirk Grayson and Nils Wessell (eds.), 'The Soviet Threat: Myths and Realities', *Proceedings of the Academy of Political Science* (Special Issue), Vol. 33, No. 1, 1978.

W. E. Griffith (ed.), *The Soviet Empire: Expansion and Detente* (Lexington, Mass., 1976).

James Kuhlman (ed.), *The Foreign Policies of Eastern Europe: Domestic and International Perspectives* (Leiden, 1978).

R. Szawlowski, *The System of the International Organizations of the Communist Countries* (Leiden, 1976).

Jan F. Triska and Paul M. Cocks (ed.), *Political Developments in Eastern Europe* (London, 1977).

Philip Windsor, *Change in Eastern Europe* (Chatham House Paper, London, 1980).

(ii) *Economic Co-operation*

A. Abonyi and I. J. Sylvain, 'CMEA Integration and Policy Options for Eastern Europe: A Development Strategy of Dependent States', *Journal of Common Market Studies*, Dec. 1977, pp. 132–54.

Nora Beloff, 'Comecon Blues', *Foreign Policy*, No. 31, Summer 1978, pp. 159–79.

Jochen Bethkenhagen, 'Comecon Energy Problems and the West', *NATO Review*, Feb. 1978.

Jozef M. van Brabant, *Essays on Planning, Trade and Integration in Eastern Europe* (Rotterdam, 1974).

J. B. Bracewell-Milnes, *Economic Co-operation in East and West* (London, 1976).

Z. M. Fallenbuchl, 'Comecon Integration', *Problems of Communism*, Vol. 8, Mar.–Apr., 1973, pp. 25–39.

Werner Feld, 'The Utility of the EEC experience for Eastern Europe', *Journal of Common Market Studies*, Vol. XV, No. 3, Mar. 1976, pp. 236–61.

P. H. Glendenning, 'Comecon: Progress and Prospects', *NATO Review*, June 1977, pp. 15–19.

Franklyn D. Holzman, *International Trade Under Communism: Politics and Economics* (New York, 1976).

John Pinder, 'Integration and Trade Negotiations', *Government and Opposition*, Vol. xiv, No. 2, Spring 1979, pp. 149–71.

Guiseppe Schiavone, *The Institutions of Comecon* (London, 1981).

Alan H. Smith, 'Plan Co-ordination and Joint Planning in CMEA', *Journal of Common Market Studies*, Vol. XVIII, No. 1, Sept. 1979, pp. 3–21.

Uwe Stehr, 'Unequal Development and Dependency Structures in Comecon', *Journal of Peace Research*, 1977, Vol. xiv, No. 2, pp. 115–28.

(iii)   *The Warsaw Pact*

Peter Bender, 'Inside the Warsaw Pact', *Survey*, No. 74/75, Winter/Spring 1970, pp. 253–8.

W. R. Kintner and W. Klaiber, *Eastern Europe and European Security* (New York, 1971).

R. Kolkowicz, 'The Warsaw Pact: Entangling Alliance', *Survey*, No. 70/71, Winter/Spring 1969, pp. 88–101.

A. Korbonski, 'The Warsaw Pact', *International Conciliation*, No. 573, May 1969.

J. Malcolm Mackintosh, 'The Warsaw Pact Today', *Survival*, May–June 1974, pp. 122–6.

N. Edwina Moreton, *East Germany and the Warsaw Alliance: Politics of Détente* (Boulder, Colorado, 1978).

Robin Alison Remington, *The Warsaw Pact: Case Studies in Communist Conflict Resolution* (Cambridge, Mass., 1971).

Jutta and Stephen Tiedke, 'The Soviet Union's internal problems and the development of the Warsaw Treaty Organization', in Egbert Jahn (ed.), *Soviet Foreign Policy: Its Social and Economic Conditions* (London, 1978).

8. Other European Organizations

(i)   *The United Nations Economic Commission for Europe*

ECE, *The Work of the Economic Commission for Europe, 1947–1972* (New York, 1972).

G. Myrdal, 'Twenty Years of the United Nations Commission for Europe', *International Organisation*, Vol. 22, No. 3, Summer 1968, pp. 617–28.

Jean Siotis, 'The Secretariat of the United Nations Economic Commission for Europe and European Economic Integration: The first ten years', *International Organisation*, Vol. 19, No. 2, Spring 1965, pp. 177–202.
Jean Siotis, 'The ECE in the Emerging European System', *International Conciliation*, No. 561, Jan. 1967.

(ii) *Benelux*

Jacques van Damme, 'BENELUX and its Relationship with the EEC', in M. Bathurst, K. Simmonds, N. March Hunnings and Jane Welch (eds.), *Legal Problems of an Enlarged European Community* (London, 1972).
R. C. Riley and G. J. Ashworth, *Benelux: an economic geography of Belgium, the Netherlands and Luxembourg* (London, 1975).
G. L. Weil, *The Benelux Nations and the politics of small-country democracies* (New York, 1970).

(iii) *The Council of Europe*

Council of Europe, *Twenty-five Years of Activity in the Social Field* (Strasbourg, 1975).
Oliver Crawford, *Done This Day: The European Idea in Action* (London, 1970).
F. E. Dowrick, 'Juristic Activity in the Council of Europe', *The International and Comparative Law Quarterly*, Vol. 23, 1974, pp. 610–41.
J. E. S. Fawcett, 'The Council of Europe and Integration', *International Affairs*, Vol. 50, No. 2, Apr. 1974, pp. 242–50.
Heribert Golsong, 'The Council of Europe', in Stephen M. Schwebel (ed.), *The Effectiveness of International Decisions* (Leiden, 1971).
W. Horsfall Carter, *Speaking European: The Anglo-Continental Cleavage* (London, 1966).
Graham Kelly, 'The Council of Europe and Local Government', *Local Government Studies*, July–Aug. 1980, Vol. 6, No. 4, pp. 63-70.
A. H. Robertson, *The Council of Europe: Its Structure, Functions and Achievements* (London, 2nd edn., 1961).
A. H. Robertson, *The Relations Between the Council of Europe and the United Nations* (New York, 1972).

(iv) *OECD/OEEC*

Ernst H. van der Beugel, *From Marshall Aid to Atlantic Partnership* (London, 1966).
Miriam Camps, *'First World' Relationships: The Role of the OECD* (Paris, 1975).
Richard D. Challener (ed.), *Extension of the European Recovery Programme* (New York, 1980).
William Diebold, *Trade and Payments in Western Europe: A Study of Economic Co-operation, 1947–1951* (New York, 1952).
European Yearbook, 'Organisation for Economic Co-operation and Development', Vol. 22, 1974, pp. 248–365 (The Hague, 1976).
Jean Gimbel, *The Origins of the Marshall Plan* (Stanford, 1976).
Lincoln Gordon *et al.*, *From Marshall Plan to Global Interdependence: New Challenges for Industrialised Nations* (Paris, OECD, 1978).

Nicholas Hutton, 'The OEEC and the OECD: A Comparative Analysis', *Millenium*, Vol. 3, No. 3, 1974–75, pp. 234–51.

Mallet, 'The History and Structure of OEEC', *European Yearbook*, Vol. 1, 1948–53 (The Hague, 1955).

OECD, *OECD: History, Aims, Structure* (Paris, 1973).

OECD, *At Work for Europe: An Account of the Activities of the Organisation for European Economic Co-operation* (Paris, 3rd edn., 1956).

W. Wentholt, *Some Comments on the liquidation of the European Payments Union and related problems* (Amsterdam, 1959).

(v)   *WEU*

Paul Borcier, *The Political Role of the Assembly of the WEU* (London, WEU, 1963).

Paul Borcier, *The Assembly of Western European Union: Its contribution to the defense and building of Europe since 1955* (Paris, 1975).

R. Dobbelstein, 'Britain's European Policy and the Western European Union', in *Revue de droit international de sciences diplomatiques et politique*, 1976 (Geneva).

European Yearbook, 'Western European Union', Vol. 22, 1974, pp. 202–47 (The Hague, 1976).

Colin Gorden, 'The WEU and European Defence Co-operation', *Orbis*, Vol. xvii, No. 1, 1973, pp. 247–57.

Noel Salter, 'Western European Union: The Role of the Assembly, 1954–1963', *International Affairs*, Vol. 40, No. 1, 1964, pp. 34–46.

9. Human Rights in a European Context

(i)   *General*

J. W. Bridge, D. Lasok and R. O. Plender, *Fundamental Rights* (London, 1973).

Evan Luard, 'Human Rights and Foreign Policy', *International Affairs*, Autumn 1980, Vol. 56, No. 4, pp. 579–606.

David Owen, *Human Rights* (London, 1978).

A. H. Robertson, *Human Rights in the World* (Manchester, 1972).

L. Scarman, *English Law: the New Dimension* (London, 1974).

L. B. Sohn and Th. Buergenthal, *International Protection of Human Rights*, 3 vols. (New York, 1972).

(ii)   *The Council of Europe and Human Rights*

R. Beddard, *Human Rights and Europe* (London, 2nd edn., 1980).

I. Brownlie, *Basic Documents on Human Rights* (Oxford, 1971).

F. Castberg, *The European Convention on Human Rights* (New York, 1974).

James Fawcett, *The Application of the European Convention on Human Rights* (Oxford, 1969).

F. G. Jacobs, *The European Convention on Human Rights* (Oxford, 1975).

A. H. Robertson, *Human Rights in Europe* (Manchester, 2nd edn., 1977).

Yearbook of the European Convention on Human Rights, annually since 1955 (The Hague).

(iii)   *Human Rights under European Community Law*

Commission of the European Communities, 'Accession of the Communities to the European Convention on Human Rights', Commission Memorandum, *Bulletin of the European Communities*, Supplement 2/79.

T. C. Hartley, *EEC Immigration Law* (Amsterdam, 1978).

F. G. Jacobs (ed.), *European Law and the Individual* (Amsterdam, 1976).

R. Lecourt, *L'Europe des Juges* (Brussels, 1976).

Bernard Paulin and Mary Minch, 'The European Community and the European Convention on Human Rights', *Government and Opposition*, Vol. 15, No. 1, Winter 1980, pp. 31–47.

P. S. R. F. Mathijsen, *A Guide to European Community Law* (London, 2nd edn., 1975).

10. Monetary Co-operation

The Banker, 'The Problem of EMS', Jan. 1979.

P. Coffey and J. R. Presley, *European Monetary Integration* (London, 1970).

Peter Coffey, 'The European Monetary System', *Three Banks Review*, Dec. 1979.

W. M. Corden, *European Monetary Integration* (London, 1976).

G. E. J. Dennis and D. T. Llewellyn, 'The European Monetary System', in Banker Research Unit, *Trends in International Banking and Capital Markets* (London, 1979).

Geoffrey Denton, 'Reflections on Fiscal Federalism in the EEC', *Journal of Common Market Studies*, June 1978, pp. 283–301.

Geoffrey Denton, 'European Monetary Co-operation: the Bremen Proposals', *The World Today*, Vol. 34, No. 11, Nov. 1978, pp. 435–46.

Federal Trust/UACES Study Group Report, 'The Administrative Implications of Economic and Monetary Union within the European Community', *Journal of Common Market Studies*, Vol. XII, No. 4, 1974, pp. 410–45.

Michele Fratianni and Theo Peeters (eds.), *One Money for Europe* (London, 1978).

Rainer Hellmann, *Gold, the Dollar, and the European Currency Systems: The Seven Year Monetary War* (New York, 1979).

Roy Jenkins, 'European Monetary Union', *Lloyds Bank Review*, No. 127, 1978, pp. 1–14.

H. G. Johnson, 'Problems of European Monetary Union', *Euromoney*, Apr. 1971.

Douglas Kruse, *The European Monetary System: History and Prospects* (London, 1980).

G. Magnifico and J. H. Williamson, *European Monetary Integration* (London, 1972).

Jocelyn Statler, 'The European Monetary System: From Conception to Birth', *International Affairs*, Apr. 1979, pp. 206–25.

Philip H. Trezise (ed.), *European Monetary System: Its Promise and Prospects* (Oxford, 1980).

R. Triffin, *Europe and the Money Muddle* (Oxford, 1957).

L. Tsoukalis, *The Politics and Economics of European Monetary Integration* (London, 1977).

L. Tsoukalis, 'Is the Re-Launching of Economic and Monetary Union a Feasible Proposal?', *Journal of Common Market Studies*, Vol. XV, No. 4, June 1977, pp. 231–47.
R. Vaubel, 'Choice in European Monetary Union', *Institute of Economic Affairs*, Occasional Paper No. 55, Jan. 1979.
Ernest Wistrich, 'A Political Guide to Monetary Union', *New Europe*, Vol. 6, No. 3, Summer 1978, pp. 46–52.

11. Cultural Co-operation

Henri Brugmans, *Towards a European Cultural Policy* (Brussels, 1978).
Wilhelm Cornides, 'Problems of a European policy in the cultural field', *Annuaire Européen*, 1957, pp. 92–111.
Council of Europe, *Cultural Development Thesaurus* (Strasbourg, 1976).
Council of Europe, *European Cultural Convention* (Strasbourg, Treaty Series No. 18, 1978).
Council of Europe, *The Cultural Dimension of Development*, Discussion Paper, Conference of European Ministers, Athens, Oct. 1978.
Francis Doré, *Europe Regained* (Brussels, 1978).
European Commission, 'Community Action in the Cultural Sector', *Bulletin of the European Communities*, Supplement 6/77 (Brussels, 1977).
A. Haigh, *Cultural Diplomacy in Europe* (Council of Europe, Strasbourg, 1974).
Journal of World History, 'European Cultural Policies', Vol. xiv, No. 3, 1973 (Special Number).
S. Lewis, *Principles of Cultural Co-operation* (UNESCO, Paris, 1971).
UNESCO, *Inter-governmental Conference on Cultural Policies in Europe* (Paris, 1972).

12. Britain and Community Europe

(i)   *The Path to British Membership*

David Butler and Uwe Kitzinger, *The 1975 Referendum* (London, 1976).
Miriam Camps, *Britain and the European Community, 1955–1963* (Oxford, 2nd edn., 1963).
Carol Cosgrove, *A Reader's Guide to Britain and the European Communities* (London, 1970).
Anthony King, *Britain Says Yes: The 1975 Referendum on the Common Market* (Washington, 1977).
Uwe Kitzinger (ed.), *The Second Try* (Oxford, 1969).
Uwe Kitzinger, *Diplomacy and Persuasion: How Britain Joined the Common Market* (London, 1973).
Lynton Robins, *The Reluctant Party: Labour and the EEC* (Ormskirk, Lancs., 1980).
Avi Shlaim, *Britain and the Origins of European Unity, 1940–1951* (Reading, 1978).
Kenneth J. Twitchett, 'Britain and Europe: Together at Last?', *International Relations*, Nov. 1973, pp. 410–17.

(ii)   *Problems of British Membership*

R. Bilski, 'The Common Market and the growing strength of Labour's left wing', *Government and Opposition*, Vol. xii, 1975, pp. 200–15.

L. Collins, *European Community Law in the United Kingdom* (London, 2nd edn., 1979).

David Coombes *et al., The British People: Their Voice in Europe* (Farnborough, 1977).

Peter Ebsworth (ed.), *Europe: A Socialist Strategy* (Edinburgh, 1979).

European Commission, *Scotland and Europe* (Edinburgh, 1978), p. 29.

Martin Fetherston, Barry Moore and John Rhodes, 'Some Effects of EEC Membership on the UK Economy', *Cambridge Journal of Economics*, January 1980.

Wyn Grant, 'Industrialists and Farmers: British Interests and the European Community', *West European Politics*, Vol. I, No. 1, 1978.

Martin Kolinsky and David Scott Bell (eds.), *Divided Loyalties: British Regional Assertion and European Integration* (Manchester, 1978).

The Labour Party, *The EEC and Britain: A Socialist Perspective* (London, 1977).

The Labour Party Common Market Safeguards Committee, *The Common Market: Labour and the General Election* (London, 1978).

Labour Party Common Market Safeguards Committee, *Enough is Enough* (London, 1980).

D. E. S. Lewis, *Britain and the European Economic Community* (London, 1978).

Mathew McQueen, *Britain, the EEC and the Developing World* (London, 1977).

New Europe, 'Europe: What the Parties Say', Winter 1979, Vol. vii, No. 1 (Special Issue).

Alan Norton, 'Relations between the European Community and British Local Government', Report on a Seminar, Local Government Studies, Jan.–Feb. 1980, pp. 5–15.

M. Ryan and P. Isaacson, 'Parliament and the European Communities', *Parliamentary Affairs*, Vol. 28, 1975, pp. 199–215.

J. Taylor, 'Great Britain's Membership of the European Community: The Question of Parliamentary Sovereignty', *Government and Opposition*, Vol. x, 1975, pp. 278–93.

Kenneth J. Twitchett, 'Britain and Community Europe, 1973–1979', *International Relations*, Nov. 1979, pp. 698–714.

Angelika Volle and William Wallace, 'How Common a Fisheries Policy', *The World Today*, Vol. 33, No. 2, Feb. 1977, pp. 62–72.

William Wallace (ed.), *Britain in Europe* (London, 1980).

Which, 'Britain and the EEC', Feb. 1981, pp. 101–5 (Special Report.)

Index

255

Brazil, 15
Bremen European Council, 1978, on EMS, 205
Briand, Aristide (1862–1932), and French tradition of Europeanism, 56
Brinkhorst, L.J., Dutch Sec. of State for Foreign Affairs 1973–77, 130
Britain and the European Communities, an economic assessment, White Paper, 27
Brunner, Guido, FDP politician, 61, 67
Brussels Treaty, March 1948, 39
BSP (PSB) Belgian Socialist Party, 150–1, 165

CALLAGHAN, JAMES, former Prime Minister, 19, 30
Canada, 28
CAP; Belgian modernization and, 158; British entry and, 27, 32; Denmark and, 175, 180–1, 188; Dutch and, 135–8, 141; France and, 44, 45, 52–4, 71, 72–3; Germans and, 71; Ireland and, 195, 199, 204, 211, 216; Italy and, 89, 100, 101, 105, 109; reform of, plans for, 2, 54, 73, 113, 116, 232–3; Spain and, 227
Carli, Guido, Italian industrialist, 95, 103
Carrington, Lord, British Foreign Sec., crisis consultation machinery plan, 21–2
CCEIA, Dutch co-ordinating committee, 129–31
CDA, Dutch Christian Democrat Alliance, 140, 141, 144
Centre Democrat Party, Denmark, 185,187, 188
CET, 11, 12, 14
CGIL, economic grounds for support for Europe, 112
Cheysson, Claude, French Commissioner; Lomé Convention and, 48; Minister for External Relations, 58
Chile, EEC resolution on human rights, 20
Chirac, Jacques, French politician, 55; outburst against Spanish EEC membership, 225
Chiti-Batelli, Andrea, Italian Senate official, 87
Christian Democratic Party, West Germany, 60, 77
Christian People's Party, Denmark, 185, 187, 188
Churchill, Winston, 25
CIPE, Italian interministerial committee, 95
Cold War, 64, 83, 86, 87, 108, 111

Colombo, Emilio, Italian DC politician; European Parliament elections, 114, key figure in Italian Community relations, 92–3
COMECON; Belgian attempt to improve EEC relations with, 149; Portuguese CP hopes of, 222
Common Commercial Policy, EEC, for Eastern Europe, 76
Common Fisheries Policy, June 1970, 14, 33; Denmark and, 180, 188; Faeroes and, 182–3; Greenland and, 175–6; Ireland and, 196, 197, 199, 202, 210, 211, 215
Communist Party, Denmark, 185, 187
Communist Party, France, 38, 41, 56, 63, 77, 219
Communist Party, Portugal, opposes EEC and Eurocommunism, 222–3
Commonwealth, British; loyalty to, 26, 27, 28; links with EEC, 13, 48; see also 'decolonization'
Conservative Party, Britain, 31
Conservative Party, Denmark; coalition proposal for Nordek, 174; entry to EEC and, 177, 178, 185, 187, 188
Constancio, Vitor, Portuguese politician, on national hopes for EEC, 221–2
Copenhagen Declaration, 1973, 51
COREPER, 7; Belgians and, 148; EEC machinery bypass, 19, Italy and, 98
COREU telex network, 17, 19, 22
Cossiga, Francesco, former Italian Prime Minister, Pres. of European Council, 21–2
Council of Europe, 39, 62, 191
Council of Ministers; de Gaulle and French walkout, 45, 126; Dutch and, 128, 140
Craxi, Bettino, PSI politician, 114
Crosland, Anthony, former British Foreign Sec.; death of, effect, 19; on EEC enlargement, 219
CVP (PSC) Belgian Social Christian Party, 149–50, 164, 165
Cyprus; EEC agreement, 1972, 14; Greek stance on, 228
Czechoslovakia, 1968 invasion as impetus for EEC enlargement, 64

D'66, Democraten '66, 140, 141, 144
Dahrendorf, Ralf, European Commissioner, 61, 70–74
Davignon Report, 1970, 17, 50, 67, 68, 127
Davignon, Vicomte, Commissioner for Industrial Policy, refutes Portuguese